Teaching in lifelo

Teaching in lifelong learning

A GUIDE TO THEORY AND PRACTICE

Edited by James Avis, Roy Fisher and Ron Thompson

 Open University Press

Open University Press
McGraw-Hill Education
McGraw-Hill House
Shoppenhangers Road
Maidenhead
Berkshire
England
SL6 2QL

email: enquiries@openup.co.uk
world wide web: www.openup.co.uk

and Two Penn Plaza, New York, NY 10121-2289, USA

First published 2010

A catalogue record of this book is available from the British Library

ISBN-13: 978-0-33-523468-4 (pb) 978-0-33-523469-1 (hb)
ISBN-10: 0-33-523468-2 (pb) 0-33-523469-0 (hb)

Library of Congress Cataloging-in-Publication Data
CIP data has been applied for

Typeset by RefineCatch Limited, Bungay, Suffolk
Printed in the UK by Bell and Bain Ltd, Glasgow

Fictitious names of companies, products, people, characters and/or data that
may be used herein (in case studies or in examples) are not intended to
represent any real individual, company, product or event.

Mixed Sources
Product group from well-managed
forests and other controlled sources
www.fsc.org Cert no. TT-COC-002769
© 1996 Forest Stewardship Council

The *McGraw·Hill* Companies

Contents

Part 2

Teaching in the lifelong learning sector

8 Learning and learners
Margaret McLay, Louise Mycroft, Penny Noel, Kevin Orr,
Ron Thompson, Jonathan Tummons and Jane Weatherby

9 The curriculum in the lifelong learning sector
Roy Fisher, Amanda Fulford, Bernard McNicholas and
Ron Thompson

10 Practical teaching
Liz Dixon, Josie Harvey, Ron Thompson and Sarah Williamson

11 Teaching with technology
Liz Bennett, Alison Iredale and Cheryl Reynolds

List of boxes

List of figures

List of tables

Notes on the contributors

The editors and all contributors are currently at the School of Education and Professional Development at the University of Huddersfield except as indicated below:

Amanda Fulford, Leeds Trinity and All Saints College, formerly School of Education and Professional Development, University of Huddersfield

Ann Jennings, Leeds City College

Louise Mycroft, Northern College

David Neve, formerly School of Education and Professional Development, University of Huddersfield

Sandra Rennie, educational consultant

Barbara Reynolds, formerly Harrogate College

Dave Swindells, formerly School of Education and Professional Development, University of Huddersfield

Jonathan Tummons, University of Teesside

Jane Weatherby, Northern College

Keith Webb, formerly School of Education and Professional Development, University of Huddersfield

Preface

We have aspired to create a text with wide appeal, of interest to all concerned with the broad field of teaching in lifelong learning. Many readers will come to the book through initial teacher training and, in the main, will be following courses such as the Certificate in Education, Professional Graduate Certificate in Education or Postgraduate Certificate in Education. Others may be undertaking awards such as the Diploma in Teaching in the Lifelong Learning Sector. We intend the book to be useful to a wider readership, including qualified teachers and those following academic courses in education requiring a text focusing on post-compulsory education.

This book is subtitled 'A guide to theory and practice'. It has been our ambition to provide a resource that addresses practical aspects of teaching and training. The day-to-day work of teaching does not take place in an atheoretical vacuum, but is contextualized by complex social and political relations. The book aims to encourage readers to engage with the growing body of literature on post-compulsory education.

We hope that you enjoy this book. We and our contributors would be grateful for comments that might be helpful to us in developing our ideas and, perhaps, informing a future edition.

James Avis, Roy Fisher and Ron Thompson

Acknowledgements

This book involves contributions from a range of institutions and people, too many to list individually. Our thinking has been informed by teacher education colleagues, trainee teachers and others in the member colleges of the Consortium for Post-Compulsory Education and Training (CPCET), together with the many institutions and individuals in the sector who provide placements and other support to our students. We thank CPCET for encouragement and support. Similarly, we acknowledge the Huddersfield University Distributed Centre for Excellence in Teacher Training (HUDCETT) and its constituent organizations, of which there are over eighty throughout England.

Colleagues at the Bath Spa University, the University of Greenwich and the University of Wolverhampton were founder members of the *Associate Online* project and have informed our thinking. Professor Terry Hyland of the University of Bolton, a visiting professor at Huddersfield, was a member of the University of Huddersfield-funded research project *The College Experience – Work Based Learning and Pre-service PCET Trainee Teachers*, which was the genesis for this book.

We are also grateful to Dalia Dasgupta, Head of Human Resources and Higher Education, South East Essex College, Southend-on-Sea; Lorraine Higham, Director of People and Performance, Accrington and Rossendale College; and Emma Richardson, Professional Development Manager, at Nelson and Colne College.

We thank Angela Johnson, a PGCE student at the University of Huddersfield, who kindly agreed to the use of her lesson plan in Chapter 10.

Alison Iredale prepared the list of abbreviations and acronyms. David Powell, another Huddersfield colleague, provided a helpful commentary on the draft text.

We wish to thank the Centre for Research in Post-Compulsory Education and Training at the University of Huddersfield for support.

We are grateful to Taylor and Francis publishers for permission to adapt Fisher, R. and Webb, K. (2006) Subject specialist pedagogy and initial teacher training for the learning and skills sector in England: the context, a response and some critical issues, *The Journal of Further and Higher Education*, 30(4): 337–49. An abridged and amended version formed the basis of Chapter 14. The website for *The Journal of Further and*

Higher Education can be found at http://www.tandf.co.uk/journals/carfax/0309877X. html

The editors would like to thank our partners for their forbearance during the preparation of this book.

Finally, we wish to express our appreciation to Fiona Richman and Donna Edwards of McGraw-Hill, and our copy editor, Maureen Cox, for their patience and guidance.

Abbreviations and acronyms

Please note that not all these refer to current concepts/organizations, and that not all entries appear in the book. We have tried to supply a guide to the bewildering range of abbreviations and acronyms that the reader might meet elsewhere.

AB	Awarding Body
ABE	Adult Basic Education
ACL	adult and community learning
AD(H)D	Attention Deficit (Hyperactivity) Disorder
AE	Adult Education
A Level	General Certificate of Education at Advanced Level
ALI	Adult Learning Inspectorate
ALLaN	Adult Literacy, Language and Numeracy
ALP	Association of Learning Providers
AoC	Association of Colleges
APEL	accreditation of prior experiential learning
APL	accreditation of prior learning
APLA	accreditation of prior learning achievement
AS	General Certificate of Education at Advanced Subsidiary Level
ASD	Autistic spectrum disorder
ATL	Association of Teachers and Lecturers
ATLS	Associate Teacher Learning and Skills
BEC	Business Education Council
BECTA	British Educational Communications and Technology Agency, established in 1998, now with a wider remit
BERA	British Educational Research Association
BESDA	behavioural, emotional or social difficulties
BIS	Department for Business, Innovation and Skills
BME	Black Minority Ethnic
BSA	Basic Skills Agency
BTEC	Business and Technology Education Council
CAL	Computer aided learning

CATs	Credit accumulation and transfer scheme
CBET	Competence Based Education and Training
CBL	Computer based learning
CBT	Computer based training
CEL	Centre for Excellence in Leadership
Cert Ed	Certificate in Education
CETL	Centre for Excellence in Teaching and Learning
CETT	Centre for Excellence in Teacher Training
CGLI	City and Guilds of London Institute
CIF	Common Inspection Framework (for post-16 Education and Training)
CLS	Centre for Longitudinal Studies
CNAA	Council for National Academic Awards
CoVE	Centre of Vocational Excellence
CPCET	The Consortium for Post-Compulsory Education and Training
CPD	continuing professional development
CRB	Criminal Records Bureau
CSCI	Commission for Social Care Inspection
CTLLS	Certificate in Teaching in the Lifelong Learning Sector
CYP	Commonwealth Youth Programme
DCSF	Department for Children, Schools and Families
DDA	Disability Discrimination Act
DES	Department of Education and Science
DFEE	Department for Education and Employment
DfES	Department for Education and Skills
DIUS	Department for Innovation, Universities and Skills
DPA	Data Protection Act
DTLLS	Diploma in Teaching in the Lifelong Learning Sector
E2E	Entry to Employment
E2L	English as a Second Language
E and D	Equality and Diversity
EAL	English as an Additional Language
EBD	Emotional and Behavioural Difficulties
ECM	Every Child Matters
ECRE	European Council for Refugees and Exiles
EFL	English as a Foreign Language
EIA	Equality Impact Assessment
EMA	Education Maintenance Allowance
ERIC	Educational Resources Information Centre
ESOL	English for speakers of other languages
ESRC	Economic and Social Research Council
EYM	Every Youth Matters
FdA	Foundation Degree Arts
FDL	flexible distributed learning
FE	further education
FEDA	Further Education Development Agency

FEFCE	Further Education Funding Council for England
FEFCW	Further Education Funding Council for Wales
FEI	Further Education Institution
FENTO	Further Education National Training Organization
FETT	Further Education Teacher Training
FEU	Further Education Unit
FfE	Framework for Excellence
FHEA	Further and Higher Education Act 1992
FHEQ	Framework for Higher Education Qualifications
FLLN	Family Literacy, Language and Numeracy
FOI	Freedom of Information
FTE	Full-time equivalent
GCE	General Certificate of Education
GCE A	General Certificate of Education Advanced Level
GCE AS	General Certificate of Education Advanced Supplementary
GCSE	General Certificate of Secondary Education
GFE	General Further Education
GLH	Guided learning hours
GNVQ	General National Vocational Qualification
GTC	General Teaching Council for England
HE	higher education
HEA	Higher Education Academy
HEFCE	Higher Education Funding Council for England
HEI	higher education institution
HESA	Higher Education Statistics Agency
HMI	Her Majesty's Inspector
HMIC A	Her Majesty's Inspectorate of Court Administration
HNC/D/Q	higher national certificate/diploma/qualification
HRM	human resource management
HSE	Health and Safety Executive
HUDCETT	The Huddersfield University Distributed Centre for Excellence in Teacher Training
IAG	Information, Advice and Guidance
IALS	International Adult Literacy Survey
ICT	Information and Communication Technology
IfL	The Institute for Learning
ILB	Industry Lead Body
ILO	International Labour Organisation
ILP	Individual Learning Plan
ILT	information and learning technology
ILTHE	Institute for Learning and Teaching in Higher Education
IQER	integrated quality and enhancement review
ISA	Independent Safeguarding Authority
IT	information technology
ITB	Industrial Training Board
ITE	Initial Teacher Education

ITT	initial teacher training
JANET	Joint Academic Network
JISC	Joint Information Systems Committee
JISC CETIS	JISC Centre for Educational Technology Interoperability Standards
JVET	Journal of Vocational Education and Training
LA	local authority
LEA	Local Education Authority
LGBT	lesbian, gay, bisexual and transgender
LLL	Lifelong Learning
LLN	Literacy, Language and Numeracy
LLS	lifelong learning sector
LLUK	Lifelong Learning UK
LSC	Learning and Skills Council
LSIS	Learning and Skills Improvement Service
LSN	Learning and Skills Network
LSS	learning and skills sector
LSRN	Learning and Skills Research Network
LTSN	Learning and Teaching Support Network
MHF	Mental Health Foundation
MIS	Management Information System
MoE	Ministry of Education
MSC	Manpower Services Commission
NATFHE	National Association of Teachers in Further and Higher Education (now UCU)
NCE	National Commission on Education
NCF	National Curriculum Framework
NCVQ	National Council for Vocational Qualifications
NEET	not in education, employment or training
NFER	National Foundation for Educational Research
NGfL	National Grid for Learning
NIACE	National Institute of Adult Continuing Education
NILTA	National Information and Learning Technologies Association
NQF	National Qualifications Framework
NRDC	National Research and Development Centre for Adult Literacy and Numeracy
NSA	National Skills Academies
NUT	National Union of Teachers
NVQ	National Vocational Qualification
OCR	Oxford, Cambridge and RSA Examinations
OECD	Organisation for Economic Co-operation and Development
Ofqual	Office of the Qualifications and Examinations Regulator
Ofsted	Office for Standards in Education, Children's Services and Skills
OLASS	Offender Learning and Skills Service
PCET	Post-Compulsory Education and Training
PDP	Personal Development Plan

PGCE	Professional Graduate Certificate in Education *or* Postgraduate Certificate in Education
PTTLS	Preparing to Teach in the Lifelong Learning Sector
QA	Quality assurance
QAA	Quality Assurance Agency for Higher Education
QCA	Qualifications and Curriculum Authority
QCDA	Qualifications and Curriculum Development Agency
QCF	Qualifications and Credit Framework
QE	Quality enhancement
QIA	Quality Improvement Agency
QTLS	Qualified Teacher Learning and Skills
QTS	Qualified Teacher Status [in relation to schools]
RACs	Regional Advisory Councils
RAPAL	Research and Practice in Adult Literacy
RSA	Royal Society for the Encouragement of Arts, Manufactures and Commerce
S4L	Skills for Life
SATs	Standard Assessment Tests
SCAA	School Curriculum and Assessment Authority
SEN	special educational needs
SENDA	Special Educational Needs and Disability Act 2001
SFA	Skills Funding Agency
SLD	Severe Learning Difficulties
SLDD	Students with Learning Difficulties and Disabilities
SMT	senior management team
SpLD	Specific Learning Difficulties
SSC	Sector Skills Councils
SSR	Staff-student ratio
SVUK	Standards Verification UK
T2G	Train to Gain
TDA	The Training and Development Agency for Schools
TDLB	Training and Development Lead Body
TEC	Training and Enterprise Council
TEFL	Teaching English as a Foreign Language
TERG	Technical Education Resource Group
TESL	Teaching English as a Second Language
TLC	Transforming Learning Cultures
TP	Teaching Practice
TQEF	Teaching Quality Enhancement Fund
TQM	Total Quality Management
TTA	The Teacher Training Agency
TTG	Train to Gain
TVEI	Technical and Vocational Initiative
UCAS	Universities and Colleges Admissions Service
UCET	Universities Council for the Education of Teachers
UCU	University and College Union

UfI	University for Industry
UNESCO	United Nations Educational, Scientific and Cultural Organisation
VAK	Visual, auditory, kinaesthetic
VET	vocational education and training
VLE	virtual learning environment
VTC	Virtual Teacher Centre
WBL	work-based learning
WEA	Workers' Educational Association
YCW	Youth and Community Work
YOI	Young Offender Institution
YPLA	Young People's Learning Agency
YTS	Youth Training Scheme

Mapping the chapters to the domains of the LLUK standards

The *New Overarching Professional Standards for Teachers, Tutors and Trainers in the Lifelong Learning Sector* (LLUK 2007a) are structured within the six domains shown below (see Chapter 3). This mapping indicates the chapters of most direct relevance to each domain; however, the nature of teaching and learning in the sector means that there are many inter-relationships between chapters and between the domains making up the standards. Readers are advised to consult the standards so that they can identify chapters in this book of particular value in developing their practice in relation to specific standards.

Domain	Chapters relevant to the domain
A: Professional values and practice	1, 3, 4, 5, 6, 7, 8, 9, 15, 16, 17, 18, 19, 20, 21
B: Learning and teaching	6, 7, 8, 9, 10, 11, 12, 14, 16, 17, 19
C: Specialist learning and teaching	3, 7, 9, 14
D: Planning for learning	8, 9, 10, 11, 12, 13, 17, 19
E: Assessment for learning	4, 8, 9, 10, 13, 21
F: Access and progression	2, 3, 7, 8, 9, 16, 17, 22

PART 1

Introduction to the lifelong learning sector

1

Introduction

Roy Fisher and Ron Thompson

> **In this chapter:**
>
> - Using this book
> - Education, the market and globalization
> - The agenda for reform in the learning and skills sector

Using this book

This book is aimed primarily at teachers and trainee teachers working in the lifelong learning sector (LLS); nevertheless, bearing in mind the weakening boundaries between different phases and sectors of education, it seeks to address its subject matter broadly. While dealing extensively with matters of practice, the book critically engages with theory and recognizes that education as a system and teaching as an activity are complex and demanding processes, resistant to simple analysis and 'quick fix' solutions. The authors have a commitment to social justice and inclusion; this is fundamental to the thinking that frames our practice.

The book has three sections. In Part 1, we set out the scope of the LLS, in terms of its institutional composition and some key concepts. Part 2 is concerned with learning, the curriculum, teaching, assessment and associated issues. In Part 3 we deal with organizational and career factors that constitute the environment in which teachers work and which are confronted and negotiated daily. There is, of course, overlap between sections. We have provided a linear order of subjects which lends itself to progression from this point to the end. Many readers, however, will steer around the chapters in ways that suit themselves. Although we have aimed to be comprehensive in our coverage, this book should not be used in isolation from other texts. The ideas presented should be examined in the light of the reader's experiences as a teacher and as a learner, and the book invites discussion and debate.

This book is a team effort, with over thirty contributors. This brings a wide range of experience and perspectives. Different chapters present their content according to the judgements of their authors, and one of the strengths of the book is that it provides access to a collection of 'voices' that present ideas based on their particular expertise.

There are now many textbooks available which have been written specifically for those working in the LLS, and we hope that you will seek out some of these. We also encourage the selective exploration of books dealing with education more broadly. Beyond textbooks and scholarly monographs is the world of academic journals. Most trainee teachers will have electronic access to these, providing an opportunity to seek out the latest thinking. In addition, the Internet provides a convenient and rapid window on a vast range of knowledge – though this should be used with caution. The refereeing process of academic journals provides a degree of 'quality assurance' which *can* be absent in web-based materials.

Education, the market and globalization

Educational institutions exist in wider economic and political systems, which both facilitate and limit the ways in which they respond to individual and societal needs. Throughout the modern era education has been seen as a process with huge potential to transform lives and to build positive futures, and this vision of education as an engine of progressive social change has been adopted by ideologies across the political spectrum. More recently, there has been some recognition that the progressive potential of education is circumscribed. Indeed, a number of authors have argued that education is a vehicle for the reproduction of social and economic structures rather than for social mobility. For example, Bourdieu (1974: 32) suggests that 'It is probably cultural inertia which still makes us see education in terms of the ideology of the school as a liberating force . . . even when the indications tend to be that it is in fact one of the most effective means of perpetuating the existing social pattern'. Bowles and Gintis (1976: 265) express this even more starkly: 'The education system . . . neither adds to nor subtracts from the degree of inequality and repression originating in the economic sphere. Rather, it reproduces and legitimates a pre-existing pattern in the process of training and stratifying the workforce'.

In other analyses, education has been seen as perpetuating repressive political structures. Louis Althusser (1918–90), in his essay *Ideology and Ideological State Apparatuses*, outlined his model of how 'Ideological State Apparatuses' and 'Repressive State Apparatuses' contrive to cement capitalistic power relations. He stated: 'I believe that the ideological State apparatus which has been installed in the *dominant* position in mature capitalist social formations . . . is the *educational ideological apparatus*' (Althusser 1971: 144–5).

The determinism of writers such as Althusser or Bowles and Gintis is at odds with more recent postmodern conceptions of a relatively fluid and unpredictable social world. Jean-François Lyotard (1924–98), in *The Postmodern Condition* (1984), contended that modernist science employed grand narratives (or 'metanarratives') as a means of legitimating scientific knowledge (see Chapter 9). The positioning of science as the key to progress means the State can control education in the name of freedom and economic development. This displaces the traditional role of the universities and applies particularly to the field of teacher education and training which, in the UK, is now heavily regulated.

The later decades of the twentieth century witnessed not only the collapse of the 'socialist bloc' countries, but a concomitant triumph of neo-liberal capitalism which was seen by Fukuyama (1992) as signalling the end of ideological struggle. This claim is now recognized as premature, but capitalist economies have grown in power and influence, and large corporations have become internationalized. The globalization of industries and technology is accompanied by the globalization of culture, both through media conglomerates and the power of certain cultural forms (such as cinema, popular music and 'cybercultures'). The largely unanticipated international economic crisis of 2008/09, though deep, and leading to the effective nationalization of major institutions, did not threaten capitalism as a system, and neo-liberalism is largely unchallenged as the mainstream way of thinking about economic and social issues, including education.

The term 'globalization' is now commonly used to describe a process of transition from national and regional economies towards global trade and markets and the increasing power of large multinational corporations; a decline in the importance of geographical and national boundaries and greater connectivity between people arising from developments in technology; an exponential increase in global economic and cultural flows; and a compression of time and space across the planet. Undoubtedly, certain features of life in the developed world are objectively different than they were in the past, and in addition many people *feel* differently about their relationship with the rest of the globe. However, as Lauder et al. (2006: 31) point out, for some writers 'globalization is primarily an "ideological" construct that is being promulgated to support a neo-liberal agenda'. This ideological dimension is increasingly apparent in debates about education, in which globalization is often used to justify increasing government control. Our only defence against global economic forces, it is argued, lies in providing the 'right kind' of education and training to large numbers of people, and only by bringing the education system under close state direction can this provision be guaranteed.

The globalization of markets and relations has therefore had direct consequences for education. These include its increasing commodification, through which learning has come to be regarded as a product to be sold and purchased like any other, with students positioned as consumers. The curriculum has been co-opted as a vehicle of 'economic progress', with largely unchallenged assumptions about its purposes as a means by which industry can be provided with efficient and pliable workers. While UK higher education (HE) has expanded through policies aimed at 'widening participation' as a means of enhancing economic competitiveness and social inclusion, this has been in the context of a rhetoric of marketization and individualism.

This rhetoric arises from the current dominance of *neo-liberalism* as a political and economic philosophy whose impact is acutely felt in the sphere of education but spreads far beyond its boundaries. Briefly, neo-liberalism consists of a set of core assumptions or approaches, including a belief that economic success depends on allowing individuals to pursue their own interests and that the operation of a competitive 'free market' will always lead to superior economic outcomes. At the same time, free-market approaches are not envisaged as arising of their own accord – individualized, competitive and market-driven policies are enacted by the state in order to create the 'right' environment. In addition, although neo-liberalism acknowledges that the least successful in society should be supported, this must be with the minimum of state intervention and at a level that provides an incentive for the individual to do better (for a more detailed discussion of neo-liberalism, see Lauder et al. 2006: 25–8).

Although neo-liberalism has attained the status of orthodoxy in the UK and many other countries, its effectiveness in creating social justice is questionable, to say the least. This book contains many references to critiques of the neo-liberal agenda, particularly in relation to its educational implications.

In post-compulsory education, neo-liberalism and globalization have led to a system which has been shaped by processes which Ritzer has called 'McDonaldization' (see Ritzer 2008). The largely vocational nature of the further education (FE) system means that the impact of these trends is amplified in colleges and the LLS. Such processes have been documented in the work of Apple (1990, 2000, 2006), Ainley (1993), Brookfield (2005) and Avis (2009) among others. For studies which focus on British developments, see Education Group (1981, 1991), Avis et al. (1996) and, more recently, Ball (2008). Teachers have found their work more scrutinized and regulated, with an associated negative impact on their autonomy leading to a crisis about their professional identity and status.

The agenda for reform in the learning and skills sector

A period of turbulent change within lifelong learning has affected teacher education, and teaching and learning more generally. Much of this arises from the broader agenda of successive New Labour governments, which reflects the assumptions of a 'political era' dating back (at least) to the late 1970s and based on neo-liberal conceptions of education. The consultation document *Equipping Our Teachers for the Future* opened with 'The post-16 learning and skills sector is pivotal to our aim of bringing social justice and economic prosperity to everyone' (DfES 2004a: 3), and related proposals for a 'step-change' in initial teacher training to *Success for All* (DfES 2002a, 2002b), the government's overarching agenda for reform in what was then being called 'the learning and skills sector'.

The 'agenda for reform' takes up the theme of education as a key element in economic competitiveness and social inclusion, setting out perceived inadequacies that must be addressed if the UK is to prosper. It draws attention to under-funding and excessive bureaucracy, as well as variability of standards based on a neglect of pedagogy: 'While there is some excellent quality provision, this co-exists with too much poor provision. And across the system as a whole, insufficient attention has been given to improving teaching, training and learning . . . For too long, further education and training has been the forgotten sector in education' (DfES 2002b: 10). To redress this neglect of teaching and learning, two of the four elements of the reform agenda set out in *Success for All* are concerned with pedagogy and the professional development of teachers: 'putting teaching and learning at the heart of what we do' and 'developing the leaders, teachers, trainers of the future' (DfES 2002b: 5).

Teacher education is at the heart of policy for the LLS. Although this is broadly to be welcomed, the reform agenda has been accompanied by increasing central control and the imposition of uniform approaches to teacher training (Simmons and Thompson 2007). One aim of this book is to enable an informed evaluation of these reforms. A major determinant of the quality of educational provision is the knowledge, skills, enthusiasm and commitment of teachers. The ideas discussed in this book are not imposed by central control; they are generated by an enormous variety of social and historical contexts. It is for each reader to critically consider them.

2
What is the lifelong learning sector?
Roy Fisher and Robin Simmons

In this chapter:

- Development of the lifelong learning sector
- The further education sector
- Local authorities
- Lifelong learning in the public services
- Private training providers
- Higher education
- Some key institutions
- The need for perspective

Development of the lifelong learning sector

Post-compulsory education and training (PCET) in England is notable for its complexity. Numerous types of provider offer diverse opportunities to people over the age of (currently) 16, including school sixth forms, sixth-form colleges, FE colleges, universities and adult education services run by local authorities (LAs). Specialist colleges cater for subjects such as art and design, performing arts and land-based studies. Other colleges serve learners with special needs or adult learners. Further diversity has been promoted through encouraging private companies to enter the marketplace. This landscape is governed by a network of rapidly changing regulatory bodies.

A large proportion of PCET provision takes place in FE colleges. Foster (2005: 58) points out that FE has been the poor relation of English education – 'the neglected middle child between universities and schools'. Historically, there has been little central guidance, and funding has been inadequate. Many FE institutions trace their roots to the mechanics' institutes of the mid-nineteenth century and most were established under the *laissez-faire* spirit that then characterized the English approach to education. Until the late nineteenth century, the majority of the population were without formal education (Pratt 2000).

In response to economic competition, the last quarter of the nineteenth and the early years of the twentieth centuries saw a burst of activity that encouraged growth of technical and commercial post-school education. It was not until the 1944 Education Act that post-compulsory education received more attention and a statutory duty was placed on local education authorities (LEAs) to provide 'adequate facilities' for what then became known officially as 'further education' in England. However, the duty placed on LEAs was open to interpretation and there was variation in provision. For an account of the development of English FE after the Second World War, see Richardson (2007).

Following the 1944 Education Act, LEAs were given responsibility for the 'general educational character' of colleges. How this responsibility was discharged depended on the 'local ecology' (Waitt 1980: 402). Provision was influenced by local communities and labour markets, and was also shaped by personalities, politics and culture. This affected the level of commitment towards FE within each authority – some LEAs created extensive provision, while others did not (Lucas, 2004).

LEAs dominated the educational landscape for over forty years after World War Two. Since the 1980s there has been a reversal of this process; LAs have become disempowered and their role in planning education has reduced (Ainley 2001). From the early 1980s a series of reports criticized the management, organization and culture of LAs. Official discourse came to characterize LEAs as pedestrian, unresponsive and divorced from the 'real world'. Subsequently, the White Paper *Education and Training for the 21st Century* (DES 1991) portrayed the sector as in need of reform. Following this, the 1992 Further and Higher Education Act removed FE, specialist and sixth-form colleges from LA control, recreating them as self-governing institutions directly accountable to the state. This was generally regarded as 'freeing' colleges from municipal bureaucracy.

The decision to end LEA control should be understood in the context of a belief that the use of market mechanisms is the most effective way to raise standards and reduce costs. From the 1980s onwards successive governments viewed public sector organization as inherently inefficient and unfairly protected from competition (Kessler and Bayliss 1998). Even before their 1997 election victory, New Labour placed 'education, education, education' at the heart of their policies. This was seen as the key to success in the global marketplace. A successful economy would contribute towards social justice, prosperity and well-being for all (Allen and Ainley 2007; Avis 2009). In the context of 'lifelong learning' individuals would be required to continuously reinvent, 're-skill' and 'up-skill' themselves. For Brine (2006: 652), this discourse places workers in a 'state of constant becoming': a readiness to retrain for whatever employment becomes available.

Since New Labour came to power in 1997, policy towards lifelong learning has emphasized its economic function (Foster 2005; Leitch Review of Skills 2006). A feature has been the creation of a mixed economy of semi-privatized state sector organizations alongside a plethora of state-subsidized private sector providers (Ainley 2001). Institutions formerly having a public service ethos are now expected to behave like private businesses: performance indicators are set; funding is tied to targets and managerialism is commonplace (Coffield 2006). Education is regarded as a commodity that can be provided cheaply and efficiently by organizations imbued with an ideology of enterprise (Allen and Ainley 2007). Nevertheless, Keep (2006) describes the regulatory systems that govern PCET in England as being the most complex and centrally controlled in the world, and Coffield (2006) argues that we are witnessing a growing accountability framework.

PCET is now characterized by commercialized public-sector institutions in a quasi-marketplace where private companies receive funding to deliver accredited courses. The proposals of the 2007 Education and Skills Bill sought to extend this by introducing public funding for employers who provide work-based training (DfES 2007). Such developments reflect a conception of learning as taking place, not only inside the traditional structures of the education system but, increasingly, in an eclectic range of settings (Jarvis 2004).

The term 'lifelong learning' is commonplace, but it is not a straightforward concept. It can be understood as a process in which the individual continues to engage in education and training throughout life. Traditionally, education was associated with the formative years but current discourse attempts to alter such assumptions. Orr (2008) argues that, according to New Labour, all social formations but especially education, must conform to the economic stringencies of globalization. Individuals are expected to take responsibility for their learning which can take place in a variety of contexts. The term 'lifelong learning' is often used to encompass learning that takes place in settings beyond the education system (Jarvis 2004). Below is a consideration of autonomous learning, followed by sections which provide a brief overview of some of the main components of the 'system' of lifelong learning.

The further education sector

FE is the largest and most diverse part of the LLS, currently serving over four million students. There were 376 colleges in 2008 (DIUS 2008a). Many of today's colleges have rich but diverse histories. A unifying thread is that, for almost 50 years after the end of World War Two, the majority of colleges were under LEA control. General FE colleges are the most common kind – in 2008 there were 196 of these in Britain (DIUS 2008a). Although they vary in size, the largest have over 50,000 students. Most general FE colleges have strong links with industry, and a tradition of teaching the theory and practice of skills used in everyday occupations; as Ainley and Bailey (1997) point out, their work has focused on vocational learning. General FE colleges, however, usually offer a broad curriculum attracting a diverse profile of students. Typically this includes basic skills and courses for those with special educational needs; English for speakers of other languages (ESOL); and work-based learning for people following apprenticeships.

Notwithstanding the vocational orientation of FE colleges, traditional academic subjects have a significant place in their provision. Many students in general FE colleges undertake degree level courses, including professional qualifications. Increasingly, foundation degrees – work-related HE qualifications designed in conjunction with employers – are offered. These cover a range of occupational areas including media, retail, sport, hospitality and construction. In combining academic and work-based learning, foundation degrees can be seen as similar to the established higher national certificate (HNC) and diploma (HND) courses. Some larger general FE colleges with substantial HE provision are now designated as 'further and higher education colleges', sometimes referred to as 'mixed economy colleges'.

General FE colleges are complex organizations, serving fragmented and diverse interests. As a result, it is difficult to describe a 'typical' general college (Ainley and

Bailey 1997; Hyland and Merrill 2003). The other institutions that comprise FE are more easily defined, as they concentrate mainly on particular groups of learners or subject areas. Traditionally, sixth-form colleges were regarded as part of the school sector. To the surprise of many, alongside other colleges, they were removed from LA control following the 1992 Further and Higher Education Act and reclassified as part of FE. To a large extent, sixth-form colleges remain distinct from other FE institutions, mainly due to their academic curriculum and the relative social advantage of their intake (Foster 2005). Sixth-form colleges focus mainly on courses that prepare their students for entry to HE and the prevailing ethos is one of examination success.

A range of FE colleges concentrate on specific subjects or vocational areas. In 2008 there were four FE arts colleges offering courses in art and design, music and performing arts; 17 land-based studies colleges focused chiefly on agriculture, horticulture and related areas; and 14 specialist colleges, some of which were residential, offered provision mainly for people with special needs. This includes those with learning, emotional and behavioural difficulties and students with physical disabilities (DIUS 2008a). There was also a small number of adult residential colleges with a tradition of providing opportunities for adults unable to take advantage of education earlier in their lives – these included Coleg Harlech in Wales, Northern College (near Barnsley), and Ruskin College in Oxford. They offer provision ranging from short introductory courses through to HE, and tend to specialize in areas such as trade union studies and community regeneration.

Local authorities

The Further and Higher Education Act of 1992 ended an era of LA control for FE. Although losing responsibility for the majority of post-compulsory education in the early 1990s, LEAs retained some involvement at its margins – for example, providing non-vocational adult education classes. Furthermore, the Government has recently suggested that responsibility for FE in England, at least for 14–19-year-olds, be returned to local authorities in 2010 (DCSF/DIUS 2008). However, this does not imply a return to the days of municipal dominance, and colleges will retain significant levels of autonomy. From 2010, LAs will have a planning and coordinating role. They will be required to ensure that young people have access to a range of learning opportunities and to manage performance locally (DCSF/DIUS 2008). LAs will be responsible to the Young People's Learning Agency (YPLA), which will ensure that central government priorities are carried out. Furthermore, colleges will retain their corporate status and there are no plans for LAs to be involved with education and training for those over the age of 19. This will be the responsibility of a national Skills Funding Agency (SFA).

Most schools have remained under the aegis of local authorities and many of them provide education for adults, with classes often taking place on school premises in the evening. Nowadays, these courses are usually certificated – for example, by the Open College Network – and they encompass a range of vocational courses in addition to learning that is orientated towards leisure and general interest. The curriculum offer can range from information technology (IT) and business administration, to courses in car maintenance, cookery, modern languages, flower arranging and yoga. In addition, LAs are involved in responding to various government-led agendas on lifelong learning through schools. For example, the Family Learning initiative aims to give parents and carers the opportunity to find out how their children are taught at school, to share ideas and to develop their own knowledge and skills, particularly in areas such as literacy, numeracy and 'healthy living'.

Lifelong learning in the public services

Public service organizations such as the NHS, Police, and Fire and Rescue Services, have a tradition of providing structured professional development. This includes extensive 'in-house training' programmes, or can take the form of day or block release attendance at colleges or universities and, increasingly, structured partnerships providing recognized qualifications. Employees are expected to undertake professional development and to continuously update their knowledge and skills.

Regional police services have training schools that provide opportunities in a range of vocational areas for officers and support staff. Examples include courses in IT, management, forensic science and crime detection as well as areas of specialist policing such as public order, firearms and driver training. There are also courses of study for formal examinations to gain promotion. These require officers to gain high levels of knowledge, skill and understanding in a range of operational and strategic competencies and to undergo a variety of assessments. Similar arrangements exist in the fire and rescue service, the ambulance service and other areas of the public services.

Private training providers

Private training organizations vary in size and expertise. It is, however, possible to identify some common characteristics. Rather than covering a range of subjects catering for a broad cross-section of students, most private training providers focus on vocational areas such as business, IT or language training. These providers also offer courses for the unemployed, or individuals who are otherwise disadvantaged or socially excluded. For example, 'Entry to Employment' (E2E) provision aims to support young people not in education, employment or training. Private training companies are also significant providers of the state funded work-based learning programme 'Train to Gain'.

The Government intends private training organizations to play an increasing role in the provision of lifelong learning in the UK. This is encouraged by the White Paper *Raising Skills, Improving Life Chances* (DfES 2006), and new competitive arrangements have been introduced to support such providers by providing development and revenue funding as well as capital incentives. The White Paper claims this will: 'promote dynamism and innovation . . . where significant expansion of high quality provision is needed' (DfES 2006: para. 32). Such claims indicate a belief that involving private companies in education and training will improve quality and responsiveness through increasing competition. The proposals of the 2007 *Education and Skills Bill* went further than this. It was suggested that employers offering accredited training for young workers (between the ages of 16 and 18) will be able to access public funds for this purpose. Where training is not accredited there is an intention to introduce 'flexible and low burden' ways to allow it to be recognized for funding purposes (DfES 2007). Pilot programmes are currently trialling such arrangements, with large companies such as McDonald's and Flybe taking part. This takes the mixed economy of private and public lifelong learning providers a step further and blurs the boundary between them. In effect, the traditional flow of funding, with employers expected to pay 'training levies' for the state to provide education and training has been reversed.

Higher education

In 2009, there were over 130 British higher education institutions (HEIs), with various institutional titles – 'university' being the most common. Although HE is normally understood to incorporate foundation degree, first degree and postgraduate provision, its detailed structure is complex. As mentioned above, a significant amount of HE is located in FE colleges, with approximately one in ten HE students studying in FE.

In general, HEIs offer a different culture to that found in FE and elsewhere in the LLS. The background to English cultural attitudes towards the vocational was outlined long ago by Weiner (1981), and the strongest antipathies are found within the great English universities which have for centuries held sway over the intellectual climate. Higher education in North America lacked the legacy of medievalism which lingered in the ancient European universities, and was therefore more able to embrace technocratic knowledge. The instrumental and applied nature of vocational education is at odds with the liberal traditions of the traditional English university, and this is something which still permeates HE in Britain.

The implicitly hierarchical division of HEIs into 'pressure groups' such as the 'Russell Group' (founded at the Russell Hotel, London in 1994 and currently comprising 20 research intensive universities), the 'Million+ Group', and the 'University Alliance' underscores differences now compounded by a performative obsession with league table positions. The 'modern universities' are mainly former polytechnics (redesignated as universities in 1992), often with roots in the former colleges of technology. Those wishing to know more of the history of HE in Britain should consult a specialist work such as Anderson's (2006) *British Universities Past and Present*. Barnett (2003) provides a critical but accessible analysis of the trajectory of HE from an elite to a mass system, in the context of globalization, postmodernism and the crisis of knowledge. More recently, Deem, Hillyard and Reed (2007) explore the impact of 'audit culture' and managerialism on HE. There can be no doubt that the move to mass HE has changed its nature: however, the balance of negative and positive consequences is not easily weighed, although most would agree that widening participation in HE is, on a number of levels (not least social inclusion), part of a democratizing process.

Some key institutions

The framework of institutions that manage and monitor British education has been in a state of great flux since New Labour began to implement its reforms in the late

1990s. The system is littered with the remnants of superseded agencies and, for the uninitiated, baffling acronyms. It is not intended to provide a comprehensive overview of all these agencies here. Readers are advised to regularly check websites to monitor changing names and policies; in all probability some of the details below will have changed by the time this book appears.

The Department for Business Innovation and Skills

The Government's short-lived Department for Innovation, Universities and Skills (DIUS) was, together with the Department for Children, Schools and Families (DCSF), and the Department for Business, Enterprise and Regulatory Reform (DBERR), set up on 28 June 2007. DIUS and DCSF, effectively, replaced the DfES – itself at the end of a sequence of re-brandings that can be traced back beyond the former Ministry of Education (previously known as the Board of Education). The three departments newly created in June 2007 clearly had some closely related responsibilities and, given the increasingly overlapping curriculum boundaries of schools and FE, and of FE and HE, it was always likely that further change would follow quickly. The Department for Business, Innovation and Skills (BIS) duly came into being on 6 June 2009 following a merger of DIUS and DBERR. The dropping of 'Universities' from the title of the new department was seen by some as indicative of a culture whereby education was regarded as incontestably in the service of business. BIS has responsibility for all post-19 learning. The management of funding for 16–19-year-olds was to be transferred to local authorities, and BIS would work closely with DCSF.

The Qualifications and Curriculum Authority and the Qualifications and Curriculum Development Agency

Following a merger of the National Council for Vocational Qualifications (NCVQ) and the School Curriculum and Assessment Authority (SCAA) the Qualifications and Curriculum Authority (QCA) was established in 1997. The QCA is responsible for development of the National Curriculum and associated assessments, tests and examinations in England and Northern Ireland. There are devolved arrangements in Scotland and Wales. The QCA reports to the Secretary of State for Children, Schools and Families. With oversight of the operation of over 120 awarding bodies the QCA's remit is a large one, and there have been some notable and embarrassing difficulties in relation to the operation of GCSE and GCE A Level results, as well as with the Standard Assessment Tests (SATs) in schools. These 'problems' were instrumental in the thinking which led to the transfer of the regulatory functions of the QCA to the newly created Ofqual. At this stage a Qualifications and Curriculum Development Agency (QCDA) was established to provide ministerial advice and oversee examinations.

Ofqual: the Office of the Qualifications and Examinations Regulator

In its 2008 launch document, Ofqual (2008: 2) proclaimed its role as,

. . . the new regulator of qualifications, exams and tests in England. We ensure that children, young people and adult learners get the results their work deserves, that standards are maintained and that qualifications count now and in the future. We also make sure that the qualifications available meet the needs of learners and employers.

A major aspect of Ofqual's operations will be its accountability directly to Parliament (not to Government). To achieve its goals, Ofqual will need to hold awarding bodies to account, ensuring the standardization of qualifications. A major challenge will be to enforce quality and assure the fairness of examination marking across a large and complicated system.

The Skills Funding Agency

In 2001 the Learning and Skills Council (LSC) took over the work of the Further Education Funding Council for England (FEFCE) and the regional Training and Enterprise Councils (TECs). The LSC would be a major presence in the planning and funding of post-compulsory education and training in England other than for those in universities. With headquarters in Coventry and nine regional offices it had an annual budget of £10.4 billion in 2006–07. In February 2009, the LSC identified its 'major tasks' as raising the participation of young people and adults in education; improving skills levels; lifting the quality of education and training; and improving the effectiveness of the sector as well as access to learning for all. It stated that 'Our vision is that by 2010, young people and adults in England have knowledge and skills matching the best in the world and are part of a truly competitive workforce' (LSC 2009). Following a ministerial statement issued in March 2008, in changes to begin from April 2009, the LSC would be replaced by July 2010. A major part of the LSC's role would be undertaken by the newly created SFA, an organization concerned with funding FE colleges and other providers of FE. The same statement announced the creation of the YPLA.

The Young People's Learning Agency (YPLA)

The role allotted to this agency includes the development of national funding formulae, the vetting of regional proposals, and the delivery of provision throughout the regions. The DCSF (2009) explained that:

The YPLA will have a duty to ensure national budgetary control and check plans are consistent with the concept of a 14–19 entitlement. It will be an enabling body to support local authorities in carrying out their new duties – providing a broad commissioning framework and strategic data and analysis for local authorities to use. It will have reserve powers to intervene and arbitrate in the event that local authorities cannot fulfil their new duties to ensure plans are agreed and cohere at sub-regional, regional and national level.

Office for Standards in Education, Children's Services and Skills (Ofsted)

Ofsted was established in 1992, quickly attracting controversy under the leadership of Chris Woodhead. Its main function is to inspect and report on standards in education. In 2007, Ofsted merged with the Adult Learning Inspectorate (ALI) to provide a service which inspects all post-16 government funded education excepting HEIs which are generally inspected by the Quality Assurance Agency for Higher Education (QAA). It is worth noting, however, that teacher education provision in HEIs is subject to Ofsted inspection. Also from 2007 Ofsted was given responsibility for the registration and inspection of social care services for children, and the welfare inspection of independent and maintained boarding schools. Technically, Ofsted is a non-ministerial government department of Her Majesty's Chief Inspector of Schools, from whom all its powers devolve. Similar functions exist under different arrangements in Northern Ireland, Scotland and Wales.

Whatever the controversies surrounding Ofsted, it plays a major role in the education system and, many believe, serves an important purpose. Ofsted defines its role as follows:

> We want to raise aspirations and contribute to the long term achievement of ambitious standards and better life chances for service users. Their educational, economic and social well-being will in turn promote England's national success. To achieve this we will report fairly and truthfully; we will listen to service users and providers; and we will communicate our findings with all who share our vision, from service providers to policy-makers. We do not report to government ministers but directly to Parliament (and to the Lord Chancellor about children and family courts administration). This independence means you can rely on us for impartial information.
>
> (Ofsted 2009)

The Quality Assurance Agency for Higher Education (QAA)

Established in 1997, the QAA provides HEIs with an independent service which reports on how they maintain their standards and quality. While individual institutions retain responsibility for the quality of their courses and awards, through its external reviews the QAA encourages improvement, comments on the ability of institutions to maintain standards, offers guidance to institutions and also advises government on institutional applications for powers to award degrees or to receive the title of 'university'.

Using peer review, QAA operates a range of audits. Universities and colleges of HE are reviewed through an 'institutional audit'. Until 2006/07, FE colleges providing HE underwent academic review at subject level – this has now been replaced by a process of integrated quality and enhancement review (IQER), designed specifically for the review of HE in FE.

The Learning and Skills Improvement Service (LSIS)

LSIS began work on 1 October 2008. It was created as a replacement for the Centre for Excellence in Leadership (CEL) and the Quality Improvement Agency (QIA). LSIS (2008) announced that it would '. . . focus on learners and on developing excellent and sustainable further education and skills provision across the sector'. It also stated that '[L]eadership development will underpin and form an important part of the organization's strategic role in the sector'.

Lifelong Learning UK and Standards Verification UK

Lifelong Learning UK (LLUK) describes itself as

> the independent employer-led sector skills council responsible for the professional development of all those working in community learning and development, further education, higher education, libraries, archives and information services, and work based learning across the UK. LLUK provides the strategic perspective for workforce planning and development and influences and shapes relevant policy across the four UK nations . . . LLUK is licensed by the UK governments to set standards for occupational competence in the delivery and support of learning.
>
> (LLUK 2009)

Standards Verification UK (SVUK) was established as an operating arm of LLUK and is primarily concerned with monitoring and endorsing generic initial teacher training (ITT) qualifications for the LLS in England and Wales, and those for Skills for Life practitioners in ESOL, literacy and numeracy in England. SVUK works with HEIs and awarding bodies to ensure the quality of initial training and continuing professional development (CPD).

Two further key institutions, the Institute for Learning (IFL) and the Higher Education Academy (HEA), function as the professional bodies for FE and HE respectively. They are discussed in Chapter 3.

The need for perspective

The reform and successive reorganizations that have been the hallmark of the New Labour years call for a sense of perspective. The history of the English education system has benefited from a number of significant studies which have provided a basis for understanding developments. In the important area of comparative studies, Archer (1979) still stands as a central contribution to the analysis of educational development and change. Green (1990), in his study of the rise of the education systems in England, France and the USA, recognized the significance of the social functions of the state and of the relationships of social classes to the state. Comparative studies of vocational education are fewer in number. Smithers (1993) incorporates an element of (unfavourable) comparison of English vocational education/training with the systems in France and Germany in what became a notable (if populist attack) on the 'new vocationalism'.

For a broad account of the history of education in England and Wales, Brian Simon's four-volume *Studies in the History of Education* (see 1991) presents a classic overview. Donald (1992) examines the emergence of education as a system of control in a study that draws on postmodern perspectives. Donald argues that a grasp of the associated 'social and cultural dynamics' (p. 18) requires an investigation that focuses on educational ideologies, the routines of schooling as power mechanisms and the ways in which knowledge is organized into a curriculum. Tomlinson (2005) provides an excellent overview of post-1945 education policy in Britain, including specific consideration of lifelong learning.

In the influential *Education Limited* collection (Education Group 2 1991), Green (1991) quotes a Parliamentary Select Committee of 1818 stating that 'England is the worst educated country in Europe' before citing Balfour's 1902 claim that 'England is behind all continental rivals in education' (p. 7). The best part of a century later the National Commission on Education (NCE 1993) pronounced 'In the United Kingdom much higher achievement in education and training is needed to match world standards' (p. 43). For Green (1991) the historical reasons for Britain's relative under-development in terms of a national education system lie in religious divisions and, more importantly, structural obstacles in the form of economic complacency and aristocratic opposition to educational advance. Despite the energy of New Labour, its neo-liberal reforms did little to solve these problems.

3

Teacher education for lifelong learning

Amanda Fulford, Denise Robinson and Ron Thompson

> **In this chapter:**
>
> - The growth of teacher education for lifelong learning
> - Professional standards for teaching in lifelong learning
> - A framework of teaching qualifications
> - Centres for Excellence in Teacher Training
> - The Institute for Learning and the Higher Education Academy

The key role of lifelong learning in government policy since the late 1990s has led to an intensive focus on teacher education for the sector, in marked contrast to the earlier 'history of neglect' described by Lucas (2004). Following the Labour election victory in 1997, both the Fryer Report on lifelong learning (Fryer 1997) and the Kennedy Report on widening participation (Kennedy 1997) called for a coherent, nationally recognized system of teacher training for FE. By 2001, a number of limited reforms had been introduced, including national standards for FE teachers and a statutory requirement for new teachers to hold a recognized teaching qualification. However, these reforms proved slow to take effect and there was growing evidence that the desired impact on learning had not been achieved.

The quality of ITT for FE also attracted criticism; a survey inspection concluded that 'The current system of FE teacher training does not provide a satisfactory foundation of professional development for FE teachers at the start of their careers' (Ofsted 2003: 2). As a result, the Government promised a 'step change' in the quality of ITT for the learning and skills sector – an extension of the earlier focus on FE teachers to a much wider range of contexts. Their proposals were set out in the document *Equipping Our Teachers for the Future* (DfES 2004; hereafter *Equipping Our Teachers*), which effectively introduced a national curriculum for ITT as well as a requirement for CPD. This chapter is largely concerned with discussing the system of teacher education implemented, in line with the proposals of *Equipping Our Teachers*, since September 2007. However, to understand the perceived deficiencies of teacher education for FE and the nature of the reforms, we need to consider the development of ITT in FE over a longer period.

The growth of teacher education for lifelong learning

Until 2001, FE teachers had not been required to undertake initial teacher training. Even the term *initial* training is problematic, for while school teachers are normally trained prior to employment, those in FE often receive their first experience of teacher training *in* post. Indeed, for many years it was not uncommon for FE teachers to remain untrained. In FE and the wider lifelong learning sector, it is usual to distinguish between *pre-service* and *in-service* initial training, the former normally taken full time and before finding employment as a teacher, the latter taken part time and based around concurrent teaching employment.

The explanation for this situation lies partly in considerations of labour supply. The vocational nature of much of the lifelong learning curriculum means that teachers are normally required to have work experience outside teaching; employment as a teacher often develops alongside their main occupation. At the same time, the need for up-to-date practitioners has often led employers to recruit staff without teaching qualifications. Although bursaries now exist to encourage intending teachers to train as pre-service students, this is often impractical and there has been an understandable reluctance on the part of both Government and employers to face up to the implications of compulsory pre-service training. There has also been a *cultural* tendency in lifelong learning not to fully recognize the value of initial teacher training, particularly as a pre-service requirement. Teaching skills have been seen as something to be 'picked up' through experience. As Robson (2006: 14) notes 'The assumption has been . . . that if I know my subject, I can, by definition, teach it to others'. The in-service mode of initial training remains the norm even today, and was accepted rather than challenged by the 2007 reforms.

Participation in initial training has therefore, until quite recently, been voluntary – perhaps expected by employers, but ultimately at the discretion of the individual. Nevertheless, a number of government reports since the Second World War have attempted to improve or extend FE teacher training. The McNair Report (Board of Education 1944) was particularly significant, providing the impetus for the establishment of specialist technical teacher training institutions based in Bolton, Huddersfield and London – later expanded to four by the addition of a college in Wolverhampton following the Crowther Report (MoE 1959). These reports share both a concern to increase the number of trained teachers and reluctance to accept the cost involved in a radical expansion of training. For example, the Russell Report's (DES 1966) recommendation that new teachers of 15- to 18-year-olds should be teacher trained within three years of taking up their posts was rejected by the Government. The continuing absence of clear Government policy into the early 1990s led to a marked resistance to change in the proportion of trained teachers, which increased from 43 per cent in 1975 to just 56 per cent in 1991 (Lucas 2004: 75).

The economic crises of the 1970s led to fundamental changes in FE, together with growing intervention by central government. Given the political climate of the time, it was perhaps inevitable that market forces would penetrate FE. The 1992 Further and Higher Education Act established colleges as quasi-independent organizations in a process known as *incorporation*, and a marketized environment was created in which colleges competed with each other for students. As a result, many colleges were placed under severe financial pressure – often leading to increased workloads for staff. In the five-year period following incorporation, 20,000 teaching posts were lost while student numbers increased by over a third (Beale 2004: 469); significant numbers of part-time and casual staff were recruited to cope with the increased workloads. Because many of these new teachers were not trained, the proportion of staff with teaching qualifications actually *declined* in the years immediately following incorporation (Lucas 2004: 86–8).

The 1990s also saw a change in the nature of teaching qualifications. Until then, the major awards had been the university-validated Certificate in Education (Cert Ed) and Postgraduate Certificate in Education (PGCE), together with national awarding body qualifications such as the City and Guilds 730 – the latter often enabling progression to the university awards. However, the development of competence-based National Vocational Qualifications (NVQs) was associated with the introduction of a range of specific awards, developed by the Training and Development Lead Body (TDLB) and dealing with NVQ-related training and assessment. Vocational teachers were required to gain those awards relevant to their role as trainers or assessors, thus undermining the status of the existing generic awards and leading to a proliferation of fragmented, competence-based teaching qualifications.

Competence-based training also influenced the generic courses themselves, and many universities re-designed Cert Ed and PGCE courses to reflect the NVQ framework. However, there was considerable opposition to the idea of competence as a basis for teaching qualifications and over time universities moved away from NVQ-style approaches. Nevertheless, the formation of the employer-led Further Education National Training Organisation (FENTO) in 1999 to implement new occupational standards for FE teaching meant that a strong flavour of the competence-based model of training persisted into the new century. Although intended as descriptions of the occupational competence of experienced teachers, the 'FENTO standards' (FENTO 1999) also formed the basis for recognition of initial teaching qualifications. Both university and awarding body courses were required to undergo a process of *endorsement* against the FENTO standards, thus providing for the first time some measure of central control over all ITT curricula in FE.

As Lucas (2007) notes, the FENTO standards and others like them encouraged a mechanistic, 'tick-box' approach – although, arguably, it is the culture of surveillance and central control now widespread in education, rather than a particular curriculum model, which has the greater responsibility for this. Whatever the reason, it became clear that the FENTO standards were not helpful to the development of trainee teachers and were 'not an appropriate tool for designing ITT courses or for judging the final attainment of newly-qualified FE teachers' (Ofsted 2003: 36).

Perhaps more significant than debates over standards was the continuing unsatisfactory proportion of FE teachers holding a recognized teaching qualification. Although substantial numbers had been trained, by 2004 only 47 per cent of part-time staff and 70 per cent of full-time staff were qualified (LLUK 2005) compared with 25 per cent and 66 per cent respectively in 1996/97 (Lucas 2004: 87). This increase was stimulated by the 2001 requirement for a teaching qualification, but also reflected increasing numbers of trainees from the wider learning and skills sector. A major factor in achieving these numbers was the growth of teacher training in colleges, through partnership arrangements with universities as well as work with awarding bodies.

Several years into the new century, FE teacher training was therefore still somewhat patchy and uncertain. Although progress had been made and greater recognition of the value of teacher training achieved, the proportion of trained staff remained low. In comparison with school teaching, work in FE appeared to be of lower status and lacking a professional identity, albeit with high levels of individual commitment. In addition, central government concerns about the quality of training, together with a growing readiness to intervene at a *curriculum* level, led to a strong focus on the structure and content of courses, enforced by mechanisms such as occupational standards and endorsement (Simmons and Thompson 2007). This was the situation that the 2007 reforms attempted to address. The remainder of this chapter describes and evaluates these reforms, which comprise three main strands: new teaching standards for the lifelong learning sector; a centrally specified curriculum structure, including a framework of teaching qualifications corresponding to defined teaching roles; and measures to improve workplace learning (see also Thompson and Robinson 2008).

Professional standards for teaching in lifelong learning

From September 2007, initial teacher training courses for the lifelong learning sector (other than courses for teachers working solely in higher education) have been based on new 'professional' standards developed by LLUK, the successor organization to FENTO. The origins of this change were discussed above in relation to criticism of the FENTO standards by Ofsted, who had called for clearer standards applicable to new teachers in the sector (LLUK 2007a: i).

The LLUK standards express the 'key purpose' of the teacher in lifelong learning as being 'to create effective and stimulating opportunities for learning through high quality teaching that enables the development and progression of all learners' (LLUK 2007a: 2) and describe the skills, knowledge and attributes required. They are divided into six areas or domains: professional values and practice; learning and teaching; specialist learning and teaching; planning for learning; assessment for learning; and access and progression. Each domain is further divided into three sets of statements, relating to: professional values; professional knowledge and understanding; and professional practice. Box 3.1 shows the statements of professional values for domain D, 'planning for learning'. In Box 3.2, the statements of professional knowledge and professional practice are shown for this domain.

The LLUK teaching standards, although described as 'professional', continue the occupational-industrial approach used by FENTO, with around 150 statements describing the values, knowledge and practical abilities expected of those in a full teaching role. However, unlike the FENTO standards, they underpin a qualification framework intended to be used in course design. Course modules, known as 'units of assessment', have been constructed by LLUK from the standards and are combined in various ways to form qualifications at various levels and with more or less breadth. Awarding institutions are required to use the units of assessment to guide selection of course content and the design of assessment strategies.

Box 3.1 The LLUK teaching standards. Professional values for domain D: planning for learning

---

Teachers in the lifelong learning sector value:

AS1 Learners, their progress and development, their learning goals and aspirations and the experience they bring to their learning.

AS2 Learning, its potential to benefit people emotionally, intellectually, socially and economically, and its contribution to community sustainability.

AS3 Equality, diversity and inclusion in relation to learners, the workforce, and the community.

AS4 Reflection and evaluation of their own practice and their continuing professional development as teachers.

AS5 Collaboration with other individuals, groups and/or organizations with a legitimate interest in the progress and development of learners.

They are committed to:

DS1 Planning to promote equality, support diversity and to meet the aims and learning needs of learners.

DS2 Learner participation in the planning of learning.

DS3 Evaluation of own effectiveness in planning learning.

Source: LLUK (2007a: 10)

Although courses must be aligned with the LLUK standards, it is important to recognize the contested nature of these standards and the problematic status of some elements of the teacher training curriculum, for example the definitions of apparently orthodox terms such as 'reflective practice'. Much criticism has been levelled at the over-prescriptive nature of the standards and their inadequacy as a means of conceptualizing the activity of teachers (Lucas 2007; Nasta 2007). However, the impact of the new standards on *learning* has yet to be fully appraised.

A framework of teaching qualifications

As well as new teaching standards, the 2007 reforms also created a framework of teaching qualifications based on the standards and related to what were seen as key teaching roles – a *full teaching role,* for which teachers need to be fully qualified, and a more limited *associate teacher* role.

Corresponding to the full teaching role, the reforms introduced the status of Qualified Teacher Learning and Skills (QTLS), to be achieved within five years of entering a full teaching role in the sector. QTLS is not awarded automatically on achieving an appropriate award; it follows completion of a period of 'professional formation', a post-qualification process which requires a teacher to demonstrate competence in practice (IfL 2008a). QTLS is subject to annual renewal based on adherence to the IfL Code of Professional Practice (IfL 2008b), together with evidence of appropriate CPD; a minimum of 30 hours of CPD per year is required (for a critical review of the implications of mandatory CPD, see Orr 2008). Both the award of

Box 3.2 The LLUK teaching standards. Professional knowledge and practice for domain D: planning for learning

PROFESSIONAL KNOWLEDGE AND UNDERSTANDING	PROFESSIONAL PRACTICE
Teachers in the lifelong learning sector know and understand:	Teachers in the lifelong learning sector:
DK1.1 How to plan appropriate, effective, coherent and inclusive learning programmes that promote equality and engage with diversity.	DP1.1 Plan coherent and inclusive learning programmes that meet learners' needs and curriculum requirements, promote equality and engage with diversity effectively.
DK1.2 How to plan a teaching session.	DP1.2 Plan teaching sessions which meet the aims and needs of individual learners and groups, using a variety of resources, including new and emerging technologies.
DK1.3 Strategies for flexibility in planning and delivery.	DP1.3 Prepare flexible session plans to adjust to the individual needs of learners.
DK2.1 The importance of including learners in the planning process.	DP2.1 Plan for opportunities for learner feedback to inform planning and practice.
DK2.2 Ways to negotiate appropriate individual goals with learners.	DP2.2 Negotiate and record appropriate learning goals and strategies with learners.
DK3.1 Ways to evaluate own role and performance in planning learning.	DP3.1 Evaluate the success of planned learning activities.
DK3.2 Ways to evaluate own role and performance as a member of a team in planning learning.	DP3.2 Evaluate the effectiveness of own contributions to planning as a member of a team.

Source: LLUK (2007a: 10–11)

QTLS and the monitoring of CPD is the responsibility of the IfL. Although it is analogous to Qualified Teacher Status (QTS) in schools, QTLS is sector-specific: its possession does not entitle the holder to work in schools as a qualified teacher. Conversely, a school teacher with QTS who transfers to a further education institution must achieve QTLS by completing appropriate professional formation.

A further, more limited status exists, known as Associate Teacher Learning and Skills (ATLS), and intended for those in an associate teacher role. This role, which institutionalizes the trend towards limited (and usually lower paid) posts to support learning or assessment under the supervision of those in a full teaching role, is defined as involving significantly less than the full range of responsibilities ordinarily carried out by a teacher with QTLS (HM Government 2007), and requires a more limited base of knowledge, understanding and application. The qualification and professional formation requirements for ATLS are correspondingly less than those for QTLS, but are broadly similar in nature (IfL 2008a).

The main awards contained in the qualifications framework, and the roles for which they are intended, are described below, together with the most common university awards.

Preparing to Teach in the Lifelong Learning Sector (PTLLS)

This award is an induction to teaching and must be achieved within one year of taking up a first teaching post. Effectively, PTLLS is the 'passport to teaching' announced in *Equipping Our Teachers* and is a short, intensive course requiring around thirty guided learning hours. It carries six credits at Level 3 or Level 4 in the National Qualifications Framework (NQF; see Chapter 9). As with earlier reforms, PTLLS represents a compromise between a desire for at least some pre-service training and pragmatic considerations of labour supply. Although PTLLS is offered by awarding bodies as a stand-alone course, in university Cert Ed and PGCE courses it is normally integrated within the first stage of the award. As well as written assessment, PTLLS requires a satisfactory standard of practical teaching, often assessed by means of a 'microteaching' exercise. Once a new entrant has completed PTLLS, they must achieve the status appropriate to their teaching role (ATLS or QTLS) within five years.

Certificate in Teaching in the Lifelong Learning Sector (CTLLS)

This qualification is for those in an 'associate' teaching role who aspire to ATLS. Normally worth 24 credits at Level 3 or Level 4 in the NQF, CTLLS requires around 120 guided learning hours and the satisfactory completion of assessed teaching practice. A significant difficulty with CTLLS is the disparity between this qualification and those appropriate to QTLS; a teacher holding a CTLLS award must complete a substantial number of further credits, and develop academically to a considerable degree, in order to achieve a qualification appropriate to QTLS.

Diploma in Teaching in the Lifelong Learning Sector (DTLLS)

The Diploma is a full teaching qualification, as required for QTLS. It is worth 120 credits at Level 5 in the NQF, and normally requires two years of part-time study. Holders of PTLLS and CTLLS awards may be able to complete the Diploma in a shorter time; those with other awards may be eligible for some form of accreditation of prior learning. A 'minimum core' of knowledge of language, literacy, numeracy and ICT (consisting of pedagogical knowledge as well as personal skills) is included in the diploma (LLUK 2007b, 2007c).

Certificate in Education and PGCE

These are university awards and are full teaching qualifications as required for QTLS. A Cert Ed is worth 120 credits; in most cases this will be at Level 5 in the NQF but may be higher. As with DTLLS, a minimum core of language, literacy, numeracy and ICT is incorporated in these courses. In some institutions, the PGCE is available at two levels: a Professional Graduate Certificate at Level 6 in the NQF and a Post-graduate Certificate at Masters level (Level 7 in the NQF). These awards normally require two years of part-time study or one year full time. Accreditation arrangements will often enable suitably qualified and experienced teachers to complete in-service programmes in a shorter time. Some universities use different titles for their awards to those given above; however, the content and academic levels tend to be similar to those outlined here, whatever terminology is used.

Centres for Excellence in Teacher Training

Concern over the work-based learning of trainee teachers stemmed from the survey inspections conducted by Ofsted (2003), which found inadequacies in the integration of practical skills with the more theoretical elements of training. Comparing FE with training for schools, Ofsted concluded that this was due largely to weaknesses in mentoring and poorly developed links between teacher educators and staff in FE colleges. The survey inspections also highlighted the often limited experience of the lifelong learning sector gained by trainees. Because in-service training is the norm, 'teaching practice' is linked to the job role of individual trainees, who may therefore find it difficult to broaden their experience. Access to local and national networks for the promotion of teaching and learning is therefore likely to improve training in the sector.

Improved mentoring and access to national networks were also seen as relevant to another weakness identified by Ofsted – inadequate development of subject-specific teaching skills and knowledge. Due to the reliance on local delivery of in-service courses discussed earlier, trainee numbers in a particular location are rarely large enough for subject-specific groupings to be viable. Some providers have developed alternative strategies based on study days or summer schools, and virtual networks such as Associate Online (see Chapter 14) show great promise. However, the belief in local mentoring arrangements as the fundamental strategy for improving the work-based learning of trainees – in particular its subject specific aspects – has become institutionalized, highlighting the need for high-quality training and support for mentors.

In response to these concerns, the 2007 reforms established a network of Centres for Excellence in Teacher Training (CETT). The rationale underpinning the Centres is expressed in *Equipping Our Teachers* as follows:

Comprehensive support for teachers in the workplace is fundamental to turning [the proposed reforms] into reality. The vast majority of teachers in the learning and skills sector are trained in-service and model their future practice by observing colleagues and mentors who teach the same subject or vocational area.

Without good role models of teaching and comprehensive support, their development is severely inhibited . . . Effective partnerships linking colleges, higher education institutions and other providers are also critical to effective initial training.

DfES (2004: 11)

Each CETT is a partnership of organizations involved in ITT and CPD in the learning and skills sector. Although there are different emphases, their activities focus mainly on developing and supporting ITT and CPD. The CETTs cover different areas of England, although a small number also have a national remit for certain specialist activities.

The Institute for Learning and the Higher Education Academy

The Institute for Learning (IfL) was officially recognized as the professional body for the learning and skills sector in 2004. The 2007 reforms give IfL a key role in the FE system, with the responsibility to register FE teachers and award QTLS or ATLS status where appropriate. The Institute monitors CPD activity and also operates disciplinary procedures relating to professional misconduct. Although government regulations on teacher training only apply directly to FE, teachers in work-based learning and adult and community learning are incorporated on a contractual basis through the LSC. As with their colleagues in FE, these teachers are required to join IfL.

The idea of a professional organization for FE teachers is not new, and its development over time reflects the slow move towards recognition of teaching in the sector as a professional activity. Trade unions such as the National Association of Teachers in Further and Higher Education (NATFHE) and its successor, the University and College Union (UCU), had a strong professional focus. Employer- or sector-based organizations – for example, the former Further Education Development Association (FEDA) – promoted the discussion of staff and professional development issues. However, none of these organizations could be regarded as a professional body in the sense discussed in Chapter 5, as they lacked regulatory power and did not encompass all staff teaching in the sector.

In HE, perhaps even more so than in the FE sector, traditional views of teaching and learning have prioritized subject knowledge over pedagogy. The emphasis on research as a distinctive feature of the activity of HE teachers provides a further 'pull' away from pedagogy as a core concern for many HE teachers, and career progression in HE has often been perceived as dependent far more on scholarly output than on teaching ability. However, the emphasis on widening participation has brought about significant change in the student body, with expectations and backgrounds ranging from the purely scholarly to the strongly vocational. As a result, attention has focused much more urgently in recent years on issues of teaching and learning in HE.

The Dearing Report (NCIHE 1997) called for a more student-centred approach in HE, supported by greater professionalism in HE teaching. A specific recommendation, duly accepted by the Government, was to establish an Institute for Learning and Teaching in Higher Education (ILTHE), conceived as a professional body for HE teachers and intended to accredit HE teacher training programmes, commission research into teaching and learning, and stimulate innovation in teaching. The HEA was formed in 2004 by merging the Institute with two other organizations with a teaching and learning focus within FE, the Learning and Teaching Support Network (LTSN) and the National Co-ordination Team for the Teaching Quality Enhancement Fund (TQEF). The HEA manages a range of professional networks, and offers accreditation to appropriate teacher-training courses. Individuals can apply for HEA membership at three levels: Associate, Fellow or Senior Fellow.

In the FE system, occupational standards are set by LLUK – essentially a government body – while regulation and support for individual teachers is provided by IfL, the professional body. By contrast, the HEA is responsible for both of these functions (albeit in consultation with employer bodies) and has developed the *UK Professional Standards Framework* (HEA 2006). In this framework, teaching is conceptualized in terms of six 'areas of activity' relating to planning, preparation and delivery; 'core knowledge' relating to subject and pedagogy; and 'professional values'. Three standards are defined, corresponding to different levels of involvement and responsibility in the areas of activity. Within this broad framework, there is considerable freedom for individuals or course designers to choose how to demonstrate their abilities, knowledge and understanding in the areas of activity. The higher education standards are therefore less prescriptive, and arguably more attuned to professional development, than those applying elsewhere in lifelong learning.

4

Theory and practice
James Avis and Kevin Orr

In this chapter:

- Policy science and policy scholarship
- Theorizing education: socio-economic and political context
- Theorizing education: contingency and complexity
- Expansive practice
- Conclusion: what about practice?

This chapter explores the relationship between theory and practice. On one level this is self evident: how we make sense of learning and teaching informs practice. The manner in which we construct learners and understand learning will frame notions of effective teaching and what it is to be a 'good' teacher. Policy scholarship shifts understandings of practice away from a narrow focus on classroom processes to their wider context. Educational processes are always theorized – even denying the salience of theory represents a theoretical standpoint. It is important to engage with theory, to deconstruct and interrogate it for its uses. How far can theory take us? Does it raise important questions? What are its limits and possibilities? What does it say about pedagogy and social justice? What are its politics?

Policy science and policy scholarship

Consider any college mission statement, or policy addressing teaching and learning, and we encounter well-rehearsed phrases that place the learner at the centre of educational processes. Continuous improvement will enhance standards and address the needs of learners more closely. This is the terrain of policy science which sits alongside a number of related currents: evidence informed practice, value for money, customer satisfaction, and so on. These may be drawn upon to inform and develop practice. For example, providers may call upon particular strategies to enhance the performance of learners or to improve 'customer satisfaction'. These activities can be placed under the remit of policy science whereby providers are deemed able to intervene in educational practices, achieving the desired outcomes.

Policy science readily folds over into interventions that focus upon individual colleges, particular classrooms or teachers, and the type of community from which learners are drawn (Grace 1995). It can veer towards an analysis that pathologizes the practices of particular teachers, colleges or communities. Paradoxically, policy science can sit alongside approaches that emphasize the possibility of intervening in practice and making a difference in a particular context. This can be seen in the case of those interventions linked to school effectiveness or improvement. The difficulty is that such approaches pay scant attention to the wider socio-economic and political context of education and learners. In ignoring the political context policy science works with the status quo, securing the interests of those with power.

Policy science can easily become preoccupied with descriptive accounts of initiatives and questions of implementation. We could use this type of approach to think about any current policy initiative – the implementation of 14–19 Diplomas at an institutional or classroom level, for example. The questions with which policy science is concerned are attractive. It avoids the apparent obfuscations of theory, having a concreteness in its direct relationship to action and practice. In addition, its technicist orientation leads it to portray itself as offering a rational and value-free approach – a problem is identified and a solution proposed.

An approach to educational practice orientated towards making a difference is no bad thing. But there are costs associated with the framework within which policy science is placed. The ground upon which interventions are to be made has been determined elsewhere. It is in this context that the language of managerialism, effectiveness and efficiency has gained ascendancy. Education, and in particular the LLS, must address the needs of the economy and there is a blurring between the needs of industry and individual learners. While the State may suggest a straightforward parallel between the interests of learners and of capital, this is by no means the case. It is important to recognize that labour creates the surpluses required for capital accumulation. The necessity for economic competitiveness may be a common refrain among policy makers, but the outcomes will be unevenly distributed, with some gaining the rewards and others bearing the costs (Avis 2007a).

Policy scholarship develops an analytic framework beyond that of policy science, placing its analyses within a wider context (Grace 1995). There is a necessity to examine the politics and underlying ideologies that inform policy making. For example, such a stance would explore how the ideas of the New Right have informed the development of educational policy, or the manner in which New Labour has appropriated neo-liberalism. This approach may be castigated for its distance from everyday educational practice, but it raises important questions about the wider socio-economic context as well as the political implications of what takes place within the LLS. It seeks to render visible contradictions and tensions. Policies and practices concerned with widening participation that seek to transform learning cultures may hold progressive possibilities, yet by not challenging class structure these are ameliorative and serve a deeply ideological function (Ainley 2008). They may offer benefits to those involved but do little to transform the wider social structure. A policy scholarship analysis would construe the inequalities related to race, ethnicity, class and gender as structural phenomena rather than arising out of discrimination or prejudice. To interrupt the processes through which these inequalities are generated, it is necessary to move beyond the individual and address the social practices through which these are reproduced.

It could be argued the dichotomy between policy science and policy scholarship is overdrawn, and that rather than a duality there is a continuum containing an interrelationship between agency and structure. Much social theory suggests a dialectical relationship between agency and structure. Marx (1968) suggested that while people make history, they do not do so in conditions of their own choosing. Similarly, Giddens's notion of *structuration* (Giddens and Pierson 1998) illustrates how social interactions re-produce social structures – by interacting with others we are simultaneously creating structure. Bourdieu's analyses emphasize the dialectical relationship between *habitus* and *field*. James and Diment note:

> '[habitus] names the characteristic dispositions of the social subject. It is indicated in the bearing of the body and in deeply ingrained habits of behaviour, feeling, thought' (Lovell 2000: 27). Habitus engages with the field, which is conceptualised as 'a structured system of social relations, at micro and macro level, rather like a field of forces in which positions are defined . . . in relation to each other'
> (James and Bloomer 2001: 5, cited by James and Diment 2003: 409)

Human agency can make a difference, but constraints must be recognized. Paradoxically, research and state interventions into education often play down the salience of structure, folding over into individualistic and technicist positions that deny the politics of engagement. This has an affinity with policy science which implicitly operates with a consensual model of society. If we all share similar goals, as in the discourse of competitiveness, technicized and individualistic solutions become readily available. This position denies the existence of social antagonism in which the interests of particular groups are in fundamental contradiction, as with capital and labour. The result is that systemic contradictions, patterns of exploitation and oppression become sidelined. Policy scholarship points towards a political understanding of the policy process, raising questions about the role of the state. It works with a conflict model of society and state, in which both are riven by antagonisms that are not necessarily amenable to rational solutions that benefit all.

Theorizing education: socio-economic and political context

The socio-economic and political context frames practices within lifelong learning. It shapes and impacts on qualification structures, models of assessment and the curriculum. This is an uneven process, accented differentially towards particular learners and educational sectors. Nevertheless there is a relationship between this wider context and educational practice. It has an influence on the skills learners should develop, such as the capacity to become lifelong learners or team players. It also has a bearing on what counts as the form of knowledge that education is to deliver. None of this is innocent but derives from particular understandings of society, the economy and, somewhat tautologically, the role of the learner and what it is to be a teacher in lifelong learning. Underpinning these ideas are theorizations of educational relations. The following, from the White Paper *Opportunity, Employment and Progression*, raises several key themes: '*Skills* are now a key driver to achieving *economic success* and *social justice* in the *new global economy*' (DIUS/DWP 2007: 30, our emphasis).

The development and enhancement of skills is seen as pivotal to economic success and the well-being of society in the 'global economy'. The pursuit of these aims also delivers social justice through opportunity, as well as providing the resources that can be used to benefit. These are key elements in New Labour's stance towards competitiveness, that allocates particular roles to education, teachers and learners. There is a resonance with New Labour's notion of rights and responsibilities. Gordon Brown, the current British prime minister has stated:

> The Britain I believe in is a Britain of fairness and opportunity for all. Every British citizen with every chance to make the most of themselves – every community fair to every citizen – *if you work hard, you're better off. If you save, you're rewarded. If you play by the rules, we'll stand by you* . . . responsibilities required in return for rights; fairness not just for some but all who earn it.
>
> (Brown 2007, unnumbered, our emphasis)

Or in the words of Tony Blair:

> It is a simple equation – we give opportunity, we demand responsibility, and that's how we build strong communities . . . Our goal is a Britain in which nobody is left behind; in which people can go as far as they have the talent to go; in which we achieve true equality – equal status and equal opportunity rather than equality of outcome.
>
> (Blair 2002, unnumbered)

An emphasis on rights and responsibilities lends itself to a particular understanding of the role of the State. It is no longer the archetypal social democratic State concerned with redistribution; rather it facilitates individual engagement with opportunity. Giddens (1998: 100–1) describes this as the social investment state:

> . . . redistribution must not disappear from the agenda of social democracy. But recent discussion has . . . shifted the emphasis towards the 'redistribution of possibilities'. The cultivation of human potential should as far as possible replace after the event 'redistribution'.

The way the socio-economic context is understood leads to the suggestion that there are boundless possibilities for those who avail themselves of the opportunities these 'new' conditions offer. Indeed, we all have a duty to take advantage of the opportunities that arise for the benefit of ourselves, our families and society as a whole. The State becomes an enabling body offering each individual the opportunity to develop – it becomes the social investment state embodying social justice. Underpinning these ideas is the notion that the social formation is based on consensus. These ideas or theorizations not only describe the socio-economic context but constitute it, resting alongside allied conceptualizations of the social formation and the role individuals play within it. This constitutes a *regime of truth*. 'Each society has its regime of truth, its general politics of truth: that is, the types of discourses which it accepts and makes function as true' (Foucault 1980: 131).

Such theorizations also shape the way in which we understand educational achievement. There are numerous ways in which we can make sense of under- and over-achievement in education. Early work in the sociology of education drew upon the notion of educability, a theme echoed in state policy.

> This [improving the schooling of working-class children] would undoubtedly be the most effective way of eliminating the social problems of the so-called delinquent areas, a name that masks a much wider social problem – the failure to integrate the unskilled and semi skilled working class into a society which is becoming predominantly governed by the values and standards of the professional middle class.
>
> (Vaizey 1962, cited by Education Group CCCS 1981: 78–9)

This resonates with current policy, which resurrects in various guises the deserving and undeserving working class. In some writing we confront notions of an underclass or a racialized section of the white working class who fail to take up the opportunities that are available to them (Preston 2003). Consider the following passage:

> [T]he risk of non-participation [learning or work] is higher for young people if:
>
> * Their parents are poor or unemployed
> * They are members of certain minority ethnic groups
> * They are in particular circumstances which create barriers to participation
>   i   They are carers
>   ii   They are teenage parents
>   iii They are homeless
>   iv   They are or have been in care
>   v   They have a learning difficulty
>   vi   They have a disability
>   vii They have a mental illness
>   viii They misuse drugs or alcohol
>   ix   They are involved in offending
>
> (Social Exclusion Unit 1999: 48)

While this hints at a structural explanation it also veers towards an underclass model that uses the language of cultural pathology to explain differential educational achievement. This results in an 'othering' of those who do not participate in education: they are different and we need to take steps to ensure their inclusion. Accordingly, we need to disrupt and undermine their 'irrational' culture which is antithetical to education. This stance is reflected in the Fryer Report: 'In our country today, far too many people are still locked in a culture which regards lifelong learning as either unnecessary, unappealing, uninteresting or unavailable' (1999: 8).

Particular forms of white working-class culture are deemed atavistic and out of step with the needs of modern society. The same can be said of certain groups within the black working class. The logic is to castigate such groups for their failure to grasp the opportunities available. It views as irrational the cultural defences of these groups and renders rational the orientations of the middle class (Davies et al. 2008). Ainley (2008) suggests that the call to widen participation in university education is a 'con'; rather than promising upward mobility, it represents in effect the proletarianization of the professions. If this is the case, how should we make sense of the 'poor' who do not go to university? Is this irrational?

Theorizing education: contingency and complexity

Policy scholarship recognizes the complexity of educational processes. Government exhortations to 'eliminate failure' (DfES 2006: 56), or an emphasis on 'best practice' reduces the significance of contingency and over-simplifies the LLS. At classroom level, what works with one group may not work with another; a student engaged by one tutor may 'switch off' for his or her colleague (Hodkinson 2008). Even at the most fundamental level of what we teach, or what knowledge is, there is complexity. Young (2003: 554) wrote: 'we have a national curriculum, a post-compulsory curriculum and even a higher education curriculum, all of which take for granted the assumptions about knowledge on which they are based'. Young had earlier asserted that the idea that 'all knowledge is socially produced for particular purposes in particular contexts is by now relatively uncontentious' (1998: 1), but this may over-state the level of agreement. In a 2003 interview the then British education minister, Charles Clarke, was critical of the study of classics, stating that 'education for its own sake is a bit dodgy' and that students 'need a relationship with the workplace' (BBC 2003). Clarke saw it as his role to evaluate knowledge, and then promote and fund what he considered worthwhile. Young (1998: 1) went on to ask: 'does this mean that what counts as knowledge in society or what is selected to be included in the curriculum at a particular time is no more than what those in positions of power decide to be knowledge?' The answer must be, no: there is always dispute and unevenness. For example, the radical Chartist movement in the nineteenth century used the term 'really useful knowledge' to describe the type of education they promoted. Richard Johnson explains:

> 'Really useful knowledge' was a knowledge of everyday circumstances, including a knowledge of why you were poor, why you were politically oppressed and why through the force of social circumstance, you were the kind of person you were, your character misshapen by a cruel competitive world.
>
> (Education Group 1981: 37)

Apple and Beane (2007: vii) noted 'the growing dissatisfaction on the part of educators in so many places with curricula that have little relationship with the cultures and lives of the students'. They endorse how engaged practitioners can challenge received notions of knowledge by (re)connecting it to 'the communities and biographies of real people' (2007: 151). Teachers have the autonomy, despite the constraints they face, to emphasize particular aspects of the curriculum according to their values. The curriculum is a social construct that reflects society in all its complexity, and the manner in which it is interpreted is complicated by individual biography and belief.

Even when considering practice, to describe particular objective circumstances may not adequately predict or explain what takes place or how individuals may react. As an illustration, here are extracts from interviews with two trainees on a PCET teacher training course who were asked to describe their experience of the staffroom.

Trainee A

[I]t's fantastic . . . It's really good. You've got like space to breathe . . . and everybody's friendly . . . and very cooperative . . .

I've been . . . given a desk and a computer . . . I mean, everybody has access to the computer . . . if I'm working at that desk they tend not to disturb me . . . They go and use other computers . . . which is brilliant 'cause . . . I am a student . . . but they have really valued me and I don't feel like a student sometimes.

Trainee B

Well, first of all we went into the department, the manager wasn't there so it was a case of oh, you know, everyone looking up and staring at you, and the first greeting was, 'Bring your own tea . . . bring your own coffee. You don't touch anyone else's. You can't sit anywhere that's anyone else's seat; you won't have a seat of your own . . .'

These trainees were describing the same staffroom, in the same college at the same time, which suggests that a relationship between situation and biography (including expectations) formed contrasting reactions to an ostensibly similar experience. Such complex relationships influence perceptions throughout lifelong learning. To quote Law (2003: 3), simplicity 'won't help us to understand mess': the LLS is characterized by messy contradictions.

Even messy contradictory situations may seem normal to those experiencing them. Reeves, writing in the 1990s, describes circumstances still recognizable today: 'The structure of further education is so immediate and enveloping that, far from seeing any absurdities or contradictions, most staff and students who work within it undertake without any question what is expected of them' (1995: 93). Bourdieu may help us to understand this apparent myopia. He described *doxa* as 'the coincidence of the objective structures and the internalized structures which provides the illusion of immediate understanding, characteristic of the familiar universe, and which at the same time excludes from that experience any inquiry as to its own conditions of possibility' (1990: 26).

We absorb the way the world around us works, however messy, so that incongruities become familiar and unnoticed. This underpins the need to delve beneath the obvious, which conscious theorization allows. Analysing education with the benefit of a coherent theoretical approach avoids a paralysing relativism that says educational situations are too complex to explain. If it is impossible to explain, then any explanation is equally valid, and education cannot meaningfully be changed. So, to acknowledge that many contingencies may interact within a given set of relationships is not to say that analysis is pointless. Rather, the point is to adopt an analysis that is sophisticated enough to comprehend complexity. Consider, for example, what Bourdieu wrote about the role of the teacher in France:

> Agents entrusted with acts of classification can fulfil their social function as social classifiers only because it is carried out in the guise of acts of academic classification. They do well what they have to do (objectively) because they think they are doing something other than what they are doing, because they are doing something other than what they think they are doing, and because they believe in what they think they are doing. As fools fooled, they are the primary victims of their own actions.
>
> (Bourdieu 1996: 39)

Bourdieu argues teachers make decisions about students that may appear impartial and based on academic progress or ability. Yet, what is happening is more nuanced because teachers do not stand outside society, and their decisions are not only shaped by the norms of society, but also perpetuate them. Teachers may think they apply objective criteria, however, those criteria reflect an unequal society where certain types of knowledge and expression are valorized and they perpetuate social division. Elsewhere Bourdieu writes

> If the freedom the educational system allows the teacher is the best guarantee that he will serve the system, the freedom allowed to the educational system is the best guarantee that it will serve the perpetuation of the relations prevailing between the classes, because the possibility of this re-direction of ends is inscribed in the very logic of a system which never better fulfils its social function than when it seems to be exclusively pursuing its own ends.
>
> (Bourdieu and Passeron 1990: 125–6)

The education system does not need to be closely controlled by the State because in pursuing its own goals it follows those of an inegalitarian society, which it then helps to reproduce. The role of education or the teacher can only be understood in relation to the values of society, the culture of the organization and its socio-economic structure.

To extract educational practice from its context is to misrepresent it, even if we are trying to understand what works in the classroom. Coffield and Edward (2008: 2), in a critique of 'best practice', suggest that to improve the quality of teaching and learning in the LLS:

> The first task is to appreciate the implications of the complexities of teaching and learning in specific localities and only then to devise policies to respond to those implications. We need an approach that constructs policy, based on a deep understanding of the central significance of what happens in classrooms, e.g. by first assessing the needs of learners, tutors and institutions, the demands of practice, the conditions of the labour markets and how these (and many other) factors interact differently and dynamically in particular areas.

Best, or even good practice cannot be passed around like a handout, because successful learning is conditional on many factors, each of which can differ from setting to setting. To suggest otherwise not only fails to explain, but sets up unreasonable expectations on teachers and learners alike. A 14-year-old student who comes to an FE college because they have not succeeded at school may similarly not succeed at college. Is that because of the failings of the staff, or the failings of an unequal society that produces teenagers who are alienated and disengaged? Apple and Beane (2007) rightly extol inspirational, engaged teachers, but the selfless commitment of individuals cannot always counterbalance the weight of a complex, hierarchical and unequal society.

Classroom practice can develop through being informed by contingency, as Coffield and Edward describe above, because teachers retain some agency to affect what happens in their classroom or workshop. This, however, demands more than a perfunctory description of 'best practice'. Indeed, the 'Transforming Learning Cultures' project, which rigorously researched learning in FE, stressed that the role of the tutor is a crucial element in successful learning.

Expansive practice

The section above explored issues that bear on the complexity of educational relations, and indeed on the importance of 'happenstance' or contingency in relation to the forms of capital and habitus that learners and lecturers carry with them. The significance of this is that there are no easy and straightforward answers of the type suggested by the technicization embedded in policy science. Inevitably the interventions we make into educational relations are formed by our values. However, while accepting the complexity and messiness of these processes it is important that we lodge them within a framework that can move beyond relativism. If, for example, we stop at an exploration of pedagogic relations that views these as ultimately arbitrary, in that 'what works for one learner or lecturer doesn't for another', this can become debilitating and overly individualistic. It is necessary to place educational processes within a relational context. We need to locate education within the social relations of class, gender, race, sexuality, age and disability, together with the institutional and wider socio-economic context. Bourdieu's work points towards the importance of these interconnections deriving from his conceptualization of the relational in education and social processes.

One of the benefits of a relational approach that locates classroom processes in a wider context is that it can avoid the 'pathologization' of the practices of learners and teachers while constituting education as a site of struggle. Some years ago Troyna (1984) sought to contest understandings of black (predominantly male) educational underachievement. His position was that in a social context in which racist processes restricted access to the labour market educational disengagement could not be understood through a simplistic lense of underachievement. A more complex process was taking place and although we may question the political efficacy of young people's disengagement from education, nevertheless such a stance does embody a particular rationale. Ironically, when such disengagement leads to civic disturbance this may bring with it positive interventions for the community involved.

Much has been written about the performative context within which FE teachers work and the consequence of this for their morale as well as the different responses this might engender (see Chapter 18). These may mirror those of disengaged youth, or may be concerned with some sort of survival strategy, and while some of these responses may be deemed anti-educational, so is much of the associated policy context. The tendency to individualize the failing of particular teachers needs to be set within this understanding. If this prognosis is somewhat bleak the same argument could be made in relation to what constitutes 'good practice', as well as ideas about learner engagement. Successful learners may serve to sustain the illusion of meritocracy and thereby perform an important ideological role (Althusser 1971). In addition, the very notion of success is a relational concept. Success within a low ranked institution will not necessarily carry the dividends associated with a high ranking one, although the abilities and potential developed may be greater in the former. It is at this juncture, and with some force, that society's inequitable social structures are encountered. Ainley's (1994) work illustrates this process. In his study of HE, students from a new university found it difficult to obtain the type of graduate employment that those from prestigious universities gained. For Ainley, this reflected class processes – the recruitment 'of those like us'. For his students however, this was misrecognized and was felt to indicate their own failings in developing the types of transferable skills required in employment.

Educational practices cannot be thought through in isolation but need to be located in their wider context, and classroom processes need to be set within their wider institutional context. The college itself needs to be related to the social relations of education, that is to say the relations between educational providers and the implicit status attached to particular qualifications. This articulates with the patterning of social relations in terms of class, race and gender within society. If we wish to engage in educational practices underpinned by a commitment to social justice, we need to consider a number of different sites of struggle and potential alliances. These include the classroom and practices that contribute to learning. Here we may encounter the contradictions of our own practice and its unintended consequences. Reflexivity is important at this level but has to be set within a wider context, otherwise we can exaggerate the efficacy of our teaching or alternatively blame ourselves for the underachievement of our students, with all the emotional cost that that incurs (Colley 2006). The point is that the classroom is just one site of struggle among many. This is why an expansive understanding is important. Such a practice acknowledges the relational context in which education is placed, the varied sites of intervention within and outside education, and the potential for alliances with progressive social movements concerned with social justice.

Conclusion: what about practice?

Earlier we argued that the way we think about what constitutes 'good practice' will be informed by the manner in which we construct knowledge, the learner and learning, the teacher and teaching, as well as the socio-economic context. These are political questions in as much as answers will inform our orientation to pedagogic practice and our understanding of the relationship of education to wider society. We have argued that classroom processes are a form of social practice that must be set alongside those taking place outside. It is because of this that an expansive notion of practice is important. This suggests that an interest in doing the best for our learners involves engagement with social practices beyond the classroom. This is not to deny the salience of the classroom but to place it in its relational context. At the same time it is important not to construct the teacher as some sort of 'super hero' actively engaging on multiple fronts in the community, professional association, unions, as well as social movements. Such expectations are unreasonable, gendered and in the long term untenable, failing to recognise that teaching is among other things paid employment – a job.

Research that has explored the experiences of newly qualified lecturers or those undergoing FE teacher training, whether as pre- or in-service trainees, characterizes these groups as holding an ethos of care, as well as a real desire and hope of giving something back to the community (Avis and Bathmaker 2004, 2006). However, the way in which community is conceived varies: for those rooted in occupational and vocational cultures it is the trade or profession, while for others it is to stand as a role model for those drawn from disadvantaged communities of what it is possible to achieve. Such orientations connect with an interest in doing the best for students, and in facilitating learner development to enhance life chances. This is in spite of the difficulties that derive from the socio-economic and institutional context in which teachers and learners labour. Underlying such commitments rests a particular orientation to practice. It is here that the writings of Hodkinson and colleagues are important. Hodkinson argues that learning in college is directly influenced by:

- the positions, dispositions and actions of the students;
- the positions, dispositions and actions of the tutors;
- the location and resources of the learning site which are not neutral, but enable some approaches and attitudes, and constrain or prevent others;
- the syllabus or course specification, the assessment and qualification specifications;
- the time tutors and students spend together, their interrelationships, and the range of other learning sites students are engaged with;
- issues of college management and procedures, together with funding and inspection body procedures and regulations, and government policy;
- wider vocational and academic cultures, of which any learning site is a part;
- wider social and cultural values and practices, for example around issues of social class, gender and ethnicity, the nature of employment opportunities, social and family life, and the perceived status of further education as a sector.

(2008: 11)

Teachers' agency and social practice will be framed by these conditions. For those with a professional and vocational commitment the wider context in which learners labour frames life chances and the possibilities for social justice. The desire of these teachers to do the best for their students necessitates a consideration of the wider social context which in turn articulates with an expansive notion of practice. At the same time, the desire to do the best reflects teacher commitment and agency and thus offers a politics of a kind – a politics of hope. To conclude, we draw upon Apple and Beane (2007: 12–13) who suggest that what distinguishes progressive from democratic schools is that the latter's vision

> extends beyond purposes such as improving the school climate or enhancing students' self-esteem. Democratic educators seek not simply to lessen the harshness of social inequities in school, but to change the conditions that create them. For this reason, they tie their understanding of undemocratic practices inside the school to larger conditions on the outside.

Such an orientation recognizes the need for an expansive practice that locates educational processes within the wider context, acknowledging their contribution to social justice as well as offering a politics of empowerment.

5

Professionalism

James Avis, Roy Fisher and Ros Ollin

In this chapter:

- The professional teacher
- Professional values and codes of conduct
- Inter-professionality in the LLS
- Research and scholarship

The professional teacher

Before considering this concept, it is necessary to examine the nature of 'professionalism', a much abused term, with many occupational groups aspiring to such a label. Historically, the term 'profession' has been applied to elite occupations within medicine, the church and law. If, however, we consider the way it is used today many occupations seek to attach the appellation 'profession' for the status it accords, consequently it has become relatively meaningless with diverse groups describing themselves as such. There are many ways to theorize the professional and below we comment on three important approaches.

Initially, we examine the trait and functionalist approaches which take at face value the self-presentation of the professions (Barber 1963; Millerson 1964). The trait approach argues that the professions have a number of characteristics that set them apart from other occupational groups. For example, professions are thought to possess particular skills and expert knowledge, acquired through training, which should be used for the benefit of society. Because of the high levels of skill and knowledge involved, only members of the profession are in a position to judge whether this has been used appropriately, with conduct being governed by codes of practice. Professions are thought to be marked by altruism orientated towards meeting the needs of clients and thereby society more widely. In order to be able act in an appropriate manner professional autonomy is a necessity. A trait approach lists the characteristics of the professions, pointing to elements such as: high levels of skill and knowledge, codes of conduct, altruism and autonomy, among others. The difficulty with this approach, as is the case with any list, is why these factors and not others?

Functionalist approaches resolve this difficulty by theorizing the relationship between particular characteristics. If 'professional' occupations have specialized knowledge and skills that are to be used for the benefit of society rather than any particular group, this claim can legitimize the necessity for autonomy. There will typically be an ethos of altruism as well as professional control through the application of a code of practice. In other words, the high status and value accorded to professional occupations is necessary if these groups are to operate effectively and meet the needs of society. The difficulty with this argument, as is the case with any functionalist argument, is that it is essentially conservative and ends up supporting the status quo. In an early contribution to the debate Johnson (1972) presented an alternative to the trait and functionalist positions which raised questions of power. He argued that the professions are those occupations able to define their relationship with clients. He suggested those occupations that recruit members from powerful social groups in wider society are more likely to be able to do this.

The continued salience of Johnson's (1972) work is that it forces us to consider power and to question the manner in which professions present themselves. Not only does Johnson remind us of historical contingency, in that in specific conditions particular occupations may be able to attain a degree of autonomy and control over their labour, but that this is pivotally related to questions of class. If members of a particular occupational group have at their disposal class power this can be used to secure professional status and influence. Witz (1992) highlighted the way in which classed processes intersect with those of gender in her discussion of occupational divisions in medicine.

The notion of professionalism and the ability of an occupational group to attain autonomy are intimately connected to historical contingency as well as processes of class and gender. Indeed, it could be argued that the apogee of the professions is past, being a feature of the nineteenth and early twentieth century. Currently the so-called professions are located within large organizations, their work determined by managerial and institutional diktat. Teachers have always had a somewhat ambivalent relationship to professionalism. It has been drawn upon as part of an occupational strategy that sought to gain autonomy and control over the labour process, and yet this claim to professionalism has rested alongside another strategy located in trade unionism. Both of these strategies have sought occupational control (Ozga and Lawn 1981), being shaped by the prevailing economic conditions of the time.

In the following we explore teacher professionalism. The years between the First and Second World Wars saw the development of legitimated teacher professionalism, a very particular form of professionalism. Teachers were deemed to possess expert curricular and pedagogic knowledge which was enacted in the classroom. Legitimated teacher professionalism embodied this idea, with teachers being granted autonomy in the classroom on the basis that politics were kept out of education. These ideas were developed in the socio-economic context of the 1920s and 1930s, in which the political Right was fearful of socialists gaining control of the state. During this period, teachers were seen as a bulwark against the incursion of socialist ideas into education (see White, cited in Grace 1987: 207).

The outcome was the suggestion that school and education lie outside politics. This in itself is a deeply political act that served conservative interests of the time. Teachers were granted autonomy in the classroom based on the evacuation of politics from education. At this time there were a range of politics surrounding education some of which were related to class, gender and ethnicity. The significance of this argument is to acknowledge historical contingency as well as the construction of teachers as a conservative force.

Legitimated teacher professionalism was hegemonic following the Second World War. It was during this period that the curriculum was described as a 'secret garden'. Curriculum and schooling were seen to be controlled by teachers. Paradoxically two contradictory arguments were applied during this period – from the Left, teachers, curriculum and pedagogic processes were critiqued for their complicity in reproducing inequality and failing to deliver social justice (Young 1971). Initially these were raised in relation to social class but were followed by concerns about gender and ethnicity (Meighan and Siraj-Blatchford 1997). At the same time writers on the Right were becoming anxious about the apparent entryism of leftist teachers (Education Group 1981). These teachers were critiqued for their attachment to the tenets of progressive education, as well as their 'anti-business' orientations.

The result of these critiques, particularly those from the Right, was to re-focus an interest in teacher professionalism, the ramifications of which are still being felt today. The curriculum has become open to view through the introduction of the National Curriculum for schools, with a focus on transparency and increasing surveillance by the state of teachers' practice. Within FE and the LLS more generally these developments are reflected in external processes of review and inspection and are also present in moves towards self-regulation and self-assessment. The development of occupational standards reflects a particular construction of what it is to be a teacher. While such frameworks cannot completely determine what goes on in the classroom, they do set the terrain in which teachers practice.

There is an influential body of work that examines the labour process of teachers in FE. This research agrees on a number of elements:

- loss of control
- intensification of labour
- increased administrative loads
- perceived marginalisation of teaching
- stress on measurable performance indicators

(Avis 1999: 251)

Wahlberg and Gleeson (2003) in their study of FE business lecturers reflect these tensions where lecturers feel 'caught in a fast changing policy-practice dynamic in which their status has been "casualised" and deprofessionalised by a process of market, funding-led and managerialist reform' (2003: 438).

There has always been a struggle over teacher professionalism and its inherent politics. Various notions have been developed that seek to move professionalism in progressive directions, the learning professional, dialogic professionalism and other models rooted in Habermassian theory (Gleeson et al. 2004). However, these come up against the preferred model of the state which construes the FE teacher in particular as a service provider, at the behest of the market, one who will acquire earned autonomy as a 'trusted servant' of the state (Avis 2003a). Ainley (2008) reminds us that state interest in professionalization often becomes a veneer for proletarianization.

Professional values and codes of conduct

Much writing on professionalism moves beyond mere description of professional behaviour to discuss more fundamental values and beliefs underpinning professional action. This work locates professionalism in a broader set of relations between the practitioner and society, in which 'professionalism' indicates attitudes and responsibilities demonstrated within a specific social context. Implicit is the notion that professionalism is more than individual satisfaction, but relates to the 'common good' and that such values remain to some extent independent of government policy changes or shifts in the economy.

In the past professions operated within slow moving social contexts, with little change in public expectations or the prevailing social order. Professional values could remain constant and unchallenged, although they might also be relatively untested in a climate of self-regulation and protectionism. In contrast, the current social environment is characterized by rapid change, with the public having higher expectations of professionals and increased awareness of individual and societal rights. In this context, professionals are exposed to public scrutiny and the necessity to justify decisions and actions. The paper-trail of documents produced to provide evidence supporting decisions in case of audit, inspection or legal action is one manifestation of the current cultural climate of managerialism. It is not surprising that the tension between personal and professional values and the need to be seen to be accountable to the public are at the root of much writing on professionalism.

The potential impact on professional values of managerialist cultures operating within complex regulatory and legislative frameworks is discussed in RSA (2002), which considers whether values are context specific or whether there is an overarching set of values applicable to all professions. The 'trait' approach to professionalism has been criticized for the arbitrary nature of the traits identified, with different socio-cultural contexts placing a higher value on some rather than others. If professionalism involves working towards the 'common good', then it is likely that some core values will underpin different professions, although they may be accorded more or less prominence. They may also be subject to different interpretations according to the socio-cultural-historical context in which they operate. The following examples of how different educational bodies tackle the notion of professional values suggests these are not neutral, but reflect particular contexts, types of discourse and 'a particular ideology of experience and service' (Evans 2008: 24).

In its 'Statement of professional values and practice for teachers' (GTC 2006), the General Teaching Council for England emphasizes that school teachers are 'skilled practitioners', placing the learner at the heart of what they do. It also refers to the legislative framework within which school teachers must work, the value and place of the school in the community and the importance of partnership with parents, carers and colleagues. A commitment to equality of opportunity is detailed as 'challenging stereotypes, opposing prejudice and respecting individuals, regardless of age, gender, disability, colour, race, ethnicity, class, religion, marital status or sexual orientation' (GTC 2006: 2). School teachers have to qualify through the achievement of professional standards set out by the Training and Development Agency for Schools (TDA). These do not include values but professional 'attributes', as well as professional knowledge and skills and a responsibility for CPD.

In HE the HEA identifies the following core professional values:

1   Respect for individual learners
2   Commitment to incorporating the process and outcomes of recent research, scholarship and/or professional practice
3   Commitment to development of learning communities
4   Commitment to encouraging participation in higher education acknowledging diversity and promoting equality of opportunity
5   Commitment to continuing professional development.

If we consider the values suggested by the GTC and the HEA, some appear more generic than others, while some reflect the cultural context of each sector. While both bodies use the term 'communities', in the case of school teachers this refers to the community where they are physically located and which they 'serve', whereas the HEA uses a broader notion of 'learning community'. Although the notion of promoting equality of opportunity could be a generic value, inclusion in the school setting is explicitly linked to social justice. In contrast, the term 'participation' in HEA standards reflects Government discourse within the 'widening participation' agenda which seeks to increase the number of students from under-represented groups in HE. Both refer to CPD. While school teachers have a 'responsibility', suggesting a social orientation to the discourse, HEA uses a more individualized notion of 'personal commitment'. Interestingly the HEA makes no mention of any legislative framework within its values, suggesting a level of autonomy and independence which contrasts to the strict regulatory requirements of the compulsory sector.

The IfL, the professional body for teachers in the LLS, has developed a code of professional practice (2008b) which cites seven key 'behaviours'. Similar to the TDA's term 'attributes', 'behaviours' suggests measurable actions rather than underpinning values and may indicate a bias towards public accountability rather than individual integrity. The IfL's behaviours are as follows:

Behaviour 1: Professional integrity
Behaviour 2: Respect
Behaviour 3: Reasonable care
Behaviour 4: Professional practice (providing evidence of compliance with CPD requirements)
Behaviour 5: Criminal offence disclosure
Behaviour 6: Responsibility during Institute investigations
Behaviour 7: Responsibility

Notably, professional integrity includes upholding the reputation of the 'Institute' and to 'not knowingly undermine' its views. In other words, professional integrity includes not criticizing the IfL. A difference from HEA's values is the reference to behaviour in organizational contexts. Respect for the rights of learners is not only in accordance with legislation, but with 'organization requirements'.

LLUK's (2007a) professional standards for teachers, tutors and trainers in the lifelong learning sector explicitly state that practice is underpinned by a set of professional values. Domain A of these standards identifies what 'teachers in the lifelong learning sector value' as follows (2007a: 3);

1   All learners, their progress and development, their learning goals and aspirations and the experience they bring to their learning.

2   Learning, its potential to benefit people emotionally, intellectually, socially and economically, and its contribution to community sustainability.

3   Equality, diversity and inclusion in relation to learners, the workforce and the community.

4   Reflection and evaluation of their own practice and their continuing professional development as teachers.

5   Collaboration with other individuals, groups and/or organizations with a legitimate interest in the progress and development of learners.

As with the GTC and HEA, the learner is central to the values underpinning practice. Notably LLUK's discourse explicitly mentions the link between education and economic benefit.

Inter-professionality in the LLS

In imagining the 'lecturer of the future', more than a decade ago, Young et al. (1995) identified 'inter-professional knowledge' as a key requirement. The rationale was based on the ways in which the trend towards resource-based learning was bringing teachers into increasing contact with non-teaching colleagues who actively supported the new modes of learning. These might include specialists in assessment, information technologists, librarians, career guidance specialists and counsellors. It was reasoned that to be effective teachers would need to have knowledge of these roles, and how best to utilize and work with them collegially to optimize learning. In more recent years learning support workers, mentors and learning coaches have taken on a higher profile, becoming part of a range of colleagues with whom teachers need to liaise. These organizational and communication trends have clear implications for the ways in which teachers need to orientate to their work (see Robson and Bailey 2009).

Inter-professional collaboration is relatively well established in the health service. Social work has also established a tradition of 'inter-agency' working. Historically teachers have mostly worked as 'lone operators', and consequently the culture of teaching is often premised on the idea of an individual being in sole charge of a class. It was not until the 1980s that FE teachers began to systematically 'design and deliver' the curriculum in more collaborative ways, with teams from different subject specialisms working closely in a more problem-based approach to learning. Effective inter-professionality presents challenges to institutional structures and to human resource management, but perhaps more profound are the ways in which it requires teachers to think differently about how they design, organize and implement learning cooperatively with others who have an important stake in the learning process and in supporting learners. In practical terms this involves active networking, inter-departmental planning and a spirit of inclusivity that reaches beyond traditional boundaries. It is fair to say that in many cases institutional mechanisms do not always currently facilitate such ways of working, and this is sometimes true of individual attitudes and departmental cultures. In some respects, the vision set out by Young et al. (1995) remains an aspiration, but it is one which is even more crucial now than it was at the time. Professional identities are never static, and are constantly negotiated in the context of changing technologies and relations to associated forms of labour.

Research and scholarship

Research is almost universally held in high esteem regardless of the educational sector in which it is conducted. However, the way in which research and scholarship are marshalled can reflect diametrically opposed political positions, holding divergent understandings of society and education. At its most basic level scholarship can refer to the necessity to keep up to date with one's discipline and in the case of practitioners, to acquire recent and relevant experience. Similarly, research can be construed as important in keeping the practitioner up to date with pedagogic research that can be drawn upon to inform practice. It may also point towards the importance of engaging in action research as a reflective practitioner. All of these practices sit quite comfortably with the state's interest in using research to improve educational practice and to validate evidence informed practice (Avis 2003b, 2009).

For some time now the State has sought to promote educational research that can be used to enhance practice. The thrust of state policy, however, has been to validate particular types of educational research, namely that which addresses questions of teaching and learning and that actively contribute towards the enhancement of prac-tice. State policy is concerned with the production of 'useful knowledge'. As a result of the critiques of writers such as Tooley and Darby (1998), and latterly Gorard (2002), who question the validity of much qualitative educational research, there is a tendency to fall back on traditional and common-sense models that resonate with forms of positivism. Hodkinson (2004) has argued that there is a new orthodoxy that validates improvement orientated research located within a spurious 'scientificity'. There is a struggle over the nature of educational research and the type of contribution it makes to society. For writers such as Pring (2000), education is an applied discipline that directly addresses pedagogic and educational questions. This means that research engaging theoretical questions that have no immediate practical implications is seen as something other than educational, being possibly sociological or psychological. The difficulty rests with where this particular division is drawn, and how narrowly or broadly we think about research and practice.

The interest in systematic review and 'scientifically' orientated research derives from its supposed capacity to generate findings that can be disseminated to practi-tioners to improve classroom practice (EPPI 2001; Evans and Benefield 2001). For some, the goal is to produce a 'crib sheet' which specifies the findings of research, the conditions in which these are operable, and the exceptions and alternative strategies that may be deployed (Davies 2000). Resting within this aspiration is the suggestion that universal solutions are possible. However, Hodkinson and James (2003) have shown that what constitutes effective learning and teaching is situationally located and cannot be straightforwardly associated with universalized models of good practice. This argument raises questions about the use of observational check lists to measure effective teaching, and calls for a nuanced approach when making judgements about learning and teaching.

Much of the ethnographic research that has examined learner experiences in further education has related these to the cultural capital and habitus that students carry into the classroom (Hodkinson and James 2003). Learners hold particular forms of cultural capital that may articulate with the educational processes encountered. Similarly their habitus will inform the dispositions carried into the classroom and will influence responses to pedagogy. A significant current in post-compulsory research is concerned with widening participation. Some of this work explores learner experience and suggests ways in which classroom encounters could be rendered relevant and accessible for such learners. Furedi (2003), Ecclestone (2004) and Hayes (Ecclestone and Hayes 2009) argue that such practices can easily fold over into a form of 'therapy culture' that encourages learners to feel good about themselves rather than developing educationally (see Chapter 6).

Within educational research we find a number of ambivalent and cross-cutting currents. For example, one strand of action research may operate with a restricted understanding of pedagogic practice yet empower the practitioner; this may in turn contrast with models of action research rooted in either a positivist paradigm or in Habermassian critical theory. To conclude we consider two key issues: first, how broadly or narrowly can we view the remit of educational research and, second, its politics – is it necessarily a political practice? What goes on in the classroom, college or training organization cannot be fully understood without setting it in its wider societal context. This is particularly the case if we believe that education should hold a commitment to social justice. Such a stance validates research that seeks to relate educational relations to wider society. This position would also suggest that we cannot escape the politics of educational research – research is inevitably a political practice. Lest we are accused of naivety and of promulgating an overly simplistic argument, it is important to recognize the significance of contingency, contradiction and a general 'messiness'. While any research practice will necessarily contain a politics, its exact form will not necessarily derive from the way in which such work represents itself. The politics of research are subject to analysis and deconstruction by others.

6

Theorizing the work-based learning of teachers

James Avis, Kevin Orr and Jonathan Tummons

In this chapter:

- Theories of work-based learning
- Socially situated practice
- Bourdieu's field and habitus
- Communities of practice and WBL
- Communities of practice in FE
- Conclusion

Theories of work-based learning

Many writers have drawn upon notions of occupational socialization or entry into particular communities of practice (Avis et al. 2002). While this work points towards the salience of work-based learning (WBL), much of its analysis stops short of a full engagement with processes of learning arising in the workplace. This chapter seeks to remedy that and to critically engage with the theorization of work-based learning and the progressive possibilities it holds.

Work-based learning has been central to government policy since New Labour's election in 1997 and constitutes a substantial proportion of vocational education and training (VET). Teachers in lifelong learning may be involved in WBL with their students on placements or on day-release courses. WBL is also an important element of initial teacher training in FE and is an integral part of its curriculum, thus fostering a dual perspective on the processes involved as trainee and trainer.

Socially situated practice

Avis and Bathmaker have considered the experience of trainee FE teachers on 'teaching practice' placements and how this has shaped both their professional identity (Bathmaker and Avis 2005) and attitudes towards pedagogy (Avis et al. 2002b; Avis and Bathmaker 2004). These authors highlight the importance of trainee biographies and while finding evidence of involvement and commitment to teaching, there was little real integration with existing teachers at their placements. One trainee commented, 'Sometimes I feel like I am sneaking around' (Bathmaker and Avis 2005: 54–5). Like Wallace (2002a), they also found a discrepancy between the hopes and expectations of trainees and their experience of placements. A sense of purpose and social justice had attracted a number of these trainees to FE teaching, which on occasion was at odds with teaching experience and the attitudes of college staff (Avis and Bathmaker 2006). Avis et al. (2002: 187) quote one trainee as saying, 'I think that they [existing teachers] forget that at the end of the day, these students are human beings.'

The work of Avis and Bathmaker and of Wallace suggests that trainees' previous experience is fundamental to understanding how FE teachers develop as well as their engagement with WBL more generally. Colley and James (2005: 11) suggest, 'There is certainly no such thing as "FE tutor" separate from the complex, wider lives that [teachers in FE] have lived and are living'. The marginalization of trainees is a recurring feature of research addressing pre-service trainees in FE and informs what is absorbed through their lived experience on placement, influencing the way in which they cope and subsequently develop.

The definition and limits of the term 'work-based learning' are disputed. Learning that is related to work has been divided into three elements: learning about work, or how organizations operate; learning for work, or developing skills appropriate for work; and learning through work, or using the workplace as the context for learning (Huddleston and Oh 2004: 85). We concentrate on the latter here, though to define WBL as learning that takes place in the workplace alone may be to over-simplify what can be a complex and subtle process.

Conceptually, this dichotomy between college- and work-based learning can be misleading. This is especially the case where formal classes and college placements form part of the course – as with vocational trainees such as plumbers, solicitors and teachers, in a blurring between on- and off-the-job learning. As Hodkinson (2005: 524) notes: 'Workplaces and educational institutions merely represent different instances of social practices in which learning occurs through participation . . . to distinguish between the two . . . [so that] one is formalised and the other informal . . . is not helpful'.

Such an approach considers learning as a process that is situated within a particular social setting, and any knowledge derived is contingent upon that social situation. It emphasizes learning as a process of *becoming* through participation in the social practices of a group or culture. This means that 'learning a subject is now conceived as a process of becoming a member of a certain community. This entails, above all, the ability to communicate in the language of this community and act according to its particular norms' (Sfard 1998: 6).

This emphasis on participation can be useful in understanding WBL where the customs, habits and even language used by particular vocational groups are never formally taught, but are acquired by newcomers as they work alongside established workers. Through its emphasis upon the situation this approach considers what is learnt to be situated and thus not transferable. However, it may also ignore the transferable knowledge and skills trainees acquire in the workplace. Arguably, some of these transferable skills, such as the use of a computer keyboard, may not be strictly situated nor related to a sense of 'becoming'.

Aspects of formal learning exist in both educational institutions as well as the workplace. The notion of informal learning is frequently applied to WBL; however, Billett (2002a: 457) challenges this position: 'Workplace experiences are not informal. They are the product of the historical-cultural practices and situational factors that constitute the particular work practice, which in turn distributes opportunities for participation to individuals or cohorts of individuals'. For Billett a significant consideration in WBL is the availability or lack of opportunity for participation in the workplace, and the bearing this has on learning. In his own investigations of learning at work Billett (2001: 209) found 'learners afforded the richest opportunities for participation reported the strongest development, and that workplace readiness was central to the quality of experiences'.

The key contributors to successful learning for the trainee were 'engagement in everyday tasks'; 'direct or close guidance of co-workers' and 'indirect guidance provided by the workplace itself and others in the workplace'. Billett (2002b: 30) argues that, 'the negotiation with and resolution of these (even if it is partial) has cognitive consequences as these activities transform individuals' knowledge'. For Billett, the workplace is understood as being defined by rule-bound structures that are only informal in so far as these rules are unwritten. These socially constructed structures pre-date any training placement and their form determines what the trainees are able to do. Billett (2002b: 36) writes that, 'Contingent workers', among whom we would include teacher trainees, 'are particularly susceptible to securing only limited workplace affordances'. Indeed, those structures can be formed to prevent the full participation of in-comers and just how formal these unspoken structures are becomes clear when people threaten or go beyond them.

Similarly, Beckett and Hager (2000: 300) ask, 'What do practitioners actually do at work from which they learn?' In seeking to examine what is learnt in workplaces they eschew the frequently used notion of 'tacit knowledge' (see Eraut 2000): 'In attempting to de-mystify such knowledge, the danger is that ascription of "tacitness" re-mystifies it' (Beckett and Hager 2000: 302).

More generally, their questioning of assumptions about the purpose of WBL helps to ' "get beneath the surface of experience", rather than merely report it' (Beckett and Hager 2000: 303). A trainee teacher, for example, learning to effectively navigate the social constructs of the workplace, in other words learning to 'fit in', is not necessarily learning to teach well but rather to accommodate to work-based cultures. More fundamentally, Young (2003: 555) questions the value of experiential learning, 'because the world is not as we experience it, curriculum knowledge must be discontinuous, not continuous with everyday experience'.

If we only learn what we experience, we may learn very little. Nevertheless, learning of one kind or another occurs in the workplace. For example, Gleeson and Shain (1999: 482) define as *strategic compliance*: 'innovative strategies for dealing with the pressures of income generation, flexibilization and work intensification while at the same time, continuing their [the FE teachers'] commitments to educational values of student care, support and collegiality'. In other words, teachers can learn how to comply with what is necessary, even if they do not value it, in order to carve out space for what they consider is important. Whatever happens in the workplace, Wenger (1998: 8) suggests, 'Learning is something we can assume – whether we see it or not, whether we like the way it goes or not, whether what we are learning is to repeat the past or shake it off. Even failing to learn usually involves learning something else instead'.

What trainees learn from participation in the workplace has a lot to do with their own biography and predispositions, which is another area of contention and dispute. How much individual agency do people have within a situation they have not created? How much does the situation form the individual? This relationship between person and environment echoes Marx, who contends that human beings make their own history, but not in circumstances of their own choosing (Marx and Engels 1968: 96). This relationship is at the heart of much of the discussion of WBL.

Bourdieu's field and habitus

In the following we examine two of the most common conceptualizations used to analyse WBL. It is useful to consider Bourdieu's work, and how his conceptualizations relate to FE as well as WBL. We begin with a consideration of Bourdieu followed by a discussion of Lave and Wenger's notion of communities of practice.

The wide-ranging Transforming Learning Cultures (TLC) research project investigated student learning in FE over a period of three years and at a variety of learning sites throughout England (James and Biesta 2007). It sought to identify and authentically describe what enabled successful learning so that such conditions could be further encouraged and enhanced. The researchers used Bourdieu's concepts of *field* and *habitus* to explain the transformations involved in learning. The TLC team describe 'learning as becoming' (Colley et al. 2003: 471) and used the term 'learning culture' (James and Biesta 2007: 4) to express the interplay between an individual student and the college environment.

Bourdieu's concepts illuminate how this dynamic process of learning, enculturation and mutual influence occurs through a series of relationships. His central concern is to overcome the dichotomy between a subjectivist emphasis on individual consciousness and an objectivist emphasis on social structures by explaining how the two are interconnected (Jenkins 1992: 66).

Bourdieu describes a person's set of individual dispositions and behaviour as their *habitus*. This is 'a product of the incorporation of objective necessity'; it is like having a 'feel for the game' (1990: 11). What constitutes that objective necessity or the game itself is the *field* within which a person lives and operates. Jenkins (1992: 85) defines Bourdieu's term *field* as 'the crucial mediating context between where external factors are brought to bear on individual and institutional practice'. It is the contested area where social forces interplay and struggle over resources such as capital, prestige or intellectual distinction.

Bourdieu describes how people adapt to the structures and relationships they find around them, internalizing rules which they may be unaware of and which may never have been formally constituted. At an almost palpable level, in a college with no dress code, the staff in one staffroom may wear suits while those in another wear jeans. '*Habitus* contributes to constituting the field as a meaningful world, a world endowed with sense and with value, in it which is worth investing one's energy' (Bourdieu 1989a: 44). Habitus is 'essentially the internalization of the structures of that world' (Bourdieu 1989b: 18) and is as much to do with physical composure as with attitude.

However, people enter a *field* with their existing *habitus* formed elsewhere, which either helps or hinders their incorporation into the new *field*. This can lead to feeling out of place or unsure of how to deport oneself as the dispositions and behaviour that are acceptable or have status in one vocational area may be regarded as inappropriate elsewhere.

Bourdieu stresses that individuals are not controlled by the *field*, and that they maintain individual agency; indeed, the *field* will itself have emerged through social interaction. The expectations and routines on a construction site from the 1970s, while recognizable today, have also evolved and changed over time. Similarly, what exists today will feel normal to today's construction workers. Bourdieu explains how the social practices involved in any situation have an objective reality (conditions on building sites have altered) and a subjective reality (those conditions feel normal to those who work on today's building sites).

Applying these concepts to WBL is fruitful as it acknowledges the dynamism of the relationship between the individual and the situation with all its complexity and contingency. Bourdieu (1989a: 40) sets out how the *field* can be analysed. First, the *field* must be considered in relation to the external *field* of power. The divisions between academic and vocational education may be pertinent, or the relationship of a group in a company to senior management. Second, the objective structure of the relations between the individuals (or agents) competing for authority within the *field* must be described and, third, the specific *habitus* of the individual needs to be analysed.

> What must be emphasized is . . . that the external determinations that bear on agents situated in a given field (intellectuals, artists politicians, or construction companies), never apply on them directly, but only through the specific mediation of the specific forms and forces of the field . . .
>
> (Bourdieu 1989a: 41)

This describes a subtle, contingent process of influence that can only be understood within a specific situation. People learn to improvise according to what is around them and in so doing internalize, or learn, attitudes and behaviour. Such a conceptualization understands learning as a socially situated process that reflects the immediate situation as well as broader society.

Within a large FE college there will be several fields which interact: the wider culture of the college and the vocational fields of departments or sections. This may be viewed, or heard, in contrasting registers of language: managers may use terms from business (audit, quality, benchmarking, performance indicators) while teachers in a staffroom may use the language of their vocational area, or that of pedagogy. All of these *fields* sit within or alongside that of FE nationally with its policy initiatives and hierarchies.

Bourdieu also uses the terms "cultural" and 'social capital' to describe how the knowledge and experience that people assimilate as well as their social networks have differing currency according to the values and mores of those around them. For example, an education system that applies the same criteria to all students may be seen as promoting equal opportunities. However, when those criteria reflect middle-class behaviour (for example linguistic expression) and values, working-class students are disadvantaged. Their *habitus* holds different, less esteemed cultural and social capital, which also helps explain the status of vocational education vis-à-vis the academic.

Bourdieu's conceptualization is a valuable tool in analysing WBL because it helps us to understand the changes that take place in an individual, for example from the commencement of work to the time when he or she becomes established in the *field*. Moreover, it explains how conflict can arise from the relative positions of individuals in relation to the *field* according to the distribution of power. Above all, Bourdieu's approach suggests how participation within a culture shapes individual disposition and physical behaviour in relation to their situation and the *field*. Thus a person gets a feel for a situation which may look like the result of rational consideration, yet it is not based upon reasoning, but upon an unstated, usually unnoticed incorporation of culture, which is simultaneously shaped through individual participation.

Communities of practice and WBL

Communities of practice, as a way of thinking about what learning is and how it happens, have been interpreted differently by different writers. Indeed, Wenger has modified his conceptualization in significant ways. At the same time, other writers have drawn on complementary theories to enhance or expand the community of practice framework (Barton and Tusting 2005). In this section, the focus is on learning within the community of practice itself. We draw on the original work of Lave and Wenger (1991) and Wenger (1998), as distinct from later work that loses sight of the central role of learning within a community of practice and which focuses on issues to do with organizational membership and identity.

Learning is a process that takes place almost all the time, in all kinds of places and does not necessarily involve teachers in a formal sense. Frequently, people are shown how to do things by friends or work colleagues, or work out how to do things by reading a book, manual or website, or they experiment to see how something works, based on their experiences of using a similar object or item. For some, learning is something that happens in a formal educational setting, whereas for others, learning happens in the home or workplace. All of these places are sites of learning, and the process of learning is the same even though what is being learned will vary considerably.

What does 'learning' actually mean in this sense? Put simply, learning is an inevitable consequence of participation within a community of practice, which is a way of describing a collection of people who are engaged in any number of similar or less-similar activities. Communities of practice are found in places of work as well as in places of leisure. They might be small and local, such as a community of model railway enthusiasts, or large, distributed across geographic distance, such as a community of online game players. Groups of communities, known as constellations, might exist within large and complex organizations such as insurance offices or FE colleges. Communities can be formal, such as those found in the workplace, or informal, such as those of hobbyists. Membership of any community of practice entails learning of some kind as a consequence of that engagement. Such learning may be more or less profound or difficult and may be more of less transferable to other contexts.

Through participating in communities of practice, members learn how the community works and how it talks to its own members as well as to others. Members learn about the history of the community, and how it goes about doing what it does. They learn how to engage and contribute to the practices of the community, and perhaps how to change them as well. They also learn how to use the resources, tools and artefacts the community has built up over time in order to carry out its practice. Such engagement in the practices of a community has learning as an integral component, and is described as *legitimate peripheral participation*. A member of a community is a participant, who is engaged in legitimate, authentic and meaningful participation (actually doing the work of the community, not simply being told about it or reading about it or observing it). The new participant is in a peripheral position, and moves to fuller participation as he or she learns, through participating, more about the practice of the community.

Any community of practice, irrespective of scale, consists of three fundamental aspects. For Wenger (1998) these involve:

1 *Mutual engagement:* In any community of practice people will work together, in complementary and overlapping ways, at some kind of activity or number of activities.

2 *Joint enterprise:* The work of the community is shared but need not be uniform. Participants will negotiate their understanding of the enterprise and its effect on their lives.

3 *Shared repertoire:* Within a community, participants work with a shared repertoire of tools, artefacts, and ways of talking, writing and behaving.

Communities of practice in FE

An FE college is too large and complex to be considered a single community of practice. Rather, it consists of multiple communities arranged in a constellation, each with their own way of doing things, their own shared stories and meanings. These communities might be situated within staffrooms, workshops or classrooms. Some participants are experts and others are apprentices, while some are members of more than one community. For the trainee teacher, a staffroom or department will be a community of practice. A workshop or classroom will be another community of practice. Other communities of practice within an FE college, relating perhaps to senior management or the estates department, would not be participated in although a trainee teacher might occasionally come into contact with them. Clearly, these communities all work in different ways.

A community of practice within a staffroom rests on a very different kind of mutual engagement than one within a workshop or classroom. Indeed, any talk of formal educational structures is somewhat at odds with the notion of communities of practice as originally envisaged by Lave and Wenger (1991), who rejected the concept of pedagogy or formal instruction as being incompatible with a social model of learning. In later work, however, Wenger (1998) proposed the idea that an *architecture* could be created that might provide the opportunity for more formalized learning within a community. Such an architecture might include the right resources or the right people, for example, but he stresses that there will always be uncertainties between designing a learning architecture and how it will work in practice. Drawing on this concept, a community of practice within a formal learning and teaching environment can be seen as resting on a learning architecture made up of the syllabus, the physical environment of the college workshop or classroom, the books and hand-outs, the equipment, and the teachers.

The staffroom

What might be termed 'the community' of the staffroom rests on engagement within an institutional architecture. A trainee or new member of staff will learn about the workplace through taking part in the joint enterprise of the work that is being done and talked about: planning lessons, admissions procedures, discovering how to get some photocopying done, good strategies for dealing with learners who come late to class, obtaining passwords for the college's information and learning technology (ILT) systems and so on. This is a process which will be facilitated to a greater or lesser degree by other, more established members of the staffroom community. It is also a process that can be limited by the trainees themselves, who may choose to engage in these practices at more or less profound levels, or to focus on some activities in preference to others. Fundamentally, however, the learning that takes place rests on trainee participation in the community. At first this is only a peripheral process, but over time the trainee becomes more fluent and confident in using the shared repertoire of the community (the forms, the procedures and the paperwork as well as the in-jokes). That is, the trainee becomes a fuller participant in the community. However, it is important to note that for a trainee on a teaching placement, this learning journey (or *trajectory*) will only ever be peripheral. The trainee is a temporary member of the community, and after the placement is over, will leave. It may only be a short time before they get a job in another college. The process of learning will have to begin again to some extent as no community of practice is the same, although some are related. The newly-qualified teacher's new staffroom may have some famil-iar features, but many other aspects of their engagement, enterprise and repertoire will be different and will need to be *negotiated* afresh.

The workshop or classroom

A classroom of basic skills students, or a workshop of trainee car mechanics, or even a classroom of trainee FE teachers, is also a community of practice, albeit very differently constituted to the staffrooms that have been previously discussed (Tummons 2008). Members engage in the community in a number of ways: the daily or weekly meeting of the class; the shared workload of class and assignment preparation; perhaps the use of a virtual learning environment (VLE). The efforts of the students and teachers are focused on a quite specific joint enterprise: successful negotiation of the course or programme of study, leading to the award of a certificate or other form of credentialed achievement. And as the teachers and students work, they draw on a shared repertoire of artefacts: worksheets; course handbooks; PowerPoint presentations; technical drawings; tools; textbooks; websites; individual learning plans; and so on.

These are not communities of practice that have emerged solely as a response to localized conditions, needs or wants. Beyond the sector as a whole, a range of both political and professional interests have combined to create a need for these courses, which arrive at the college more or less fully formed. Teachers and students work with course handbooks or packs that are generated by the awarding body. Assessment activities are explicated in detail within such documents. These materials and procedures can be seen as the conceptual architecture (Wenger 1998: 230), a collection of things that can encourage the development of a community of practice, encompassing the joint enterprise, mutual engagement and shared repertoire of the community.

For the teacher, membership of such communities can be seen as providing opportunities for participation, and hence for learning, in two distinct ways. First, as a teacher (whether trainee or employee), teaching a course allows the teacher to learn about being a teacher in that specific college. Some of this learning will be transferable to other contexts, other communities. Second, the teacher will learn more about that specific community of practice, as indeed will the students through their engagement, though in the latter case this will be accented differently. In this sense, the learning journeys or trajectories of students are different from those of teachers. For example, on a plumbing course, the students are learning to become plumbers within a community of practice of trainees. Eventually they will go into the world of work – encountering and becoming participants in workplace communities of practice. These workplace communities will share some of the engagement, enterprise and repertoire of the 'trainee community'. The more successfully the plumbing course 'authentically' reflects the world of work, the more successful the transfer of learning will be. However, in the trainee community the role of the teacher is to facilitate the students' participation to engage with the practice and repertoire of the community.

There is one crucial difference between the community of the real world of work and that of the college course: pedagogy. A college course is a formal learning environment involving teaching and assessment. Assessment and the preparation for it, as aspects of pedagogic activity, do not sit comfortably within the community of practice model as initially posited by Lave and Wenger, who argue: 'in a community of practice, there are no special forms of discourse aimed at apprentices or crucial to their centripetal movement toward full participation that correspond to . . . the lecturing of college professors' (1991: 108). However, by drawing on some of the key concepts of community construction proposed by Wenger (1998), it is possible to explain how assessment might fit into an educational community of practice situated in a formal learning environment.

Assessment demonstrates the students' fuller competence and experience in the practice of the community (Wenger 1998: 216). It can be seen as a signpost or a marker that students can successfully negotiate and travel along their learning trajectory. For some students, however, learning how to pass an assignment – about how to be a successful student for the purposes of accreditation – is all that they wish to do. It is the piece of paper, the end qualification that counts. For other students, assessment can be a way of learning about the practice of the trainee community and other communities the student is in or likely to join. This learning moves beyond the instrumental, as participation in the trainee community impacts on their identity in such a way that they carry this learning with them as they travel through the community and into other communities of practice in their chosen sector of work or industry.

For some students, assessment is part of learning, whereas for others assessment is a mechanistic, instrumental process to be completed and promptly shelved. As Lave and Wenger point out, there is a contrast between learning to know and learning to display knowledge for evaluation (1991: 112). If assessment is a reified form of activity within the community of practice, then it embodies the 'double edge of reification' (Wenger 1998: 62). That is to say, it can (but need not necessarily) be reduced to a procedure, and the meanings and purposes of the procedure might be lost sight of. So where does the learning happen? Wenger (1998) draws a distinction between newcomers to a community and those who have been members for a longer time and have a greater expertise. Newcomers can learn from the longer standing members and from each other. What is important is that learning is happening in an authentic community of practice with people learning through participation in practice.

Conclusion

This chapter has drawn upon conceptual resources that can be used to explore WBL generally, and more particularly that of trainee teachers in LLS. We have commented upon learning as a socially situated and participatory process but also sought to set this within a wider context by drawing upon Bourdieu's notion of *field* and *habitus*. While the *field* is socially constituted it also provides the context in which agency is enacted and is indicative of Bourdieu's attempt to go beyond the dichotomy of agency and structure. We drew on Lave and Wenger to explore the notion of community of practice seeking to emphasize aspects of learning within such communities addressing the relationship between college- and work-based processes.

In this chapter we have pointed towards a number of implicit tensions. Throughout we have focused upon processes of 'becoming' a teacher through participating in a community of practice. This has resulted in the marginalization of participatory and learning processes that underscore the way in which a member of a community of practice moves from a position of centrality to the periphery and exits that particular community. Colley et al. (2007) have described this as a process of 'unbecoming'. It is important to acknowledge that this process of 'unbecoming' a teacher is as much a participatory process as becoming one, and that conceptualizations of *habitus*, *field* and communities of practices can help us to make sense of this (Colley et al. 2007).

We have also sought to acknowledge the constraints that frame socially situated practice and to refer to the relationship between WBL and the wider curriculum and assessment contexts in which FETT is located. The tensions and contradictions surrounding work-based practices and the *habitus* of trainees as well as their responses to the communities of practices they inhabit, first as trainees and then as practitioners, provide the context in which they can struggle to assert agency. It is important to recognize this, for otherwise analysis can fold into a model of unreflexive socialization into the teaching role, denying the possibility of agency and therefore change.

7

Equality and diversity

*Lyn Ashmore, Julie Dalton, Penny Noel,
Sandra Rennie, Emma Salter, Dave Swindells
and Paul Thomas*

In this chapter:

- Equality and diversity in lifelong learning
- Faith and religion
- Anti-racism
- Anti-sexism
- Lesbian, gay, bisexual and transgender issues
- Mental health
- Equal opportunity in practice
- Conclusion

Equality and diversity, like many of the concepts in this chapter, are contestable and can be interpreted in different and sometimes contradictory ways. In particular, the notion of equality is more complex than it appears; one way to illustrate this is to consider equality of opportunity. Do we offer equality if we provide equal access to a differentiated education system that is selective on the basis of ability or interest? How are notions of ability and interest understood? Can they be treated separately from social and cultural background? Do they by default serve to reproduce inequality? One of the difficulties with equality of access is that it ignores such questions. This has partly been addressed by concerns with equality of outcome, which examines *what actually happens to people* in relation to categories such as class, race or ethnicity, gender and disability. The outcomes of particular categories are compared and if there are significant differences these suggest the presence of inequality. Often the comparison is with the white male middle class and can be used to point to discriminatory educational practices. Paradoxically, however, this category becomes the 'norm' against which others are compared, and the 'others' who underachieve can implicitly be construed as in some ways inadequate. A possible response is to recognize and value diversity in relation to race/ethnicity, class, gender, sexuality, religion, age, disability and so on. Diversity becomes an all-embracing concept that nevertheless seeks to acknowledge and value difference and otherness and calls upon us to consider the interrelationships between these categories. Such analyses are reflected in the concern to increase access and widen the participation of disadvantaged groups in further and higher education.

In the context of lifelong learning, valuing diversity means creating a learning and workplace environment that includes and respects difference and otherness. It means recognizing the unique contributions individuals can make. By nurturing, embracing and valuing diversity institutions can create an environment that maximizes the potential of all. Such arguments suggest a consensual framework whereby valuing diversity and difference is in the interests of all. But is this possible, and how can we reconcile antagonistic interests or incommensurate difference?

Equality and diversity in lifelong learning

'How diverse is the LLS?' This is a difficult question with only a partial answer. Although legislation requires public authorities to monitor race, gender and disability, there is no shared understanding in the sector about the importance or scope of diversity. In their assessment of barriers to increasing the diversity of the LLS workforce, Cummins et al. (2006: 10) found that 'independent providers often lack a basic understanding or any empathy with the issue of workforce diversity'. In addition, there are significant difficulties in collecting reliable data.

The concept of 'diversity' is complex and involves multiple understandings. For instance, Lumby et al. (2005: 71) found: 'The starting point is to use the term diversity to describe different "kinds" of people working or studying in the organisation. Most often it is used to designate "others" as different from themselves. Thus the term is frequently used to categorise individuals in terms of visible difference'. Discussing workforce diversity, Kandola and Fullerton (1998: 8) use an inclusive definition recognizing both 'visible and non-visible differences'. If we accept this, the question arises: which differences should be used to measure diversity? Inherent difficulties with a singular approach are suggested by Grayling (2007):

> a person is not one thing (a Muslim or a Jew only, or an Arab or an American only) but many: a parent, a mathematician, a tennis player, a Bangladeshi, a man, a feminist, a Muslim – all these things at once, and thus a multiple and overlapping complex being, whom the politics of singular identity reduces to a mere cipher and crams into a small box with a single simple label stuck on it.

Furthermore, there may be a discrepancy between self and institutional definitions of that individual as a member of a particular category (Rennic 2006). However, in relation to discrimination and inequality, not all aspects of identity carry the same import. Monitoring the number of tennis players in the LLS is unlikely to tackle disadvantage, whereas monitoring other aspects of identity may indicate necessary action. Differing aspects of identity are highlighted within the equality and diversity policies of LLS providers. These may include; age, gender, ethnicity, race, disability, national origin, religion and belief, marital status, sexual orientation, transgender status, social class and political opinion. The focus upon certain aspects of identity involves value judgements. Embedded within the rhetoric of diversity policy are judgements about which categories should be represented proportionately. Ironically, such values will not necessarily be shared across categories. A survey undertaken for the Cabinet Office *Equalities Review* into prejudice in Britain explored how far this is rooted in relationships between specific social groups, finding 'prejudices do correspond to intergroup differences of interest or perspective' (Abrams and Houston 2006: 56).

Within the LLS a number of identity categories are monitored, often as a legal requirement, and much of the resulting data, although incomplete, is updated annually and publicly available. However, for many of the aspects of identity highlighted above there is little or no comprehensive data, and many people may not identify with the category with which they are labelled. Even those who do may be uneasy about providing information, particularly if they feel prejudice exists. Awareness of this type of prejudice and the impact that it may have on monitoring is made explicit in guidance issued by the Equality Challenge Unit:

> While general best practice suggests that staff and potential staff should be monitored on the grounds of sexual orientation, experience has proven that staff . . . have been reluctant to declare their orientation because they are not convinced that the information will be kept confidential or that it is relevant. There is also suspicion that any declaration will result in prejudice or will not be used in a constructive way.
>
> (ECU 2004: 36)

While the purpose of monitoring is to ensure the elimination of discrimination is measured and appropriate action implemented, this process is not unproblematic and diversity profiles are incomplete.

Diversity, equality and learners in the LLS

The LSC (2007a) provides yearly updates on learner numbers in the LLS. Minority ethnic young people are more likely to stay on in full-time education at 16, and are more likely than white learners to enter FE or sixth-form college, rather than remaining in school (Connor et al. 2004). FE has a relatively high proportion of minority ethnic learners, almost one in five students in 2006–07, where they are more highly represented than in local populations. For the same year the proportion of minority ethnic learners in former adult and community learning (ACL) providers was 12 per cent, in WBL around 7 per cent; the smaller numbers taking work-based routes on employment or government-supported training reflects their greater proportion in education. Minority ethnic young people are under-represented in apprenticeships and are less likely to gain employment on completion. The Commission for Black Staff in FE, while acknowledging in its report on FE that 'major progress has been made where learners are concerned' (2002: 8), draws attention to witness concerns:

> Despite the fact that the students are predominantly Asian the syllabus does not reflect this, for example, in music technology, they study mostly European music . . . At one college, there had been 30 exclusions, 26 of whom were Black students. The reasons given were not consistent and appeared to take a

stereotypical view of students . . . Muslim staff and parents emphasised the need for a separate common room for girls at the college, as well as for a prayer room for staff and students. Food to meet the specific cultural and religious dietary requirements of our community is still not provided.

(p. 64)

The tendency to equate the dialect and accent of some Black learners with literacy or English language needs.

(p. 65)

There has been some progress in the sector. Reporting on race equality, Ofsted (2005a) found that 'Nationally, the success rates of groups of Black and minority ethnic (BME) learners of all ages have improved at an above average rate' (p. 1) and note:

Learners identified as strengths in their colleges friendly and supportive teachers, the safe and secure environment, the respect with which they were treated as individuals, and the support and opportunities they were provided with. The quality of teaching and learning was also important to them, as was a good atmosphere in the institution. Learners gave very few examples of problems relating to race.

(p. 4)

Ofsted drew attention to the too few colleges 'actively and systematically instigating change to improve race equality at the rate which might be expected' (p. 1).

The gender mix of FE learners closely mirrors that of teachers, with almost 58 per cent being female. Similarly, the student gender mix in former ACL provision reflects that of its teachers, with 75 per cent being female. Conversely, WBL and Train to Gain (TTG) have a higher proportion of male learners with only one in fifty apprentices being female. Throughout the sector, subject segregation by gender is pronounced. Apprenticeships in construction, plumbing and the motor industry are overwhelmingly male, whereas more than 90 per cent of hairdressing apprentices are female. The same pattern of subject segregation characterizes FE (see Table 7.1).

Stereotypical attitudes to subject choice post-16 are well established before school-leaving age. Tomlinson (2004) found that 'the uptake of Year 10 work experience placements is highly gender stereotypical and, instead of broadening pupils' horizons, their perceptions of the adult workplace are frequently being reinforced by work experience practice' (p. 84). The persistence of this segregation does little to reduce the gender pay gap as women continue to be disproportionately represented in low-paid employment.

LSC statistics for 2003–04 show that over 500,000 learners across the sector identified themselves as disabled (including students with learning difficulties), 11 per cent of full-time equivalents, with the majority aged over 19. As noted earlier, disclosure can create anxiety. Data was unavailable for around 15 per cent of students but the full extent of non-disclosure remains unknown. FE has the highest number of disabled learners, with the proportion who self-identify increasing over time. A review

Table 7.1 Learners by gender on LSC-funded FE provision 2006–07

	Women		Men	
Selected sector subject areas	*Thousands*	*%*	*Thousands*	*%*
Retail and commercial enterprise	118	78	34	22
Health and public services and care	309	77	94	23
Languages, literature and culture	101	66	51.5	32
Business administration and law	113	62	67	38
Science and maths	54	60	36.5	40
ICT	191	56	149	44
Engineering and manufacturing technologies	12	10	119	90
Construction, planning and built environment	5	5	94	95

Source: LSC (2007a)

of disabled students in higher and further education in London (Barer 2007) identified little difference between the level of study of disabled students and those with learning difficulties, with both studying at a lower level than other students, the implication being that disabled learners underachieve. Clearly, disabled students with academic potential do study at higher levels; however, there are many enrolled only at level 1. Disabled people have drawn attention to the importance of flexibility in relation to the learning environment, highlighting a number of barriers (GLA 2006). For example, potential learners have expressed concern about the loss of benefits that learning may entail, particularly as disabled people are significantly more likely to face barriers to employment. Lack of access to appropriate support has been identified as another obstacle. Disabled learners have reported 'unhelpful and even hostile staff attitudes' (p. 81) and of teasing by other students. The lack of consistency experienced by disabled learners is illustrated below:

> I'm going to the college in October and this is only really possible because they are giving me relevant support. This whole experience for me is possible because I will be given a PA, tape recorder, a copy of notes. All the tools to be able to contribute to the course.
>
> (p. 83)

> I was taking a community care course and as soon as they realised I was disabled they took me off the course. They said that I did not have the aptitude to pass . . . So I left, I was very upset. I could have done the course, if they'd helped me.
>
> (p. 85)

Whereas HE is concerned with the representation of differing social classes this is less so within LLS, and when class is used it is associated with disadvantage and deprivation. An explanation for this derives from a perception of the LLS as predominantly working class. Thompson (2009), analysing the youth cohort study, found substantial middle-class representation in the sector. While these middle-class participants have tended to be school 'failures' they nevertheless access the more prestigious courses, whereas their working-class counterparts are less likely to attend. In other words, those working-class young people who have had some success at school are likely to attend while those who have failed are less likely to do so. In addition the class structure is mirrored by the sector's tripartitism embedded in its academic, technical and work-readying streams (Gleeson 1983).

The analysis of diversity and equality across the sector is not straightforward. Data is missing or incomplete, and the notion of diversity is elusive. However, the examination of diversity in relation to staff and learners indicates that there is some way to go in achieving proportional representation of diverse communities. Foster (2005) observed that FE 'colleges have a strong commitment to social inclusion and inclusive learning' and that 'they attract a higher proportion of disadvantaged learners than the local population average' (p. 27). He also cautions that 'Demographic changes and an increase in local diversity will mean that the numbers of learners from under-represented groups is set to increase and colleges will need to adapt to their changing requirements' (p. 27). This is pertinent to all LLS providers. Adaptation must include improvement in staffing to reflect local communities, being better able to identify and respond to differing needs, and therefore more likely to attract and retain under-represented learners.

Faith and religion

Here we discuss why and how teachers and colleges might accommodate the religious needs of students. We also outline teachers' employment rights under the Employment Equality (Religion or Belief) Regulations 2003.

What counts as religion?

Outside specialist forums 'religion' is used to describe prescribed beliefs and customs associated with generally recognized religious faiths. However, identifying the boundaries of legitimate religious observance is not straightforward. This should not fall to individual teachers, but be part of a whole college policy that ensures students and staff are not disadvantaged because of their religious beliefs. It is each teacher's responsibility to be aware of college policy so that all students are treated fairly.

Why accommodate students' religious observances?

In 2004, France reinforced its secular position by banning religious symbolism in public arenas. Muslim girls were not allowed to wear the hijab [headscarf] to school. Opinions within and without the Muslim community vacillated between support for the legislation and its claim to foster citizenship, and repugnance at the ban which was perceived as racist and an infringement of human rights. In contrast, the UK embraces secular liberalism rather than the secular conservatism of the French. This means we foster citizenship through inclusion by 'celebrating diversity'. At least, that is the current public face of multicultural Britain. In practical terms college commitment to secular liberalism means that it enables students to express their religious identity as far as it is reasonable without compromising other students' learning.

Colleges have a political incentive and, arguably, a moral duty to support students in their religious observances while at college. There are also legal obligations. Admissions policies for FE are regulated by the Employment Equality (Religion or Belief) Regulations 2003 which makes it illegal to discriminate against an employee (or applicant) because of their religion or belief, or lack thereof. These Regulations do not clarify precisely what qualifies as religion, but they make a distinction between religious and political belief, the latter not being covered by the Regulations. The University and College Union provides clear information about the Regulations on its website (http://www.ucu.org.uk). Employers, and by extension admissions policies, are exempted from these Regulations when it can be demonstrated that affiliation to a particular religion or belief is a necessary quality in an employee or applicant. In 2004, after consultation with relevant parties, the Secretary of State approved an amendment to the Regulations that permits Catholic sixth-form colleges in England and Wales to prioritize Catholic applicants to non-vocational courses, where those courses are over subscribed, in order to maintain a Catholic ethos.

Religious literacy in the classroom

Here the 'classroom' is used to refer to any teaching environment. Teachers have a professional obligation to treat students fairly and equally, and to enhance the learning of all. In terms of religious literacy, this means being aware of how students' religious affiliation may affect their learning so that schemes of work can be planned accordingly. Teachers are not required to become experts in world religions, but some awareness and forward planning is good practice. The BBC Religion and Ethics website (http://www.bbc.co.uk/religion/) provides a good overview. Other sources of information include *Faith Guides for Higher Education* (Blunt, series editor) and the Multifaith Centre at the University of Derby (http://www.multifaithcentre.org). Although religious literacy may be desirable for teachers, discretion is advisable. Hypersensitivity towards religious backgrounds could accentuate difference and hinder learning. It is important to avoid stereotyping; all religions have internal diversity and those who subscribe to a religion may have varying levels of observance.

A primary consideration for the teacher is planning schemes of work. The Western calendar is tailored around the main Christian festivals of Easter and Christmas; consequently those of non-Christian students often fall during term time. Significant events such as field trips, visiting speakers or examinations should not be scheduled when students may be absent due to religious observance. This may require forward planning if the class includes a range of religions. Most academic diaries have a list of religious festival and dates. It can be useful to highlight those of relevance. The BBC website publishes religious calendars and the Shap Working Party (http://www.shapworkingparty.org.uk) produces wall charts and calendars. Schemes of work are easier to manage where the student body is predominantly or exclusively of the same faith, for example, if the college population is largely Muslim it may choose to suspend formal teaching during Eid and provide students with independent study tasks. Or in the case of a Jewish student who cannot attend Friday afternoon classes during winter months because he or she has to reach home before sunset to observe the Sabbath, the most obvious solution would be to re-timetable the class.

Another consideration is the types of activity students feel comfortable with. Physical contact between girls and boys such as in 'ice-breakers' during induction, are best avoided. Some girls may follow dress codes and prefer to wear an adapted PE kit, covering arms and legs. Some Muslim students may not want to draw images of people or animals, while Buddhist, Hindu and Jain students may not want to practise animal dissection or handle meat products. The cow is sacred in Hinduism, which means devout Hindus may prefer not to handle leather goods. Jains and some Buddhists also avoid leather. Jewish and Muslim students may wish to avoid products derived from pigs. Christian, Jewish and Muslim students may be offended by blasphemy, however casually expressed. Rephrasing the exclamation, 'God!' to 'Goodness!' or something similar may avoid causing offence. Student behaviour may also be affected by particular religious observances, for example, during Ramadan Muslims refrain from eating and drinking during daylight hours, which could affect concentration.

Religious literacy in the whole college

College resources may govern the extent to which religious needs can be met. Nevertheless, accommodating religious observances within reasonable limits should form part of an equality and diversity policy, and reflect the needs of its student population. It is important to recognize the difference between direct and indirect discrimination. Direct discrimination is where someone is openly disadvantaged; indirect discrimination is where an individual is disadvantaged due to official or unofficial institutional policy. This can be less apparent, particularly when the individual teacher, or college as a whole, is unaware of a student's religious observances. Offering the Jewish student no alternative to his or her Friday afternoon classes could be classified as indirect discrimination because the student's learning will be disadvantaged through missed lessons. Organizing timetables to accommodate religious observances would be a good example of implementing secular liberalism.

There are a variety of ways to support religious diversity. These include providing access to appropriate pastoral and chaplaincy services, as well as careers and progression advice that is culturally sensitive and relevant. Library resources could include journals and newspapers that reflect students' cultural and religious backgrounds, for example, *Q News* or *Eastern Eye*. Most colleges provide canteen facilities. While the feasibility of providing Kosher and Halal food is likely to be dependent on local stockists, the canteen menu should at least provide a range of options suitable for Muslim and Jewish students. Provision of worship facilities can be particularly contentious as colleges rarely have space, and if given to one group others may feel entitled to make similar demands.

Religious dress has become an issue for schools with uniform policies. In 2008 a Sikh teenager was excluded from school for wearing a kara (steel bangle worn by Sikhs) because it violated uniform policies. The High Court ruled in her favour, stating that she had been unlawfully discriminated against on the grounds of race and religion. In a more complex case a Muslim girl was excluded from school for wearing the jilbab (loose fitting dress worn by Muslim women). The school argued this posed a health and safety risk and that the girl had refused to wear shalwar kameez (loose fitting trousers and top) as a uniform option (Muslims' opinions about appropriate religious dress differ and can be associated with cultural beliefs as well as religious interpretation). The courts initially found in the girl's favour, but in 2006 this ruling was overturned by the House of Lords. Although it is illegal to discriminate against someone because of their religion, these examples illustrate how interpretations of religious dress rest with the courts.

In FE, uniform policies are likely to apply only to certain vocational courses, but there may also be implicit dress codes for students following academic courses. As colleges need to treat all students fairly, there must be good reason for permitting some forms of religious dress and not others. In some learning environments, for example, kitchens, laboratories, workshops or salons, loose fitting garments could present a genuine health and safety concern.

The thesis that religion has shifted from the public to the private sphere and is a personal matter is now questioned. Religion has re-emerged, claiming recognition in the public domain; Casanova (1994) describes this as the 'deprivatization of religion'. This presents a challenge to secular organizations, who because of equality legislation, have to consider not just one familiar religion, but a range of often unfamiliar religions each with its own internal diversity. Gilliat-Ray (2000) noted that religion is fundamental to many young people's identity, particularly among minority ethnic groups, and that 'an individual's identity becomes more sharply defined when it is not recognised by the institution' (p. 55). Combined with secular liberalism and developments in equality legislation, this means that harmonious college environments depend in part on accommodating religious observances to a reasonable degree. If religious identity is accepted as inextricably part of the person, then religious literacy becomes an important aspect of a teacher's ability to meet the professional obligation of employing strategies to ensure the best learning experience for students.

Anti-racism

Anti-racism, or 'political multiculturalism', became a significant policy approach following the 1981 urban disturbances that exposed the systematic racial discrimination and inequality faced by non-white people in Britain (Scarman 1981; Solomos 2003). Anti-racism provides a critique of 'race relations' policies of multiculturalism that focused on sharing cultural practices and overcoming individual prejudice and ignorance. In contrast, anti-racism stresses the structural nature of racism within British society, and the role of colonialism, slavery and Empire in creating racism. Rather than focus on individual attitudes, anti-racism is concerned with patterns of discrimination and unequal outcomes for disadvantaged ethnic groups. For anti-racists, these are non-white and share a common experience of white prejudice, discrimination and violence, as well as institutional bias. Here, the over-representation of African-Caribbean young men in school exclusions, the under-achievement of some non-white school pupils, and the over-representation of non-white young men in all aspects of the criminal justice system are not simply due to the prejudices of racist teachers or police officers, but rather to 'institutional racism' whereby assumptions, practices and inherited traditions combine to produce unequal outcomes for non-white people (Solomos 2003).

The importance of policy

The response of anti-racists has been to campaign for, devise and implement equal opportunities policies and procedures designed both to counter past bias and to make future practices open and transparent, with the expectation that this will eventually produce more equal outcomes (Bhavnani et al. 2005). Initially championed by left-wing LAs from the early 1980s, anti-racist and equal opportunities policies have become increasingly mainstream in both public and private sectors. The development of 'ethnic monitoring data', particularly the inclusion of an ethnicity question in the 1991 Census, has produced information on the experiences of different ethnicities in all aspects of society, thus enabling targets for improvement, such as increasing the numbers of ethnic minority police officers and fire-fighters. While British legislation specifically outlaws positive discrimination or quotas (as used in the USA), it does allow 'Positive Action' efforts to encourage more qualified candidates from under-represented ethnic groups through processes of training, mentoring and preparation. Allied to this have been fair recruitment and selection policies, and measures against racial harassment and violence in schools, colleges and the community. Following the racist murder of Stephen Lawrence and the Macpherson Inquiry (1999), there have been significant improvements in the recording, acknowledgement and investigation of racial incidents and crimes. This number has steadily increased since the mid-1990s, and arguably is due to improved reporting mechanisms and increasing confidence among ethnic minorities to report incidents, rather than to an increase in racism. Alongside this has been the strengthening of anti-discriminatory legislation, with the Race Relations (Amendment) Act 2000 requiring public bodies to carry out Equality Impact Assessments in the expectation that this will expose and undermine implicitly racist practices and assumptions. While non-white groups continue to lag behind white people on a range of socio-economic indicators, significant advances have been made by non-white minorities as a result of these measures.

Problems with anti-racism

While many of the assumptions and priorities of anti-racism have become mainstream, difficulties have emerged. One key problem has been a simplistic understanding of ethnic relations, with white people characterized as powerful and dominant and all ethnic minorities portrayed as victims of racism and inequality. While this picture carried weight in 1976 when the Race Relations Act came into force, it is less recognizable in the ethnically diverse Britain of today. Some non-white ethnic groups are outperforming white children in schools and, as a result, accessing high-status jobs. Modood et al. (1997) conclude that Chinese and African-Asians (mainly Hindus and Sikhs arriving in Britain from Africa) cannot be characterized as 'disadvantaged' in any meaningful way. Education and employment data suggests the severe educational and economic disadvantage faced by other Asian groups, particularly Pakistanis and Bangladeshis, is as much to do with class, economic background and qualifications as with racial discrimination. The concentration of these communities in the Midlands and North of England where de-industrialization has occurred is relevant.

Alongside this came an unravelling of an over-arching 'Black' identity crucial to the development of anti-racism. Increasingly, Asian-origin commentators highlighted how 'Black' identity focused more on Afro-Caribbean experiences, failing to reflect the concerns and priorities of Asian communities. This came to a head with the *Satanic Verses* crisis of 1989 when anti-racist alliances fractured over Muslim demands for the banning of Rushdie's book (Modood 2005). These new demands by specific ethnic and religious communities could be seen as an inevitable outcome of LA funding of facilities and organizations aimed at specific ethnic groups in the name of 'anti-racism'. Such practices fractured previous multi-racial alliances in the fight against racism (Sivanandan 2005).

The fundamental importance of economic factors in explaining disadvantage has been downplayed by anti-racism's over-concern with ethnicity and 'race'. Some understandings of ethnicity have obscured the role of class, gender and place in creating and maintaining the identity of individuals and communities. This approach of measuring experience by ethnicity rather than income has served to obscure the severe educational and economic disadvantage faced by the poorest white working-class communities, a failing now starting to be addressed (JRF 2007). Alongside this have been concerns about a 'white backlash' to anti-racist policies and curriculum approaches within schools, colleges and youth work.

Attempts to challenge racist attitudes and behaviour have often been 'clumsy' and less than even-handed, with persistent allegations that mixed-race fights are seen as an expression of white racism, while the same judgement is not applied to non-whites. While this reflects the lack of confidence and clarity of practitioners (CRE 1999), it also highlights fundamental problems with anti-racism. These include a belief that 'racism' is something that only white people do to non-whites, and that incidents the other way round cannot be characterized in the same way. However, the reaction of established ethnic communities to recent migrants questions this assertion. Anti-racist educational approaches have focused unduly on white people learning about the (essentialized) 'cultures' and religions of ethnic minorities, with little concern for cultures and traditions of white communities, as shown by recurring concerns over whether public displays of St George's flag are 'racist'. Research shows that white English-origin young people have less understanding and confidence in their own 'culture' than any other ethnic group (Nayak 1999).

Multiculturalism, integration and community cohesion

Kundnani (2002) suggests that there has been a significant shift in the concerns and priorities of 'race relations' policies (Solomos 2003). This shift has been characterized, negatively, as a retreat from 'multiculturalism' towards 'integration', one less concerned with difference and the promotion of ethnic diversity. Rather than replacing 'multiculturalism' in general, the current policy approaches of integration or community cohesion represent a move away from one particular type of multiculturalism or political anti-racism, towards a 'critical multiculturalism' concerned with holistic forms of citizenship (May 1999).

The 2001 disturbances in Oldham, Burnley and Bradford were a turning point in government approaches to 'race relations'. Following these a new policy concept, 'Community Cohesion', was rapidly deployed. The report of the government enquiry (Cantle 2001) paid scant attention to the actual events, suggesting they were a symptom of much deeper malaise concerning ethnic relations. Local authorities were instructed to measure the impact of Community Cohesion; all schools now have a duty to promote cohesion. The bombings of July 2005 and the subsequent policy concern with 'preventing violent extremism' have re-emphasized this agenda.

The central premise of Community Cohesion is that entrenched ethnic segregation is a reality in many areas leading to 'parallel lives' (Ritchie 2001), little contact between ethnic groups and a lack of shared values and understandings. Such segregation is seen as causing ethnic tension and distrust, the solution being a greater focus on bringing people together around common issues, identities and values. Implicit within community cohesion is a critique of anti-racist policies since the late 1980s, which are seen as being unduly focused on difference and with the concerns of specific ethnic groups, rather than on common problems. These policies did not cause segregation, were necessary in the 1980s, but more recently have had the unintended consequence of exacerbating ethnic segregation (Cantle 2005). It is suggested that anti-racism has been more concerned with 'equality' for specific ethnic groups than with relations between groups or the overall common good.

Thomas (2006) has shown that 'meaningful direct contact' between young people of different ethnic backgrounds is central to this policy agenda. Such interventions focus on shared, common identities and enable cooperation in safe spaces that allow 'rooting and shifting' (Yuval-Davis 1997), the re-thinking of cultural understandings and identities without one's own identity being threatened. This type of activity supports 'contact theory', the belief that to break down ethnic divides and prejudices, action needs to be based on groups rather than individuals and to take place over a period of time (Hewstone et al. 2007). Such activity develops 'bridging social capital' (Putnam 2000) between strong, segregated monocultural communities, suggesting that individuals and communities take some responsibility to foster integration that government cannot create on its own (Giddens 1998).

Criticisms of community cohesion

A key criticism of integration approaches is that placing the responsibility for overcoming segregation on communities and individuals implicitly blames them for segregation (Kundnani 2002). This has been fuelled by the emphasis of some politicians on the agency of Asian communities, with pronouncements on increased use of English, trans-continental marriages and Islamist political activity. There is much less concern with White 'flight' or self-segregation, and growing support for the far-right BNP (Alexander 2004), which can suggest community cohesion is a return to the failed 1960s policy of 'assimilation'; the idea that all ethnic minority communities should give up their distinct cultures and integrate. Arguably, the practice of community cohesion suggests this is not the case. The Cantle Report (2001) acknowledged the reality of diversity, and the need to continue developing race equality measures, such as the Race Relations (Amendment) Act 2000 and the associated

Equality Impact Assessments. Thomas (2006) argues this approach to integration works with the reality of difference and rather than being the 'death of multiculturalism' (Kundnani 2002), is a rejection of one type of multiculturalism/anti-racism, with an emphasis on a new 'critical multiculturalism' (May 1999). This recognizes ethnic difference but rejects essentialized and fixed notions, highlighting other forms of identity. Community cohesion is arguably concerned with divisions of class, income, community and 'territory' as well as ethnicity, seeing these as relevant to the realities of segregated and 'tense' communities. Community cohesion's focus on integration and common identity is part of wider attempts by New Labour to create de-centred and inter-sectional identities, 'cooler' or multiple identities, rather than 'hot' ethnic identities that lead to tension (McGhee 2005).

Anti-sexism

Women's representation in public life and employment has improved dramatically since the 1975 Sex Discrimination Act. Consequently there has been a tendency to assume that gender discrimination has been eradicated or, if it still exists, people may claim 'the pendulum has swung the other way', pointing to the underachievement of boys in GCSEs and under-representation of male teachers. However, there is still a gender pay gap, women are not fairly represented in the judiciary or in Parliament, and are under-represented in top level management. Anti-sexist practice moves beyond quantitative demands for political and financial sex equality and looks instead at the qualitative aspects of how we live our lives and how our gender enhances or detracts from the potential richness of experience. For education, the major issues in anti-sexist practice are how to enable a fulfilling work–life balance and how to ensure gender does not force girls/boys and women/men into stereotyped subjects and careers.

Organizations like the UK Resource Centre for Women in Science aim to improve the recruitment of women into science, engineering, construction and technology. They recommend that, in order to attract more women into construction, advertisements and course design should be more focused on women. The same may well apply in areas of male recruitment into health and social care. Ensuring an anti-sexist environment is particular necessary for learners recruited to occupational areas not traditionally associated with their gender. From the beginning of a course, sexist or gender-stereotyped language should be identified as unacceptable with the teacher ensuring it is dealt with appropriately. When, at the outset, the teacher has negotiated rules of acceptable language with the whole class, students will often take on the responsibility of identifying gender-stereotyped words and suggest alternatives.

Students should be able to encounter learning materials showing images of people of diverse appearance, both male and female. Posters presenting diverse images are available from organizations such as the Equality and Human Rights Commission. Where possible language used in learning materials should be gender neutral, for example use 'staffed' instead of 'manned'. Advice on language use is available from the Equality Challenge Unit (www.ecu.ac.uk). To avoid creating a culture where only one gender feels comfortable, teachers may need to modify their interaction with students. A male Construction lecturer may slip into a familiar way of talking to apprentices and say, 'Right then lads . . .' but this could exclude female apprentices. Similarly a female Hairdressing lecturer should avoid chatting about 'a girls' night out' as this may exclude male students.

Gendered assumptions about learners' social and family lives should be avoided. For example, we should not assume that a woman will need time off for family responsibilities and a man will not. Positive support and encouragement is the most important factor in retaining women and men in non-traditional subjects. Learners are encouraged if teachers create a cooperative learning environment rather than a competitive milieu. By working on cooperative tasks, students in a mixed-sex environment are more likely to take the risk of revealing what they do not know.

Learning or assessment tasks should aim to draw on contexts familiar to both sexes. For example, an engineering task might involve designing and building a baby buggy or a bicycle rather than a model racing car. No subject, not even science or mathematics, can claim to be completely value free and objective. Part of the teacher's role is to ensure that values and feelings are discussed with respect. For example, when learning about motor vehicle maintenance it might become relevant to discuss the social and environmental implications of choosing one type of vehicle rather than another. A value-based approach to scientific subjects can make these more attractive to some learners.

Lesbian, gay, bisexual and transgender issues

Hunt and Jensen (2006) found homophobic bullying, involving verbal and physical abuse, was prevalent and largely unchallenged in schools and in some cases even condoned by teachers and support staff. They found that 65 per cent of lesbian and gay pupils had experienced bullying and that many teachers failed to respond to homophobic language. Homophobic language does not just consist of intentional abuse, but includes regular off-hand comments that go unnoticed and unaddressed by teachers. For example, the phrases 'that's so gay' or 'you're so gay' are used negatively to indicate that something is useless. Such language is so pervasive that most people think it is 'natural' and do not recognize that it is abusive and can reflect institutional heterosexism and the presumption of its normality. The consequence of institutional heterosexism is that lesbian, gay, bisexual and transgender (LGBT) people may feel excluded and not fulfil their learning potential. In their study Hunt and Jensen commented that school work was affected by homophobic bullying and half of those bullied said they had missed school as a result.

For some LGBTs sexual orientation may be central to their educational experience. Vicars (2007: 21) suggests:

> Cultural homophobia . . . refers to social standards and norms which dictate that being heterosexual is better than being lesbian, gay or bisexual . . . Often heterosexuals do not realise that these standards exist while lesbian, gay and bisexual people are acutely aware of them. This can result in lesbians, gays and bisexuals feeling like outsiders in society.

In some workplaces LGBTs are expected to keep their sexual orientation and family life secret, whereas in others they may be forcibly 'outed' irrespective of their wishes.

The Sexual Orientation Regulations do not undermine an individual's right to privacy – staff or students have the right not to discuss their sexual orientation or have it discussed by others. Some workplaces may profess a commitment to equality policies, but there is still a prevalent culture of heteronormativity, whereby partners are assumed to be of the opposite sex. This can be seen in the way family photographs are displayed, trips and social events advertised and time off from work or study is structured to allow for domestic responsibilities. Consequently LGBTs may feel unable to talk naturally about family life or participate fully in the social milieu of college.

Harassment of LGBTs in colleges and the workplace can take many forms from unintentional to intentional exclusion, and if unchallenged, may result in verbal insults and physical abuse. This could include comments overheard in canteens or corridors, graffiti scrawled on walls and posters, or physically pushing people out of a group of learners in the classroom. The teacher needs be alert to harassment and abusive language, and needs to be familiar with relevant policies in their institution so that their response can be appropriate. Learners' behaviour towards each other and how they respect each others' identity are matters for all teachers and learning support staff.

Mental health

According to the Mental Health Foundation (MHF), one in four people will experience some mental health disorder in the course of a year (MHF 2009).

Teachers may approach the topic of mental health in three ways:

1   dealing with students' mental health conditions and their effects on teaching and learning;

2   maintaining and promoting students' mental health and not causing undue stress or exacerbating difficulties while teaching;

3   maintaining their own mental health by striking a work-life balance, promoting well-being and taking active steps to avoid stress.

Learners may present with recognizable, diagnosed and disclosed conditions. Some learners will not yet have been diagnosed and others will develop conditions during their studies. Clearly, learners must not be coerced into disclosure and the stigma of mental illness must be considered. Teachers involved with prison education should be aware that 90 per cent of prisoners have a recognized mental health condition. Other providers may have contracts to work with mental health and voluntary groups to deliver provision for learners with specific difficulties.

What can practitioners do?

1   Learners with existing conditions:
    •   Research conditions and strategies.
    •   Talk to experienced colleagues.
    •   Attend awareness training.
    •   Read *Introducing Access for All* (DfES 2003a).

- Expect the unexpected, but not the worst.
- Consider classroom organization and management issues.

2   Promoting mental health and well-being:
- Allow space for active listening and opportunities for one-to-one interaction to detect issues and refer to appropriate support.
- In class, build in anti-stress activities such as relaxation techniques.
- Be aware of referral procedures and when and how to make these within the institution and community.

3   Promoting teachers' own mental health:
- Find ways to relax and maintain a healthy work-life balance.
- Use de-stressing techniques as listed above.
- Be aware of triggers to negative feelings and adopt effective coping strategies.
- For all the above seek professional support.
- Discuss issues with a line manager, equality and diversity representative or union official.

Equal opportunity in practice

Colleges collect information about disadvantaged groups represented among staff and students in accordance with legislation and to enable forward planning to redress under-representation. For the teacher, this should not just be 'box-ticking'. Cowan (2006: 8) suggests: 'Monitoring for the sake of it is generally unsuccessful. Before sexual orientation monitoring is introduced, it is important that employers identify why they want to ask about sexual orientation, what they want to find out and what they will do with the information'. Questions about disability, ethnicity, sexual orientation and religion are particularly sensitive and are significantly under-reported, because some see these as a personal matter and not relevant to education.

Inclusivity and differentiation

Inclusive teaching means recognizing and meeting the learning needs of all students. Ideally inclusivity should involve the whole class working and learning together in which there are no 'outsiders' – easier to say than do, as most social groups develop insiders and outsiders over time. Teachers have to perform a difficult balancing act ensuring learners are made to feel their needs are recognized, while making sure differences are not highlighted by constant reference. For example, it would not be helpful to ask a male care student, 'As the only man in the room, what is your opinion on fatherhood?' or to say to a learner with dyslexia, 'I have prepared this handout on coloured paper especially for you'. It would be more appropriate to allow the male student to decide his contribution in whatever role he identifies with. Similarly, it would be more inclusive to allow the dyslexic student the opportunity to select materials in the appropriate format from a display of handouts.

Providing the option to select handouts from a range of different formats and media is also an opportunity to become familiar with the particular learning needs and preferences of students. Many disabled students wish to avoid unwanted attention and public 'fuss' around them reinforces their perceived difference and contributes to social isolation. When planning lessons teachers should consider how to differentiate teaching and provide learning facilities according to the needs and characteristics of learners. Listed below are possible indicators of inclusivity and differentiation in learning situations.

- Does the teacher draw on the individual experience of all group members?
- Does the teacher direct questions to and seek responses from a range of different learners?
- Does the teacher encourage harmonious relationships between different groups of learners?
- Does the teacher challenge the use of inappropriate language by learners?
- Are learners encouraged to work with others from different backgrounds through group work?
- Are all learners actively engaged in the lesson?
- Do learners show that they expect to be treated differently but with equal respect?
- Is the language used in learning materials and by the teacher appropriate?
- Is the learning support equipment used sensitively and appropriately?
- Is the assistance of learning support workers e.g. signers, amanuensis, bilingual support workers, etc., used appropriately?

Equality and diversity in teaching

All educators are expected to embed equality and diversity in teaching. This may be easier in some subjects than others. Social scientists may feel that these concepts are an integral to their discipline. Similarly, artists have a tradition of drawing on other cultures and different life experiences as source material. This may be more challenging in other subjects. How is diversity embedded into teaching a task like changing a gear box or calculating percentages? A teacher concerned with spreading awareness and respect for diversity needs to consider where their subject interfaces with human beings. For example, the teacher of motor vehicle mechanics might discuss clutch pedal adjustments and adaptations and their suitability for drivers with disabilities. Mathematicians could ask learners to calculate percentages of male and female apprentices who chose care courses compared with construction. The contribution of different cultures to the development of academic disciplines can also be discussed. For example, different cultures have given us different number and calculations conventions, including Arabic numerals, Pythagorean triangles and the division of the hour into 60 minutes.

In judging whether an educator is promoting equality, diversity and inclusion we need to consider the values and culture of the learners and the teacher, the physical environment and the learning materials. Some indicators are given below:

1   Culture and values:
    - Are learners aware of their rights and responsibilities?

- Are the assessment methods valid and varied?
- Is individual progress in learning identified and celebrated?

2 Physical environment:
- Do the displays and images used give an impression of an organization that values diversity?
- Are the accommodation and facilities suitable for disabled learners?

3 Learning materials:
- Do learning materials avoid stereotyping and reflect the diversity of learners?
- Do learning materials reflect the cultural diversity of British society?
- Are other cultures considered and used as examples in learning?

Conclusion

This chapter set itself a wide ranging brief and touches on a number of important debates, locating this discussion within the context of practice. It considers the way in which we make sense of equality and diversity, exploring this in the context of the LLS. It examines issues of anti-racism, anti-sexism and LGBT as well as the salience of faith and religion in educational settings, with later sections turning more directly towards practice. Throughout there is recognition that many of the terms are contestable and that there is a constant struggle to sustain practices committed to social justice. We need to recognize that educational processes cannot simply be viewed from an institutional position and that they need to be placed within the relational setting in which education is located as well as its wider social context.

PART 2

Teaching in the lifelong learning sector

8

Learning and learners

Margaret McLay, Louise Mycroft, Penny Noel, Kevin Orr, Ron Thompson, Jonathan Tummons and Jane Weatherby

---

In this chapter:

- What is learning?
- Classifying types of learning
- Deep, surface and strategic learning
- Factors influencing learning
- Theories of the learning process
- The learning styles debate
- Widening participation
- Adult learners and 'adult learning'
- Learners from other countries
- Students with learning difficulties or disabilities
- Gifted learners
- Learners aged 14–16

What is learning?

The professional standards for teachers in lifelong learning (LLUK 2007a: 3) require teachers to value learning and to understand 'ways in which learning has the potential to change lives'. However, learning is not easy to define: quite often, what is meant by learning will depend on the way the process of education is viewed. Rather than being a straightforward idea, the concept of learning may require a great deal of elucidation. This chapter begins by introducing some ways of looking at learning, with the aim of highlighting a number of issues to be taken up in more detail later.

One approach is to begin with specific examples. Learning the names of the bones in the human body, learning to swim and learning to judge the quality of a poem would all seem to be appropriate uses of the word 'learning', yet they are quite diverse in nature. Ramsden (1992: 26) cites research on adult students' conceptions of learning, which distinguished five 'common-sense' categories:

1   learning as the acquisition of knowledge;

2   learning as memorizing;

3   learning as the acquisition of skills;

4   learning as making sense or meaning;

5   learning as interpreting and understanding reality in a different way.

A distinction can also be made between learning as a *product* (what is its outcome?) and learning as a *process* (how it occurs and sustains itself over time). Conceiving learning as a product often involves focusing on the behaviour of an individual thought to have learned something. For example, if a student has learned to play a musical scale on the piano, they might sit down and play that scale. An observer could then *infer*, from the student's behaviour, that learning had taken place. Alternatively, someone who had learned what causes earthquakes might be expected to have the ability to explain how earthquakes are caused, and to answer questions about this. Once again, observable behaviour leads the teacher to conclude that learning has taken place.

Robert Gagné (1977: 3) defined learning as 'a change in human disposition or capability, which persists over a period of time, and which is not simply ascribable to the process of growth'. It is worth considering this definition further. All learning relates in some way to change. However, not all change can be ascribed to learning – for example, physical growth can change our capacity for certain activities. Interestingly, Gagné does not ask for a change in behaviour as such, but of 'disposition' or 'capability' – that is, of the potential for behaviour. You may learn to swim but never be observed swimming; nevertheless, if challenged, you would be able to do so!

In contrast to the product model of learning, David Kolb emphasizes the nature of learning as a continuing process and a characteristic of the human ability to understand and shape the environment: 'Learning is a holistic process of adaptation to the world ... learning is *the* major process of human adaptation' (Kolb 1984: 31–2). Influenced by the pragmatist philosophy of John Dewey (see Chapter 15), Kolb argues that learning evolves in response to our development as individuals and to changing circumstances. Learning outcomes indicate only what we *knew* at a particular time in the past, not what we know and can do now: 'Learning is best conceived as a process, not in terms of outcomes ... learning is an emergent process whose outcomes represent only historical record, not knowledge of the future' (Kolb 1984: 26). Related to this idea of learning as an adaptive process is the idea of learning as knowledge construction and of actively making sense or meaning from experience; this view is known as *constructivism*.

The process of learning may also be thought of as a *social practice*. In their study of learning in further education, James and Biesta (2007) draw on a *cultural theory of learning*, 'a theory which conceives of learning not as something which happens in the heads, minds or brains of students, but sees it as something that happens in and "through" social practices' (p. 21). Building on the ideas of the influential French sociologist Pierre Bourdieu and the work of Lave and Wenger (1991; see Chapter 6), James and Biesta argue that the cultural context of learning is not merely a backdrop to the educational experiences of learners; rather, learning must be understood as a cultural practice in its own right.

James and Biesta (2007: 23) define a learning culture as 'the social practices through which people learn' and note that learning is not merely 'done' but is 'done with others', in a community which influences, and is influenced by, its individual members. This leads to the idea of 'learning as becoming' (Colley et al. 2003), in which the self is transformed by a particular learning culture, developing socially approved ways of thinking, feeling and behaving. As Lave and Wenger (1991: 53) observe, 'learning involves the construction of identities', so that knowledge, social membership and identity are inextricably linked.

It should now be clear that there is no single answer to the question 'What is learning?' However, the different perspectives outlined can be seen as complementary, and providing different insights suited to differing contexts and purposes of education and training. The implications of these perspectives will be explored in more detail within this chapter.

Classifying types of learning

The discussion above indicates that there are different types of learning outcome and different learning processes. The nature of the learning process may relate to the type of outcome involved, although learning outcomes do not always capture what is of value in learning. Indeed, *how* something is learned can sometimes be more important than *what* is learned. Furthermore, individuals can learn in various ways at various times. Each of these observations is important in its own way, and will be pursued further in this chapter. For the moment, however, different types of learning outcome will be considered in more detail.

Gagné (1977: 27) identifies five major categories of learning outcome: intellectual skills, verbal information, cognitive strategies, motor skills, and attitudes. This highlights the fact that attitudes can be learned as well as knowledge or skills. Gagné also draws attention to hierarchical structures in learning: for example, within the category of intellectual skills he identifies four levels: discriminations, concepts, rules and problem solving, each of which draws on those below it in the hierarchy.

Bloom (1956) developed a more detailed classification of learning outcomes in his *Taxonomy of Educational Objectives*. This taxonomy is used extensively in planning for student learning, particularly when the teacher or trainer writes behavioural objectives (see Chapter 10). Bloom's taxonomy classifies learning outcomes depending on the type of learning which they represent, using three *domains*: Cognitive, Affective and Psychomotor. As with Gagné, each domain contains a hierarchy of levels, beginning with the simplest and moving towards more complex and challenging types of learning.

Cognitive learning comprises the acquisition and use of knowledge and is demonstrated by knowledge recall and intellectual skills: comprehending information, organizing ideas, analysing and synthesizing data, applying knowledge, choosing among alternatives in problem solving, and evaluating ideas or actions. This domain predominates in academic courses. Bloom identified six levels within the cognitive domain, from simple recall or recognition of facts, through increasingly more complex and abstract cognitive behaviours. Examples of verbs representing intellectual activity on each level are listed in Box 8.1.

Affective learning relates to emotions, attitudes, and values: for example, enjoying,

---

Box 8.1 Levels of learning in the cognitive domain

Knowledge: recognizing and recalling information. Appropriate verbs would be: arrange, define, label, list, name, recall, state.

Comprehension: interpreting, translating or summarizing given information, principles and concepts. *Appropriate verbs*: classify, describe, discuss, explain, identify, locate, recognize, restate, select, translate.

Application: using information, principles and concepts in a context different to the original learning context. *Verbs*: apply, choose, demonstrate, dramatize, illustrate, interpret, practise, schedule, solve, use.

Analysis: separating a whole into parts and making clear their functions and the relationships between them. *Verbs*: analyse, calculate, compare, contrast, differentiate, distinguish, examine.

Synthesis: combining elements to create something different from the original. *Verbs*: arrange, compose, construct, create, design, develop, manage, organize, plan, prepare, propose.

Evaluation: making decisions and judgements based on stated criteria. *Verbs*: appraise, argue, assess, choose, compare, defend, estimate, support, evaluate.

Source: Gronlund (1970)

---

respecting and supporting. The affective domain is important in planning learning which involves working with people; its structure is shown in Box 8.2. *Psychomotor learning* (Box 8.3) involves a range of physical skills and requires atributes such as coordination, dexterity, grace and balance. Its applications cover subjects such as art and dance as well as vocational areas like construction or motor vehicle engineering.

Ausubel (1963) draws attention to the tendency for Bloom's taxonomy to be used in a mechanistic way which emphasizes the lower cognitive levels because they are

---

Box 8.2 Levels of learning in the affective domain

Receiving: showing awareness and attention, for example by listening.

Responding: meeting expectations by responding to stimulus, for example by commenting sympathetically on something said.

Valuing: behaving consistently with stated single beliefs, values and attitudes.

Organizing: behaving consistently with a given system of values and beliefs.

Characterizing: behaving consistently with an internalized value or belief system.

Source: Gronlund (1970)

Box 8.3 Levels of learning in the psychomotor domain

Imitation: observes a skill and tries to repeat it.

Manipulation: performs a skill according to instruction rather than observation.

Precision: accurately and independently reproduces a skill.

Articulation: combines one or more skills in sequence with harmony and consistency.

Naturalization: completes one or more skills with ease and becomes 'automatic'.

Source: Gronlund (1970)

---

straightforward to measure. However, it can be invaluable to the teacher when designing programmes of study, framing learning objectives and planning for assessment.

The distinction between the cognitive and psychomotor domain can be related to the difference between *knowing that* and *knowing how*. The philosopher Gilbert Ryle expressed this distinction as follows:

> Learning how or improving an ability is not like learning that or acquiring information. Truths can be imparted, procedures can only be inculcated, and while inculcation is a gradual process, imparting is relatively sudden. It makes sense to ask at what moment someone became apprised of a truth, but not to ask at what moment someone acquired a skill.
>
> (Ryle 1949: 58)

For a surgeon, extensive medical knowledge is necessary, but far from sufficient: 'excellence at surgery is not the same thing as knowledge of medical science; nor is it a simple product of it. The surgeon must indeed have learned . . . a great number of truths; but . . . must also have learned by practice a great number of aptitudes' (Ryle 1949: 48–9).

A particular characteristic of learning in the psychomotor domain is that it can be very difficult to express 'knowing how' in language or any other symbolic form. The knowledge is *tacit* rather than explicit (Polanyi 1983) and is not understood in terms of formal procedures or codes. Someone may know how to give an injection but may not be able to explain how they do it. Although in some cases, this may be due to incomplete understanding, it may also be a feature of the knowledge itself rather than of how an individual knows it. Tacit knowledge may only be transmissible by means of observation or by the learner becoming immersed in the social practices of a particular organizational culture. In this way, tacit knowledge is acquired by becoming part of a community of practice (Wenger 1998; see also Chapter 6).

Deep, surface and strategic learning

Many teachers will have observed that students have varied attitudes to learning. One student may be thoroughly committed to learning for its own sake, and be passionate about understanding as much as possible about a particular field; another may want to do a bare minimum of work. Such tendencies are often classified in terms of *deep* and *surface* learning (Marton and Säljö 1976).

Deep learning is associated with a commitment to learning for its own sake, in which the student wishes to acquire an extensive knowledge and understanding that is relational as well as factual – that is, based on principles and relationships. The deep learner is likely to ask awkward questions and to want to know why a method works rather than being content with correctly applying it; they would be unhappy to be fobbed off with superficial explanations.

Surface learning, as its name implies, is the opposite of deep learning and is character-ized by an avoidance of reasoning, explanations or underlying principles. 'Just tell me what I need to know' is an attitude associated with surface learning, which might also be very narrow and instrumental (that is, directed towards a specific and immediate goal).

Strategic learning is perhaps the most commonly observed approach from students, and is closely associated with assessment regimes and learning cultures. Students may be largely concerned with obtaining a qualification, or perhaps simply with staying on a course for financial reasons. Such students may be strongly influenced by what is required of them, particularly by the surrounding learning culture. If learning for its own sake, and a commitment to higher level learning outcomes, are not reflected in assessment requirements or in the learning culture, students may simply adopt a surface approach. When immersed in a different, more demanding culture, they may well be able to adapt, taking on the characteristics of deep learning because this is now required of them.

Factors influencing learning

A number of factors can be responsible for how quickly and effectively an individual learns, or even whether they learn at all. Some are transient, relating to the individual or the immediate learning environment; for example, the learner's physical state, the perceived relevance of a topic or their response to learning activities. Other short-term factors may include the timing and length of a learning session or peer group behaviour. Many of these factors may be under the control of the teacher; however, more permanent influences on learning may have greater impact and be more difficult to address. These include confidence and self-esteem, motivation and cogni-tive development. A learner may have deep-rooted beliefs about learning and their own relationship with education. Peer group pressure and the expectations of teachers, parents or employers are also important. Furthermore, structural issues of race, gender, disability and class can have a considerable impact on learning. These wider social factors are discussed in more detail later in this chapter and in Chapters 4 and 7; this section concentrates on individual differences which influence learning.

Motivation is a key factor in learning, both in its own right and as an underlying element in a number of other factors. For example, the reason *why* peer group pressure influences the learning of an individual can be attributed to more general elements in the motivation of their behaviour. Abraham Maslow developed an influential theory of motivation which can be useful in understanding the inter-relationships between some of the factors noted above – it is illustrated in Figure 8.1. According to Maslow, a hierarchy of needs underlies the motivation for human behaviour. Belonging, and psychological safety, are important elements of this model, so that learning behaviours which mark a student as 'standing out from the crowd' or which could expose them to embarrassment, might be expected to be avoided. In a similar way, several points noted above as factors influencing learning (for example, self-esteem, classroom environment and peer group pressure) can all be related to aspects of motivation in Maslow's hierarchy.

It can also be useful to distinguish between *intrinsic* and *extrinsic* motivation – that is, what comes from within (such as a desire to learn or find job satisfaction) as opposed to motivation from outside (for example, receiving praise, being admonished or financial reward). Child (2004: 192) cites evidence that praise has a more beneficial long-term effect than being admonished or chided. Intrinsic motivation is more likely to result when students attribute their achievement to internal factors under their control, such as the amount of effort they make, or when they believe they have *agency* in reaching desired goals (achievements are not determined by

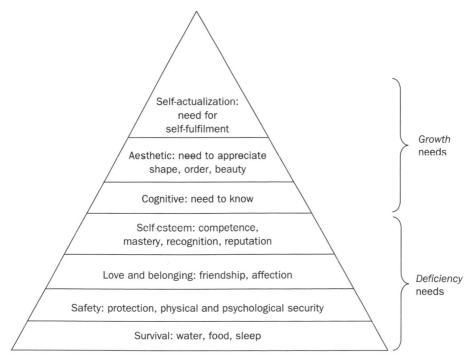

Figure 8.1 Maslow's hierarchy of human needs
Sources: Maslow (1970); Child (2004)

luck). Conversely, students may deliberately not stretch themselves so that they may attribute failure to lack of effort rather than ability (Seifert 2004). Extrinsic motivation can certainly be effective; however, an overemphasis on extrinsic rewards may lead to a reduction in intrinsic motivation.

Reinforcement is 'rewarding' learned behaviour with desirable outcomes (positive reinforcement) or removing undesired outcomes (called negative reinforcement by Skinner, although some authors use negative reinforcement to refer to punishment). Reinforcement is related to behaviourist models of learning: successful learning is rewarded with something desirable and is therefore more likely to occur again. Equally, unsuccessful learning associated with undesirable outcomes (failure or rejection, for example) can lead to behaviour that prevents learning – it damages confidence, for example. Adult learners often show signs of this when returning to education in later life.

Expectation is a very important influence on learning, whether on the part of a teacher, parents, peers or the student themselves; expectations of success or failure are very often borne out. The 'halo effect' is well known and should put teachers on their guard against 'labelling' groups or individuals. These points are often linked with issues of equality and diversity: where certain groups are labelled as less likely to succeed, they may be given less challenging work, taught less rigorously and given restricted opportunities.

Learning style theories have been influential since the early 1990s, and have more recently taken hold as a way of ensuring that the individual needs of learners are addressed. These theories propose that, although people learn differently, their preferred ways of learning tend to fall into identifiable categories. There are numerous schemes for classifying learning styles, and many educational institutions use them to identify the styles of students as a diagnostic tool. It is claimed that tutors need to be aware of the learning styles of their students, and alert to possible preferences and weaknesses, in order to provide learning activities that cater for the range of existing learning styles within a learning group. However, it is important to understand that learning styles have come to be seen as problematic; the debates surrounding them are discussed in more detail later in this chapter.

Theories of the learning process

Theoretical discussion of education dates back at least as far as the Greek philosopher Plato. Both the word 'education' (from the Latin *educare*, meaning to bring up or draw out) and the word 'pedagogy' (from the Greek word for education but now used to mean the theory of educating), have ancient roots. However, the systematic investigation of how learning occurs in individuals is relatively recent, developing from the general considerations of philosophers such as John Dewey but also from a tradition of empirical research into learning. Within this tradition, the work of the Russian physiologist Ivan Pavlov on conditioned reflexes, in the early years of the twentieth century, can be seen as originating behaviourism – one of the main theories of individual learning. The following section gives a brief sketch of this important area.

Behaviourism

Behaviourism attempts to approach learning scientifically, with a cumulative growth of knowledge based on repeatable and verifiable experiments. Pavlov's well-known experiments on dogs are an early example of this approach, in which he demonstrated that an initial *unconditioned response* – in this case, salivation when presented with food – could be transformed into a *conditioned response* by repeatedly accompanying the food with a characteristic sound. The original unconditioned stimulus (the food) eventually was not needed to produce salivation; instead, the dogs salivated on hearing the sound (conditioned stimulus). See Figure 8.2 for a description of this process of *classical conditioning*.

Whether this experiment is relevant to the study of learning is debatable; Carr (2003: 88) discusses the limitations of conditioning as a model of learning, an obvious one being that what has been developed is more akin to a reflex than to the voluntary, conscious behaviour we would normally associate with learning. This criticism is partly addressed by the work of E.L. Thorndike (using cats this time) on what later became known as *operant conditioning*. In Thorndike's experiments, animals 'learned', through a process of trial and error, to escape from a cage – being rewarded with food, as well as freedom. In this case, there seems at least to be an element of purposeful behaviour, directed towards intelligible goals.

Thorndike deduced two principles of learning: the 'law of exercise', which emphasizes the importance of frequent repetition, and the 'law of effect', which introduced the concept of reinforcement discussed above. According to the law of effect, rewarding success increases the effectiveness of learning. In these findings, a fundamental concept of behaviourism appears: the idea of a stimulus-response (S–R) link. In Pavlov's experiment, the link is direct and essentially constitutes a conditioned reflex action; however, in Thorndike's model, the link is indirect and mediated by the organism (S–O–R), the role of reinforcement and goal-directed learning indicating an element of purposive behaviour on the part of the learner.

Experimenting with dogs and cats is all very well, but does any of this relate to

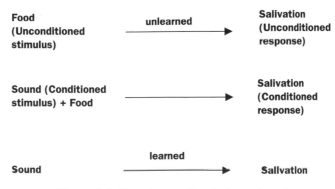

Figure 8.2 Pavlov's conditioning experiment

humans? Another well-known experiment, conducted by J.B. Watson, shows that conditioning can apply to humans – the infamous case of 'Little Albert'. In this experiment (Watson and Rayner 1920), Watson presented a small child of 11 months, Albert B., with a variety of small animals and objects. On each occasion, the researchers frightened Albert by, for example, striking a metal bar with a hammer. Not surprisingly, Albert was soon conditioned to be afraid of the objects themselves. Clearly, then, conditioning does work with humans – an important finding, but perhaps less significant than the illustration this case gives of the need to apply ethical standards to educational research.

Another key figure in behaviourism is B.F. Skinner, who developed Thorndike's ideas into a sophisticated theory of operant conditioning. Skinner believed that almost anything could be taught by conditioning, and famously taught pigeons to play table-tennis by breaking down the game into a sequence of actions, reinforcing each one separately whenever the pigeons displayed an approximation to the particular action. More generally, Skinner saw this process as representing how learning could be induced – analysing a task into behavioural components and then systematically reinforcing each component in its proper sequence. The later development of *programmed learning* owes a lot to Skinner, and even today a great deal of training follows the principles laid down in his development of operant conditioning.

Skinner distinguished between respondent and operant types of behaviour. The first type is essentially a predictable reflex, such as drawing one's hand away from a flame, whereas the second is a spontaneous act of the individual and may have no obvious cause. Operant behaviour may therefore be directed to a goal not obvious to an observer, something desired or valued by the individual. Skinner argued that operant behaviour can be created or modified by controlled stimuli associated with appropriate reinforcement. A reinforced behaviour will be progressively selected in preference to other behaviours.

Although behaviourism has been hugely influential, it should be clear from the brief discussion above that it has severe limitations, both conceptual and moral. Its explicitly scientific approach means that behaviourism consciously limits itself to observable, repeatable facets of human behaviour. It thus diminishes the richness of learning and makes it difficult to transfer findings to the complex situations encountered in real-life education and training. All but the most controlled and pre-scribed situations will therefore be very imperfectly represented by behaviourist approaches. In particular, although the agency of an individual is recognized in terms of instrumental learning and motivation, there is no account of how an individual makes sense of their experience – a key element of later theories. Nor is there any recognition of the social aspect of learning. Arguably, behaviourism is also morally deficient in that human beings are treated as little more than mechanical systems; the treatment of Albert B. is an example of what this approach can lead to.

For an interesting discussion of the philosophical limitations of behaviourism, see Carr (2003: 90–3). He notes that behaviourism cannot account for the ways in which people grasp the *sense* or *meaning* of knowledge and social practices. Although learning may involve causal processes such as the establishment of S–R bonds, it cannot be reducible to *only* these processes. For example, a pigeon could be taught to press a red disc to obtain food, in preference to discs of other colours. Does the pigeon *know* that the disc is red? And what would it *mean* to say, 'The pigeon knows that the disc is red'?

Nevertheless, it would be a mistake to dismiss behaviourism. The important concept of reinforcement, when interpreted in the human terms of praise, satisfaction and a sense of achievement, indicates the importance of the benefits (material and intellectual) of learning. The potential of classical conditioning for creating undesired learning, such as Albert's fear of animals, also suggests possible explanations for the fear and anxiety often reported by adult learners returning to education following difficult experiences at school. Furthermore, the emphasis on careful analysis of a task or topic to be learned and the systematic reinforcement of each aspect is clearly important in building up an understanding of how to go about planning learning.

Cognitivism

Cognitive psychology attempts to remedy the shortcomings of behaviourism by giving an account of human learning 'in terms of the active construction and imposition of principles or rules on experience' (Carr 2003: 94). Its roots lie in the work of the early twentieth-century Gestalt psychologists (Gestalt is a German word meaning 'shape'), who investigated the nature of perception and the ways in which people construct meaning from sensory impressions. Their aim was to discover general laws determining the way objects are perceived; however, unlike behaviourists who break down learning into discrete components, Gestalt psychologists wanted their principles to account for the 'breakthrough' moment in which we perceive something as a whole. Many of the examples used in Gestalt psychology have become familiar: for example, the picture of a duck that, perceived differently, suddenly emerges as a picture of a rabbit. In such cases, we experience sudden discontinuities in the way we perceive them; we do not learn to see them differently through a sequence of S–R bonds – or at least it does not *feel* that we do.

Cognitivism is concerned with structure: both the intrinsic structure of knowledge and the structures 'within our heads'. For the cognitivist, going beyond mere information requires that we organize and re-organize facts, concepts and principles in cognitive structures. Ideas are related to other ideas, and individual facts acquire meaning by being subsumed into broader, principled structures. A key figure in cognitivism is Jerome Bruner, who describes how his interest was stimulated by reflecting on the *activity* of cognition. 'Knowing, it soon became clear, was not just passively receiving and associating stimuli from the world and then responding in conformity with rewards or "reinforcements" from outside . . . much of *learning* was guided by how you thought about what you were encountering' (Bruner 2006: 1).

Bruner originated the term *spiral curriculum*, meaning a way of organizing the curriculum so that fundamental concepts are introduced at an early stage of a course in a simplified way, and then revisited one or more times to bring out their full complexity. For Bruner, this is not merely a matter of teaching technique; it is bound up with the hypothesis that 'any subject can be taught effectively in some intellectually honest form to any child at any stage of development' (Bruner 2006: 47). It follows that anything not worth teaching in a developed form to adults is not worth teaching to younger or less experienced students; 'a curriculum ought to be built around the

---

Box 8.4 Some key themes of cognitivism

---

1   Bodies of knowledge, like the sciences, cohere by dint of ideational structures that serve to organize and give meaning to their empirical details.
2   Understanding any particular body of knowledge requires grasping the under-lying intellectual structure that renders its empirical details comprehensible.
3   Such structures vary from the highly intuitive and informal to the deductive-mathematical . . .
4   In the course of coming to understand any particular body of knowledge, we tend naturally to begin with an initial intuitive grasp and progress with its help to a more formalized and verifiable form of understanding.
5   Indeed, the course of human mental growth itself typically progresses from an earlier intuitive stage to a later, more formalized and explicit form of verifiable reasoning . . .
6   It follows then that any body of knowledge, whatever the subject, can be taught to anybody at any age in some initially intuitive form that does it justice.

Source: Bruner (2006: 2–3)

---

great issues, principles and values' of a society (Bruner 2006: 56). Hence, the spiral curriculum approach is a way of maintaining these central issues in the foreground of education while recognizing the cognitive structures used by a learner.

Bruner's name is particularly associated with his advocacy of *discovery learning*. He argues that 'Mastery of the fundamental ideas of a field involves not only the grasping of general principles, but also the development of an attitude towards learning and inquiry . . . toward the possibility of solving problems on one's own' (Bruner 2006: 41). Developing this attitude, Bruner says, cannot be done by 'mere presentation'; learners must actually participate in the excitement of discovery. By contrast, David Ausubel is critical of discovery learning and regards *expository* or *reception* learning as wilfully under-rated by some authors, resulting in students being 'coerced into mimicking the externally conspicuous but inherently trivial aspects of scientific method' in order to 'rediscover or exemplify principles which the teacher could have presented verbally and demonstrated visually in a matter of minutes' (Ausubel 1963: 141).

Ausubel emphasizes the idea of meaningful learning, in which new material is related to existing knowledge, and advocates the use of *advance organizers* in present-ing new content. As their name implies, these help the learner to fit new knowledge into their cognitive structures and aid the development of new structures. Advance organizers should indicate how existing relevant concepts are either basically similar, or essentially different, to the new ideas and information being presented. However, an advance organizer is not quite the same thing as a summary or overview of what is to be learned, but a way of making sense of it. Thus an advance organizer for a lesson on the storage and display of cakes might use the general principle that cakes go stale because of drying out, and also indicate similarities and differences to the principles for storing biscuits learned previously. This will help learners to integrate the specific knowledge gained within a broader conceptual scheme.

Humanist theories of learning

Whatever their relative merits, the theories discussed above share a *detachment* in which their subject matter, although concerned with human learning, might as well be the motion of planets or the multiplication of bacteria. Although this is laudable as science, it fails to recognize that its subjects are people and can lead to a *technocratic* approach which is fundamentally undemocratic and alienating. As a student, how you learn is determined by experts, who know best what you need because they have the theoretical keys to the learning process. By contrast, humanist theories of learning contest this viewpoint, drawing on the work of Dewey (1938) as well as on humanist psychology to take a person-centred approach in which true learning comes from within. Particularly associated with the work of Abraham Maslow and Carl Rogers, humanist theories have influenced many theoretical and practical developments in education, including student-centred learning and the andragogy of Malcolm Knowles (Knowles et al. 2005).

Humanistic psychologists claimed that behaviourist and cognitivist approaches excluded from psychology much of what makes us human. They aimed to emphasize the notion of 'self' and to cultivate the development of human potential. This viewpoint is associated with Maslow's concept of self-actualization and connects learning with individual desires. Rogers and Freiburg (1994: 35) state the humanist position eloquently:

> I want to talk about learning, but not the lifeless, sterile, futile, quickly forgotten stuff that is crammed into the mind of the helpless individual . . . I am talking about *learning* – insatiable curiosity that drives the adolescent mind to absorb everything he can see or hear or read about a topic that has inner meaning. I am talking about the student who says 'I am discovering, drawing in from the outside, and making what I discover a real part of me.'

Maslow's work in particular is based on assumptions of human-centredness, personal autonomy, the idea of human dignity and a sense of personal responsibility. These assumptions have all found their way into mainstream practice in lifelong learning, particularly through the precepts of andragogy but also within pedagogical principles concerned with younger learners, such as the idea that students should 'take responsibility for their own learning'. Rogers emphasizes the importance of personal relationships between teachers and learners and advocates the creation of a human climate in the classroom, based on empathy, trust and respect. Furthermore, he rejects the idea of learning as based on pre-determined outcomes, instead encouraging teachers to create an environment that facilitates broader experiential and largely self-directed learning.

Critics of humanistic psychology have argued that its assumptions are unjustified, leading to a romanticized view of the possibilities for self-actualization in contemporary society (Pearson and Podeschi 1999). In particular, the validity of assuming personal autonomy is questioned, on the basis of the critiques of individualism discussed in Chapter 4 in the context of structure and agency. Some of these criticisms are especially pertinent to the current discourse of individual responsibility in lifelong learning: 'Those who fail to reach the heights described by Maslow may feel that they are personally to blame for their discontent . . . The individualization of success and failure can also result in blaming those who suffer from social injustice for the hardships they face' (Shaw and Colimore 1988: 60).

Experiential and reflective learning

Experiential learning is much more than the observation that all learning comes from experience, whether of sitting in a classroom or of more general day-to-day activities. An experiential approach to learning is implicit in humanistic theories; Rogers in particular often equates person-centred or humanistic classrooms with the practice of experiential learning. In fact, experiential learning is a complex integration of theory and practice, based on a view of learning as essentially democratic and inclusive. It is based on an 'education of equals' rather than on 'education from above' (Gregory 2002: 95) and involves personal commitment, interaction with other people and a willingness to engage one's emotions and feelings (Boud et al. 1993: 1). Some of the central tenets and assumptions of experiential learning are shown in Box 8.5.

Experiential learning aims to involve the whole person in an encounter with learning; the experience is of immersion in knowledge, action and practice. Heron

---

Box 8.5 Characteristics of experiential learning

Learning is best conceived as a process, not in terms of outcomes.

Learning is a continuous process grounded in experience.

The process of learning requires the resolution of conflicts between dialectically opposed modes of adaptation to the world: for example, between concrete experience and abstract concepts or between observation and action.

Learning is an holistic process of adaptation to the world.

Learning involves transactions between the person and the environment . . . books, teacher and classroom cannot substitute for the wider environment of the 'real world'.

Learning is the process of creating knowledge by the transaction between objective, accumulated human cultural experience and the subjective life experiences of the individual person.

Source: (Kolb 1984: 25–38)

The whole person, both in feeling and in cognitive aspects, is part of the learning event. Self-initiated involvement is essential for significant learning.

Learning is pervasive – it affects the behaviour, attitudes and even personality of the learner.

The learner's evaluation of a learning event is with reference to the learner – the element of meaning to the learner is built into the experience.

Source: Rogers and Freiberg (1994: 36)

(1989: 13) states that 'Experiential knowledge is knowledge gained through action and practice. . . . It is manifest through the process of being there, face-to-face, with the person, at the event, in the experience'.

However, experience must somehow be transformed for learning to occur. Indeed, Kolb (1984: 38) *defines* learning as 'the process whereby knowledge is created through the transformation of experience'. Building on the work of Dewey (1933), Kolb developed a well-known model of how this transformation takes place in an *experiential learning cycle* (see Figure 8.3).

According to this model, experience is first *grasped* and then *transformed* into strategies that guide future actions. Experience may be grasped through its immediate impact or be mediated by concepts and theories. The transformation of experience may take place through internal reflection or by actively experimenting and manipulating the environment. The process of experiential learning therefore consists of a four-stage cycle involving four learning modes – concrete experience, reflective observation, abstract conceptualization and active experimentation. Kolb (1984: 41) pairs these modes as opposites, concrete experience being 'dialectically opposed' to abstract conceptualization and active experimentation to reflective observation.

In Figure 8.3, the four modes of Kolb's 'cycle' are shown, together with the four types of knowledge arising from these modes. For example, *assimilative* knowledge results from grasping experience by means of abstract concepts and transforming the experience so grasped by reflective observation. On the other hand, *accommodative* knowledge derives from apprehending the immediate qualities of experience, which is then transformed into knowledge by the results of active experimentation.

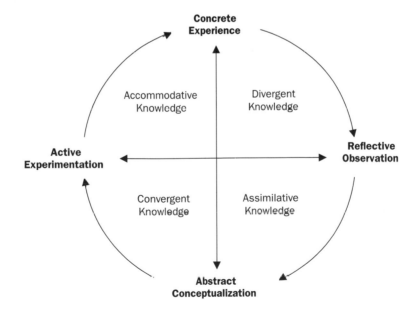

Figure 8.3 Kolb's Experiential Learning Cycle
Source: Kolb (1985: 42)

It should be clear from this discussion that Kolb's model is not necessarily a sequential cycle; it may also be regarded as a model of different preferences for grasping experience and transforming it into knowledge. This leads to the idea of a *learning style*, in which Kolb was a pioneer. He regards learning styles as originating in our preferences for certain types of experience: 'Through their choices of experience, people program themselves to grasp reality through varying degrees of emphasis on apprehension or comprehension' (Kolb 1984: 64). Similarly, they program themselves to transform their grasp of reality through reflection or experimentation. This self-programming, according to Kolb, determines which parts of the learning cycle receive the greatest emphasis in a particular individual.

Using a *learning styles inventory*, a person's orientation to learning can be assessed, classifying their learning style along the same lines as the different types of knowledge discussed above. Thus, Kolb's inventory assigns one of four learning styles: convergent, divergent, assimilative or accommodative (Kolb 1984: 77–8). In view of current debates on learning styles (see pages 173–6), it is important to note that Kolb does not advocate 'catering for' particular learning styles – in fact, he regards each mode as being incomplete: 'more powerful and adaptive forms of learning emerge when these strategies are used in combination' (Kolb 1984: 65). The highest level of learning occurs when all four modes are combined in a balanced and appropriate way.

Following Kolb's work, the reflective learning mode has received a great deal of attention, and numerous authors have developed models of this particular aspect of the learning cycle. In a famous quotation, John Dewey (1933: 6) defines reflection as, 'Active, persistent and careful consideration of any belief or supposed form of knowledge in the light of the grounds that support it, and the further conclusions towards which it tends'. More recently, Boud et al. (1985: 19) define reflection as 'a generic term for those intellectual and affective activities in which individuals engage to explore their experiences in order to lead to new understandings and appreciations'. They propose a model of reflection in which experience (the left-hand circle in Figure 8.4) is transformed into learning outcomes (the right-hand circle) by means of a three-stage process.

The first stage, *returning to experience*, is the description of relevant events. Boud et al. (1985: 27) regard this descriptive activity as crucial in re-presenting events to the mind and recommend that judgements should be avoided at this stage; the aim is to provide data for reflection, not to jump to conclusions. However, feelings and judgements made at the time should be noted as an important part of the data. In the second stage, *attending to feelings*, past and present emotional responses are evaluated either as aids or barriers to learning. Being able to recognize the role of feelings is essential, otherwise entrenched perspectives may prove difficult to surmount due to affective rather than cognitive barriers, for example, if new ideas conflict with cherished values or beliefs.

These two stages establish the foundations for *re-evaluating experience*. In this third stage, new data are related to what is already known. An important element of this stage is validation and appropriation – reconciling the new ideas and feelings with one's own identity and integrating them into new cognitive and affective structures.

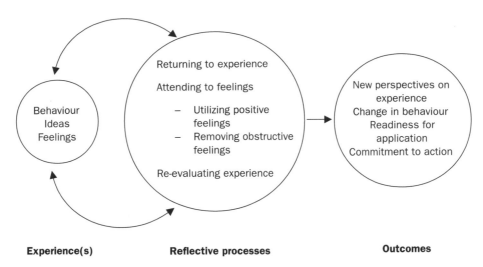

Experience(s)   Reflective processes   Outcomes

Figure 8.4 Three-stage model of reflective processes and their role in reflective learning
Source: Boud et al. (1985: 36)

The learning styles debate

Learning style theory has been widely promoted as a strategy for supporting learning, with organizations such as DfES, Ofsted and QCA advocating its use (O'Toole and Meyer 2006: 17). It is argued that some learners may be disadvantaged if teachers do not take their preferred ways of learning into account. Although this idea has an intuitive appeal, notions of 'learning style' are problematic. The term itself is variously defined and used interchangeably with other expressions such as *thinking style, cognitive style* and *learning orientation*. Cassidy (2004: 420) draws attention to the 'variety of definitions, theoretical positions, models, interpretations and measures of the construct'. However, Nixon et al. (2007: 40) describe all learning style models as built around three principles:

> The first principle claims that an individual's behaviour demonstrates a pattern of preferences or habitual ways of acting. That is, the learner's behaviour will follow certain predictable patterns if confronted with a given set of stimuli. Second, these patterns of preferences can be identified and then organized into a classificatory scheme . . . Finally, it is claimed that reliable and insightful diagnostic tools can be devised to link learners to particular preferences.

Teachers are faced with a bewildering array of models. Coffield et al. (2004: 2) note that 'In many ways, the use of different inventories of learning styles has acquired an unexamined life of its own, where the notion of learning styles itself and the various means to measure it are accepted without question'. One popular model involves the identification of *learning modalities* based on the use of a visual, auditory, kinaesthetic (VAK) learning style analysis, in which individuals are said to have a preference for learning through a specific perceptual channel. Teachers are advised to match curricular activities to the needs of students who have been identified as visual, auditory, kinaesthetic or multi-modal learners (for example, see Duckett and Tatarkowsky 2005).

The VAK model has been subject to rigorous challenge, and its supposed benefits are disputed. For example, Klein (2003: 48) argues that curricular activities cannot be categorized by modality because 'many and perhaps most kinds of knowledge appear to involve representations of more than one modality'. For example, consider the suggestion that one sign of a kinaesthetic learner might be that they enjoy making things and using their hands (Duckett and Tatarkowsky 2005: 14). This involves over-simplifying the process of 'making something'; for most people, making something also involves the use of visual information – and much else besides.

Coffield et al. (2004) draw attention to the beliefs upon which specific learning style models are built. A number of approaches involve the assumption that learning styles are fixed, inherited traits, although some models stress the influence of contextual, personal and environmental factors. The view that learning style is innate carries the risk of students being labelled – sometimes literally – by means of badges identifying their learning style. Hargreaves (2005: 11) suggests that the uncritical use of learning styles is reminiscent of the 'now largely abandoned notions of fixed and inherited intelligence'. Learning style instruments may be specific to culture, gender or age and can lead to the incorrect assessment of learners from different backgrounds. If a diagnostic tool fails to take account of language variation, responses may be misinterpreted.

In spite of the deficiencies of learning style theory, there are benefits to a critical awareness of learning styles: 'instead of talking about different types of learner we recommend discussing different approaches to learning . . . different orientations to learning . . . different models of learning . . . and different emotions associated with learning' (Coffield 2005: 6). This requires teachers who are 'knowledgeable . . . about learning itself'. In particular, Coffield et al. (2004: 36–9) identify two specific advantages of introducing learners to the idea of learning style: first, it encourages them to engage in *metacognition* – considering their own approaches to learning and knowing; second, it can provide a language for talking about learning as called for by Hargreaves. Although at present the evidence is conflicting, the deliberate mismatching as well as matching of learning activities to individual learning styles may enable learners to develop a more rounded and balanced approach to their learning (Coffield et al. 2004: 40–1). Much research remains to be carried out in these areas, but educational institutions and teachers would be well advised carefully to consider the issues before applying labels to learners which may be inappropriate to their development.

Widening participation

This section, and those that follow, consider a number of specific groups of learners who face particular challenges and opportunities, including adults, learners from other countries, students with disabilities or learning difficulties and gifted learners. These sections should be read in conjunction with Chapter 7, which discusses broader issues of equality and diversity such as class, race and gender.

The Kennedy Report (1997) highlights the role of *widening participation*, which explicitly seeks to promote a more diverse social profile of learners. Kennedy described how colleges could tackle social and economic inequality through drawing a wider community into education; a commitment to social justice by means of education throughout life, or *lifelong learning*, was coupled with enhancing Britain's economic competitiveness in a globalized world by improving workforce skills. This approach places FE at the centre of government policy. In particular, the objectives of the Department for Innovation, Universities and Skills (DIUS 2008b) included aspirations to improve the skills of the population throughout their working lives and to build social cohesion. Improving literacy and numeracy is a key element of widening participation strategies, including the *Skills for Life* agenda developed through numerous policy documents such as *Success for All* (DfES 2002b).

Encouraging access to education beyond school has a long history in Britain. However, economic competitiveness and social inclusion motivate today's policy, as 'the twin pillars of lifelong learning' (Hyland and Merrill 2003: 30). New Labour has funded FE more generously than previous governments, but it has also directed the sector more closely than before, focusing on tightly defined skills rather than a broader education. Widening participation has therefore gone hand in hand with a narrowing of the curriculum, which has become more vocational and increasingly fragmented.

One of the most significant and ambitious widening participation targets is for 50 per cent of 18–30-year-olds to experience Higher Education (HE) by 2010. Part-time students accessing HE in an FE context, especially through Foundation Degrees, will provide much of the intended increase. Funding for increased participation has also been provided for marginal groups such as those who are not in education, employment or training (NEET). Young people aged 16–18 in full-time education can receive the means-tested Educational Maintenance Allowance (EMA), provided they regularly attend college. Another example of such focused funding, in this case for adults, is the National Employer Training Programme (NETP), which receives public funding to provide free training at NVQ level 2.

The overall impact of widening participation has been to increase greatly the numbers in education and training. Much of this increase has been in part-time courses, often at lower levels, which have a key skills or 'employability' element. The development of 14–19 education has brought in new learners, as has the extension of 'HE in FE'. The rate of growth has been rapid, and the nature and content of many courses has changed. Nevertheless, the recent developments associated with widening participation can be considered as evolutionary and not a radical break from the history of FE.

The concept of *inclusive learning* is also important in this context. The Tomlinson Report of 1996, on integrating students with learning difficulties and disabilities, argued that for inclusion to work effectively, it must be seen as applying to *all* learners, not just those with disabilities. Tomlinson (1996: 4) defines inclusive learning by asserting that 'we want to avoid a viewpoint which locates the difficulty or deficit with the student and focus instead on the capacity of the educational institution to understand and respond to the individual learner's requirement'. This involves creating an environment of trust, safety and acknowledgement of individual needs and aspirations.

Adult learners and 'adult learning'

Changing political and social circumstances have led to a varied population of adult students in formal education or training. The aspirations and experiences of adult learners are equally diverse. Some may want a qualification relevant to their work in the community, voluntary or trade union sectors; some are taking their first steps back into education after a long break; some hope eventually to gain a university degree. Many adult learners have had less than positive experiences of education in the past. Each arrives with attitudes to learning which shape their aims and expectations; very often, these attitudes are based on constructing education as difficult, hard to access or constraining. Adult learning, therefore, is partly concerned to introduce new ideas about what it means to be a student, about the nature of knowledge, the value of experience and the transformative potential of education. This may entail changing the learner's perspective from a view of education as a potentially dispiriting experience to something which is associated with success rather than failure:

> So, what if we adopted a different perspective, one that placed learning in the context of our lived experience of the world? What if we assumed that learning is as much a part of our human nature as eating or sleeping, that it is both life sustaining and inevitable, and that – given a chance – we are quite good at it?
>
> (Wenger 1998: 3)

Theories of adult learning

Many concepts, theories and models currently inform discourses of adult learning. However, a number of common themes or assumptions – often associated with the term *andragogy* – can be identified (Knowles et al. 2005; Morgan-Klein and Osborne 2007; Osborne et al. 2007):

1   *Adults can learn how to learn*: tutors can facilitate this process in order to make learning more effective and meaningful.

2   *Adult learning is self-directed*: that is, adults are or have the potential to be autonomous learners.

3   *Adult learning is purposeful*: adults choose to learn for reasons to do with their lives outside the classroom or workshop.

4   *Drawing on experience is a fundamental property of adult learning*: life or family or work are all valid contexts from which to draw in an experiential learning process.

5   *Adults reflect on their experiences and learn from them*: reflective learning as an individualized form of learning can be facilitated by a tutor.

In many ways, the assumptions and commitments of andragogy can be seen as reflecting more mainstream concerns with inclusive learning, or discourses of 'learning to learn' and 'employability', all of which are also relevant to younger learners. It would be difficult to argue that children do not wish to relate learning to their lives; learn from reflecting on their experiences; and so on. Research about the ways in which young people learn how to play computer games would suggest that their learning is indeed self-directed and involves learning how to learn (Gee 2003, 2004). However, the legal, social and financial independence of most adults is perhaps a key factor in marking out the assumptions of andragogy as applying with greater intensity to adult learners.

Practices of adult learning

Much adult education practice draws on the assumptions outlined above. That is to say, the ways in which mature students are accommodated are often directly influenced by andragogy. For example, the motivation of mature students is often assumed not to be a significant issue in education and training, compared with the motivation of 16-year-old students within a further education college. At the same time there is also a longer standing philosophical and political approach to adult education and training that still has an impact today and which has been influential in forming attitudes around the social implications of adult learning (A. Rogers 2002; J. Rogers 2007; Wallis 1996). Once again, common themes can be discerned:

1   Problem-based learning and teaching activities are well-suited to mature students.
2   Learning and teaching strategies should help build the confidence of mature students if they have been away from formal education and training for some time.
3   The biographies of mature students can have a considerable impact on their learning.
4   Mature students return to learning for all sorts of reasons that might not be directly concerned with the actual subject or topic being taught.
5   Barriers to participation by mature students may be bound up in the practicalities of their lives: childcare; transport; reconciling work commitments with study.

As noted earlier, the assumptions of andragogy are not always treated critically, and the issue of motivation is not necessarily different between adults and younger students. The rise of 'welfare to work' policies such as New Deal has brought large numbers of adults back into learning who are there more or less by compulsion, further questioning the assumptions of andragogy, so that new approaches to both theory and practice in adult learning may be needed.

Many adult educators would acknowledge that instrumental motivations are often responsible for a return to learning, but seek to subvert the notion of workforce development as purely functional education for a series of 'economic units'. Thus students wishing to gain qualifications in sectors, such as childcare and community development, where a competence-based approach dominates, may also be encouraged to adopt a more reflexive standpoint. Adult education practice can therefore embody a 'third discourse' which synthesizes instrumental and transformative education (Moore 1999: 132).

Learners from other countries

Approximately 5.3 million residents in England are foreign-born: the great majority are based in London and the South-East. This figure includes three million foreign nationals, of whom around 40 per cent are from Europe (LSC 2007a: 5). Many migrant learners engage in Skills for Life provision, particularly English for speakers of other languages (ESOL). In 2004–05, £279 million was spent on ESOL classes, funding 538,700 'learning opportunities' (NIACE 2006: 4). However, most ESOL learners are from UK-born minority ethnic groups (LSC 2007: 14), so the number of learning opportunities is an inaccurate measure of migrants' participation in ESOL provision. Nevertheless, the LSC (2007: 13) estimates that 15 per cent of ESOL learners are asylum seekers. Moreover, the expansion of the European Union has brought in many learners from Eastern Europe. Conversely, the number of students entering the UK from outside the European Economic Area has declined in recent years (LSC 2007: 4).

The skill levels of migrants differ widely: for example, 33 per cent of African migrants and 31 per cent of Chinese migrants have a degree. Sachdev and Harries (2006: 39) conclude that the majority of migrants from the European accession states are highly qualified but lack sufficient English language ability to access employment opportunities commensurate with their qualifications.

The European Council for Refugees and Exiles (ECRE) asserts that 'Education is the key to integration' (ECRE 1999: 5). In England and Wales, NIACE (2006) specifically recommends that ESOL teachers should be involved in providing general advice and guidance to new migrants, particularly relating to employment – partly in recognition that many ESOL teachers already act unofficially in this role.

Students with learning difficulties or disabilities

Social attitudes towards people with disabilities are changing, underpinned by government initiatives and legislation, and excluding disabled students from mainstream educational opportunities is no longer socially acceptable. The notion of inclusive learning, introduced earlier in this chapter, is a major step forward in this respect and highlights the ability of institutions to respond to learner needs rather than locating the difficulty or deficit with the learner. Recent legislation is based on this viewpoint and emphasizes the responsibility of education providers to anticipate and adjust to individual requirements; in particular, discrimination against students with disabilities in post-compulsory education is illegal.

According to this legislation, known as the Disability Discrimination Act (DDA) Part Four (DRC 2007), discrimination against a student may come about in two ways: failing to make *reasonable adjustments* for a student with a disability; or treating a student with a disability *less favourably* for a reason related to that disability. These provisions are important to bear in mind in course planning, as potential students are not obliged to disclose a disability and may therefore only have support needs identified once on course.

Teachers' practice can be adjusted in a number of ways to support students with disabilities. For example, a partially sighted student could use a computer with a magnified screen display, or may benefit from access to printed materials with larger font sizes, or a magnifying reading lamp. A student unable to create written documents due to restricted mobility could be provided with a computer having speech recognition software, while furniture in a room may need to be altered for a learner who uses a wheelchair. Some disabilities are 'unseen' and may not be obvious to the tutor or other students. For example, a student with a mental health difficulty may need additional tutorial support because they find it difficult to take part fully in a whole class setting. In other situations, the teacher may need to accommodate support workers – for example, a hearing impaired student may be working with a British Sign Language (BSL) interpreter.

Gifted learners

The provision of enhanced support for students with learning difficulties is largely uncontroversial. Support for students with exceptional ability, on the other hand, is much more controversial and is inextricably linked with questions concerning the relationship between education and equality. As Purdy (2007: 314) notes, 'Deciding how to educate so-called "exceptional" students is both a moral and an educational question'. She contrasts the argument that children who are not challenged may become bored and rebellious, ultimately to the detriment of society as a whole, with the democratic requirement of a common education for all children.

Programmes for gifted learners are often associated with one of two basic models: enrichment or acceleration. The enrichment approach maintains normal progression through the curriculum but attempts to provide greater depth and breadth, while acceleration allows learners to progress more quickly. Both of these models have advantages and disadvantages, and evidence for and against them is not conclusive.

Whatever model for gifted and talented provision is adopted, a crucial question is whether reliable and valid means of selecting students can ever be produced. This is particularly important given the possibility of gender, race, class and income influencing selection to gifted and talented programmes. Purdy (2007: 318) uses this as part of a moral argument for the acceleration model, which arguably can be accessible to anyone at any time dependent on performance, but whether any form of provision can be separated from injustice in selection is unlikely.

In England, the issue of gifted and talented children has been highlighted by the Government's Gifted and Talented programme. This programme has had most impact in the compulsory sector, where every school must have a strategy to 'stretch' the top 10 per cent of achievers in any subject (DfES 2005b). However, the programme extends into post-compulsory education and relates to widening participation by aiming to improve attainment, aspirations and motivation as well as the support available for gifted and talented students aged 14–19 (DfES 2004b: 24).

The Gifted and Talented programme creates a new variety of special need attracting substantial attention and resources, and raises the controversial general questions discussed above. It can be seen as an opportunity for the most able students in state education to compete with those in the independent sector for places in elite universities. However, some question whether the most successful learners really require extra help and funding, which arguably could be better directed towards students who are struggling. Tomlinson (2008: 60) states that the focus on gifted learners in England is 'reminiscent of nineteenth-century debates over gradations of mental retardation' and 'predominantly benefits white middle and upper class students'. As such it may not fit easily with the egalitarian ideals of much of the learning and skills sector.

Learners aged 14–16

The introduction of applied diplomas from September 2008 (see Chapter 9) will increase the number of students aged 14–16 in English FE colleges, where aspects of these new qualifications are taught. Many school-age students attended colleges prior to this, but the numbers involved in the new diplomas are planned to be significantly greater than anything seen before. For the New Labour government, attracting younger students onto vocationally-based courses in FE colleges derived from its two central policies: reducing social exclusion through widening participation in education and enhancing the vocational skills of the workforce. Above all, the government wished to reduce the number of young people 'not in education, employment or training' (or NEET). Providing younger students with non-academic courses earlier is part of that strategy.

The new diplomas have the title 'applied' in an effort to avoid the low status of vocational courses in Britain, and are intended to attract a broad range of younger students. However, Stanton and Fletcher (2006: 3) demonstrate a link between lower social class, poor academic attainment and attendance at colleges within this age group. Moreover, Harkin (2006: 323) found that the initial suggestion to attend a college course often came from school teachers. He described this as 'a process of benevolent herding', with schools directing their most challenging students towards FE colleges.

Nonetheless, Attwood et al. (2003), Harkin (2006) and Davies and Biesta (2007) have all found that the 14–16-year-olds who went to colleges enjoyed it, often because they appreciated the greater independence as well as the attitude of college teachers. However, colleges differ as to how they manage school-age students, with some integrating them fully and others organizing discrete provision. Similarly, teachers have varying opinions about how younger students should be treated, but many identify a need for shorter, more varied class activities. Whatever strategies are adopted, evidence from research suggests that colleges are successfully including school-age students who have been disaffected in schools.

9

The curriculum in the lifelong learning sector

Roy Fisher, Amanda Fulford,
Bernard McNicholas and Ron Thompson

What is the curriculum?

The term 'curriculum' can be defined in many ways, reflecting the complexity of an idea which encompasses meanings ranging from the specification of a programme of study, to the educational outcome of struggles between ideological forces. Some introductions to the subject begin by explaining the etymology (origins) of the word – in Latin: 'curriculum' means a course, (although originally a racecourse rather than a course of study). In a seminal text first published in 1975, Richard Stenhouse (1981: 4) tentatively offered the formulation that 'A curriculum is an attempt to communicate the essential principles and features of an educational proposal in such a form that it is open to critical scrutiny and capable of effective translation into practice'.

The Stenhouse definition takes *intent* as an essential element; however, a broader conception might contain unplanned elements which form part of the educational experience. This would incorporate factors arising from what is referred to as the 'hidden curriculum'. In essence, the term 'hidden curriculum' refers to the consequences of factors, outside formal teaching, which shape the educational experience. Institutions where learning takes place transmit attitudes, values and ways of being – some of these are intended, some are not. While some definitions of the hidden curriculum refer to it as 'unintended' and, generally, imply that it is negative, this is not necessarily the case. In some instances, the hidden curriculum might be both intended and positive, or benign, in its consequences.

Within different educational systems broad frameworks have emerged in an attempt to impose a sense of coherence and equivalence. This has been a particular need in Britain, which has seen a combination of piecemeal development and a series of reforms, especially in the area of the vocational curriculum. Figure 9.1 shows the current National Qualifications Framework (NQF) together with the Framework for Higher Education Qualifications (FHEQ). From 2009, the NQF will begin to be replaced by a new Qualifications and Credit Framework (QCA 2008a); an outline of the QCF is shown in Figure 9.2 on page 106. By 2010, all vocational qualifications are expected to be incorporated into the QCF and it is likely that GCSEs, Diplomas and GCE A levels will be part of the framework by 2013 though a QCA statement issued in January 2009 cautioned that DCSF had yet to formally commit to this (QCA 2009a).

Curriculum theory and models

The curriculum is a social product and a social practice. Curriculum Studies is a broad field informed by philosophy (particularly epistemology – the theory of knowledge), sociology, social policy, politics and psychology. There are also important questions relating to the practicalities of curriculum planning and design. This chapter will introduce some fundamental theoretical concepts; it will be selective but wide ranging in its exploration of some associated debates. The increasing interest in curriculum history points to a recognition of the significance of the curriculum in critical analysis of education. Goodson (1994: 40–1), writing specifically about schools, states that curriculum history is important because it provides insight into the way in which

> courses of study have constituted a mechanism to designate and differentiate students. It also offers a way to analyse the complex relations between school and society because it shows how schools both reflect and refract society's definitions of culturally valuable knowledge . . . curriculum history . . . enables us to examine the roles that professions – like education – play in the social construction of knowledge.

Goodson argues that the social history of curriculum subjects demonstrates how teachers have been encouraged to define knowledge in particular ways in return for status and resources.

Curriculum theory and the associated curriculum models must be placed in the context of educational ideologies. Kelly (2009) provides a detailed account of curriculum theory. Flinders and Thornton (2004) present a collection of source papers from the early years of curriculum thinking.

The traditional curriculum associated with the elite universities and academic 'school' subjects is generally regarded as having knowledge at its core. Golby (1989: 36) characterizes this model as positioning the learner as 'a postulant to be initiated into the mysteries of the subject by working at it alongside a "master" '. Modern variants of this conception have tended to derive from Liberal-Humanist approaches to knowledge. Kelly (2009: 56) has influentially referred to this approach as one of 'curriculum as content and education as transmission'. This kind of curriculum, taken to extremes, would be not much more than a list of knowledge to be passed from

National Qualifications Framework

The National Qualifications Framework (NQF) sets out the levels against which a qualification can be recognised in England, Wales and Northern Ireland.

The NQF helps learners to make informed decisions about the qualifications they need. They can compare the levels of different qualifications and identify clear progression routes for their chosen career.

It comprises nine levels (Entry level to level 8). Learners' progression routes do not necessarily need to involve qualifications at every level. Following changes to the NQF, qualification titles may have changed. However, the qualification's content and demand on the learner has not changed. Each accredited qualification has an NQF level. If qualifications share the same level this means that they are broadly similar in terms of the demand they place on the learner. However, qualifications at the same level can still be very different in terms of content and duration.

The following table shows a selection of individual qualifications and how they appear in the current NQF. It also highlights how qualifications broadly compare to the Framework for Higher Education Qualification (FHEQ) levels.

National Qualifications Framework (NQF)		Framework for Higher Education Qualifications (FHEQ)
Previous levels (examples)	**Current levels (examples)**	**Levels (examples)**
5 Level 5 NVQ in Construction Level 5 Diploma in Translation	**8** Specialist awards	**D** (doctoral) Doctorates
	7 Level 7 Diploma in Translation	**M** (masters) Masters degrees, postgraduate certificates and diplomas
4 Level 4 National Diploma in Professional Production Skills Level 4 BTEC Higher National Diploma in 3D Design Level 4 Certificate in Early Years Practice	**6** Level 6 National Diploma in Professional Production Skills	**H** (honours) Bachelor degrees, graduate certificates and diplomas
	5 Level 5 BTEC Higher National Diploma in 3D Design	**I** (intermediate) Diplomas of higher education and further education, foundation degrees and higher national diplomas
	4 Level 4 Certificate in Early Years Practice	**C** (certificate) Certificates of higher education
3 Level 3 Certificate in Small Animal Care Level 3 NVQ in Aeronautical Engineering A levels		
2 Level 2 Diploma for Beauty Specialists Level 2 NVQ in Agricultural Crop Production GCSEs Grades A*-C		
1 Level 1 Certificate in Motor Vehicle Studies Level 1 NVQ in Bakery GCSEs Grades D-G		
Entry level Entry Level Certificate in Adult Literacy		

Learners can use the National Database of Accredited Qualifications to get up-to-date information on the current NQF level for all accredited qualifications. Both the current and previous levels are shown for qualifications in the higher levels of the NQF.

Figure 9.1 Curriculum Frameworks in England, Wales and Northern Ireland
Source: Ofqual (2008)

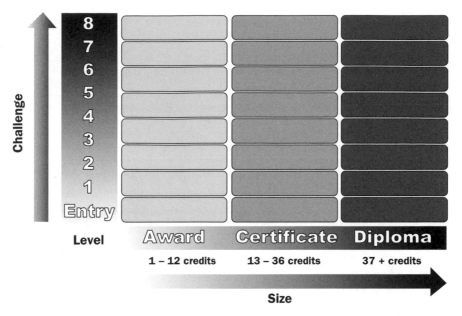

Figure 9.2 The Qualifications and Credit Framework (QCF)
Source: QCA (2009b)

teacher to student. Questions as to which knowledge exactly, and the basis of its selection, are problematic and Kelly criticizes the 'curriculum as content' model on the basis of its tendency to be culturally exclusionary and uninformed by developments in pedagogy.

Kelly (2009: 67) contrasts the 'curriculum as content' approach with a conception of the curriculum 'as product', which manifests itself in the now pervasive 'objectives' or 'outcomes' model of curriculum design. With its genesis in American behavioural psychology (see also Chapters 8 and 10), the key figures in this technocratic tradition were John Franklin Bobbitt (1876–1956) and Ralph W. Tyler (1902–94). Golby (1989: 30–1) summarizes the product approach as follows:

> The idea that decisions about designs for learning can be achieved by recourse to a means-end model of human action is fundamental here. If we are clear about what we wish to teach, and the reasons why, curriculum decisions are to be reached through the specification of clear objectives and the choice of technically apt methods for the achievement of those objectives. Clear objectives entail the specification of outcomes in terms of the learners' abilities at the end of the course . . .

Golby goes on to identify problems with this conception. Primarily these rest on its assumptions that the aims and objectives will not be for debate; that so complex a thing as learning can be reduced to behavioural statements; that the teacher will mould the learner to a 'predetermined shape' (Golby 1989: 32); and that the objectives

of a curriculum should hold primacy over content. Despite these difficulties, the objectives model of the curriculum has been immensely influential. Box 9.1 indicates Tyler's four fundamental questions, which he considered should guide curriculum development.

The conception of the 'curriculum as process' (Kelly 2009), and education as concerned with individual development rather than the needs of employer or state, might be a way to counteract some of the tendencies discussed above in relation to the 'curriculum as product' model. 'Curriculum as process' rests on the assumption that a teacher must focus on the process of learning rather than the outcome. In effect, the art of the teacher is to take the position not of an expert, but to be 'cast in the role of a learner' (Stenhouse 1981: 94; see also the discussion of humanist and experiential models of learning in Chapter 8). From this vantage point the teacher exercises judgement regarding how to enable learning, becoming a resource for learners who are stimulated to enquire. The model is nonlinear, resting on a 'specification of content rather than by pre-specifying outcomes in terms of objectives' (Taylor and Richards 1979: 72). It demands of the teacher a careful consideration of learning activities. If the curriculum as product model is concerned with ends, the process model is concerned with means, and inevitably leads to the 'student-centred learning' often associated with educational progressivism.

All curricula are the outcome of social, cultural and historical circumstances. Recent and current educational practice is substantially a product of social and cultural developments within the period of economic progress and administrative rationalization in Europe. This period, widely referred to as *modernity*, stemmed from the rise of capitalism and the massive productive power unleashed by the Industrial Revolution, and from the intellectual force of the eighteenth-century Enlightenment. The resulting philosophy, of material and social progress based on science and technology as opposed to a static society based on tradition and authority, is known as *modernism* and pervades much official thinking on education at the present day. Contemporary educational practice is situated within a social context containing critiques of modernism, in which the term 'postmodern' has enjoyed currency. The literature on postmodernism is considerable; in particular, Usher and Edwards (1994) deal engagingly with education and postmodernism. Essentially, postmodernism questions the primacy of scientific and other established forms of knowledge as a source of truth and progress, and elucidates the power and ideology associated

---

Box 9.1 Tyler's (1949) four fundamental questions for curriculum development

1   What educational purposes should the school seek to attain? *[aims and objectives]*
2   What educational experiences can be provided that are likely to attain these purposes? *[choosing the appropriate learning experiences]*
3   How can these educational experiences be effectively organised? *[organising the learning]*
4   How can we determine whether these purposes are being attained? *[evaluation]*

Source: Stenhouse (1981: 3, italics added)

with apparently neutral academic enquiry. As will be discussed subsequently, this calls into question many of the established values concerning the knowledge and culture to be expressed and transmitted in a curriculum. What we teach and how we teach it is no longer a purely technical issue concerned with selection of content and teaching method; for many, the curriculum is an expression of dominant ideologies within society in such a way that we are barely conscious that they *are* ideologies.

The remainder of this section discusses a range of analyses related to the curriculum. Beginning with a survey of older standpoints, and in particular the distinction between 'traditional' and 'progressive' conceptions of the curriculum, we move on to outline some of the ideas of postmodern writers, in particular Michel Foucault and Jean-François Lyotard.

Given the centrality of educational processes within the civil life of society, and also in the sphere of the *personal*, there is a sense in which all social theory relates to Curriculum Studies and the work of a wide range of writers might reasonably be discussed in relation to it. Morrison and Ridley (1989) identified five of the most prevalent 'schools of thought' or 'clusters of educational ideologies' relating to the curriculum. Unfortunately, these do not always have the same description or 'label', but the ways in which they are generally described are as follows:

1 *Progressivism*: places its emphasis on the individual child; also referred to as child-centredness or Romanticism.

2 *Academicism*: places its emphasis on high status knowledge for elites; also referred to as Classical Humanism or Traditionalism or Conservatism.

3 *Liberalism*: focuses on making high status knowledge accessible to all; sometimes referred to as Liberal Humanism.

4 *Instrumentalism*: aimed at improving existing societal and economic relations. This is sometimes referred to as Revisionism or Economic Renewal.

5 *Democratic*: focuses on changing societal and economic relations; also known as Reconstructivism or Democratic Socialism.

Each of the above has its own view of the theory/nature of knowledge; learning and the role of learners; teaching and the teacher's role; and implications for resources and the organization of learning situations, and for the method of assessment to be utilized. For the sake of brevity and clarity, we shall focus here on differences between the broadly 'traditional' and the 'liberal/progressive' philosophies of education which have often been summarized as opposed points on a series of dimensions. Some of these dimensions, and the oppositions of traditional and progressive values, have been summarized by Carr (1995) and are shown in Table 9.1.

Carr (1995) points out that the 'traditional' and 'liberal-progressive' educational philosophies are not 'ahistorical' and that there are areas of overlap. The vocational curriculum (meaning related to preparation for employment) in England embodies most of the characteristics associated with the liberal progressive model outlined above. Some knowledge of the philosophical underpinning implicit in Table 9.1 can be useful in making practical decisions about the kind of pedagogy to be

Table 9.1 Dimensions of Traditional and Liberal Progressive education

	Traditional	*Liberal Progressive*
Political perspective	Conservative	Liberal/communitarian
View of society	Elitist	Egalitarian
Guiding educational slogan	'Academic excellence'	'Learning from experience'
Canonical texts	Plato's *Republic*	Rousseau's *Emile*
Types of schools	Grammar	Community
Classroom organization	Rigid grouping on basis of ability	Flexible grouping on basis of needs
Curriculum content	Subject centred; rigid subject differentiation	Student centred: weak subject differentiation
Curriculum knowledge	Objective	Subjective
Teacher's role	Expert, transmitting cultural heritage	Facilitator of personal learning
Teaching methods	Formal instruction	'Discovery' methods
Assessment procedures	Traditional examinations testing knowledge	Informal evaluations of qualitative developments in understanding

Source: Adapted from Carr (1995: 55)

employed – where there is choice – or in reflecting on the kind of pedagogy that is being employed where (as is more frequently the case) there is not.

The work of Michel Foucault, at least within education, might be primarily associated with the concepts of discipline and power, and the idea of schools and of educational processes as being concerned with the construction of an obedient or governable subject. In *Discipline and Punish: The Birth of the Prison* Foucault (1991) charts how the eighteenth century saw a transition from public execution to penal retention as a technique of social control. Within this period a number of technologies associated with the control of individuals were developed. At the level of the human body, as opposed to the intellect, a requirement for control was that of physical enclosure within space and over time. By the division of buildings educational spaces took on some characteristics of the factory. These designs facilitated supervision, hierarchy and reward. Donald (1992) refers to the English monitorial schools of the early nineteenth century as illustrating the kind of architecture which Foucault described as permitting this kind of control.

Foucault referred to Jeremy Bentham's penitentiary design, the *Panopticon* (a central watch-tower from which an observer could oversee a circle of tiered cells) as ideal for surveillance. A prisoner could be observed 'round the clock' but would be unaware whether or not observation was taking place at a given time; control would thereby become 'internalized' within the mind of the individual. Many recently designed college buildings, with large overlooked atrium spaces, incorporate similar features. Another important factor in imposing control was the timetable. Time was planned, organized and controlled in increasing detail and within the curriculum this was manifested in organizing learning into lessons and terms. Foucault (1991: 178) explains that

> the workshop, the school, the army were subject to the whole micro-penalty of time (latenesses, absences, interruptions of tasks), of activity (inattention, negligence, lack of zeal), of behaviour (impoliteness, disobedience), of speech (idle chatter, insolence), of the body ('incorrect' attitudes, irregular features, lack of cleanliness), of sexuality (impurity, indecency).

Deviance from the norm was, in a sense, pathologized and as a consequence of this the systems through which people pass function as processes of normalization. Over time this required the exercise of observation and judgement, and the creation of norms and averages, of passes and fails. The means were various forms of testing and examination through which the student is allocated a grade, which defines whether or not they may progress.

Lyotard (1984) has been credited with bringing the term 'postmodernism' into general circulation; certainly his work *The Postmodern Condition: A Report on Knowledge* has been massively influential. Lyotard defines the postmodern as 'incredulity towards metanarratives' (1984: xxiv), pointing to a crisis of the status of knowledge and to the end of 'universalist' or overarching systems of thought (such as Marxism). Science has been the privileged discourse of the modern era and, as a consequence of this primacy, has dominated education and the associated pedagogic and research methodologies. The claim that science is the key to progress enables the State to control education in the name of freedom and progress. It works against the fragmentation of ideas and towards the one big truth which will 'explain'. The twin imperatives of progress and the seeking after truth constitute the two metanarratives upon which the modern university has rested. The current displacement of the role and social authority of the universities may be taken as evidence of the end of the modernist vision.

Lyotard argues that the primacy of concepts such as truth and falsehood in relation to knowledge has been replaced by issues of efficiency and inefficiency. He describes this new focus as 'performativity'. Knowledge becomes a commodity (Usher and Edwards 1994: 166). That which does not fit is disqualified and the curriculum becomes a repository of what Apple (2000) calls 'official knowledge'. The performance of 'competence' and the positioning of education as a service to business become orthodoxies of policy. A curriculum based on the performance of competencies and the development of skills, delivered through resource centres by facilitators of 'student-centred learning', would represent the culmination of processes that have been at work in the transition of learning institutions. A factor in these changes has been funding pressure that has arisen from the introduction of mass participation in FE and HE.

Curriculum design and development

Involvement in curriculum design and development may range from the creation of learning materials by an individual teacher for a particular class, to working collaboratively to design, plan and implement a major course to be delivered through a national network. Many teachers and trainers have opportunities to become engaged in curriculum design and development activities – often without consciously regarding themselves as 'curriculum developers'. Not all participants in curriculum development will be involved in every stage of the process. A formal curriculum development initiative would normally contain the following elements.

Rationale

This would outline the reasons for the course. These might concern the learning needs of the students and/or the needs of society, employers or a specific organiza- tion. For example, a tenants' association might identify a need for provision dealing with housing legislation; a teacher might identify a learner's need for a programme designed to support their difficulties in working with number; or a bank might identify its need to ensure employees were able to use new technology properly. A training needs analysis might identify broad departmental needs. A course rationale would also explain why the particular approaches to learning, assessment and evaluation had been adopted.

Aims and objectives

Depending on the philosophy of the author/team, a curriculum would normally incorporate aims and broad and/or specific learning objectives. The dominance of the product (or objectives/outcomes) curriculum model means that detailed learning objectives are often an expectation.

Content

This will normally be a description of the topics to be covered. A critical factor is to ensure that the content is designed to address the reasons identified for developing the curriculum in the first place.

Teaching and learning methods

A curriculum encapsulates the teaching and learning methods used. Questions to consider include: is the course to be delivered at a regular time? Will there be open, distance or e-learning? Will the course employ lectures, group work or other pedagogic techniques? Will the course be held in a classroom, a laboratory, in the workplace, or elsewhere? Will the course utilize specific learning materials? Crucially, what are the needs of the learners?

Assessment strategy

Assessment (see Chapter 13) is an integral part of a curriculum. An outline of the curriculum should clearly identify the assessment methods to be used. These should be designed to check that learning outcomes/objectives specified have been met and that content has been covered. The form of assessment should be appropriate for the students and for the nature of the subject.

Resources

What are the staffing, learning technologies, equipment, material and other needs of the programme? A further important question to consider is the environmental impact of the course – how does the course design fit with a commitment to sustainability? Recent years have seen an increased recognition of the importance not only of making ecologically sensible decisions in relation to the use of resources, but also of the raising consciousness of sustainability issues within the content of the curriculum (see Blewitt and Cullingford 2004; Gough and Scott 2004).

Evaluation

Curriculum planners need to consider how they can best determine whether or not the curriculum is successful – that is, how to evaluate the curriculum (see Chapter 21). The curriculum will normally include, for example, mechanisms for gathering evidence from students, teachers and employers about the effectiveness of the learning programme. 'Performance indicators' are sets of criteria against which to measure the curriculum – for example, whether it has recruited to target, levels of student satisfaction, assessment results and so on.

Vocationalism and parity of esteem

The term 'vocationalism' is generally used in relation to the curriculum movement associated with work-related learning – it can be used approvingly, pejoratively or as a neutral technical term. Successive reforms of the vocational curriculum have failed to gain the recognition accorded to the 'gold standards' of the General Certificate in Secondary Education (GCSE) and the GCE Advanced Level (GCE A). The Diploma courses, available from September 2008, are the latest such initiative, following a succession of 'new' vocational awards that began in the late 1970s (see Fisher 2004).

High culture in England has held an antipathy, manifest in the curriculum of the elite public schools and universities, towards the vocational. Beyond this, the implications of new modes of production, information technologies, and the associated new industries for the vocational curriculum have not been fully articulated. That vocational courses have tended to exhibit characteristics associated with progressive education has been a problem in relation to parity of esteem. GCE A Levels fit received notions of what might constitute the preparatory stage of an education leading to the production of some form of 'intellectual', but that term is not one which can be used with conviction in relation to the aspirations of vocational curricula.

In 1923 in Italy, Mussolini was implementing educational reforms that attacked the traditional 'instruction' of the old curriculum, arguing for 'active education'. This was opposed by the leading Marxist Antonio Gramsci. Writing during the 1920s, Gramsci (1971: 40) argued that,

Schools of the vocational type . . . are beginning to predominate . . . The most paradoxical aspect of it all is that this new type of school appears to be advocated as being democratic, while in fact it is destined not merely to perpetuate social differences but to crystallise them . . . The labourer can become a skilled worker, for instance, the peasant a surveyor or petty agronomist. But democracy, by definition, cannot mean merely that an unskilled worker can become skilled. It must mean that every 'citizen' can 'govern' . . .

In criticizing the spread of this particular instance of vocationalism, Gramsci was expressing fears similar to those which would exercise liberal and radical educationalists in Britain during the 1980s and 1990s as attempts were made to promote vocationalism. The idea that education at all levels should align itself more closely with the needs of business became known as the 'new vocationalism'. The argument that education should concern itself with equipping young people and adults with economically valuable skills has a strong hold on public opinion. In a society which places different values on different knowledge and skills, to acquire a particular set of skills to the exclusion of others is to be allocated a particular position in society. Avis (1995: 68) refers to 'a tendency to technicise skills and to separate these from their social and cultural location . . . Perhaps the most significant of all these issues is that the notion of a learning society rests upon an acceptance of capitalist hegemony . . . We have here the construction of a regime of truth'.

Gramsci (1971: 41) was also critical of the 'active learning' approach which was associated with vocationalism: 'It is noticeable that the new pedagogy has concentrated its fire on "dogmatism" in the field of instruction and the learning of concrete facts . . .'. More recently, Avis (1995: 63) identifies the creation of a framework within which 'teachers become transmogrified into facilitators of the learning process, [and] professional and disciplinary knowledge becomes marginalised. The emphasis in these new teaching relations is on the student 'learning how to learn'. Studies which chart and analyse vocational provision are vital to the formulation of a *theory* of these forms of curricula.

Lyotard (1984: 4) identified 'a thorough exteriorization of knowledge with respect to the "knower" at whatever point he or she may occupy in the knowledge process'. The vocational curriculum in England presents such a point. The relegation of knowledge in the face of skill has clashed with the goal of parity of esteem. The vocational curriculum occupies a difficult place in the field of educational classification and hierarchies. Official positions speak reassuringly of its equivalence to courses such as GCSE and GCE A Level, and its acceptability for entry to university or professional training. Alongside these official positions are the personal beliefs of various 'gate-keepers'.

The vocational curriculum is regarded as necessary and worthwhile, yet it is circumscribed by its instrumental nature. It is the individual recognition of limits which is part of what it means to be rendered governable, and that is still the prime need for effective vocational deployment. Foucault (1991: 194) suggests that power 'produces reality; it produces domains of objects and rituals of truth'. A curriculum may well be seen as an instrument, or a machine, which is situated within domains and power structures, which is filled with rituals, and which manufactures *kinds* of truth.

The evidence of the vocational curriculum experience, however, is that while it may empower by enhancing life chances, and by developing knowledge and skills, it *can* also repress and it *can* be exclusionary in its consequences for some people. Different curricula are not the same and some are, in Orwellian terms, more equal than others.

14–19 education and training

The *14–19 Education and Skills White Paper* (DfES 2005a), which emerged from the Working Group on 14–19 Reform chaired by Sir Mike Tomlinson, proposed an ambitious ten year plan and transition for 14–19 education and training. The concept of a 14–19 continuum was proposed by the Manpower Services Commission (MSC) in the early 1980s. It was supported by a group known as the 'Conservative Modernisers' (Chitty 2004) with proposals highlighting the ideological war that had been raging in England since James Callaghan's speech at Ruskin College in 1976 (Callaghan 1976). The so-called 'Great Debate' surrounding education can be viewed as signalling a change in the way education policy would be formed and administered. More recent developments in the 14–19 arena still reflect debates which originated in the 1970s.

Chitty (2004) highlights the increased political focus on education following the Great Debate by comparing the volume of legislation before 1976 and after, identifying 30 Education Acts between 1979 and 2000 as opposed to only three between 1944 and 1976. The prevailing ideology has been a 'utilitarian' view that places education at the forefront of attempts to 'deliver the skills and knowledge essential . . . for an economy seeking a strong position in a globalised political world' (Lumby and Foskett 2007: 87).

The Working Group on 14–19 Reform (DfES 2004b) was widely expected to recommend the replacement of GCSEs and GCE A Levels with an overarching Diploma. While this did not happen, many of the Group's proposals were accepted, and the reforms that emerged reinforced the new vocationalism synonymous with New Labour, including the proposal for a new 'specialized' Diploma qualification. Previous attempts at reform had been undermined by 'deep-seated historical institutional, curricular and organisational features' (Hodgson and Spours 2006: 325).

As Stasz and Wright (2007: 157) suggest, 'Forming a picture of policy for 14–19 education in the United Kingdom is a bit like the proverbial blind man confronted by an elephant. It is possible to understand specific parts, but the size, shape and sheer complexity of the elephant remains obscure'. This complexity was understandable given the fragmented nature of policy initiatives and the entrenched academic-vocational divide based on selection at 16+ along institutional, curriculum and assessment lines. The 14–19 curriculum reforms being implemented at the turn of the first decade of the twenty-first century sit alongside other fundamental changes. These include the introduction of the QCF, the raising of the age of compulsory education or training to 18 by 2015 (see Simmons 2008), and the emphasis on a learning entitlement for all 14–19-year-olds from 2013. The requirement for a consortium approach to delivering the new Diplomas attempts to address some of the tensions between collaboration and competition that previous reforms encountered

(Hodgson and Spours 2006). By 2010 funding of 14–19 provision will sit within the control of local authorities – a key factor in the reforms. It would be imprudent to equate current reforms with previous attempts since the prospects have been transformed by some robust administrative and legislative mechanisms.

The role of education as a function of the economy was highlighted with the twinning of the White Papers *14–19 Education and Skills* (DfES 2005a) and *Skills: Getting on in Business, Getting on at Work* (DfES 2005c). Proposals included strengthening of the GCSEs and GCE A Levels, an expansion of apprenticeships and the introduction of a new Diploma route. These three routes would be offered at levels 1, 2 and 3 with the apprentice route being mostly offered at 16+. There would also be the introduction of a new Foundation Tier at levels 1 and 2, which would allow achievements at these levels to be recognized. Existing key skills were to be replaced by 'functional skills' in English, Maths and ICT which would be embedded in all three routes. The 'specialized' Diplomas were the defining element to the 14–19 curriculum proposals, whereas the existing traditional and apprenticeships routes were to be modified in an attempt to create a coherent and cohesive offer allowing movement between routes.

The new Diplomas were originally to be offered across 14 lines of learning, subsequently increased to 17 with the inclusion of academic Diplomas, to be phased in over a period of four years from September 2008. Achievements were to be recognized at all three levels: Foundation (Level 1), Higher (Level 2) and Advanced (Level 3). Each Diploma line was to consist of three components: principal learning, generic learning and additional and specialist learning. There would also be a compulsory element of experiential learning with a minimum of ten days work experience incorporated within the generic learning at all levels (QCA 2008).

The first five Diploma lines were introduced in September 2008. There were concerns about uptake, with reports that fewer than 12,000 14–19-year-olds had commenced the course, many short of the 40,000 hoped for. Concerns over the credibility in HE of the new Diplomas were eased slightly by the announcement that the Universities of Oxford and Cambridge would accept the new engineering Diploma for entry. Notwithstanding the additional requirement of Physics GCE A Level, this was still seen as an important step forward. It will, however, be some time before the impact and success of these reforms can be evaluated.

Literacy, numeracy and ESOL

The words 'literacy' and 'numeracy' are no longer the preserve of the classroom, the inspectorate report, or of the latest policy briefing – they have now become part of everyday discourse. This derives from increased media attention on the attainment of school leavers and on methods of teaching young children how to read, as well as concerns about low levels of literacy and numeracy within a workforce facing intense global competition. Initiatives such as family literacy programmes, where children learn alongside parents or carers in educational or community settings with the support of specialist staff, have increased adults' and young people's skills. In addition, they have improved adults' understanding of the requirements of literacy and numeracy curricula in schools and related pedagogical approaches.

Despite growing awareness of issues surrounding literacy and numeracy in the general population, there is debate over the nature of what, if any, difference exists between literacy and the curricular subject of English, and similarly between numeracy and the subject of mathematics (Medway 2005; Green 2006). While it might be argued that literacy and numeracy are concerned with the practical application of skills and knowledge for everyday tasks and effective participation in civic life and the workplace, perceived distinctions are often not clear either in research or in policy. In the latter case, for example, specialist teaching qualifications for the learning and skills sector (LSS) introduced against new professional standards in September 2007 (LLUK 2007a) had the curious titles 'Level 5 Diploma in Teaching English (Literacy) in the LLS' and the 'Level 5 Diploma in Teaching Mathematics (Numeracy) in the LLS' (LLUK 2007b).

Such difficulties are less pronounced when considering courses for learners whose first language is not English. In this area, though the terminology is no less complex, the distinctions are clearer. The terms English as a Second Language (E2L) and English as an Additional Language (EAL) generally refer to provision for school children studying in British education and accessing the National Curriculum who have varying levels of English, and who may be receiving additional support and teaching to develop their spoken and written English language skills. This is distinct from English as a Foreign Language (EFL) provision that typically refers to courses for visitors to Britain, many being young people on short intensive programmes, who wish to develop their English language skills. English for Speakers of Other Languages (ESOL) is provision mainly, though not exclusively, delivered to adults studying in adult and community or FE settings to develop their skills in spoken and written English and reading for a wide variety of purposes. These might include gaining a qualification or passing the 'Life in the UK' test and becoming a British citizen. ESOL qualifications are offered at the same levels of the NQF as the related national literacy (and numeracy) awards, namely entry levels 1 to 3 and levels 1 and 2.

Literacy, numeracy and ESOL, though distinct curricular areas, share a number of important features: established methods and tools for initial and diagnostic assessment of skills; subject standards; curricula; and a national system of assessment. This provision is essential given that not only are the skills learned required for effective participation in a wide variety of social contexts, but they are also the means of access to all other curriculum subjects. Notwithstanding this, seeing these subjects primarily in terms of skill acquisition – a predominantly government driven policy viewpoint – continues to be problematic (Pahl and Rowsell 2005; Papen 2005).

Criticism from practitioners in the field tends to focus on the narrow curriculum and the methods of testing, which can lead to teaching directed solely towards passing national tests in order to reach achievement targets and secure funding. Research highlights the performative culture that pervades much literacy, numeracy and ESOL provision (Pahl and Rowsell 2005; Papen 2005). In challenging this performative focus and in proposing a social theory of literacy, a framework for thinking that has come to be known as the 'New Literacy Studies' (Barton, Hamilton and Ivanič 2000) has been developed, turning attention to the relationship between, particularly, literacy and wider social practices:

The traditional view of literacy as the ability to read and write rips literacy out of its sociocultural contexts and treats it as an asocial skill with little or nothing to do with human relationships. It cloaks literacy's connections to power, to social identity and to ideologies, often in the service of privileging certain types of literacies in certain types of people.

(Gee 1996: 46)

Skills for Life

In March 1999 an influential report was published (DfEE 1999), dealing with the literacy, language and numeracy skills of Britain's adults. Commonly known as the 'Moser Report' (after Sir Claus Moser who chaired the working party), this found that one in five adults was not functionally literate, that is, they did not have the literacy skills of the average 11-year-old. In terms of the number of adults with the very lowest level of literacy skills, only two developed countries were then ranked worse than Britain. A higher number still of adults had serious difficulties with numeracy and were only able to operate at the very lowest level.

The Report did not consider definitions of 'literacy' or 'numeracy', matters regularly discussed in other studies (Papen 2005; Hamilton and Hillier 2006). The still under-researched notion of what was meant by, for example, being literate or numerate was similarly not examined as part of the Working Party's research. The emphasis of the opening sections of the Report was on the results of skills assessments devised by organizations including the Centre for Longitudinal Studies (CLS) and the Organisation for Economic Co-operation and Development (OECD), and on analysis of results from the International Adult Literacy Survey (IALS). In response to what could have been considered alarming statistics on the low levels of literacy, language and numeracy skills, the Report proposed a ten element national strategy for Britain's adult basic skills. This covered all aspects of provision including planning, delivery and assessment for post-16 literacy, language and numeracy. New achievement targets were set; the statement of an entitlement to learn was compiled; proposals for a new curriculum and system of qualifications were planned; and an overhaul of specialist teacher training and related qualifications was recommended.

The Government's response to Moser, in the form of a national strategy for adult basic skills, was far reaching and its title, *Skills for Life* (DfEE 2001), is now suggestive of a whole range of teaching and learning in adult basic skills. These skills are defined as literacy and ESOL (reading, writing, speaking and listening), numeracy (the basic mathematical skills of number; measures, shapes and space, and handling data) and most recently, information technology. One of the initial responses to the recommendations of the Moser Report was the writing of sets of standards for the respective skills at levels one and two of the NQF, and, below these, at entry levels 1, 2 and 3 (QCA 2000). Following on from these, specialist curricula were devised which drew heavily on units for the key skills of communication and application of number as devised by the QCA, on international curricula, but also on the frameworks for teaching literacy and numeracy as elaborated in the National Literacy and Numeracy Strategies in the statutory schools' sector.

The terminology surrounding *Skills for Life* has, in recent years, seen a number of different acronyms emerge including ALLaN (Adult Literacy, Language and Numeracy), LLN (Literacy, Language and Numeracy), as well as the more dated term, 'basic skills'. The idea of functional skills draws together the notion of the provision itself with considerations of delivery, resourcing and assessment. The White Paper *Skills: Getting on in Business, Getting on at Work* (DfES 2005c) was the impetus for the idea of 'functional skills', which were subsequently described as 'practical skills in English, mathematics and information and communication technology (ICT) that allow individuals to work confidently, effectively and independently in life' (QCA 2007).

Though the move to functional skills might be suggestive of a significant change in this curriculum area, the standards to be covered and skills in literacy, numeracy and ICT that learners are required to demonstrate, and indeed the overall purpose of these elements of the curriculum, seem little changed from that articulated by the report of Moser's Working Party nearly a decade earlier. Moser's vision for literacy and numeracy had been one of an 'ability to read, write and speak in English, and to use Mathematics at a level necessary to function at work and in society in general' (DfEE 1999: foreword). This may seem modest enough but it remains a necessary aspiration.

10

Practical teaching

Liz Dixon, Josie Harvey, Ron Thompson and Sarah Williamson

In this chapter:

- Planning learning sessions
- Aims and objectives
- Learning activities
- Using questions to promote learning
- Learning resources
- Differentiation
- Lesson plans and schemes of work
- Teaching groups of learners
- Managing challenging behaviour
- Tutorials and pastoral support

Planning learning sessions

Planning a learning session involves making a number of decisions about: content and learning objectives; learning activities and resources; support for individual learners; how to deal with key skills issues; and how learning will be assessed. In making these decisions, the teacher should draw on the theoretical perspectives discussed in Chapter 8 and also take into account specific factors such as those shown in Figure 10.1. Learning sessions will normally follow a basic structure consisting of an introduction, followed by development of the main learning themes and finally a conclusion. Although such a format may seem an obvious one to use, it is worth discussing this structure in a little more detail.

Introduction: This phase should be fairly short; however, it is important because it provides an opportunity to cover basic issues such as registers, health and safety, and returning assessed work. Learning from a previous session is often revisited (a 'recap' or recapitulation of key elements, usually involving some form of assessment such as a quiz). The teacher will introduce the session, often by displaying the main learning objectives and providing a brief overview of the lesson content, why it is important

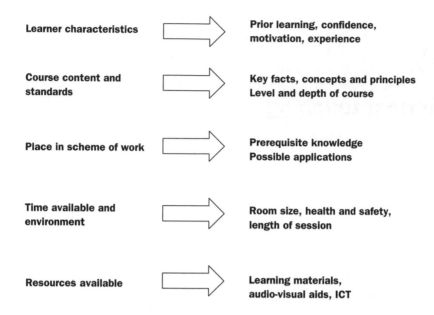

Figure 10.1 Factors influencing decisions in lesson planning

and how it relates to previous learning. An advance organizer may be used. The introduction may also include a 'starter' activity – a short but stimulating learning activity intended to get learners in the right frame of mind for the session.

Development: In this phase, the main content is developed through a series of learning activities. It will therefore occupy the majority of the lesson time. It is important to ensure that all learners are involved and that the teacher is in a position to assess progress. How many activities are included in this phase will depend on a number of factors, including the time available and the characteristics of the learners. As Child (2004: 50, 159) points out, attention span is limited and the position of information within a session can affect its retention.

Conclusion: In the final phase of the lesson, the main ideas are reviewed and related to the aims and objectives stated in the introduction. There will normally be a recap of the learning achieved and some evaluation of the learning processes in the session. In some situations, learners will need to reflect formally on what they have learned and record their reflections in an individual learning plan or record of achievement – if this is the case, plenty of time should be allowed. The conclusion will often look ahead to the next session and cover issues such as 'homework' if this has not already been dealt with.

Transitions between learning activities

In most sessions, the development phase will include more than one learning activity. This makes the issue of *transitions* between activities important – each one will need to be concluded effectively and the next activity introduced. As well as practical considerations such as collection and distribution of learning materials or equipment, learners need to understand where they are in the session and where they are heading. The basic structure outlined above therefore becomes embedded in miniature within the development phase. It is helpful to think of this phase in terms of a reflective learning cycle as in Figure 10.2, so that learners are able to reflect on and make links between different learning activities.

Although evaluations of quality in teaching and learning are to some extent subjective and even ideological, it can be helpful when planning lessons to bear in mind current inspection frameworks relevant to lifelong learning. For many teachers in the sector, external judgements of their teaching will be made according to the *Common Inspection Framework* for post-16 education and training. Features of a 'good' lesson, within this framework, are shown in Box 10.1 overleaf.

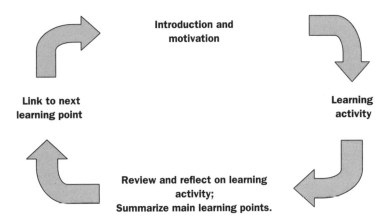

Figure 10.2 Cyclic structure for the development phase of a learning session

Aims and objectives

In almost any teaching session, learning of some form will take place. However, the learning that occurs might not be intended, or even desirable. How can the teacher judge whether to be satisfied with the session? One possibility is to state in advance the intended learning outcomes and then to assess the extent to which they have been achieved. This section deals with the formulation of learning outcomes by means of behavioural objectives, drawing on the discussion in Chapter 8 of behaviourist theories of learning and of Bloom's taxonomy of learning.

Behavioural objectives have a number of advantages. For example, they help in the process of lesson planning, by requiring the teacher to make explicit the nature of the intended learning outcomes and the relevant subject content. They are important for lesson evaluation – it is often pointed out that it is difficult to know when you have arrived if you have no idea of where you are going! For similar reasons, learning objectives are a useful tool for ensuring the validity of assessment.

Box 10.1 Features of a 'good' lesson according to post-16 inspection criteria

---

- setting of clear objectives which are made known to the learners;
- enthusiastic and interesting teaching which provides an enjoyable experience for learners;
- activities that are suitable for all learners, whatever their age, ability and cultural background, and which are suitably demanding;
- awareness of different individuals' needs;
- effective questioning of learners to check their understanding;
- learners demonstrating their achievements through improved knowledge, understanding and skills;
- skilful leadership of discussions to ensure that learners' contributions are encouraged and valued;
- clear explanations, particularly of the links between theoretical knowledge and its practical applications;
- accurate and up-to-date technical knowledge;
- sensitivity to and promotion of equal opportunities issues;
- clear writing on whiteboards and overhead projectors;
- interesting and relevant use of technology to support learning;
- good quality handouts that are well produced, free from errors and which contain references where appropriate;
- sufficient coverage of ground in the topic;
- effective management of any transition between individual and group work;
- a crisp end to the lesson, summarizing what has been learned and avoiding 'tailing off'.

Source: Ofsted (2008a: 84)

An *aim* is a general statement of aspiration, usually associated with a course or subject as a whole. For example, 'the aim of humanities teaching is to forward understanding, discrimination and judgement in the human field'. Aims often focus on teacher behaviour, such as providing certain types of learning experience; for example, 'the aim of this customer care unit is to provide trainees with simulated experience of dealing with abusive clients'.

A *general objective* is a broad statement of what the learner is expected to achieve as a result of the learning session. A *specific objective* is a precise and verifiable statement of expected learner behaviour or potential. For an individual learning session, there would normally be a single general objective and a small number of specific objectives (typically four or five).

Since a general objective is meant to be a broad statement of the overall learning outcome from a unit of study, some care is needed to achieve the right level of generality. For example, consider the three statements below (adapted from Gronlund 1970: 10):

1   Writes clear, effective English.

2   Applies correct punctuation to sentences.

3   Uses the full stop to terminate sentences.

The first would normally be too general for a single lesson, although it could be adapted for a more extended period of learning. The third is probably too specific for use as a general objective for a complete learning session. The second is probably the most appropriate, although factors relating to the course content and the learners would need to be taken into account in making this decision.

When writing behavioural objectives, the key words are verbs describing intended learner behaviour or potential. Gronlund (1970: 10) suggests that, for general object-ives, appropriate verbs describing learning in the cognitive domain would include: applies, comprehends, knows, understands, uses. For example, 'understands the principle of the lever' would be an appropriate general objective for a science or engineering lesson.

As its name implies, a specific objective is meant to be more particular than a general objective, and to be directly verifiable. Specific objectives are therefore written using verbs describing observable learner behaviour. They are now often referred to as SMART objectives. This acronym is derived from the words Spe-cific, Measurable, Achievable, Realistic and Time-related; although 'achievable' and 'realistic' may seem to overlap, the distinction usually made is between being achievable in principle and realistically achievable given the available resources and conditions.

A specific objective consists of up to three parts. It begins with an indication of the behaviour that will provide evidence that the learner has met the objective, for example 'defines correctly the terms "profit" and "interest" '. Often, the objective consists *only* of this indication. However, in the interests of clarity, it can be helpful to describe the conditions under which this behaviour is to be demonstrated (for example, 'making use of reference books' or 'without the use of a calculator'). In addition, the objective may include criteria for an acceptable level of performance (for example, 'state correctly at least three of the following points . . .' or 'within a tolerance of ten per cent'). Some complete examples are given in Box 10.2 overleaf.

Identifying appropriate learning objectives is not easy, and the teacher requires a clear understanding of how a particular topic can be analysed. In broad terms, the objectives approach asks the teacher to interpret the question 'What do learners need to *know*?' in terms of the question 'What should learners be able to *do* as a result?' Bloom's taxonomy can be helpful, by encouraging the teacher to take into account the appropriate domain of learning and the level within this domain. For example, within the cognitive domain, relatively simple learning outcomes relating to knowledge, comprehension and application may be reflected in objectives that use verbs such as 'states' or 'calculates'. However, uncritically adopting these simple verbs may lead the teacher to overlook opportunities for higher level learning involving analysis, synthesis and evaluation, or to underestimate the learning that is actually taking place.

This highlights a broader issue relating to the use of behavioural objectives: do they actually diminish our view of learning by reducing it to observable behaviour?

Box 10.2 Examples of general and specific behavioural objectives

---

General objective: Apply Pythagoras' Theorem to plane right-angled triangles.
Specific objectives:

1　State Pythagoras' Theorem with reference to a given diagram.
2　Use Pythagoras to calculate, correct to three significant figures, the length of the hypotenuse of a right-angled triangle given the other two sides.
3　Use Pythagoras to calculate, correct to three significant figures, a side of a right-angled triangle given the hypotenuse and one other side.

General objective: Understand the role of a receptionist in a beauty salon.
Specific objectives:

1　State four of the main responsibilities of a beauty salon receptionist.
2　Explain why it is important for the reception desk to be staffed whenever the salon is open, giving at least three reasons.
3　Identify situations where the receptionist must pass enquiries to a qualified beauty therapist.

We saw in Chapter 8 that Kolb regards learning as a dynamic process which is difficult to capture in terms of learning outcomes. Rogers and Freiberg (1994: 188) give an example of learning expressed as an outcome and as an experiential process:

- The students will list five contributions of ancient Egypt to modern world societies.

- Class members will design, plan and go on a field trip to the ancient Egyptian collection at a museum.

He argues that the process-driven approach provides a broader learning experience and does not predetermine the learning that will take place. Although we might reply that his process example is perfectly consistent with achieving the learning outcome, and other outcomes could be constructed to reflect a broader view of learning about Egypt, Rogers is concerned that the outcomes approach contains an inherent tendency to reduce expectations and limit learning to low-level threshold skills.

Learning activities

The range of learning activities available to the teacher can seem bewildering at times, particularly in view of the difficulty of basing the selection of activities on hard evidence. Although a number of studies of the effectiveness of different learning methods have been carried out, they need to be used with care, bearing in mind the observation of Hodkinson and James (2003: 401), that learning in FE appears to be strongly culture and context dependent: 'what works, or is deemed good practice in one learning site may not work or be good practice in another'.

Hattie (2009) provides a careful synthesis of over 800 'meta-analyses' which consider the impact on learner achievement of a range of educational interventions. In a meta-analysis, the outcomes of an intervention over a number of research studies are reduced to a common measure, known as 'effect size'; the effectiveness of the intervention can then be compared with other interventions, and with the influence of factors such as home background and individual learner characteristics. A positive effect size of 0.5 is equivalent to an increase of one grade in achievement at GCSE level (Black et al. 2003: 9). Hattie (2009: 17) argues that an effect size of 0.4 constitutes a 'hinge point'; below that level, the benefits of an intervention may not justify the effort or expense involved.

Table 10.1 shows the effect sizes of some teaching methods in common use, together with information on the number of studies included in the meta-analysis and the degree of variability between studies (high variability would suggest considerable sensitivity to context). Note the impact of direct instruction (*not* didactic instruction!) on learning and the effectiveness of learners teaching others. Table 10.2 overleaf shows, for comparison, the effect sizes of some other factors influencing achievement.

Selecting learning activities can be made easier by distinguishing between teacher-centred and learner-centred activities. This distinction is based on who is the main focus of the activity, particularly in terms of the balance of control and decision making between teacher and learner. It has been expressed by Minton (1991) as a matrix of control for various learning activities, as shown in Figure 10.3 overleaf.

Learning activities which are directed by the teacher, and in which the teacher is considerably more active than the learners, lie near the teacher-centred extreme of this matrix. The teacher may feel 'safe' with these activities, as they are able largely to determine what happens next. Teacher-centred activities are predictable and may be valuable in situations where new material is to be covered. However, the learners will be relatively passive and it may be difficult to ensure that all are involved and focused on the activity. On the other hand, the teacher may feel that learner-centred activities,

Table 10.1 Effect sizes of selected teaching/learning methods

Method	Effect size	Variability	Number of studies
Formative feedback	0.73	Medium	1,287
Direct instruction	0.59	High	304
Worked examples	0.57	Medium	62
Peer tutoring	0.55	High	767
Small-group learning	0.48	Not given	78
Questioning	0.46	Medium	211
Computer-based instruction	0.37	Medium	4,875
Simulations	0.33	High	361
Audio-visual methods	0.22	Medium	259
Team teaching	0.19	Medium	136
Web-based learning	0.18	High	45
Mentoring	0.15	Medium	74

Source: Adapted from Hattie (2009)

Table 10.2 Effect sizes of factors not related to teaching method

Factor	Effect size	Variability	Number of studies
Own estimate of achievement	1.44	Low	209
Teacher–student relationships	0.72	Low	229
Prior achievement	0.67	High	3,607
Socio-economic status	0.57	Low	499
Peer influences	0.53	Not given	12
Parental involvement	0.51	High	716
Motivation	0.48	Medium	327
Quality of teaching	0.44	Medium	141
Teacher expectations	0.43	High	674
Class size	0.21	Not given	96
Gender (Males–Females)	0.12	Low	2,926

Source: Adapted from Hattie (2009)

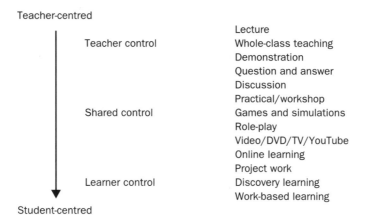

Figure 10.3 Minton's Matrix of Control
Source: Adapted from Minton (1991: 112)

in which learners work individually or in groups, at their own pace and generating their own ideas, are 'risky' and may result in learners heading in unexpected directions or in important learning being missed out. However, only by giving learners the opportunity to express their own ideas and solve problems on their own can their true level of understanding be explored and enhanced. Carl Rogers encourages the teacher to take on the role of facilitator, creating a community of learners rather than passive recipients: 'I see the facilitation of learning as the function that may hold constructive, tentative, changing *process* answers to some of the deepest perplexities that beset humankind' (Rogers and Freiberg 1994: 153).

Using questions to promote learning

Dialectic, or the method of seeking knowledge by means of question and answer, has a long and distinguished history, dating back to the Greek philosophers and to Socrates in particular – in fact, it is often referred to as the 'Socratic method'. Asking questions of learners provides a simple and immediate way of monitoring progress and under-standing in a learning session; it can also be used to develop understanding and promote reasoning. However, some skill and patience is required if questioning is not to be simply a means of checking low-level rote learning or enabling a few articulate students to show off their knowledge.

Oral questioning provides a way of turning a quite passive and teacher-centred activity, such as whole-class teaching or a demonstration, into something much more interactive and challenging. It allows the teacher to draw on the knowledge and experience that learners bring to the session, to seek opinions and contradictory views, or to collaboratively explore a problem. In addition, it encourages students to contribute ideas who might otherwise have remained silent. However, anyone who has asked a question and then waited in deafening silence for an answer will know that there are pitfalls and disadvantages for both students and teachers. Apart from varied levels of involvement from different group members and the anxiety caused by being 'put on the spot', there are problems related to the structure of the questions them-selves – what *kind* of knowledge do they develop and assess, and how can teachers know whether a correct answer is a valid indicator of knowledge?

The simplest technique is to ask an *overhead* question. This means that the question is asked of the whole class, and an answer taken from anyone who responds. While being a relatively non-threatening approach, it has the obvious disadvantage that some students may dominate the session, misleading the teacher as to the level of understanding and excluding other students from the discussion. One solution to this problem is to ask the question of a specific learner – a *nominated* question. However, this can be quite stressful for many students and is often avoided by teachers. Another strategy is to pose the question and ask students to discuss it in pairs; after a few minutes the teacher nominates several pairs to answer the question and their ideas are compared and discussed. This can be particularly helpful if the question is open-ended, with many possible answers. Nominated questions can also be useful when asking students to talk about their own experiences, as clearly they will know the answer – reducing, although not eliminating, the pressure on them.

A variation on nominated questions is *redirection*. The teacher asks a question with a number of possible answers, nominates a student to answer, then a second student and possibly a third. Other students are invited to comment on and evaluate the answers, followed by some evaluation from the teacher. The teacher may also employ *reflected* questions: when Student A asks the teacher a question – for example, 'What does the word "numerator" mean?' the teacher passes on this question to Student B, who then has the opportunity to explain the concept to the class. The teacher may also simply pass the question back to Student A – a *reversed* question – but if this is done frequently some students find it frustrating.

One consideration when using nominated questions is that naming the student before asking the question can be a signal to other students to 'switch off' and not even listen to the question, let alone think about its answer. To counteract this tendency, the teacher may give time for all students to think about the question before asking a particular student to answer it.

Using question and answer in the classroom requires confidence and patience from the teacher. A common failing is to give too little time for students to think – five seconds of silence can often seem a long time, and can tempt an intervention too early. Re-phrasing the question can help if contributions do not flow, but another common failing needs to be avoided – asking what lawyers would call leading questions. A question such as, 'Can understanding play types help childcare staff to identify limitations in a play environment?' may get a correct response, but does not indicate understanding as the answer has been effectively 'fed' to the student. A further weakness of this example is that it gives no scope for the student to express ideas – it is a *closed* question.

Closed questions have a yes/no answer or a strictly limited set of answers; for example, 'What are the main constituents of air?' They are useful for checking factual knowledge, but will give little indication of deeper understanding. By contrast, *open* questions have no predetermined answers and may provide considerable scope for different explanations, interpretations or opinions. A question such as, 'How may the concept of play types help childcare staff to plan activities with young children?' will have a number of different answers, all equally valid, and each one will require some understanding of the concept under discussion and its application. Closed questions may be thought of in terms of a behaviourist approach (see Chapter 8), their advantage being that they are straightforward to ask and can be quite specific in nature. This allows frequent reinforcement, for example by praising correct answers, and enables the discrete behaviours characteristic of this approach to learning to be developed and chained together. However, closed questions will tend to emphasize lower cognitive levels in Bloom's taxonomy, rather than higher level cognitive behaviours such as evaluation and synthesis.

Open questions, on the other hand, ask students to relate learning to their own experience, to make connections between different areas and to imaginatively explore the implications of what they are learning. It is not difficult to translate closed questions into open ones – for example, simply by inserting the word 'why'. A question such as, 'What is the capital city of the United States?', which asks for a trivial item of general knowledge, transforms into, 'Why did Washington become the capital city of the US?', a much more challenging exploration of historical, political and geographical factors. Questions based on imagining the consequences of certain states of affairs – 'What if?' questions – are also useful in terms of a cognitivist approach to learning. Thus, a closed question such as, 'Name the principal arteries supplying the heart with blood and state their functions' would become, 'What would happen if one of the arteries supplying the heart became blocked?'

Learning resources

Learning resources can range from equipment, models and real objects for use by the teacher to materials designed to be used by the learner, either in the learning session or independently. Well designed resources can engage learners and add variety to a lesson.

They aid conceptualization and offer communication through different channels – for example, visual resources help learners to 'see' and understand more clearly. Learning resources can be analysed from various theoretical perspectives, including behaviourist, cognitivist, humanist and social learning theories. For example, do resources:

- Help structure information, develop concepts or provide 'advance organizers' (Cognitivist)?
- Focus attention, provide practice and feedback or enhance reinforcement (Behaviourist)?
- Support learners in identifying and achieving their own goals, promoting intrinsic motivation (Humanist)?
- Provide enhanced opportunities to learn from tutors or other students, and to create a community of practice (Social learning)?

The development of new technologies means that there is an ever-increasing range of multimedia tools available for use as learning resources, and these are discussed in Chapters 11 and 12. This section reviews other teaching and learning resources and offers guidance for their use.

Whiteboards

Because most classrooms have a whiteboard, the ability to use one effectively is essential. Advance preparation of the whiteboard, with a welcome message and general notices and reminders, is an effective way to instantly personalize a room to a group of learners. 'Setting up' in advance also allows legibility and spelling to be checked. Writing the lesson objectives on the board provides a useful visual focus at the start of a lesson. It can also help learners who arrive after the start.

The size of lettering is important – writing a few words and then checking for legibility from all parts of the room is important. Visual separation or emphasis of different points through colour can be very helpful to learners. Content should be visually organized, using bullet points, boxes, sub-headings and other indicators to make information clear. Talking to the whiteboard while writing is a common error, and as well as making the teacher inaudible will also result in the teacher's back being to the learners. As a matter of courtesy to colleagues, the whiteboard should be left clean at the end of the session, unless important information needs to be retained.

Handouts

Handouts are a commonly used resource and are useful in organizing information for students. However, giving a handout to learners does not guarantee that learning will take place. Handouts which require learners to engage with them in some way are likely to be the most effective. Incomplete (or 'gapped') handouts have spaces for learners to complete – for example, diagrams to be labelled or space for notes, comments and answers to questions.

Layout and design are important. Large blocks of text can be off-putting; leaving 'white space' allows room for learners to annotate and personalize a handout with their own notes. Overuse of upper-case letters is best avoided, as the shapes of words in lower case are an aid to reading. Teachers often develop a consistent style for all materials produced for a particular group of learners, possibly with a heading or logo, rather than new designs for every session – this helps learners to recognize handouts for a certain unit or module more easily. Illustrations and clipart can break up text and make handouts look more interesting and attractive. However, some learners may feel patronized by excessive use of certain types of illustration.

Coloured paper, rather than colour printing, can be a relatively inexpensive way to introduce colour. Pastel tones may also be helpful to learners with literacy difficulties, while a bright colour can be used to highlight the importance of a certain handout. Learners can be asked to read handouts in advance and to make summary points for discussion in class. This helps learners with literacy difficulties who may find it hard to read quickly in class. Using 'committed space' can be helpful and guide responses to tasks and activities; for example, a handout may ask learners to 'list five reasons in the space below'.

Learning materials may be tested for readability, for example by using the FOG index. In this method, a sample of 100 words of text is taken. The number of complete sentences in this 100 word sample is counted, together with the number of words contained in the complete sentences. From this information, the average sentence length, L, can be calculated. The next step is to count the number of words, N, of three or more syllables in the 100 word sample. Finally, the FOG index is calculated using the formula

$$\text{FOG Index} = 0.4 \times (L + N)$$

For example, suppose the 100 word sample of text contained five complete sentences containing a total of 86 words. Then $L = 86 \div 5 = 17.2$; if the sample also contained six words of three or more syllables, then $N = 6$ and

$$\text{FOG Index} = 0.4 \times (17.2 + 6) = 9.3$$

correct to one decimal place. For comparison, newspapers such as the *Guardian* have FOG indexes of around 12–14; text aimed at most learners should normally fall into the range 6–10, although this would vary depending on the level of the course. The FOG index is designed to correspond to US school grades; to convert a FOG index to an approximate reading age, add five to the value of the index.

Overhead projectors and transparencies

An overhead projector (OHP) allows an overhead transparency (OHT) to be projected onto a screen. Although gradually being replaced by data projectors, they have the advantage of being relatively cheap and can be very effective when properly used. It is possible to achieve a good quality of production with a mixture of text and images, particularly if a digital printer is used to prepare transparencies.

The most effective transparencies are clear, bold and simple. Key words and short phrases are preferable to full sentences as space is limited with a readable font size. A useful guideline is to limit text to six to eight lines, with six to eight words in each line. A square central area on the transparency should be used, as the top and bottom can be out of focus when projected.

The size of text is important and at least 18–20 points will be necessary in most rooms. Handouts are not suitable for conversion to transparencies as handout text will normally be far too small. Permanent or non-permanent felt pens are available for writing on transparencies and can be used by learners to add detail to 'gapped' slides, or to record points from group work to project and share with the whole class. To project the transparency at the required size, the projector needs to be positioned correctly and then focused. An effect called 'keystoning', in which a square will appear wider at the top and narrower at the bottom, is common with projectors and the solution is to incline the screen so that light falls 'flat' onto it. On each transparency, points can be revealed one at a time, or further information introduced with an overlay.

Data projectors, presentation software and electronic whiteboards

Using presentation software, such as Microsoft PowerPoint, with a data projector has become a popular method of communicating, presenting and sharing knowledge. However, a long series of slides presented to a passive audience should be avoided. The inclusion of photographs, other images and diagrams as well as sound and video clips can be effective and add a multi-sensory dimension.

Colour schemes need to be carefully considered as contrasts which are easily readable on a PC screen may be illegible when projected on a screen. Two or three colours on a slide are quite enough for most purposes and rainbow effects or colours similar in tone should be avoided. It is tempting to include a plethora of animations, transitions, word art and sound effects. However, these can be intensely irritating for learners and detract from the points being made. The teacher should have a printed copy of the slides to refer to, so that reading from the screen is avoided and eye contact with the learners is maintained.

Electronic whiteboards are becoming increasingly common. These boards allow handwritten text to be captured and include a variety of software tools to enable the teacher to increase the interactivity of presentations and other whole-class activities.

Flipcharts

Flipcharts are portable and can be just as effective as more sophisticated equipment. They are useful in community settings and their lack of formality or technology can be helpful where learners are returning to education and confidence may be an issue. Individual flipchart sheets can be torn off a pad and used for group activities, then pinned up for presentation, feedback and reference.

As in the case of whiteboard pens, visibility of colours must be checked. Strong, dark colours are effective; orange and yellow will not show up clearly on a white ground. Flipcharts can be prepared in advance with key points in sequenced pages and also saved for further use, while sticky notes can be used to 'book mark' pages on a flip chart pad. Faint pencil lines can be ruled onto sheets to provide guide lines and aid neatness.

Audio-visual resources

Audio-visual resources such as DVDs, videos and sound recordings can be used to enhance and support learning in many ways. For example, they can 'set the scene', shock, stimulate discussion, give a wider perspective and demonstrate a particular technique or expertise. Digital technology now enables a wide range of material to be searched and used effectively in a classroom. For example, YouTube offers a wealth of short film material, and some television channels offer 'replay' facilities online.

The teacher should ensure that learners remain engaged and active as they view or listen to the resource. For example, an incomplete handout can be used, learners can be asked to note down specific examples or points, or a film stopped at regular intervals for review and discussion. DVDs and videos should be viewed in advance so that the teacher can check and become familiar with their content. Starting points for DVDs and tapes need to be set up so that time is not wasted looking for them in a lesson. The teacher should, of course, always check *in advance* that they know how to use the audio-visual equipment.

Differentiation

For many years, education in England has been attempting to come to terms with changing social and economic circumstances which have been reflected in the social makeup of schools and colleges. These changes have been reflected in curricula, but also in the recognition that individual learners must be supported in achieving their potential. The Warnock Report (1978: 5) sets out the key idea of differentiation for all learners: 'The purpose of education for all children is the same; the goals are the same. But the help that individual children need in progressing towards them will be different'. Differentiation is therefore about the ability of institutions and teachers to respond to the varying needs of individual learners, to help them achieve appropriate outcomes.

> Differentiation is not a single event, it is a process. This process involves recognising the variety of individual needs within a class, planning to meet those needs, providing appropriate delivery, and evaluating the effectiveness of the activities in order to maximise the achievements of individual learners.
>
> (NCET 1993: 21)

Maker (1982) has developed a model of curriculum differentiation for teaching gifted students, which can also be applied to work with other learners. She suggests that the curriculum should be differentiated in four ways, in terms of modifications to the *learning environment*; the *content* of learning; learning *processes*; and learning *products*. Differentiation may therefore take a variety of forms, each one adapted to particular circumstances.

Differentiation may occur by *task*, either by different learners undertaking different tasks or with all learners undertaking a single task which has been graduated in difficulty. Extension material may also be provided for the more able or experienced learners. In a graduated task, not all learners will be able to achieve all parts, but the task must be structured so that every learner can successfully complete a significant part of it. Differentiation may also take place by *outcome*; learners all undertake the same task, responding to it in different ways and achieving at their own level.

Creative writing provides an example of differentiation by outcome, as different learners could respond to the same title or stimulus material, but produce markedly different compositions. Differentiation by outcome may also be achieved by varying the nature of learning and assessment tasks – for example, by giving learners a choice of forms in which to present their work. Thus an assignment could be presented using posters or web pages rather than by a conventional written report; different presentation methods could also be used for different assignments. See Jones (2006) for further discussion and examples of differentiation by task and outcome.

In differentiation by *support*, learners with different needs are given different forms or levels of support. This may be informal and within the context of the teacher's normal activity, such as individual help given during learning activities. More formally, group work may be planned so that stronger learners are paired with those less able – an example of peer support – or additional help may be provided in the form of tailored resources or support from a teaching assistant or other colleague. Writing frames can be helpful in some situations by providing key words or phrases to act as 'scaffolding' for learners undertaking an assignment. Effective writing frames will structure the content of learners' work by providing prompts to ensure that all key areas are covered, but may also be used to help learners achieve higher cognitive levels in their work. One way of doing this is for the writing frame to explicitly direct learners to discuss evidence for their views and strengths or weaknesses in theories that they use.

For some learners, *additional time* may allow them to successfully complete a learning activity. Differentiation may also be achieved through the *feedback* provided following assessment – in this case, the feedback relates to the individual starting points and goals of the learner, giving advice on how to get from one to the other. This approach to differentiation is associated with the idea of *assessment for learning*, which is discussed in detail in Chapter 13.

Lesson plans and schemes of work

Lesson plans

There are many ways of recording the plan for a learning session. Teachers may be free to devise their own approaches but often institutions will adopt a standard format to be used by all teachers. Wherever possible, lesson plans should be adapted to the nature of the teaching and learning taking place, as an approach suitable for formal classes in an academic subject may be inappropriate for an engineering workshop or training carried out in a hospital ward.

The most common format for lesson plans is a cover sheet containing brief details about the course and learners, together with one or more pages in the form of a grid setting out the structure of the session (see Figures 10.4 and 10.5 overleaf for an example of this format). The cover sheet may state the time and location of the session and should outline strategies for assessment and differentiation, unless these are

Class/Group: NVQ Level 2 Children's Care, Learning and Development

	Room: PF1/09	**Tutor Name:** Angela Johnson

Topic or reference to scheme of work
Providing a safe and effective childcare environment

	Day: Tue	**Date:** 2 Nov 2009
		Time: 10.15–12.15

No. on Register: 13	**Module:**
No. in attendance: 12 (11F, 1M)	002/202

General aims	**Understand key principles and procedures involved in providing a safe childcare environment which promotes learning and positive behaviour.**
Specific learning outcomes for the session:	• Know how to prepare and maintain a safe and healthy childcare environment • Be able to follow procedures for accidents, emergencies and illness • Explain procedures and methods that safeguard children from abuse • Suggest ways of encouraging children's positive behaviour
Anticipated inclusive learning issues and differentiation strategies for the lesson	Variety of student placements can be used to relate learning to individual experiences; however some learners have limited practical experience as yet. The lone male student in the group can feel isolated at times. I will adapt approach to individual needs through discussion, one-to-one support, and mixing experienced/less experienced learners in group work.

Assessment planned for during session, including key skills:
Observation of student practical activity, question and answer, discussion of paragraphs written by individual students. Drawing activity will allow practice and observation of numeracy skills. Group discussion enables development of communication skills. Written paragraph develops literacy skills.

Figure 10.4 Sample cover sheet of a lesson plan for a childcare class

Time	Topic	Teacher Activity	Learner Activity	Resources
11.15	Introduction	Welcome learners, take register. Brief recap of previous session. Introduce unit it is about keeping children safe during day to day activities.	Take part in Q/A.	Aims and objectives on whiteboard
11.20	Responses to accidents, emergencies and illness	Explain key principles and procedures, using Q/A to involve learner's and encourage them to contribute from own knowledge and experience.	Take part in Q/A; share placement experiences.	Whiteboard; teacher's notes.
11.30	Practical activity: produce diagram showing placement safety equipment	Ask learners to draw layout of their placement setting, label rooms, add furniture. Example on whiteboard using Q/A.	Take part in Q/A; make initial drawings and share with others.	Workbooks, sharp pencils, rulers.
11.45	Practical activity continued	Ask learners to add furniture, play/learning equipment and safety equipment.	Complete drawings and discuss safety hazards and reasons for position of safety equipment with others in group.	Workbooks, sharp pencils, rulers.
12.00	Write a paragraph about how the rooms are organized	Explain activity.	Write paragraph, including discussion of safety factors. Refer to p. 31 in textbook.	Course textbooks
12.10	Conclude first part of session	Review key points; check understanding of first objective by Q/A. Thank learners for contribution and link to next part of session.	Take part in Q/A.	

Figure 10.5 Extract from a lesson plan for a childcare class

indicated elsewhere in the plan. The grid pages usually give rough timings for key phases in the session and have headings such as content, learner activity, teacher activity, assessment and resources. Columns for learner and teacher activity are sometimes merged to avoid repetition, but it can be useful to keep them separate as scanning up and down the learner activities can indicate whether a lesson involves the learners appropriately.

The scheme of work

A lesson plan should not stand alone; it should form part of a coherent sequence of learning expressed in a scheme of work. The use of schemes of work allows individual learning sessions to be placed in a wider context and related to the overall aims and content of a unit of learning. Knowledge, understanding and skills can be shown building up systematically over a period of time, and the role of language, literacy, numeracy and ICT in a course of study can be made clear.

A scheme of work will normally cover an extended period of learning, particularly for groups meeting once or twice a week throughout an academic year. However, the concept can also be applied to more intensive courses, such as a one-week residential induction for newly-appointed trade union workers. Whatever the time period, the scheme of work will show the sequence of learning sessions, together with brief details of the general objective for each session, key learning activities and resources, and the schedule of assessment to be used. A sample scheme of work is shown in Figure 10.6.

There are several ways of deciding on a learning sequence for the scheme of work. In subject areas where there is a hierarchical organization of knowledge – with more advanced concepts and principles building on simpler ones – it is necessary to pay careful attention to the precedence of particular topics, so that concepts and methods are available when needed. The sequence may therefore be constructed from an analysis of prerequisite knowledge at each stage. However, even in a highly structured subject area, a purely logical development may not always be the best pedagogic approach. These considerations lead to the contrast between a *depth-first* approach, in which a particular topic is explored in detail before moving on to the next one, and a *breadth-first* approach in which a topic is taken only as far as is needed to be used in other topics. The breadth-first approach allows a broad survey of a subject or occupational area to be established at a relatively early stage, thus encouraging holistic learning. The topics can then be revisited in more depth later on, achieving the spiral curriculum approach advocated by Bruner (see Chapter 8).

Rather than use a topic-based approach, in some cases it may be better to adopt a thematic structure for the scheme of work. For example, 'climate change' is a theme that could draw together different topics in a science course, integrating otherwise abstract ideas and showing how they may be applied.

Teaching groups of learners

In lifelong learning, groups can take many forms, ranging from a class meeting regularly several times a week in a college to work-based learning groups attending for a specific training event. Different types of group may need different approaches,

Date	Content	Learning Activities	Resources	Embedding Language, Literacy, Numeracy and ICT	Formative Assessment
Term One					
30 Sep	Introductions. Role of the teacher.	Group work Presentations	Role of teacher handouts Flipchart paper	Developing communication skills	By trainee presentation/discussion
07 Oct	Factors influencing learning. Learning styles.	Tutor input; Group discussion Completion of Learning Style Inventory (LSI)	Factors handouts Powerpoint; LSI	Statistics analysing LSI	LSI; Q&A Presentations on group work
14 Oct	Theories of the learning process	Tutor input; Group discussion Posters on learning theories	Powerpoint; YouTube video; Theory handouts	Using YouTube for educational purposes	Q&A Poster presentations
21 Oct	Planning learning sessions and schemes of work	Tutor input Small group work Differentiation case studies	Powerpoint Example lesson plans Trainees' own plans	Giving constructive feedback to peers	Q&A Own lesson plans
28 Oct	Library induction or e-resources	Librarian input Hands-on practice	Research activity handout	Use of online journals; Referencing	Completion of activities
04 Nov	Teaching and learning methods and materials	Group work; game Group discussion Tutor input	Materials for game; Powerpoint; Handout on effectiveness of teaching methods	Percentages, effect sizes for teaching methods	Q&A; reflection on issues raised by game

Figure 10.6 Extract from a scheme of work for a Certificate in Education class

appropriate to varying circumstances learner characteristics. Many teachers emphasize the importance of high expectations from the very beginning of their work with a learning group, advocating the model of the *confident professional* (LSDA 2007: 20) who expects, and is generally rewarded with, good social behaviour.

Tuckman and Jensen (1977), in their classic model of group development, suggest that all groups move sequentially through five different stages: *forming, storming, norming, performing* and *adjourning*. More recently, a seven-stage model for learning groups has been proposed by Johnson and Johnson (2006: 28). According to their model, group development begins with three initial stages: *defining and structuring procedures, conforming to procedures and getting acquainted* and *recognizing mutuality and building trust.* These early stages, when a group comes together for the first few times, are a period of uncertainty and group members are often heavily dependent upon the tutor. Learners need to be welcomed and may need clear direction on aims, expectations and procedures.

Teachers need to establish rules and boundaries, rights and responsibilities, and routines and protocols with the group (Vizard 2007), and to then *habituate* what they establish (Rogers 2004). Negotiating ground rules with learners allows both teachers and learners to have a shared understanding. Through activities which encourage cooperation and socialization, the teacher can help learners get to know each other and can create a supportive, inclusive atmosphere in tune with Maslow's hierarchy of needs.

Rebelling and differentiating, the fourth stage of this model, can be compared to the *storming* period of Tuckman and Jensen. This phase may be short, or conversely one from which some groups find it difficult to progress. There may be conflict, disagreements and challenges or resistance to procedures. This may be exhibited openly or through passive behaviour such as minimal effort or withdrawal from collaborative learning. Johnson and Johnson see this as a natural part of the development process, a move towards independence, which should be dealt with in an open and accepting way. They recommend smoothing, reasoning and mediating while recognizing learner autonomy and individuality. It is important to repair and rebuild relationships following intervention, to prevent the erosion of relationships and damage to self-esteem (Rogers 2004).

Committing to goals, procedures and other members and *functioning maturely and productively* are the next stages of Johnson and Johnsons' model. In a similar way to the *norming and performing* phases of Tuckman and Jensen, norms are established and cohesion and commitment increased, and the group works effectively and productively. Learners become intrinsically motivated to provide support and assistance to each other and regard the group as *their* group, not the tutor's. Positive relationships exist between the learners themselves and with the teacher.

For groups that have matured into cohesive, effective units where strong friendships and emotional bonds have been formed, the final phase of *terminating* (Johnson and Johnson 2007) or *adjourning* (Tuckman and Jensen 1977) can be accompanied with some sadness. The teacher needs to recognize this and provide closure for the group in some way. Review and evaluation exercises, acknowledgement and celebration of success and achievement and opportunities to 'say goodbye' can all be valuable at this stage.

Attention to group management and the building of positive relationships between all learners can play an important part in promoting effective learning. In any group there is a complex play of relationships, which may result in an 'emotional swirl' (Jacques and Salmon (2007:11). This should not be underestimated by the tutor and indeed it needs to be proactively managed to develop and maintain a positive group culture.

Managing challenging behaviour

Different age groups may present different forms of challenging behaviour and although most problems tend to be associated with younger learners, some adults can also be difficult and demanding. Challenging behaviour includes the following:

- behaviour that disrupts routine teaching to an extent that challenges the teacher's resources and concentration of other learners; this may not be violent, offensive or dangerous, simply disruptive
- behaviour that is offensive or violent, interfering with routine activity
- offending behaviour, including offending in the criminal sense, which bullies or ridicules fellow learners and creates an intimidating environment
- extreme passivity or non-engagement in learning
- intermittent patterns of attendance.

(LSDA 2007: 2)

As a starting point, it is essential to analyse the causes of disruption. Jacques and Salmon (2007) suggest that many incidents are a consequence of a lack of structure in sessions. Transitions between activities should not leave gaps which learners can exploit to pursue their own agenda. Providing learners with appropriate tasks will also reduce opportunities for disruption. Overtly challenging behaviour can indicate disengagement from learning; it can also be a signal that learners are not placed on the most appropriate programme, or that the level of learning is inappropriate. Some learners may seek attention through misbehaviour. For some young people, 'egos are much more insecure and fragile than in fully fledged adults' (Blum 2001: 7). As a result of such factors, learners may respond to certain situations with overt resistance, avoidance, 'herd' behaviour or inertia.

Gibbs (1995) suggests three practical strategies for meeting the challenges of group management:

1   *Don't start from here*. This refers to problems which may arise because action was not taken earlier. For example, ground rules may not have been established, or initial assessment may have been ineffective.

2   *Use structures*. Both content and methods need to be structured effectively; planning and preparation are important. In addition, prior consideration of classroom organization will promote the smooth running of a lesson, including protocols for different types of work which take account of health and safety (Vizard 2007: 25).

3   *Make leadership interventions.* These are the things which teachers say and do, for example to redirect groups or defuse certain situations. Larger groups may need more emphatic intervention. Problems in groups can become part of a group culture which, if not dealt with promptly, can be very hard to change. Cliques may form and teachers need to discourage them.

First impressions with a group are important, to 'make a significant initial impact on students and to get initial interactions right' (Vizard 2007: 22). Although approaches may vary, parameters of acceptable behaviour need to be established as outlined above. Rules and routines should identify unacceptable behaviours, for example, using mobile phones; racist, sexist or other inappropriate language; and unexplained lateness. It is useful to note the difference between an authoritarian approach with imposed rules and a democratic one in which boundaries are established by both teachers and learners. Leadbeater (2005) cautions that some learners with challenging behaviour may not be able to articulate their expectations, as immediate concerns may dominate their thinking. Such learners may express anger or discontent loudly as a way of being 'heard'. However, the underlying message and cause should also be heeded, and help provided to examine and change behaviour. Vizard (2007) notes that students are often told not to behave in a certain way but are not given the skills and strategies necessary to manage their feelings and behaviour in a more positive manner.

To prevent unwanted behaviour, teachers should appreciate the importance of non-verbal communication and body language. Being aware of 'psychological geography' (Vizard 2007) and frequently moving around the classroom in a confident manner are characteristics of an effective teacher – although care should be taken not to over-control students who might otherwise settle down to work if their attention-seeking behaviour is not rewarded. Eye contact can indicate awareness of individual learners. Overtly scanning the class, using a sweeping, 'lighthouse' effect to include all learners in the field of vision, can also be effective.

It is helpful to identify in advance learner behaviour that may cause concern and to research and practise strategies. Vizard (2007: 139) suggests preparing a 'script' for response to particular types of behaviour, as 'the choice of words we use and how we say them influence the management of behaviour'. He emphasizes the need to remain assertive, giving clear instructions and avoiding emotional language, pleading or apologetic delivery. Cowley (2003) suggests that teachers will benefit from knowing exactly what they want and expect from learners (although the title of her book indicates that teacher expectations can be negative), and from maintaining a psychological distance to retain feelings of control and prevent emotional reactions. In some situations, a 'blocking' and 'broken record' technique can be helpful. 'Blocking' involves ignoring a comment made by a student while repeating a redirecting statement like a 'broken record'. Reprimands should be in private, as this removes the audience which some learners may seek, and sanctions should be applied consistently.

Learners should be aware of the consequences and sanctions embedded in institutional policies on disruptive behaviour. Allowing time for learners to conform and comply with instructions can be helpful and will give both parties some 'time out'.

Direct confrontations should be avoided wherever possible as they may cause an already difficult situation to escalate. When dealing with challenging behaviour, it is advisable to avoid making personal comments and to criticize the behaviour, not the person. Wallace (2002b) draws attention to positive and negative styles used by teachers to motivate and control challenging students (see Table 10.3). In particular, teachers should model good behaviour, reinforce positive behaviour in students through praise, and maintain standards of respect and politeness towards students.

Table 10.3 Positive and negative approaches to motivating learners

Positive teacher behaviours	Negative teacher behaviours
Motivates with praise and trust	Motivates with fear for the present or future
Rewards students to motivate them	Indifferent to learners' achievements
Focuses on the goals and expectations of learners	Focuses on own goals
Manages own behaviour effectively	Loses self-control
Builds learners' self-esteem	Undermines learners' self-esteem
Shows empathy with learners	Behaves insensitively towards learners

Source: Adapted from Wallace (2002b)

Tutorials and pastoral support

In post-compulsory education, tutorials focus on the academic and pastoral requirements of learners, as well as promoting retention, attendance and punctuality. In many cases, personal tutors will also teach their students in subject classes, generating further insight into their academic progress and pastoral needs but also blurring the boundaries between roles and possibly compromising the tutorial relationship. Tutors need to develop and demonstrate a wide range of qualities and skills to manage tutorials; being a supportive and empathic listener is important, but on occasion poor behaviour or attendance may have to be challenged.

The amount of time devoted to tutorial activity varies; for full-time students, one hour per week is common but part-time students may have significantly less. To ensure consistent tutorial support, many institutions use a common scheme of work for all groups of students. This will begin with an induction period, followed by other tutorials focusing on pastoral and academic support. Induction may be the first opportunity for students to bond with each other. Often, they are anxious about starting the course, making new friends and coping with the transition from school, college or a previous job. In higher education, this may be the first time the student has lived away from home. Icebreaker activities can be used to develop peer bonding and support, which in turn, will help to improve retention and attendance. Often, team-building events away from the college environment are organized.

Induction is also the best time to establish ground rules about conduct, attendance and punctuality, and completion of work. Treasure hunts and quizzes can be used to introduce and consolidate information about the institution and course requirements.

Induction will also provide an opportunity to inform students about enrichment activities, and the use of facilities such as library, IT and learning support. At this stage, students may also be given diagnostic assessments to identify learning support needs.

Pastoral support throughout the course will be one of the key roles of the personal tutor. Activities may focus on issues such as developing research skills, revision techniques and time management, along with careers tutorials dealing with CV writing and educational or job applications. Pastoral support will also include one-to-one supervision, requiring the tutor to establish a supportive and trusting relationship with their students. However, knowing where the tutorial role ends and specialists need to be involved is important. Unless a personal tutor is sure of their competence, it is best to refer complex issues to an appropriate support service, or involve more senior colleagues. Martinez and Munday (1998) identify the importance of supporting inexperienced tutors through staff development and sharing good practice within a course team.

Personal tutors will often be the first point of contact for students, and may offer the help and advice needed to prevent an unhappy student from dropping out. Designated times for individual tutorials will help to manage the demands on tutors, especially with large tutorial groups. Some tutors use a virtual learning environment to supplement tutorials, especially with part-time students, although students still favour face-to-face contact (Sweeney et al. 2004). Students may be encouraged to develop links within the tutorial group through social networking sites such as MySpace and Facebook.

Monitoring retention, attendance and punctuality are important tutorial roles and diligence in following up attendance or punctuality issues is essential. Students who attend irregularly soon get behind and are highly likely to fail or leave the course. In higher education, monitoring attendance is not so straightforward, as students are often living away from home and are expected to be more responsible for their actions. However, it is still important to track poor attendance as this could be the result of underlying personal problems; for the mature student, it could be the effect of combining the course with the demands of family life. Records should be kept of any calls or meetings, as these may be needed if the student is suspended or withdrawn from the course.

In some courses, an individual learning plan is a formal part of tutorial support and is used to set targets and identify learning needs. Individual learning plans are initiated early in the course, and then regularly reviewed and updated to monitor progress; in some courses, they are updated weekly or even after each learning session. When reviewing an individual learning plan, discussion should include progress since the last review and learning support needs, as well as attendance and the balance between study and social life.

11

Teaching with technology

Liz Bennett, Alison Iredale and Cheryl Reynolds

In this chapter:

- Concepts of learning technology
- Technologies for learning
- The value of learning with technology
- Designing for learning with technology
- Safety in using technology

The central concern of this chapter is the impact of newer technologies upon educational practices. That today's students are not the same as yesterday's is self-evident from how they communicate with one another, create and maintain friendships or engage in study. They are 'digital natives' (Prensky 2001), having grown up in a world pervaded by technology. If the medium is the message, the message is discursive, interactive, engaging and mobile. They are as likely to shape what they find on the Internet as well as to absorb it, to re-purpose information tools to their own ends and to find ways of exploiting technology that subvert its original intentions.

In this context, a balanced approach to the educational use of technology can be a great asset to the teacher. A willingness to try new tools, while remaining sceptical about their educational value, means that judgements about their effectiveness can be made from a position of understanding. There is an inherent semiotic coherence to contemporary software – in other words, the symbolic systems used to represent choices and actions are largely uniform across many applications. One gains an instinctive understanding of how a new application is likely to work, based on the things one has tried in the past. Grappling with new technologies becomes easier the more one engages with them, helping to develop confidence and transferable skills. Immersion appears to be the best way to transform oneself from 'digital immigrant' to 'digital native'.

An awareness of how technology impacts upon young people can therefore help us to exploit this technology to educational ends. Critical reflection upon the impact of technology on the learning process is also valuable as it puts the emphasis in the right place; on the learner rather than inside the computer. This chapter introduces some technologies for supporting learning and considers important factors in redesigning or adapting approaches to learning when using technology.

Concepts of learning technology

A range of concepts and terminology has emerged to describe the application of technology to learning (see Box 11.1). The existence of different terms for more or less the same thing indicates that this is a developing field where concepts are being refined and adapted. In this chapter, we define *e-learning* as 'any learning that uses ICT'. This definition includes learning that takes place in the classroom and learning at a distance. However, the distinction between face-to-face and distance learning is being blurred by the use of technology. Traditionally, distance learning involved studying on one's own (perhaps occasionally attending a tutorial) whereas classroom-based learning involved working with others but with the pace of the lesson dictated by the teacher. With the advent of the Internet, distance learning students may be working on a web-based group project or communicating with other students and tutors online. Even within a classroom setting, students may be working at their own pace – for example, using a laptop computer to access learning materials or to search the web for ideas and resources. This blurring of the boundaries between classroom-based and distance learning is part of the transformative potential of technology (HEFCE 2005; BECTA 2008a).

Thompson (2007: 52) argues that the term 'e-learning' is problematic because it limits our ability to conceptualize the subject. Clearly, learning is multifaceted, involving a delicate interplay between a range of factors – including national policies, institutional policies and practices, students' characteristics, teachers' skills and curriculum requirements. The use of the term e-learning creates a mystique,

---

Box 11.1 Definitions of terms relating to learning with technology

Learning technologies (LT) Technologies used to support and potentially enhance learning.

Technology supported learning The use of technology to support the learning process. This term places emphasis on the learning process which technology is trying to facilitate.

Technology enhanced learning The use of technology to improve the student's experience of the learning process. The term places emphasis on the benefits that can arise from use of technology.

Distributed learning This term focuses on remote delivery of learning or learning materials although it may incorporate some face-to-face elements as well.

Flexible learning Used often in conjunction with distributed learning; for example flexible distributed learning (FDL). Flexible distance learning means that some aspects of a course are delivered remotely.

Distance learning A term used when *all* the mandatory aspects of a learning programme are delivered remotely.

Blended learning This term is most commonly used to reflect systematic combination of delivery models that includes both face-to-face and online learning.

suggesting that the process of e-learning is new and different. This chapter analyses the various factors affecting the success of e-learning and suggests that learning with technology depends on getting the balance of these factors right – taking into account the particular context in which learning is taking place.

Technologies for learning

This section introduces some of the learning technologies currently available. Care is needed to avoid focusing on technology itself rather than on *how it can be used* to enhance learning. First, the technologies are merely tools, and concentrating on tools gives them a status that distracts from the principles underpinning their use. Second, technology can be promoted for its own sake rather than to add something useful and meaningful for the learner. A superficially attractive point of view argues that, to implement successfully a form of learning with technology, one must try out the tool in the classroom in order to evaluate and reflect upon the experience. However, this approach may be argued to be technocentric rather than pedagogical. An alternative viewpoint is that redesigning learning to use technology should be driven by pedagogy, considering students' needs, learning outcomes and other curriculum factors.

Table 11.1 overleaf outlines some of the web-based tools available for teaching and learning, indicating the *affordance* of each tool – that is, the role for which it is most obviously suited. However, the notion of affordance is problematic – is it a property of the tool or of the way it is used? An affordance is really a socially constructed property, and as a tool is used in new and imaginative ways, its affordances can change. With this proviso, Table 11.1 provides a useful starting point for understanding some tools for learning technology.

Table 11.2 overleaf provides another way to conceptualize e-learning tools by considering the type of interaction they afford. The table categorizes the tools according to the numbers of people involved in using the tool, for example, one-to-one may involve a single tutor being in contact with a student. The tools are also grouped by whether they operate synchronously or asynchronously. A *synchronous* activity requires users to be involved all at the same time, whereas an *asynchronous* activity does not. This important distinction clearly applies to the affordances of a tool: synchronous tools facilitate an immediate response but they also require more organization, whereas an asynchronous activity does not require the same commitment. In addition, the nature of the interactions is significantly different because of the temporal separation involved in asynchronous activities.

Finally, Table 11.3 on page 147 matches some pedagogical approaches to some of the technological tools introduced above. The mapping is indicative, as it is possible to apply the tools in different ways. Indeed, this chapter argues that the success of a particular learning activity depends on a number of factors rather than the particular tool being used.

Virtual learning environments (VLEs) consist of a number of the tools outlined in Table 11.1 built into a single web-based package. Chapter 12 examines VLEs and their use in more detail. Web tools which support user contributions, for example social networking tools, blogs, wikis and content sharing systems such as YouTube

Table 11.1 Web-based tools available for teaching and learning

Tool and explanation	Possible affordances
Asynchronous, text-based communication Users can post, read and respond to messages without being online at the same time (for example, discussion forums or message boards).	Record keeping in group work; learning through discussion of course topics
Wiki A website which can be edited by users.	Production of a shared resource e.g. a collaborative project
Blog An online diary where users can post entries in date order.	Reflective diary
Podcast An audio or enhanced audio file that is *syndicated*, i.e. automatically sent to a user's computer.	Delivery of lecture material; learning offsite e.g. field work
Voice over Internet Protocol (VoIP) Internet-based phone technology such as Skype.	Tool for mutual support and for voice-based communication
Chat or instant messaging Texting over the Internet by means of networks such as MSN.	Informal discussions to enhance or support learning
Virtual Classroom Combines a number of tools, such as chat, VoIP, file sharing in one application. For example Elluminate, Wimba.	Tutorials; collaborating on a project
Massively multiplayer virtual world (MMVW) An online 3D environment populated by 'avatars' – representations of human or animal form. Examples include Second Life.	Modelling real world scenarios, for example, marketing, fashion shows; online role-play
Repository A storage area for digital files that enables sharing of resources.	Finding teaching resources

Table 11.2 Collaborative tools available for learning

Type of interaction	Asynchronous	Synchronous
One-to-one, for student support or tutorials	Email; blog	Telephone; VoIP; chat
One-to-many, for teacher-led activities or group learning	Email; blog; Discussion forum; Podcast	Chat; Virtual Classroom tools; VoIP; MMVW
Many-to-many, for collaborative projects or sharing resources	Wiki; repository	MMVW; Virtual Classroom tools; VoIP

Table 11.3: Mapping technologies against approaches to teaching and learning

Pedagogic approaches	Examples of technologies
Problem-based learning	World Wide Web (activities such as web quests), online resources such as data bases, discussion boards, email groups
Resource-based learning	World Wide Web (activities such as online treasure hunts), online resources such as data bases
Contributing student model (Collis and Moonen 2001: 88)	Wiki, discussion boards, email groups
Reflective learning	Blog
Community of practice/socio-cultural learning	Discussion board, blog, wiki, chat, virtual world
Collaborative learning	Discussion board, blog, wiki
Content led learning	VLE content area, virtual classroom

and Flickr are generically referred to as web 2.0 tools. The importance of these tools is in the way that they change students' perception of and relationship to knowledge; they also are discussed in Chapter 12.

The value of learning with technology

There are many reported benefits of using technology to support learning. Its transformative potential is frequently mentioned in policy documents; for example, the *Technology Strategy for Further Education, Skills and Regeneration* refers to a 'vision of further education transformed by the confident use of technology' (BECTA 2008a: 5). However, what this transformation would entail is often left unclear. One of the few such explanations is contained in the Higher Education Funding Council for England's (HEFCE) e-learning strategy, which sets out the potential for 'using technology to transform higher education into a more student-focused and flexible system, as part of lifelong learning for all who can benefit' (HEFCE 2005: 5). Thus, student-centredness and flexibility are identified as key elements of learning with technology.

The *Technology Strategy* (BECTA 2008a) suggests that building technology into the curriculum improves engagement, retention and progression, accelerates learning and promotes more efficient teaching. In particular:

- Effective use of ICT can personalize learning by enabling greater learner choice within the curriculum, improved assessment and more learner-directed teaching.
- Technology can facilitate more effective assessment by making it easier for learners to be more involved in target-setting and for teachers to give individualized feedback.

E-learning may provide the opportunity for learners to revisit and absorb key concepts in their own time and at their own pace, in a personalized way, and linked to their individual learning preferences and preparedness. Other evidence for the value of e-learning comes from the Joint Information Systems Committee (JISC), a government-funded body whose role is to promote learning technologies within the HE and FE sectors. Their work identifies six key benefits:

- Connectivity – access to information is available on a global scale.
- Flexibility – learning can take place at any time, in any place, and allows students to reflect and to revisit material.
- Interactivity – assessment of learning can be immediate and autonomous.
- Collaboration – the use of discussion tools can support collaborative learning beyond the classroom.
- Extended opportunities – additional e-content can reinforce and extend classroom-based learning.
- Motivation – multimedia resources can make learning fun.

(JISC 2004: 7)

Another JISC-funded study examined the impact and possible benefits of using e-learning in 16 universities. Tutors in the same subject area at different institutions drew up case studies describing and analysing the use of e-learning. They also considered the potential benefits of e-learning, grouping them under six main headings:

1 Cost-saving and resource efficiency
2 Recruitment and retention
3 Employability skills
4 Achievement
5 Widening participation
6 Support for students with learning difficulties or disabilities

(JISC Infonet 2008: 14–26)

Other potential benefits included enhanced reputation, invigoration of teaching, changes to institutional policy and reinforcing face-to-face learning. The project report provides a succinct statement of the potential of e-learning:

> The most fundamental point to come out of all of the case studies is that the appropriate use of technology is leading to significant improvements in learning and teaching across the sector and that this is translating into improved satisfaction, retention and achievement. e-Learning is facilitating the expansion of the sector [and] is allowing broadly the same numbers of staff to educate a larger and more diverse student body

(JISC Infonet 2008: 33)

However, other studies have found insufficient evidence to make unequivocal statements about the impact of technology on learning (Twining et al. 2006; Condie and

Munro 2007). These studies conclude that there are many factors which impact on the success or otherwise of learning with technology. The context in which learning takes place and support within the organization are at least as important as the nature of the technology used.

Designing for learning with technology

Boud et al. (1993: 8–16) identify five propositions about learning from experience (see also Chapter 8):

1   Experience is the foundation of, and the stimulus for, learning.
2   Learners actively construct their own experience.
3   Learning is a holistic process.
4   Learning is socially and culturally constructed.
5   Learning is influenced by the socio-emotional context in which it occurs.

These propositions can help to frame a pedagogical basis for e-learning, and underpin much of the following discussion. Some studies point to the dangers of evaluating the success or failure of learning technology through the measurement of student performance (Alexander and McKenzie 1998), when it is the quality of the learning experience which is pivotal. Context is therefore crucial to understanding what makes e-learning successful and the first step in using technology to support learning is to assess the learning environment, including the needs and characteristics of the learners and the skills and attitudes of the teacher – as well as considering relevant national and local agendas.

Learners

Several recent studies explore the confidence with which people use technology. For example, a study of young people aged 16–18 (JISC 2007) found that they expected it to be used within learning. Perhaps surprisingly, many older people have similar attitudes. Creanor et al. (2006: 27) found that 'despite differences in gender, age, educational background and learning context, the learners' attitudes and opinions display marked similarities in several aspects'. Students' confidence in using technology, and their ability to select appropriate technology, are also reflected in their expectations of learning: 'They believe that technology should be used to enhance their learning and are clear that they will not engage with it if they feel it is not to their personal benefit' (Creanor et al. 2006: 26). This is echoed in the JISC study mentioned above 'They expect it [technology] to be just as present in their school life as it is at home' (JISC 2007: 29).

Developments in technology may have changed learners' attitudes to knowledge being conveyed in a didactic way. Furthermore, e-learning provides an opportunity to focus on tacit as well as explicit knowledge. Whereas explicit knowledge is largely determined, conceptual and representational, tacit knowledge is relatively shifting and uncertain and depends on a shared or a distributed understanding. Learning the rules about a subject requires a different set of skills and attributes than learning how to become a competent practitioner in the field, and it is here that the leap from explicit to tacit knowledge can be supported by e-learning. There is a need to engage learners not just with representations of explicit knowledge, but with the interface between theory and practice. Opportunities to solve real problems, finding, sharing and using information in a practical activity can all be supported by e-learning.

It has been suggested that the growth in digital technologies is changing the characteristics of young learners. For example, Prensky (2001) defines 'digital natives' as a generation that has grown up with digital technology, operating at 'twitch speed', and performing multiple activities simultaneously. Oblinger and Oblinger (2005) characterize net generation learners ('net genners') as digitally literate, Internet familiar and connected via networked media. They argue that such learners are used to immediate responses, prefer experiential learning and teamwork, crave interactivity in image rich environments and have a preference 'for structure rather than ambiguity' (2005: 27). However, this is not to suggest that all learners operate in this way or that face-to-face contact with a tutor is obsolete; on the contrary, such interactions are still accepted as vital to the learning process (Oblinger and Oblinger 2005; Creanor et al. 2006).

Although the claims made for the existence of a 'digital generation' are thought-provoking, they are in the end assumptions and should not be used to overlay individual differences with stereotypes. Learner identities, their degree of cultural capital and the contexts in which learning takes place often frustrate attempts to generalize research findings; it is important to view the learner and their approach to learning as fundamental to the success or otherwise of learning technology strategies. Entwistle and Ramsden (1983) argue that it is the experience based on practice or engaging actively with a specific task which enables learning rather than the design of the learning, and this applies irrespective of whether the learning occurs in a traditional curriculum design or in distance learning using a virtual learning space.

Teachers

Just as student attitudes and skills towards technology are key factors in the adoption of a new approach to learning, it can be argued that the teacher skills, knowledge and commitment are even more crucial. Masterman and Vogel (2007: 60), in their study of how teachers approach VLE tools, conclude that 'the process of design for learning has painted a complex composite picture that has as much to do with the dispositions and preferences of individual practitioners, their subject domains and the community pressures on them as with the availability and affordances of the tools used'. This understanding of one's own attitudes to learning technologies is a key component to their successful use in the classroom.

Dispositions towards the adoption of technology can vary considerably, and the following (somewhat light-hearted) typology may be helpful:

- The 'expert' knows a lot about learning technology but may lack experience of teaching. Their knowledge may not be embedded in an understanding of classroom subtleties.

- The 'enthusiast' has a positive approach to new technologies, but may lack critical awareness.

- The 'Luddite' has an inherent resistance to change. This may provide a critical test of new ideas; however, the Luddite may resist change out of hand, whatever the evidence in its favour.

A further type of response, perhaps with a more balanced and positive perspective, is the 'agile adopter' – the practitioner who is well grounded in existing practice but alive to experimentation with new technologies and to sharing them with colleagues. The notion of being alive to experimentation is echoed by Masterman and Vogel (2007: 61), who found that one of the conditions for effective adoption of e-learning is 'willingness on the part of teachers to experiment . . . [and] creativity in identifying opportunities to broaden their approach'. Chapter 12 explores in more detail the skills and knowledge required by teachers for e-learning.

National initiatives

There have been a number of national strategies related to technology to support learning produced by Government bodies and funding bodies. *Harnessing Technology* (DfES 2005d), also referred to as the Government's e-learning strategy, is an overarching document for schools, colleges, universities and children's centres. Other reports respond to this strategy in the context of FE (BECTA 2008a) and HE (HEFCE 2005). All make the case for e-learning in terms of how it can help institutions deliver their strategic aims. Hence the strategy for higher education focuses on meeting a greater diversity of student needs, more flexibility in provision, personalizing the learner's experience of HE, and supporting transitions between school or college and HE. For the FE system, the strategic aims also relate to personalization, flexibility and choice; however, they focus on purposes of more immediate relevance to learning and skills than to higher education such as employability and social inclusion.

Institutional policies and practices

The nature of the organization and how it supports innovation is a key factor in the successful adoption of e-learning (Condie and Munroe 2007; Masterman and Vogel 2008: 61). Hence, in order to make successful changes to practice, it is important for practitioners to understand their role within their organization, its limits and the level of support that they enjoy. Jones (2007: 177) has described three layers that affect the design of learning activities – macro, meso and micro:

- *Macro* level is beyond the control of the individual practitioner, for instance the adoption of a particular VLE. Decisions at this level usually take time to enact, and occur at a national or institutional level.

- *Meso* level – the layer beyond immediate classroom practice and involving medium-term planning and interaction with close colleagues. This is the layer most appropriate for the design of learning activities.

- *Micro* level – the interactions in the classroom. While within the control of the practitioner, the micro level is highly context-specific.

Using Jones's three levels it is possible to approach pedagogical changes using technology by focusing on the meso level and to recognize what is beyond the control of individual practitioners. Jones argues that the key to successful e-learning is to focus design on the medium term, helping to ensure that the detailed classroom or online practice is coherent with the intended outcomes of the programme or module.

Mason (1998) argues that, to maximize the success of changes to learning methods, e-learning design should be approached at the level of the whole course rather than smaller units of study such as modules. There are many reasons for this, not least that the expectations of learners are formed by their whole experience of study. It is very difficult to implement radical changes that require students to work in different ways if these changes subvert the accepted norms to which students are exposed in the rest of their studies. A whole-course redesign ensures that new approaches to learning are embedded within an overarching learning and assessment strategy.

Safety in using technology

The safe use of ICT for young people or vulnerable adults is a critical issue in institutional policy. As well as the transformative possibilities explored in this chapter, new technology carries with it a number of risks. Children and vulnerable adults may be exposed to a range of online dangers including increased exposure to sexually inappropriate content, contributions to negative beliefs and attitudes, cyber-bullying and access to sites which may promote harmful behaviours (Byron 2008). Educators have a duty of care towards young people and children in particular and towards the well-being of all learners. This section outlines the legislative framework surrounding the use of ICT, discusses some practical challenges posed by the Internet and suggests how they might be addressed. As the FE system increasingly welcomes children in the 14–16 age range to a range of provision, this is a topical issue for practitioners.

The Children Act 2004 is the main legislative framework for strategies for improving children's lives, with the overall aim of encouraging integrated services for children, and improving multi-agency working. The Act underpins *Every Child Matters* (DfES 2005e), which focuses on five key outcomes for every child and young person, including 'staying safe'. Young people must be safe from maltreatment, neglect, violence and sexual exploitation; accidental injury and death; bullying and discrimination; crime and anti-social behaviour in and out of school; and be secure, stable and cared for. These aspects of safety apply equally to the digital world as to the physical one. The challenge is heightened as younger people are taught in colleges and the distinctions between the more adult-orientated world of college and school are blurred.

The Byron Review (Byron 2008) emphasizes the need for an 'e-safety agenda'. One of its conclusions is that that e-safety is an institutional issue and is not only the domain of those who teach ICT (BECTA 2008b: 4). Byron recommends that e-safety education and digital literacy development should continue throughout life, that parents should be supported in understanding the issues and risks associated with children's use of digital technologies and that educational establishments have policies and procedures on e-safety. Teachers and support staff should be appropriately trained and ITT courses should embed e-safety training.

For the practitioner, e-safety translates into a number of responsibilities and challenges. The main responsibility is to be aware of the possible dangers and to promote safe use with learners. Not only do tutors need to ensure that they work within institutional policies, but they should also help to shape these policies so that access to valuable resources is retained where possible.

12

E-tutoring

Liz Bennett and Andrew Youde

In this chapter:

- E-learning models
- E-tutoring technologies and skills
- Conclusion

This chapter discusses support for learners studying at a distance or within blended delivery models. Writing on theory and practice in distance education, Holmberg (1989: 163) states that 'learning is encouraged by frequent communication with fellow humans interested in study'. The feeling of belonging – to a course or institution – is just as important as discussions about the subject being studied. Wenger (1998) explains that learning is derived from participation in a community of practitioners, the shared practice being central to the community and helping to form relationships and develop identities. Moore's (1980) notion of *transactional presence* refers to the connectedness a student feels to the course and tutor. Even students working online can still feel part of a community if such a relationship has developed. The strategies discussed in this chapter will help to foster transactional presence and facilitate the development of communities of practice among students.

E-learning models

This chapter draws on the work of Salmon (2003) and Laurillard (2002) to analyse and evaluate e-learning and e-tutoring. Although their models focus on different aspects of e-learning, both stress the value of communication with tutors and peers as well as interactivity in the learning process.

Salmon's five stage model

This model aids the design of online courses as well as describing the stages of learning, interactivity and socialization through which students and tutors will progress. The stages include roles and actions for the tutor and are usually developed around a VLE with asynchronous communication facilities (see Chapter 11 for a discussion of these terms). Other educational technologies such as chat, blogs and e-portfolios can be incorporated into a course designed around this model. The five stages are discussed below.

Access and motivation: The main focus of this stage is for students to access and explore the online system. Individual support from the tutor will be required, particularly for those students unfamiliar with this type of learning, as well as technical support to help resolve difficulties with access. The tutor should motivate and encourage students by welcoming them, explaining the value of participation and providing an overview of course delivery and assessment.

Online socialization: In this stage, the aim is to establish a community of practice. The tutor should provide opportunities for socialization, allowing students to develop a relationship with their peers and to understand the course requirements. Encouraging student participation is an important tutor role at this stage; Mason and Bacsich (1998) suggest that a significant number of students only read messages, with others not engaging at all. Initially, students can be encouraged simply to introduce themselves in the online environment, with course-specific activities being introduced gradually. Tutors can monitor student contributions and communicate individually with those not participating. When an understanding of the culture, technology and content of the online environment has been developed, students will begin to feel confident enough to contribute.

Information exchange: In this stage, students 'start to appreciate the broad range of information available online' (Salmon 2003: 38), while exploring course materials and undertaking learning activities. The tutor's role is support, facilitation and generally responding to individual queries. However, ensuring that all students are participating in the course and developing online relationships remains important. Personal responses to students during this stage can be very motivating, particularly if they feel their contributions are valued. Tutors can also offer alternative perspectives and identify further avenues of research.

Knowledge construction: The previous stages now provide a scaffold for learners to relate the course content to their personal circumstances, enabling them to construct their own meanings. Students will now be learning from each other, appreciating different perspectives through frequent interactions. The tutor should be able to step back and oversee the debate. However, there is still a very important role to play in what Feenberg (1989) calls 'weaving'. This is the act of pulling the debate together and can include summarizing general themes, linking similar viewpoints, and relating personal experiences to theories previously studied.

Development: Salmon highlights the importance of this stage as it supports the metacognitive process which 'promotes integration and application of learning experiences' (Salmon 2003: 38). Students need less support from tutors, with the most able students acting as moderators for the more inexperienced ones. The tutor's role is to develop critical thinking within the group and develop activities, such as evaluating a piece of student work, to support this. During this stage it is natural for the students to reflect, both on their learning throughout the course but also on the online learning experience.

There are limitations to all models of learning and Salmon's is no exception. It does not acknowledge differing learning styles and assumes that students cannot be successful while working independently from their peers (Moule 2007). It will be more difficult for part-time students to fully engage in the socialization process as other demands will restrict the time they can commit to study. Creanor (2002) explains that for a tutor to maintain participation in online courses is difficult, and there is a danger of nominally student-centred activities becoming tutor led. This can increase the tutor's workload and demotivate both tutor and students. In order to prevent this she argues that 'tutors may require a more thorough grasp of pedagogical principles than is conventionally required' (Creanor 2002: 66).

Laurillard's conversational framework

Laurillard's (2002) framework was designed for HE, but is just as applicable elsewhere in lifelong learning. It characterizes the teaching-learning process as an iterative conversation in a similar fashion to Kolb's experiential learning cycle. The framework outlines the dialogic relationships between the teacher and student and includes:

- Discursive processes – description of topic goal.
- Adaptive processes – internal to both teacher and student, adapts actions to task level;
- Interactive processes – activities to achieve task goal.
- Reflective processes – internal to both teacher and student, reflect on activity's achievement of topic goal.

The framework represents both a theory of learning and a design model for online and blended educational environments. It includes 12 types of interactions, which are seen as essential to the learning process and are based around the four process types outlined above (see Figure 12.1).

Laurillard considers that media forms have different affordances (see Chapter 11), and categorizes them into five types which mediate learning in different ways: narrative, interactive, communicative, adaptive and productive. Examples of these media forms are outlined in Table 12.1 together with the learning experiences they support.

The model allows a framework for engaging learners in online discussions and allows a tutor to evaluate the scope and variety of communications in a course. Laurillard emphasizes the importance of student feedback in the learning process but notes that it can be limited in HE environments. More generally, the conversational framework requires a level of dialogue and feedback that can be difficult to maintain with the large groups commonly found in HE and in some FE environments.

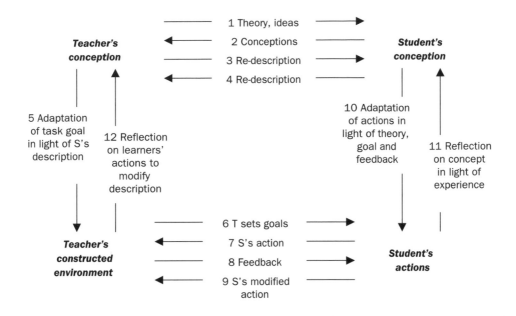

Figure 12.1 Laurillard's conversational framework
Source: Laurillard (2002: 87)

Table 12.1 Media forms and their affordances

Media forms	Learning experience	Educational technologies
Narrative	Attending, apprehending	Lecture, TV, DVD
Interactive	Investigating, exploring	CD Rom, web resources
Communicative	Discussing, debating	Discussion boards, chat
Adaptive	Experimenting, practising	Simulation
Productive	Articulating, expressing	Producing a resource, blog entries

Source: Laurillard (2002: 90)

E-tutoring technologies and skills

In this section a variety of learning technologies will be examined to outline their value to lecturers and tease out some of the 'e-tutoring' skills required to use them effectively.

Email

Email has the advantage of being freely available, either as an institutional facility or by signing up to a web-based provider. Uses of email in teaching include answering course enquiries, supplying course information or enrolment forms, answering queries from course members and submission of assignments by students. Email also provides a convenient way of contacting absentees and sending work to students who miss a class.

MacDonald and McAteer (2003) found that in both campus-based and distance learning courses email was frequently used for encouragement and assignment preparation. Supportive messages can be written to those who have not been in touch. Saved messages can allow tutors to write future communications in a more personal manner, for example, if a student has written to say they may not be in touch as they are moving house a tutor can use this at the start of any future message to ask if they have settled in well.

Email can also have a pedagogical role, for example in supporting tutorials and group work. Role play is an obvious group activity where students can adopt distinct email personas as they work together on a particular activity with their communications being saved for assessment. Video clips, images and audio content can illuminate email activities and hyperlinks can be used to distribute webquest (see p. 301) activities. As students and tutors can take time to compose messages, they are usually better informed and more clearly expressed than face-to-face discussions.

Some educational uses of email can be better addressed with different applications; for example, peer group work could arguably be better developed through a wiki. If a tutor is using email in a large part of their teaching then time management becomes important and different work patterns need to be developed. Responding to each message when it arrives can have an adverse effect on tutor efficiency. MacDonald and McAteer (2003) warn tutors about the pressure from students for quick responses and more individual attention. It is sensible to use the filters and rule features to direct incoming messages into particular folders and set time aside to deal with each folder. Tutors must take care when composing emails as it is very difficult to express, and therefore interpret, emotions. Comments intended to be humorous can be considered sarcastic or insulting. Correct punctuation, such as appropriate exclamation marks, can help students' understanding, as can 'emoticons' – graphic icons intended to convey particular feelings.

Webpage authoring

Even an inexperienced online tutor can now create quite sophisticated webpages. Word processing or presentation software will usually contain web-authoring functions that will convert the content into web format, to be accessed by students from email attachments and VLEs. A basic webpage could include some text to introduce a learning activity with hyperlinks to relevant websites for students to explore.

Laurillard (2002) warns that, without some structure to their learning, students can quickly become frustrated and demotivated and turn their attention elsewhere. There is little interactivity in basic webpages (Barker 2002) and this reduces their educational value, losing the potential multisensory richness of web resources. Webpages can be enhanced by embedding multimedia objects which are often freely available to download from the Internet. Comprehension exercises, for example, can be produced using any such object but sound and video make more use of the electronic environment and with a little imagination can offer rich learning experiences. When producing this type of material, hyperlinks to externally held media files help to prevent problems with copyright.

To structure student learning by means of a basic webpage, tutors can develop a 'webquest', defined by March (1997) as 'an inquiry activity that presents student groups with a challenging task, provides access to an abundance of usually online resources and scaffolds the learning process to prompt higher order thinking'. While webquests are susceptible to changes in external websites they can be linked to collaborative tools (for example, discussion boards and wikis) to allow an interactive aspect to the learning experience.

Asynchronous text-based communication systems

These include discussion forums, message boards and bulletin boards. The technology is widely used in online and blended learning environments and is frequently discussed in the literature (Weller et al. 2005). It forms the basis for Salmon's five-stage model and has become a frequent focus of debate. While they are a popular and widespread technology, these systems are often used ineffectively due to a 'lack of participation, resistance to participation, unfocused discussion, fractured discussion that is difficult to follow, manipulation by strongest member and so on' (Weller et al. 2005: 65). Webb et al. (2004) argue that passive or active participation in such systems is positively associated with meeting course learning outcomes, but highlight the importance of design, moderation, students' perceptions and the quality of dialogue in achieving this.

To use asynchronous systems effectively, it as advisable to follow a structure such as Salmon's model to progress students from writing introductory comments to a deep engagement with the course and the exchange of information. Topics for discussion should be clear and provide students with an opportunity to relate the materials to their own experience. Allowing opportunities for socialization can help a community of practice to develop but the difficulty in achieving this should not be underestimated. To encourage participation, contributions are often linked to formative and summative assessment. However, even with careful alignment of teaching and assessment, learners will often contribute strategically.

E-portfolios

In their most basic form, e-portfolios are an electronic storage system for students' assessments and reflections. They allow students to collate and display their work and include facilities to support reflective writing and personal development planning. Mason (2006: 30) argues that, to increase the pedagogical value of e-portfolio systems, 'course designers and tutors [should] promote a culture of reflection and self-assessment in order that the benefits of e-portfolio development can be realized'. To aid reflection, students should be encouraged to review periodically the content of their portfolios and distinguish current from out-of-date material. This process can be enriched by the use of hyperlinks within the portfolio to relate common themes across a course (Mason 2006), together with the comment and annotations tools available for student use. Tutors, peers and mentors can all participate in the evaluation of portfolios and provide feedback on the uploaded content and reflective writings.

Blogs and wikis

Blogs (the term is derived from 'web logs') are online diaries which can have quite wide pedagogical benefits. While they are usually text-based, they can also incorporate images and multimedia objects. A tutor's blog providing a brief summary of recent developments within a subject area can be a useful resource (Weller et al. 2005). For students, blogs can aid reflection and may be valuable in competence-based courses or to aid personal development planning. Blogs were initially developed as public documents; however, access can be restricted to participants on a specific course. Peer-assessment is possible, as students can be asked to comment on each others' blogs. Community blogs allow a number of participants to contribute, thus facilitating group work and aiding socialization in online environments. A tutor can monitor both individual and community blogs and provide feedback as necessary.

A wiki is similar to a blog in that it allows users to add content; however this can be edited by other users. These applications are freely available and simple to use. Their main pedagogical benefit is in supporting group work as students can collaborate on a project from a distance. Any changes made by an individual student are highlighted by the wiki, making it is easy to follow the project's development.

Chat/instant messaging

These technologies offer a synchronous and mainly text-based communication system that is freely available to both lecturers and students, either as part of an institutional VLE or a web-based application. While a chat system needs the user to open the program an instant messaging system runs continuously when a computer is in use. The pedagogical benefits of these systems are similar and can be roughly categorized into formal and informal aspects. The formal aspects involve tutors structuring the use of chat sessions around the course curriculum, usually specifying the topics for discussion. This tutorial approach (Barker 2002) can allow preparation time for all the participants and can be integrated into a formative assessment strategy. The number of participants must be chosen with care; with too many, the 'conversation' loses focus and becomes difficult to follow. Slow typists can find chat sessions frustrating as the 'conversation' may have moved on by the time they have composed their message. Tutors need to also be aware of the difficulties dyslexic students or those with poorer written English skills may encounter.

In addition to the tutorial approach, tutors can use chat as a drop-in session for individual support. Students find these sessions valuable given the speed of response, but tutors should be careful about the amount of time they are available, as this can impact on other activities. Informal chat sessions can involve tutors; however, peer-to-peer sessions foster informal learning communities and increase social interactions among the students. Nicholson (2002: 371) argues that chat can meet a need for social communication if this is not being met through other channels with a 'stronger sense of community'.

Mobile learning technologies

These include personal digital assistants (PDAs), mobile phones, wireless laptops and tablet PCs. Appropriate use of these technologies may increase the 'transactional presence' between students and their online tutor. For example, students working through course materials and exercises in a variety of locations can contact their tutors for support. Such quick communication can also benefit tutors as their students are close to their phones and email more frequently. Tutors should also be aware of the motivational benefits of these technologies as personal and motivational messages can quickly be received by students.

Mobile technologies are commonly associated with the use of *podcasts*. This is a file (audio, video or multimedia) that is downloaded from the Internet or VLE onto a computer (see Chapter 11). They can be played on a mobile device and in some instances on iPods and MP3 players. A common educational use of podcasting (defined as providing material online to download) is the recording of teaching sessions for absent students to review. There is little student interaction with podcasts and the tutor should be careful to complement their use with a variety of pedagogical approaches.

Virtual/managed learning environments

A virtual learning environment (VLE) is a software system combining a number of tools that are used systematically to deliver content online and facilitate learning (Weller 2007: 5). The particular tools available will vary and depend on the way they are implemented within a particular institution, but typically will include many of the synchronous and asynchronous tools discussed above and in Chapter 11, including discussion boards, a repository for learning resources (text-based and multimedia), email and blogs or wikis. They will also include specific areas for conferences (both synchronous and asynchronous), class lists and student homepages, assessment tools and grade books and will allow file upload for students' assessed work. A managed learning environment (MLE) will incorporate all the elements of a VLE together with the institution's student record system and other education management systems, such as attendance monitoring.

VLEs can enable tutors to improve the learning experience for students by utilizing communication and collaborative tools as well as assisting in the management and administration of the course. However, VLEs have been widely criticized for tending towards a linear, didactic and content focussed approach to learning (Weller 2007: 125). They lend themselves to being a repository for lecture slides and word-processed handouts and are often associated with behaviourist approaches. Nevertheless, as Weller argues, it is also possible to design learning activities within VLEs that reflect other models of learning – for instance constructivist, socio-cultural learning or resource-based learning (Weller 2007: 19).

Conclusion

This chapter has provided an overview of key theories in relation to e-tutoring and provided practical guidance for the effective utilization of some common educational technologies. The importance of the tutor in facilitating a successful online and blended learning experience cannot be underestimated. Smith (2004: 37) notes that in distance learning, 'Quality is influenced by the usefulness of feedback students receive on assignments and research work, the availability and accessibility of lecturers, and the promptness with which lecturers respond to and reply to students'. She emphasizes the importance of responding to questions with enthusiasm and the lecturer's ability to meet individual needs.

An online tutor must be able to foster a group identity, develop collaboration and link theory to personal experiences and practice (Creanor 2002; Salmon 2003). All the skills that lecturers in traditional classroom environments possess are essential; however, an online tutor does not have the benefit of non-verbal feedback (body language and facial expression for example). Therefore, a heightened knowledge of pedagogical principles and empathetic consideration of the students' learning environment will help an online tutor be successful.

13

Assessment

*Ros Ollin, Ron Thompson and
Jonathan Tummons*

In this chapter:

- The nature and purpose of assessment
- Assessment tasks
- Planning and designing assessment
- Summative, formative and ipsative assessment
- Providing feedback
- Norm-referenced and criterion-referenced assessment
- Validity and reliability
- Accrediting prior learning
- Moderation and standardization

The nature and purpose of assessment

Assessment often appears to be so embedded in our experience of education that we hardly stop to question its role. However, the importance of assessment lies not only in recognizing the attainments of learners. Interpretations of assessment – what it is, how it is done and what it means – are unavoidably bound up in broader assumptions about learning and teaching and may have profound individual, institutional and social consequences. Underlying the diversity of assessment processes is a variety of functions, both educational and social. These functions include the following.

Evaluation of the student's achievement

This is the most obvious reason for carrying out an assessment, and often the only one made explicit. We may wish to know whether learning outcomes have been achieved, or if the student is of the standard required to receive a certain grade. Sometimes, it is important to know how a student has performed in relation to their peers. Questions of this type are best answered at or near the end of a course of study, and require what is known as *summative* assessment. Alternatively, determining a student's development needs during a course or giving feedback designed to help the student to learn requires *formative* assessment. Unlike summative assessment, which would almost always be carried out formally using examinations or coursework, formative assessments can be informal as well as formal, and may be carried out during learning sessions.

Evaluation of the teacher or institution

Assessment may be used to provide information about a course, an individual teacher or the institution. The teacher may ask whether the learning objectives are appropriate – are they too easy or too difficult? Are the teaching methods effective? Such questions could aid reflection, or possibly inform the *appraisal* of the teacher by the institution. Assessment may also provide information relating to the *accountability* of the institution to outside organizations (such as funding or inspection bodies – see Chapter 21). Is the curriculum suitable? Is the institution effective and providing value for money?

Motivating students

Assessment, particularly in the form of external examinations, provides motivation and in particular assists in setting goals for students. Formal assessment of a curriculum area signals to students that it is important and is taken seriously both by teachers and by awarding bodies. The 'strategic learners' described in Chapter 8 may be reluctant to embrace a particular topic or skill unless they can see that it will have an impact on their success in the course.

Social regulation

Assessment plays a subtle and complex role in the social and political structure of the UK, regulating entry to various occupations or levels of education by means of specific requirements for admission to many jobs and courses. The frequent debates in the press concerning standards and status in academic and vocational qualifications attest to widespread public interest in the social and political implications of assessment. Success in public examinations is closely linked with social advantage and disadvantage; for example, in England in 2006/07, only 21 per cent of pupils eligible for free school meals achieved five or more GCSE grades A*–C (including English and mathematics), compared with 49 per cent of those not eligible (DCSF 2007). Although there are many reasons for this not connected with the ways in which learning is assessed, it is at the point of assessment that such social inequalities become visible.

Assessment tasks

There are numerous types of assessment task in common use, for example:

- written tests of various forms, including essay questions, multiple choice tests and short answer tests;

- practical assessments and simulations;
- project work;
- oral assessment;
- observation of natural performance;
- evidence-based or 'portfolio' assessment;
- online and computer-based assessment.

These tasks may be used for summative assessment, or may contribute to formative assessment. Whatever task is used, assessment involves taking a *sample of learner behaviour* and making *inferences about their learning* from this sample. The degree of trust that can be placed on assessment outcomes will therefore depend on a number of factors relating to the sampling process and the interpretation of the resulting behaviour. It will be helpful to keep this in mind when examining the particular features of each form of assessment.

Most of the examples above are *supply-type* assessments; that is, they ask the student to provide some form of response to a stimulus. Both the stimulus (for example a question, an assignment brief or a mathematical problem) and the response (for example, an essay, a calculation or a diagram) may be written or oral. However, *selection-type* assessments are often used and have the great advantage of being straightforward to mark. In a selection-type question, the candidate must select an answer from a number of alternatives. For example, in a *multiple choice* question it is usual to offer four possible answers, of which only one is correct. Box 13.1 overleaf gives some examples of selection-type questions.

Planning and designing assessment

The assessment process may be thought of as having the stages illustrated in Figure 13.1 on page 167: planning for assessment; collecting the evidence; making judgements; giving feedback; and recording achievement. Each of these stages is important, and a range of knowledge and skills is required of the teacher in order to implement them effectively. The planning stage is particularly important, and includes making decisions or assumptions about what constitutes achievement and planning an *assessment strategy* to measure this achievement. The detailed design of assessment tasks can then be undertaken, including the preparation of marking schemes or other detailed specifications for applying the assessment criteria to the selected tasks.

A teacher's degree of involvement and control in planning assessment will depend on the nature of the courses on which they teach. For external awards such as GCSE, many of the decisions outlined above will be made at national level. On the other hand, teachers involved in the delivery of courses tailor-made to suit local needs are likely to have much more responsibility for the design stage.

Assessment planning must integrate closely with the curriculum philosophy and design. The assessment strategy chosen must be consistent with the course aims and philosophy, and therefore with the model of achievement being used: for example, in a vocational course practical and interpersonal skills may be of a higher importance

---

Box 13.1 Examples of selection-type questions

Multiple choice:

In a 3-pin electric plug, the *earth* wire is coloured:	**stem**
(a) Brown	distractor
(b) Blue	distractor
(c) Green and yellow	**key** (correct answer)
(d) Red and black	distractor

Alternative choice:

If litmus paper turns from red to blue in a solution, the solution is

(a)   acid

(b)   alkaline

A variation of multiple choice using combinations of statements:

Which of the following statements is true?

(I)   A force is required to change the position of a particle

(II)   A force is required to change the speed of a particle

(III) A force is required to change the direction of motion of a particle

(a) Statement (II) only   (b) Statements (I) and (II) only

(c) Statements (I) and (III) only   (d) Statements (II) and (III) only.

---

than theoretical knowledge; it would therefore be inconsistent to design assessments which ignored these skills, or gave them an insufficiently high weighting. It follows that assessment, and curriculum design more generally, depends quite crucially on value judgements: 'What we choose to assess and how shows quite starkly what we value . . . effective assessment depends upon having a view of what it is that we are trying to do in a programme and hence of what we ought to assess' (Knight 1995: 13).

Once we have decided on what constitutes achievement it is essential to make sure that it can be measured, selecting methods of assessment which can give us information on what students have achieved. We must not emphasize certain attributes simply because they are more straightforward to assess than other, more important, areas of learning. In other words, the assessment strategy must 'make what is important measurable, rather than . . . making what is measurable important' (SEC 1985: para. 2). In addition, it is often argued that the assessment strategy should allow candidates to show what they know and can do: in other words, it should allow for differentiation so that all can succeed at an appropriate level.

Some examples of models of achievement and associated assessment strategies will now be examined.

Example 1: GCSE English

GCSE English is based on the National Curriculum for schools in England and Wales. Three areas of achievement are recognized: Speaking and Listening, Reading

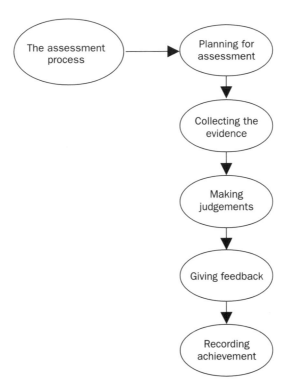

Figure 13.1 The assessment process

and Writing. Although this model of achievement may seem obvious, it is interesting to note the value judgement implied by the inclusion of Speaking and Listening. Some earlier qualifications in English (such as GCE 'O' level) were essentially academic tests, based entirely on written examinations. The inclusion of Speaking and Listening as an attainment target gives a clear message to students, teachers and employers that these skills *are* valued.

However, once an area such as Speaking and Listening is included in a model of achievement, there has to be a way of assessing it. Thus, the assessment strategy devised for GCSE English must correspond to the three areas of achievement just identified. This immediately moves us away from sole reliance on written work, and suggests that some form of continuous assessment or 'coursework' should be an element of the assessment. In particular, Speaking and Listening can most effectively be assessed through coursework. Detailed decisions on the weighting of these elements and the nature of the assessment tasks are then made in relation to the assessment objectives of the course.

Example 2: Assessment of National Vocational Qualifications

NVQs are competence based awards. The model of achievement is based on a *functional analysis* of a given occupational area. It is assumed that different levels of achievement can be identified within the occupation, so that we talk of NVQ level 1, level 2 etc. For a given occupation at a given level, the ability to do the job is specified in terms of *elements of competence* and these elements are supplemented by criteria for success (*performance criteria*) and a *range* of situations in which successful performance must be demonstrated. As in the previous example, having decided on what constitutes achievement, it is necessary to think about how this achievement can be measured. Clearly, the major source of evidence of achievement for NVQs will be actual job-related performance, so an assessor must observe candidates performing their job role. However, the requirement for a range of situations may require additional *supplementary* evidence to be used, for example oral questioning or even written tests. This may also allow *underpinning knowledge* to be assessed where appropriate. Figure 13.2 illustrates the NVQ assessment strategy.

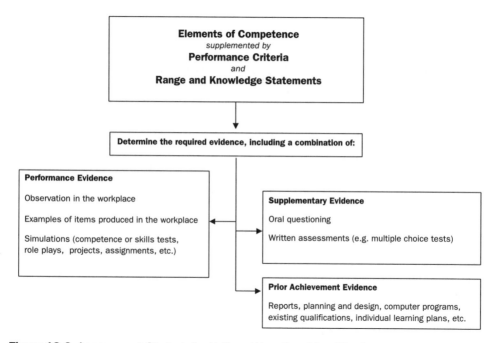

Figure 13.2 Assessment Strategy for National Vocational Qualifications

Once the broad assessment strategy is decided, detailed planning and design of assessment tasks can take place. For many teachers working on externally assessed courses, mock examinations and formative assessments provide an opportunity to be involved in planning and design even though the external assessment is determined by others. Box 13.2 gives an overview of guidelines for the design of written assessment tasks; similar considerations can be applied to other forms of assessment.

Summative, formative and ipsative assessment

Three distinct types of assessment can be identified according to the stage at which they occur and the purposes for which they are used. These types – summative,

---

Box 13.2 Design of written assessment tasks: some guidelines

A *Specifying the task*

The following questions should be asked:

- What learning is being tested? It is usually better to test a small number of objectives, one or two at a time, unless there is a specific reason for assessing a larger number of objectives at the same time.
- What *types* of objective are involved in terms of Bloom's Taxonomy? Questions will vary according to the level and type of learning involved. Often, the wording of the objective will suggest the required question (State . . . , Explain . . .).
- Does the question have an answer? A mathematical problem may have no solution; an ambiguous question may have several alternatives. A badly written question may have an (unintended) one-word answer ('yes').
- Have you given all necessary information? Unless there is a data sheet, you may need to give formulae, values of constants, etc.
- Is the language appropriate? The reading level of the question should be checked, and stereotypical images avoided.
- Is the time allocation reasonable? If graphs have to be drawn or essays written, you need to check that you have allowed enough time.

B *Designing a marking scheme*

- Make sure you supply a detailed worked answer, including acceptable alternative answers.
- Allocate marks in detail, trying for decisions like 'one mark or none', rather than 'how many marks out of five'.
- Ensure that the marks reflect the nature of the objective. Pure recall would normally deserve fewer marks than understanding.
- Check that similar tasks in the same or other questions are given similar marks.
- Consider whether to award marks for presentation. If you decide to do this, make it clear in the assessment task.
- Consider how to award marks to time-consuming but straightforward tasks such as graph plotting or drawing diagrams.

---

formative and ipsative – are not necessarily discrete: there is often some overlap or blurring of distinctions. Nonetheless, the typology provides a useful framework for analysing assessment processes.

Summative assessment

Summative assessment is used to determine whether students have acquired the skills, knowledge, behaviour or understanding that the course of study aims to provide. It gives an overall picture of performance within a complete unit of learning. Summative assessment is always a formal process, and is normally carried out at or near the end of a course or individual module.

Summative assessment normally leads to the award of qualifications: grades, diplomas and certificates. For some students, a qualification will lead to new employment or changes to existing employment. For others, a qualification may be needed for educational progression. Other stakeholders have an interest in summative assessment as well. Employers rely on qualifications and records of achievement to ascertain the skills and abilities of their new employees. Summative assessment can therefore be described as *high stakes* assessment (Knight and Yorke 2003). However, summative assessment can also be formative. Particularly in a modular curriculum, summative assessment can provide 'feed forward' in anticipation of the next summative assessment to be attempted by the student.

Formative assessment

Formative assessment is assessment for learning – it takes place during a course or programme of study, as an integral part of the learning process. Formative feedback (also known as 'feed forward'), contributes to the learning process by providing guidance to students on how to bridge the gap between current performance and desired achievement.

Any assessment activity has the potential to be formative. The kinds of activities that might be employed are similarly varied: case studies, quizzes, presentations, multiple choice tests, practical tasks and simulations. Students may be involved in their own assessment: for example, a short answer written test may be followed by peer marking and feedback. Formative assessment activities may also be a spontaneous, small scale or even unconscious part of the teacher's repertoire: for example, asking oral questions or observing student posture and body language to gauge understanding and motivation. Viewed from this perspective, it is clear that many learning and teaching strategies have an aspect of formative assessment. It is the systematic employment of these activities within a classroom or workshop that provides the key characteristics of formative assessment:

- assessing learning with the intention of making future learning more effective;
- providing information to teachers on how their students are progressing;
- providing feedback to students concerning their own progress;
- diagnosing students' needs or barriers to learning.

Formative assessment is sometimes confused with continuous assessment. In fact, these terms need to be carefully distinguished. In its correct sense, continuous assessment is a form of summative assessment that accrues over time: for example, through the gradual completion of a portfolio. Formative assessment may well take place throughout a programme of study, but it is not continuous assessment.

Ipsative assessment

This is a process in which students' own starting points are identified and targets set against which future progress can be assessed. The student can then reflect on their learning goals independently of the teacher. The ipsative assessment process will often be formally recorded, generally on paper, although web-based e-portfolios are becoming more widespread (see Chapter 12). Learners' goals may be stated or negotiated within a learning contract, and progress and achievement recorded by means of learning logs or similar documents. Where ipsative assessment is a formal part of a course, learners will often be supported – or constrained – by writing frames or other 'scaffolding' such as checklists and self-assessment proformas.

The use of ipsative assessment is now strongly embedded in education, with the increasing penetration of discourses concerning 'key skills', 'learning how to learn' and the 'self-regulated learner'. Records of Achievement and Individual Learning Plans (ILP) are common in schools and in further education, while in higher education Personal Development Plans (PDP) are widely used. These documents are updated by the student throughout a course and may be a part of the formal course assessment; students are encouraged to use them as a means of developing the ability to direct their own learning.

Providing feedback

Providing feedback to students is a crucial part of formative assessment. Unlike summative assessment, which relates to assessment *of* learning, feedback relates to 'assessment *for* learning', assessment which helps the learning process (Black and Wiliam 1998; Torrance and Pryor 1998). The skills of giving and receiving clear, constructive, developmental feedback are integral to good teaching.

In order to enhance learning, feedback should motivate the learner to do better and help to develop the ability to self-assess in the future – in other words, it teaches the learner what should be considered important and how improvement can be measured. This conception of feedback is associated with the notion of *self-regulated learning*, defined by Pintrich and Zusho (2002: 64) as 'an active constructive process whereby learners set goals for their learning and monitor, regulate and control their cognition, motivation and behaviour, guided and constrained by their goals and the contextual features of the environment'. In this definition, the reference to contextual features recognizes that self-regulated learning may operate within an environment where specific goals, such as the completion of assignments, are determined by teachers or other external agencies; nevertheless, self-regulated learners will not be passive recipients of assessment tasks but will reinterpret them in the light of their own goals.

In an influential paper, Sadler (1989) gives three conditions which must be fulfilled if students are to benefit from feedback on assessment. First of all, they need to understand what constitutes good performance in the task, so that assessment criteria must have been clearly explained beforehand and revisited in the feedback. Second, the feedback must help the student to understand how their current performance compares with good performance; and finally, the feedback must help the student understand how to close the gap between current and good performance. According to Sadler (1989: 119), this implies that students need to acquire some of the same evaluative skills as their teacher, thus emphasizing the importance of developing self-assessment skills as an integral part of student learning.

Black and Wiliam (1998) draw on Sadler's work in developing their extensive analysis of research and practice in formative assessment, making three fundamental arguments:

- Improving formative assessment can improve learning.
- There is room for improvement in formative assessment.
- There is research evidence on *how* to improve formative assessment.

These arguments are supported by extensive research; furthermore, many of the studies cited 'show that improved formative assessment helps the (so-called) low attainers more than the rest, and so reduces the spread of attainment while also raising it overall' (Black and Wiliam 1998: 3).

Weeden et al. (2000) report on research into students' experiences and expectations of feedback, involving 200 learners aged between 8 and 19 years. As might be expected, older students had experienced a wide range of different types of feedback throughout their school careers. Students of all ages felt that positive comments boosted their confidence and reported using feedback to improve their performance. However, although simple comments, ticks, smiley faces and evaluations such as 'good work' were welcomed as signifying approval, they did not help students to 'bridge the gap' between present performance and future goals. Both teachers and students preferred prompt oral feedback and discussion and felt that this improved performance.

Constructive criticism was found to be useful when it helped students understand what the task required and engaged them in thinking about their current performance and how to improve their work. Conversely, critical comments that damaged self-esteem and self-concept were unhelpful and demotivating. It is interesting to note that *criticism of effort* was found to be demoralizing and tended to be ignored or treated with hostility, especially if the student's own perception of the effort made was at variance with the teacher's. Older students expressed concerns that teachers' comments were sometimes inaccurate or unfair. 'The comment says – Not thinking about it enough – But I did!'

Black et al. (2003: 43) discuss research on comment-only marking. This research showed that, of three feedback schemes – marks only, comments only and a combination of marks and comments – the *most* effective feedback was comment only. This may be due to a number of factors, but quite often students presented with both marks and comments tend to focus on the mark at the expense of the more detailed comments.

Research into how adult learners respond to feedback (Young 2000) supports many of the findings discussed above, particularly the need for positive feedback. Young relates attitudes to feedback to self-esteem, noting that for students with lower self-esteem feedback was taken very personally and could damage confidence, even when well intentioned. She argues that, in order to 'customize' feedback to the needs of learners, it is essential to ascertain what their needs are in terms of the type of feedback that will be most helpful to them at a particular stage in the course, and that these needs will relate to their self-esteem as learners.

Feedback should be given as soon as possible after the assessment, and give a clear indication of the standard achieved. It should also be precise and detailed, giving specific examples and guidance on how to improve. Highlighting good aspects of the student's work as well as detailing what can be improved will help them to understand more explicitly what is required. Black and Wiliam (1998: 6) recommend that 'Feedback . . . should be about the particular qualities of [the learner's] work, with advice on what he or she can do to improve, and should avoid comparisons with other [learners]'. As with good teaching, feedback needs to be customized to the individual learner's personality and preferred way of learning and be expressed in a way that enables the student to understand and accept the points made.

Nicol and Macfarlane-Dick (2006: 207) identify seven principles of good practice in feedback, based on their effectiveness in strengthening students' capacity to self-regulate their own performance. These principles are:

1   Clarify what good performance is (goals, criteria, expected standards)

2   Facilitate the development of self-assessment (reflection) in learning

3   Provide high-quality information to students about their learning

4   Encourage teacher and peer dialogue around learning

5   Encourage positive motivational beliefs and self-esteem

6   Provide opportunities to close the gap between current and desired performance

7   Provide information to teachers that can be used to help shape their teaching.

Giving oral feedback to a student may benefit from additional strategies. These include giving the student first say, so that they can demonstrate their own appraisal of their performance; giving praise before criticism in a 'sandwich' approach which ends on a positive note; and focusing on just two or three key areas so that the student is not overwhelmed with information. The student also needs to be given time to think and respond – oral feedback should be a dialogue. The teacher needs to listen to how the feedback is being received and allow the student to ask questions and to put forward their own point of view.

Norm-referenced and criterion-referenced assessment

How do we know whether someone has 'done well' in an assessment? It might appear that this question has a very simple answer: I've done well in my test if I obtained a high mark, or if I've demonstrated that I have achieved certain learning outcomes, or I have performed a practical operation (such as changing a wheel) successfully. However, I may have obtained 80 per cent in a test, but still come last. Is this a good performance, or a bad one? In order to think more clearly about such matters, the concepts of norm- and criterion-referencing are helpful.

A *norm-referenced* assessment is one which contains no absolute criterion of competence; it is intended to rank students rather than to measure their achievement against a fixed scale. The test may tell us that student A lies in the top 15 per cent of the students assessed, but not whether that student has reached any definite level of attainment. Indeed, the level of attainment of the top 15 per cent (or of any other group) could vary from occasion to occasion. Obviously, the test must be a fair one, taken from the syllabus as taught and containing questions at an appropriate level. But there is no need for the entire syllabus to be covered in the test, or for the test to have exactly the same degree of difficulty every year.

A *criterion-referenced* assessment is one which measures the achievement of a student against specific criteria of competence. In this type of test, the standing of a student in relation to their peers is irrelevant. All that matters is that they meet the prescribed criteria for award of a pass or of an individual grade. A criterion-referenced test looks for mastery of skills, rather than superiority over one's peers. An example of this type of assessment would be the practical driving test.

These two methods are often described as if they were mutually exclusive; however, it is easy to see that they can never be wholly separated. For example, a norm-referenced test will always test *something*, at a level determined by some criteria, so that a high or low ranking will always be meaningful in terms of absolute attainment. Furthermore, if the test population remains approximately the same from year to year, a certain ranking will always correspond to very similar levels of competence. Although traditional exams such as GCSE and A Level are often described as being norm-referenced, the examining bodies go to great lengths to establish assessment objectives and criteria in order to ensure that a particular grade one year implies a similar level of performance as the same grade another year. At the other extreme, a criterion-referenced test needs to have realistic criteria which are within the grasp of at least some of the target population, so that the distribution of levels of competence within the population and the length of training required will help to determine criteria. We should therefore think of the *emphasis* of a test as being to one extreme or the other, rather than thinking in terms of absolutes.

Closely related to the idea of criterion-referenced tests is that of assessment based on *competence*. In this approach, a particular occupation is analysed in order to say what makes a competent practitioner at various levels. Such an analysis results in 'elements of competence' which can form the basis for units of study and ultimately of assessment, which is typically carried out in the workplace and is based on the candidate's performance in job-related activities (Ollin and Tucker 2008). In order to achieve a competence-based award, a candidate must reach a satisfactory standard in all elements of competence associated with the award. In the United Kingdom, the competence based approach is particularly associated with NVQs.

Validity and reliability

An assessment is effectively a measuring instrument, and in order to give useful information it must be both *valid* and *reliable*. The difference between these two concepts is often expressed by saying that validity is about *getting the right assessment* – that is, matching assessment tasks and judgements to what has been learned – while reliability is about *getting the assessment right*, in terms of ensuring a consistent approach to the assessment tasks and the process of making judgements and giving feedback.

Validity

A valid assessment covers the course content and is appropriate to the subject or vocational area. An assessment may be invalid if, for example, there is an inconsistency between the importance of a topic and its weighting in the assessment; there are problems which are too easy or too difficult; the questions are not relevant to the assessment objectives; range statements are inappropriate; and so on. Formative assessment involving syllabus content not yet covered in the course would also be invalid.

Clearly, a test must be reliable if it is to be valid, but a reliable test is not *necessarily* valid – think of a set of scales which consistently indicates a weight which is two kilograms out. The aim, of course, is to provide assessments which are both reliable and valid, and a number of possibilities exist to achieve this. For example, we might use commercially available tests, which are thoroughly trialled and often come with statistical measures of their reliability and validity. However, many teachers are required to design their own assessments (and this would obviously be the case for formative assessments such as homework or class tests), and need to be aware of certain elementary steps which must be taken to achieve a reliable and valid test. For example, how can teachers check the validity of a test once it has been constructed or build in validity to a test as they write it?

Some general conditions will always be necessary if assessment is to be valid. These are *sufficiency* – the assessment tasks generate enough evidence to demonstrate that all the learning objectives have been achieved; *currency* – the candidate's present level of attainment is being assessed; and *authenticity* – the performance being assessed is the candidate's and not that of someone else. In addition, various approaches to checking validity are used. They involve asking the further questions:

- Does the test accurately predict future performance in the subject (*predictive validity*)?

- Does the test provide a similar picture to other, independent measures of performance carried out at the same time, for example success at work (*concurrent validity*)?

- Does the test cover the objectives of teaching in proportion to the importance allocated to them (*content validity*)?

- Does the test actually capture the essence of what it is trying to assess (*construct validity*)? For example, do personality tests or learning style inventories actually measure something identifiable as 'personality' or 'learning style' respectively?

All four of these approaches could be useful in checking validity retrospectively. However, only content and (in a more limited way) construct validity is of much help in test design. As a simple initial test, *face* validity may be helpful before going any further – does the assessment *look* valid, or does it have some obviously invalid features?

Table of specifications

This is an aid to test design which attempts to increase content validity by making explicit the objectives to be tested and the weighting to be attached to them. These decisions are presented in a two-way table with *content* on one axis and *process* on the other. Here 'process' refers to the type of objective involved (for example, recall of knowledge, comprehension, application, etc.) and is usually related to levels in Bloom's Taxonomy.

Example: a test on food hygiene

Suppose a teacher wishes to assess a unit on food hygiene, with the following broad headings:

1   Food safety hazards

2   Food handling

3   Principles of safe food storage

4   Premises, equipment and cleaning

Inspection of the learning objectives would reveal how they relate to Bloom's Taxonomy. In this example, there would probably be categories such as recall of knowledge, comprehension and application. The teacher must now decide what *weightings*, as a percentage of the total test mark, to give to each topic and to each type of objective. In general, the weightings would reflect the importance of each topic and the nature of the objectives.

To see how this would work, suppose that the test is to be marked out of 100, and that 20 per cent of the teaching time, and therefore 20 marks, is allocated to food safety hazards. Suppose further that inspection of the learning objectives for this topic indicates that just over one-third of the objectives ask for recall, the remainder being equally divided between comprehension and application. The teacher might choose to allocate marks as eight for recall, six for comprehension and six for application. The same idea would then be applied to the other topic areas.

An example of a completed table of specifications is shown in Table 13.1. This would provide a statement of intent, which would help in designing the test. For example, the table shows that 16 per cent of the marks should be for recall of

Table 13.1 Table of specifications for a unit on food hygiene

	Recall	Comprehension	Application	Total
Food safety hazards	8	6	6	20
Food handling	12	9	9	30
Principles of safe food storage	4	3	3	10
Premises, equipment and cleaning	16	12	12	40
Total	40	30	30	100

knowledge of premises, equipment and cleaning, and the test items and marking scheme should reflect this.

Validity can also be achieved by a number of further strategies (Tummons 2007), for example: wording, explaining or defining the assessment tasks correctly, to prevent students performing activities that do not match the course objectives; setting assessments that include all relevant areas of the course and taking care not to include something that was not part of the course content; and finding ways to ensure authentic assessment.

Reliability

In an educational system where assessment takes place on a national basis across many hundreds of sites employing thousands of tutors, the need to prevent local or personal factors from affecting assessment practice is self-evident. Reliability relates to consistency in a number of ways: markers or examiners will agree on the mark or grade to be awarded to a given piece of work; there will be consistency between the students' work and the markers' or examiners' grades; students' grades or marks will not depend on where or when they were assessed; the language used in the assessment process is clear, unambiguous and inclusive; the environment in which the assessment is carried out will not affect the process; and students or candidates will not have been 'coached', that is, given preferential access to knowledge about the assessment. Thus, achieving reliability depends on building consistency into all aspects of the assessment environment.

Accrediting prior learning

Current policy in education and training emphasizes the importance of recognizing what individuals have learned through previous experiences in their lives. This is not only reflected in teaching strategies that build on learners' existing knowledge and skills, but also in formal accreditation systems which acknowledge prior learning or experience, and, as a result, provide exemption from part of a qualification. The term 'accreditation of prior learning' (APL) is often used to describe a formal process for recognizing previous learning. Accreditation of prior learning achievement (APLA) is used where the learner has some relevant prior *certificated* learning and accreditation of prior experiential learning (APEL) is used where the learner has relevant previous *experience*, which has not been formally accredited.

Processes for APL

Balancing ease of recognition and transfer for students against ensuring that standards are maintained can produce tensions within APL systems. As a result, the rigour of APL procedures can vary between organizations. However, certain common features are expected as good practice. Challis (1993: 1) states that

> The fundamental principle underpinning APEL is that learning is worthy and capable of gaining recognition and credit, regardless of the time, place and

context in which it has been achieved. It thus represents a move to accept that learning is not dependent upon any particular formal setting, and to acknowledge it as being of value in its own right.

The individual candidate must take responsibility for providing and organizing the evidence, although the amount of advice and support available will vary according to the context. In the case of APLA, the candidate will need to produce proof of formal certification and for APEL appropriate evidence of previous experience. Sometimes a claim may be based on a mixture of APLA and APEL.

Depending on the context, the claim will be assessed by an APL assessor or the tutor in charge of the course. The evidence will be considered against the outcomes or criteria in specific modules or units in the qualification (although in some contexts a broader approach that the evidence generally 'fits' is possible). The APL process will be documented in some way, so that internal and external moderators are able to confirm its reliability and validity. Box 13.3 shows some useful questions that APL assessors should ask when considering a claim. All of these conditions must be satisfied to justify the award of APL and it is important to remember that an individual who gains exemption through APL will achieve the same qualification as someone who has completed the entire course.

In addition, it is important that standards are not compromised by exempting a student from certain modules. They must be able to demonstrate knowledge and skills on completion of the qualification comparable (not necessarily identical) to a student who has studied the complete programme.

Moderation and standardization

Whatever form of assessment is used, judgements about students should depend as little as possible on who assessed the student or the particular setting in which the assessment was carried out. However, the most reliable methods of assessment are often the ones with least validity and vice versa, so procedures are needed to maintain academic or vocational standards without compromising the validity of the assessment or its ability to engage the interest of students.

Box 13.3 Useful questions when considering accreditation of prior learning

- Is the evidence valid? Does it match the learning outcomes of the modules the candidate wishes to gain exemption from?
- Is it reliable? Will two different tutors agree that the evidence meets module requirements?
- Is it sufficient? Is there enough evidence to cover all aspects of the modules for which exemption is claimed?
- Is it authentic? Is the evidence the property of the candidate?
- Is the evidence current? The evidence needs to be up-to-date, normally less than five years old.

(Tummons 2007: 16)

Moderation and standardization procedures are designed to increase the reliability of assessment through opening up the individual assessor's judgements to wider scrutiny. Assessment of students' work or performance can be subject to all kinds of bias, particularly if the assessor is inexperienced. The assessor may be inclined to favour particular students, prefer a particular way of approaching a task to others, or misjudge the required standards. This bias can be *moderated* through comparison with other people's judgements about the same work.

Different contexts and qualifications moderate student work or performance in a variety of ways. In some cases, local and informal procedures may be sufficient, but national qualifications are usually subject to a formal process of internal and external moderation. Moderation conducted internally within an organization aims to ensure that all assessors have a common understanding of course requirements; external moderation ensures that these understandings are comparable to those in other organizations. The terms used to describe these processes vary according to context. For example, 'verification', using internal and external verifiers, is often used instead of 'moderation', especially in relation to vocational qualifications. In further education, external verifiers will be appointed by the awarding body offering the qualification. In contrast, universities appoint their own external examiners from comparable institutions and subject areas.

External examinations

Written examination papers for a qualification such as a GCSE are sent directly to be marked by assessors appointed by the awarding body and so are not marked by the organization which delivered the qualification. Assessors will have been trained through marking cross-moderated samples of work and their assessments will also be subject to moderation by the awarding body.

Double marking

For internally assessed written assignments, 'double marking' is sometimes used. Each piece of work is marked twice, with the second marker often assessing 'blind' without seeing the first marker's assessment. Marks are then compared and adjusted if necessary following discussion between the two markers. Double marking is particularly useful when important decisions are to be made, for example when a student is on the pass/fail borderline or is being considered for a high grade.

Practical work or performance

The most valid forms of vocational assessment may involve practical tasks or observing performance 'on the job'; these are likely to be the major forms of assessment in work-based learning. If these assessments contribute to a qualification, then they also need to be moderated, even if the nature of the assessment makes it difficult for assessors to compare judgements – for example, when observation of performance in the workplace is involved.

When practical work leads to a product, the items produced can be moderated in a similar way to written work, in that other assessors can consider and comment on the judgements made about these products. Thus, in a workshop containing sections of wall built by NVQ bricklaying candidates, an internal verifier can moderate the assessor comments made against each candidate's work. When observation of performance is involved, moderation may entail an internal verifier observing at the same time as an assessor and then comparing the assessor's judgements with their own.

Moderation and standardization have an important role in ensuring that academic standards are maintained and are uniform across institutional, geographical and curriculum boundaries. In addition, they provide valuable opportunities for professional development, allowing teachers to 'test out' their judgements against those of their peers and providing exposure to alternative interpretations and values. In turn, this will inform not just the summative assessment practice of the teacher, but also their ability to provide constructive formative feedback and to enhance the quality of 'assessment for learning'.

14

Subject specialist pedagogy
Steve Burton, Roy Fisher, David Lord and Keith Webb

> **In this chapter:**
> - Subject specialist pedagogy in the lifelong learning sector
> - A practical response: *Associate Online*
> - Some wider considerations

This chapter introduces debates surrounding subject specialist pedagogy in the LLS, and outlines a resource created to facilitate subject specialist development (for an extended account, see Fisher and Webb 2006). In relation to the development of school teachers' professional knowledge, Goodson (2003: 7) called for 'the joining of "stories of action" to "theories of context"', arguing that 'without this kind of knowledge, teaching becomes the technical delivery of other people's purposes'. Goodson's vision is of theoretically informed practice undertaken by relatively autonomous professionals engaged in critical debate. Given the recent policy interest in teacher education for the LLS the issue of 'other people's purposes' has resonance: a particular element of this has focused on 'subject specialist pedagogy'.

Subject specialist pedagogy in the lifelong learning sector

Healey and Jenkins (2001: 3) situate disciplinary communities centrally within educational development, and suggest that the 'view that teaching is generic reduces it to the technical matter of performance . . . unconnected to the disciplinary community at the heart of being an academic'. They argue that 'different clusters of academic disciplines and their respective degree programmes have distinctive norms and values; and academics in different disciplinary clusters show wide difference in their teaching practices' (pp. 3–4).

Goodson (2003: 9) points out that 'scholars working in disciplinary modes normally develop their first allegiance to their home discipline'. In her discussion of the move towards integration of academic and vocational education in American High Schools, Warren Little (1992: 4) refers to the presence of a 'legacy of subject specialism', comprising 'intellectual orientation, social relations, emotional satisfactions, and formal organization', viewing this as a barrier. This legacy is at work in twenty-first century education in England. However, it has been eroded by new currents in knowledge production and consumption and changes in academic disciplines. Schools and HEIs still largely structure the curriculum in 'subjects'. This is less so in FE, and is not the case in the wider LLS. The idea of 'subject specialist pedagogy' remains a powerful one, but it contradicts strong intellectual and epistemological trends. Browne (2005: 3) suggests that:

> Academic curricula are being strengthened and enriched through the enlightened realization that no discipline is an island unto itself. Instead, each is a part of the curriculum mainland, to which it feeds important nutrients and from which it draws life-giving nourishment in the form of intellectual commerce and trade . . . Interdisciplinary study is a breaking down of what Marjorie Garber in *Academic Instincts* (2003) called 'Disciplinary Libido'.

Changing conceptions of knowledge, derived from postmodernism and associated ideas, have incorporated notions of interdisciplinarity. Lyotard's (1984) pronouncement of 'the end of metanarratives' and the rise of performativity in educational institutions (see Chapter 9) has altered the ways of organizing knowledge on which the force of the concept of subject specialist pedagogy rests.

In March 2003 the DfES (2003a: 1) issued its consultation document *Subject Specialism* which discussed 'how professionalism in subject specialism might be more effectively supported and developed through the school workforce'. This document argued that, 'It is a combination of deep subject knowledge and a range of appropriate teaching and learning techniques which make for the most powerful interactions between teachers and pupils' (p. 2). The GTC's response appeared the following June (GTC 2003: 1) and indicated that their own research on teachers had shown 'love of their subject' to be 'the first reason for them wanting to teach'. The GTC, however, also pointed to 'a danger in separating it [subject specialist pedagogy] from other aspects of teacher pedagogy'.

Thornton (1998: 38), discussing the issue of subject specialism in primary education, saw the concept partially emerging as a response to supposed progressivism within that sector. She cites Ball's (1995) argument that the Education Reform Act of 1988 established the National Curriculum as a mechanism designed to 'deconstruct the comprehensive modernist curriculum' putting in its place 'a political but depoliticized, authoritative curriculum of tradition'. This perception of subject specialist pedagogy as a reactionary response to progressivism is one that has interesting parallels with regard to FE and the LLS (but see Avis 1991).

An Ofsted (2003: 23) survey of FETT reported that:

> [u]nlike ITT for secondary school teachers, most courses for FE teachers are not designed to provide subject-specific or vocation-specific training, although some have done so in the past. It is assumed that trainees will already have the necessary specialist skills, or that they will receive specialist training within the college faculties or departments in which they work. While this may be true in some cases, many new FE teachers do not receive this specialist input.

The report stated that, 'many trainees who are not employed by the college in which they are doing their training receive no specialist mentoring' (Ofsted 2003: 24). A major finding was that '[t]he content of the courses rarely includes the development of subject specific pedagogy to equip new teachers with the specific knowledge and skills necessary for teaching their specialist subject or vocational area' (p. 3).

One of eight recommendations was that HEIs and awarding bodies should 'give substantially more attention to developing trainees' expertise in teaching their subject' (p. 4). The DfES (2003b: 7) response to Ofsted's report included under the heading 'Our starting point' the assertion that '[t]eachers in our sector need two sets of skills – to be expert in their subject, and to be trained to teach it'. A specific way to address the Ofsted recommendations, DfES claimed, would be through 'The introduction of formalised subject specific mentoring as part of the workplace development of trainee teachers' which 'will ensure that all trainees have access to subject pedagogy' (p. 8). Recognizing some practical difficulties DfES (2003b: 23) acknowledged:

> It will not always be possible for the trainee to be assigned to a mentor teaching the same subject. The wide variety of subjects taught in the learning and skills sector means that in some colleges and providers, more specialist subjects may have only one teacher. In such cases, the trainee should be paired with a teacher of a related subject . . . Trainees will also be able to access support materials online.

DfES (2004a: 5) issued its plans for the reform of ITT for the LLS in the document *Equipping Our Teachers for the Future*, stating that teachers in the sector would be 'trained and qualified in':

- the skills and subjects they teach at the levels appropriate to their teaching, which may be level 1 or degree level; and
- the skills of teaching their subject in the workshop, laboratory or classroom.

This thinking would be reflected in the LLUK (2007a: 8) professional standards (see Chapter 3), within which 'Domain C' was devoted to specialist learning and teaching. Teachers in the LLS need to demonstrate a commitment to:

- understanding and keeping up to date with current knowledge in respect of own specialist area;
- enthusing and motivating learners in own specialist area;
- fulfilling the statutory responsibilities associated with own specialist area of teaching;
- developing good practice in teaching own specialist area.

The standards also relate directly to subject specialism in Domain F 'Access and progression' where there is a requirement for commitment to 'Maintaining own professional knowledge in order to provide information on opportunities for progression in own specialist area' (LLUK 2007a: 14).

It is clear from *Equipping Our Teachers for the Future* that mentoring was seen as the route to subject specialist pedagogic skills and there is the affirmation that 'an essential aim of the training is that teachers should have the skills of teaching in their own specialist or curriculum area' (p. 8). The importance of teachers knowing their subject is a fundamental principle that few would dispute. Whether or not there are clear and distinct subject specialist pedagogies, and whether these should be an organizational/structural factor in teacher training for the LLS is not so clear. It is hard not to detect in DfES/DCFS and Ofsted thinking a perception of curriculum issues informed by practice in secondary schools.

Issues of subject specialist pedagogy have both epistemological and cultural dimensions. Crawley (2005) suggested that a review of an FE college prospectus would identify up to 200 subject specialisms. The wider LLS is awash with 'subject specialisms' (bearing only a passing relationship to traditional academic disciplines). The LLS and FE colleges are populated by vocational curricula. These have a tendency to 'atomize' in relation to workplace roles, while incorporating remnants of the academic disciplines from which they are derived. A typical Business Studies Diploma, for instance, might incorporate (versions of) English, mathematics and newer disciplines such as economics alongside contemporary curricula constructions such as IT, and other new 'bundles of knowledge and skills' that attract a wide range of descriptors (for example 'Managing People'). These newer 'subjects' are inter- and trans-disciplinary.

The Business Education Council (BEC), and its successor the Business and Technology Education Council (BTEC), transformed pedagogic practice in FE between 1979 and 1985 (see Fisher 2004). Lecturers were challenged to work cooperatively and to break away from traditional lecturing. To make this a possibility BEC provided advice about delivery of the curriculum reinforced by the monitoring of assignments and programmes. During the 1980s this, together with vocational progressivism, practically eliminated 'old school' subject specialist teaching in business related FE. Subjects such as economics became integrated into business studies and shifted away from their academic origins. It should, however, be noted that some academically orientated teachers may have continued to teach GCSE and GCE A Level subjects. The new style of student centred curriculum introduced by BEC and promoted by BTEC had a major impetus in changing the role of the FE lecturer from something approaching that of an instructor to that of a facilitator. Many found this transition difficult and left. FE practitioners today do not generally conceive themselves to be 'subject specialists' in the sense of working within defined academic disciplines.

The everyday experience of teaching within FE and its associated culture has seen a move away from practices that could be characterized as an 'insular model' of working, towards a 'connective model'. Lucas (1995) argued for the creation of a teacher training provision for FE which would serve the needs of the concept of the 'connective specialist'. The development of such teacher training programmes would be predicated on 'an alternative model based on a new relationship between theory and practice . . . articulating a view of the skills needed for the future' (p. 13). Lucas recognized that merely adding the concept of reflection to that of competence would not be enough because the skills required for the needs of the future could not be derived from an examination of current practice. Dimensions for the training needs of the 'lecturer of the future' identified in related and contemporaneous work by Young et al. (1995) were:

Curriculum knowledge: 'Lecturers . . . will still be subject specialists' [in our view wrongly] but this will be based on 'an understanding of how her/his subject relates to other forms of subject specialism'. (p. 32)

Learner-centred pedagogic knowledge: 'Lecturers will need . . . to be experts in the management of learning and in how to enable their students to become managers of their own learning.' (p. 33)

Inter-professional knowledge: 'lecturers will depend more and more on other professionals . . . lecturers will need to know about these different sources of expertise and how students can access them.' (p. 33)

Organizational knowledge: In a situation where they will increasingly be working in teams with very diverse memberships lecturers will need to 'develop teamwork and collaborative skills . . . they will also need negotiating skills'. (p. 33)

Connective knowledge: Lecturers will 'need to be able to help students connect their past, present and future learning as well as have enough knowledge of workplaces to be able to support a student's workplace learning'. (p. 33)

The above model has much to commend it as a framework, with the *Associate Online* facility having the potential to assist the process of connectivity.

A practical response: *Associate Online*

Associate Online provides a national online subject specialist environment accessible (currently) to trainee teachers in member institutions. This community has access to bespoke, user-generated, moderated learning materials, together with electronic access to experienced subject mentors and communication tools. The creation and initial management of this was led by the University of Huddersfield and CPCET in collaboration with Bath Spa University, the University of Greenwich and the University of Wolverhampton. It is now led by HUDCETT. The project was based on recognition that ICT could provide trainee teachers in the LLS with learning communities focused on the teaching of a particular subject or vocational curriculum, and that a fundamental element of learning is achieved through taking part in social practice (Lave and Wenger 1991).

No matter how specialized or isolated their particular teaching and/or training context, *Associate Online* can be used to bring trainees together with experienced subject tutors and other specialized resources. It directly addresses the national policy priority (DfES 2003b; Ofsted 2003) requiring greater attention to subject-specialist pedagogies. It also promotes engagement with 'e-learning'.

The application of technology has the potential for two contradictory effects: it can either be an instrument of central direction and control or, equally, a mechanism that frees developing professionals from constraints of time, place and contextual setting. *Associate Online* was concerned to construct an online learning community that empowers learners and enhances their learning by overcoming restrictions on their ability to engage with peers.

Laurillard (2002) and Liber and Holyfield (2003) are among those who have emphasized the requirement for institutional systems to adjust in order that the implementation of new technology can be successful. The centrality of e-learning in *Associate Online* ensures that participants experience the benefits of ICT. The DfES (2003c: 4) pointed out that 'e-Learning is not embedded in our teaching and learning . . . the time has come to recognise the benefits that these technologies can bring to the way we teach and learn'. This is despite the realization that such technologies can be used to 'support and encourage the revolution which has been taking place in education whereby new learning environments have been developed which are based on principles of active learning' (Jefferies and Hussain, 1998: 359). It has been claimed that such experience has the greatest impact on the practice of teachers where it is linked to their subject specialism, 'If teachers are to engage with e-learning, they must see the relevance to their own cognitive area, and surveys have shown that students gain more benefit from subject specific e-learning materials than those designed for generic consumption' (LTSN 2002).

Some wider considerations

Associate Online is addressing some important needs in innovative and positive ways. It acknowledges pedagogic issues that arise within a particular subject specialist or vocational area, but does so without adopting a reductionist conceptualization of pedagogy. At the same time, however, there is a need for caution in certain respects.

There is a clear trend towards the disintegration of disciplines and an intensified fluidity of knowledge that suggests that inter-disciplinarity is a sensible approach to research and (in a connected way) to much teaching at HE level. In many cases, this applies in FE. The atomization of the FE curriculum reflects the reality of vocational application, and the 'supercomplexity' of the LLS makes the concept of subject specialism and the associated move towards mentoring difficult to implement, especially since there is an absence of specific expertise and currently of dedicated funding to release that expertise.

The density, compactness and 'contrary directions' of the ITT curriculum for the LLS, creaking under the weight of imperatives to address literacy, numeracy and ESOL, has created the need for more 'space' than is available. It is increasingly difficult to address core educational questions and practices in a way that is appropriately critical. In one sense the key question is, 'What constitutes legitimate knowledge in this context?' Moreover, we are keenly conscious that the technologies and mechanisms that we have been describing may be open to utilization by management for monitoring, performance review and, in Foucauldian language, surveillance.

Lyotard (1984:4) referred to a trend towards 'a thorough exteriorization of knowledge'. What we have described in relation to *Associate Online* is one response to a practical issue that, we hope, may ultimately militate against this by enabling practitioners to engage directly and freely in the critical resolution of everyday problems. This engagement, we anticipate, will be in the context of an ethos that asks 'why?' as well as 'how?', and one that moves beyond the technique of subject specialist pedagogy to embrace deeper issues surrounding contemporary and future professional practice.

15

Reflective practice
Barbara Reynolds and Martin Suter

What is reflection?

> Active, persistent and careful consideration of any belief or supposed form of knowledge in the light of the grounds that support it and the further conclusions to which it tends constitutes reflective thought.
>
> (Dewey 1933: 9)

The quotation above is taken from *How We Think*, a seminal work by the philosopher and educational theorist John Dewey, considered by many to be the most important influence on notions of reflective practice. It encapsulates Dewey's belief that there are many complex situations in modern society which require choices to be made, and often no clear cut, ready-made answers. Dewey was very suspicious of any claims to easy solutions, speaking of individuals being 'confused' and 'perplexed' by the situations facing them, but proposing that through 'careful consideration' they would find solutions adapted to their particular situation. This position derives from Dewey's philosophical pragmatism, an approach that views knowledge as produced by an adaptive process in which the human organism succeeds in understanding and manipulating its environment. According to Dewey, knowledge *is* successful practice: we have knowledge in a particular context only when we can overcome the difficulties it sets for us.

It is not difficult to see the attraction of reflective practice in teaching. Writers on the subject (see Carr 1995) have argued that teaching is a complex activity, often contingent, and in which it is difficult to be prescriptive. Teachers are often faced with 'perplexities': what is the right thing to do in a particular professional situation?

What elements of professional practice, then, should receive 'careful consideration'? The use of teaching and learning strategies and resources is an obvious one. The teacher must consider the most effective strategies in a particular situation, and how to adapt them to different subjects and groups of learners. There are the learners themselves: what are the best ways to manage particular groups, motivate individuals and help learners to achieve? Policies on widening participation and social inclusion mean that the teacher must cope with varied learner needs. For example, how does the teacher differentiate between learners to ensure that learning is effective? These complexities of professional practice are compounded by the rate of curricular change. How does the individual teacher respond to such changes, for instance the embedding of literacy and numeracy in their own subject teaching? Of course, for all these elements help and guidance is available, but often it is up to the individual teacher to 'adapt' that guidance, to make it 'work' in their particular professional situation. To cope effectively with the complexities and contingencies of practice the teacher needs to 'actively' and 'persistently' consider what works in a variety of situations. In so doing, what constitutes 'best practice' must receive careful scrutiny, the teacher being wary of 'ready-made' solutions and adapting teaching and learning strategies to fit their particular situation. In lifelong learning, Dewey's suspicion of ready-made solutions is reinforced by research indicating that learning in FE appears to be strongly culture and context dependent: 'what works, or is deemed good practice in one learning site may not work or be good practice in another' (Hodkinson and James 2003: 401).

In this chapter we consider reflective practice, suggesting how a teacher might reflect on their professional situation. This is followed by an identification of the levels of reflection in which a teacher might engage, for instance the 'technical' relating to everyday classroom and workshop practice, and 'critical' reflection on the *context* within which the teacher conducts their practice. We then explore three 'models' which have strongly influenced conceptualizations of reflective practice and consider how they might guide the teacher. The chapter concludes by reviewing criticisms of reflective practice, arguing that the concept is not unproblematic, and that its limitations should be acknowledged.

The process of reflective practice

How do we reflect on practice? Figure 15.1 overleaf illustrates the basic process of integrating the practice of teaching with reflection on that practice. The process starts with 'practice': a teaching session, or other engagement with learners, after which the practitioner reflects upon the session. As a result, the teacher may decide to make some changes, perhaps introducing new learning activities and resources to better meet the needs of learners. When reflecting on the next session, the teacher considers how effective or otherwise the changes have been. Note that the cycle is not 'closed': if it were, reflective practice would be exactly the 'quick fix' to problems that Dewey rejects. On the contrary, the notion of a teacher as 'reflective practitioner' implies that reflective practice is ongoing – hence the arrow pointing towards 'further practice'. Boxes 15.1 and 15.2 overleaf provide examples of an ongoing process of reflection.

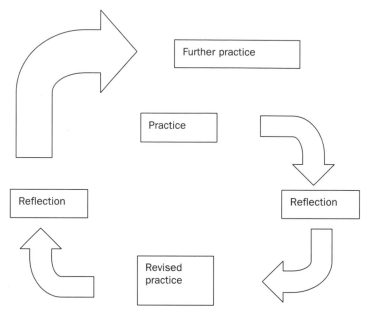

Figure 15.1 Basic model of reflecting on practice

Box 15.1 Example of reflection (1)

Chantelle teaches an 'Access to HE' class. The teaching room was laid out with the tables in rows facing the whiteboard at the front of the room. Initially, this posed no problems, but layout difficulties became evident when she attempted to engage the students in group discussion. Students at the front of the room had to turn around awkwardly to see a speaker behind them, while those at the back had difficulty in seeing the speaker at all. This resulted in a rather stilted discussion where some students made no contribution at all.

On reflection, Chantelle felt she had to make some changes to the layout. She considers group discussion to be an important learning activity and resolved to find a way of making it work effectively. Given that she had planned for a mix of 'teacher centred' and 'learner centred' activities, Chantelle decided against laying out the room for small groups, as some of the students would have difficulty seeing Powerpoint presentations and whiteboard work. She decided instead on a 'U' shaped arrangement of tables to enable a range of teacher and learner centred activities to take place.

In the next session, having made the necessary changes, Chantelle notes more effective interaction among the students during group discussion. She does note, however, that two or three students tend to monopolize the discussion and a few students make very little or no contribution . . .

Box 15.2 Examples of reflection (2)

Peter works for a charity offering training to young people not in education, employment or training (NEET). He teaches basic landscaping skills, with the object of readying learners for employment with local companies or to progress to the nearby FE college.

As part of his training role, Peter is required to ensure trainees build a portfolio demonstrating evidence of learning and achievement in literacy and numeracy skills. The trainees demonstrate their literacy skills largely by logging their progress on the course, with appropriate support and guidance from Peter. Building of the numeracy portfolio has tended to be undertaken when the weather is so inclement that the trainees cannot work outdoors, an arrangement that Peter inherited from the previous tutor. For this purpose, Peter has used worksheets he found in the cabin used by the group.

These numeracy sessions are unpopular with trainees, with much grumbling when the worksheets are produced, and many requests to visit the toilet or have a cigarette. After one particularly fraught rainy afternoon in the cabin, Peter reflected upon his own experiences as a learner. He recalled his dislike of mathematics at school, only finding 'meaning' in the use of number when he became an apprentice landscape gardener, when tasks such as calculating quantities and areas became part of the everyday job. Peter reflected that much of the numeracy work undertaken by trainees had little relevance for them, perhaps replicating negative school experiences. This led Peter to think about ways of integrating numeracy with landscaping projects. He created worksheets on linear measurement, area and volume on which the trainees could perform the calculations that any landscape gardener would reasonably be expected to perform. In this way, Peter has increased the relevance of numeracy to the trainees, with the bonus that there are fewer behavioural issues on rainy afternoons.

Reflecting on the integration of numeracy skills with project work, Peter is pleased with the results so far, but he still has the problem of how to cater for the range of abilities in his group.

In both examples it can be seen that neither of the practitioners were content to continue with situations they had inherited. As a result of reflection, effective solutions were found to the problems presented in the use of a learning activity in a particular learning situation. Notably in both cases the cycle is not 'closed'; further issues have arisen which call for reflection and consideration of ways to ensure a sound learning experience for *all* learners.

Levels of reflection

We turn our attention now from *how* we might reflect on practice to consider what a teacher might reflect *about*. There are two levels of reflective practice that, while not mutually exclusive, can nevertheless be distinguished from one another: (a) technical; and (b) critical-organizational.

Technical

This is the type of reflective practice likely to be undertaken by the practitioner on a regular basis. It is a reflection which acknowledges the complexities and often uncertainties of the learning environment. It is often thought of as a problem-solving approach, addressing issues of teaching and learning as they arise. The 'technical' level deals with the techniques of planning and delivering learning. Thus a teacher reflects upon the use of teaching and learning activities; are they effective in achieving learning outcomes? Do they help stimulate learning? Are the students motivated by the activities? Do they promote active learning? The teacher may also reflect upon the use of teaching and learning resources: are they 'pitched' at the right level for the learner? Are they designed to take into account any necessary differentiation of learning? Have they been designed to take into account any specific learning need, for example dyslexia? Box 15.3 provides an example.

Box 15.3 Example of technical reflection

Aisha teaches a 'human sciences' module on a level 3 social care course. It was evident in the first week that there is a wide spread of attainment in the 'sciences', with some students having gained GCSE Biology at 'A' grade, most having grades 'D' to 'F' and some having no science background at all. Aisha reasons that if she does not differentiate learning by content, the problems already experienced in the first week of some students not being stretched while others struggle to 'keep up', will only increase. As a result of this reflection Aisha decides to design worksheets with tasks ascending in difficulty. This she reasons would help ensure that outcomes are being achieved for all, while providing the necessary challenge for the more able learner.

Critical-organizational

This level is identified as 'critical' because it may be necessary to question the actions, decisions and opinions of others; 'organizational', because the practitioner is reflecting upon the management and deployment of teaching and learning activities, resources and learner support. Box 15.4 provides an example.

Where teaching and learning activities are concerned, a teacher might reflect upon the methods employed on a particular course, and having done so might consider that they tend to result in learner passivity. The action the practitioner might persuade the course team to take is to employ more methods that promote active learning. Crucially, it is important that they are suggesting activities that have 'worked' for the practitioner making the suggestion!

A practitioner may reflect upon the teaching and learning resources available. Perhaps there are too few resources, or the resources are not suitable for a certain type of learning. Whereas a practitioner reflecting at the technical level might try to find a way of working 'creatively' within such constraints, at the critical-organizational level the practitioner is questioning these, and working, where possible, to overcome them.

Box 15.4 Critical-organizational reflection

Louise is a trainer working for an NHS trust. Her role is to train care workers in manual handling skills and 'back awareness'. She had been required to train a group of care workers at a large home for the elderly. This was somewhat unusual, as participants in training usually attend the suite of training rooms at the Trust buildings, which are set out for the training in which Louise is engaged. In this instance however, Louise's manager felt that, given the number of participants involved from one location, it would be more efficient for Louise to deliver the training at the care home, which she duly did. The training session was less than successful. The room allocated was too small, and initially there were not enough chairs. There was not enough room to set up some of her equipment, restricting the efficacy of the training. The training was continually interrupted by participants leaving the room on work-related errands.

Louise returned to her workplace and wrote up her reflections on the session. Having done this, she approached her manager, telling her what had happened, and proposing how future training sessions for such groups should be conducted. Louise suggested that ideally all training sessions should be held in the Trust's own training suite, but if not, Louise should be able to assess the suitability of facilities 'off site', where practicable, and that an agreement should be reached with the management of the homes that participants should not be disturbed during training sessions. Louise's manager was not prepared to establish the principle that all training should be conducted in the Trust training suite, but agreed that where practicable Louise should be able to assess facilities for their suitability, and that it would be 'written into' any training agreement with management of the homes that participants should not be disturbed during training.

One important resource where there might be constraints is the spaces or environments where learning takes place. In FE colleges for instance, science practitioners might have what they consider to be limited access to laboratories, whereas other teachers might be allocated 'specialist' rooms unsuited to the learning needs of their learners.

There is a variety of learner issues upon which a practitioner has cause to reflect. A teacher might become concerned about the challenging behaviour of a group of learners. Through reflection at the technical level, he or she may find solutions that work in the learning environment. However, the teacher may reason that challenging behaviour is a more general organizational issue, and having reflected upon the reasons for this, might put forward suggestions for a 'policy' for dealing with it.

Theories of reflective practice

Donald Schön

Schön's (1983, 1987) work has had a great influence on reflective practice in teaching. This is probably because of his emphasis on the complexities of practice. In his work, Schön was critical of 'technical rationalism', the idea that there is 'one best way' to undertake a task, and that this prescription is followed at all times and in all circumstances. Greatly influenced by Dewey, Schön argued that professional practices are complex, contingent and even 'messy', and do not lend themselves to a 'technical-rational' approach.

For Schön, the professional is knowledgeable in a unique way and demonstrates through *reflection in action*, practical or personal knowledge, what he called *knowing in action*. The practical knowledge, reflection in action, has been described as the teacher 'thinking on his or her feet', being spontaneous, creative and unique. According to Schön, the professional exhibits a kind of 'artistry', building up a 'repertoire' of knowledge and skills through reflection in action. This is built up by the teacher gaining understandings of situation that inform action. When the practitioner experiences 'puzzlement' or 'confusion' in a situation, an 'experiment' is carried out to generate new understanding. A teacher will learn a range of classroom management skills, or an understanding of when learners are finding a topic difficult, by 'experimenting' with different ways of dealing with these situations, and if successful, these will be added to the repertoire. Knowing in action results in what Van Maanen (1995) has called a 'competent performance', where the teacher 'just knows' what to do.

This process of thinking on one's feet can be built upon through *reflection on action*, after the encounter with learners. Reflection on action may involve writing up reflections, or discussing our practice with a mentor or colleague. It enables a teacher to 'slow things down' (Schön 1987), to explore what happened and why, allowing the formulation of questions and development of ideas for future practice.

The attractiveness of Schön's ideas is easy to see. First, there is an acknowledgement of the complexities of teaching, and the need to build a repertoire of knowledge and skills to deal with the many and varied situations encountered. What distinguishes this from a 'craft' model of teaching (Larivee 2000) is the expectation there will be an ongoing purposeful *reflection on action*, subjecting the 'tacit knowledge' (Polanyi 1983) of professional practice to careful, sustained thought.

There are, however, several criticisms of Schön's model. First, is it always possible to 'slow things down' sufficiently for reflection to take place in busy teaching situations? Second, is it always wise for a teacher to disclose professional dilemmas and perceived limitations in their own practice? Third, does it take into account sufficiently those factors which are outside the individual teacher's control?

Tripp's critical incidents analysis

Critical incident analysis is a model of reflective practice closely associated with the work of Tripp (1993). He argues we need to explore the incidents that occur in the every day work of teaching which can be used to question teacher's own practice, enabling them to develop an understanding of the processes of teaching, and crucially, to develop their professional judgement. A critical incident is that which we interpret as a challenge in the professional context. Tripp suggests that when something goes wrong, teachers need to ask what happened and why. It is therefore important that the incidents are framed as *questions* that the teacher asks him- or herself.

The process starts by choosing a critical incident, which is not necessarily

dramatic. It might be a commonplace event, but is significant because it might indicate underlying motives, structures and processes (Pollard et al. 2005). For example, a
teacher might notice that his or her group of adult learners are reluctant to give
individual presentations to their peers. This reluctance would probably not be surprising, but in this instance the teacher has chosen to deal with it as a critical incident. The
teacher gives a careful description of it: who was involved; where it happened; what
actually happened; what the teacher's reaction to the incident was.

The next step is to analyse the description, to look for the underlying 'structures',
'motives' and 'processes'. This is where the teacher starts to ask 'why' the incident
happened: is the location or context of the incident significant? Is it something to do
with the nature of the group of learners? Was it subject related or is the teacher's role
significant? The teacher in our example might ask questions about the nature of
the presentation; students might be particularly apprehensive if it forms a summative
assessment. The background of the students may be considered. Could relatively low
levels of educational attainment in the past have resulted in a lack of confidence? The
topic of the presentation might have been significant, had the students been struggling
with the subject and feeling inadequately prepared. In considering their own role,
the teacher might reflect on the preparation given to learners and whether enough
guidance had been given on what was expected.

When the teacher has considered the questions framed on the critical incident,
the analysis continues with what can be learned from the episode and ends with what
can be done to find a resolution. However, before implementing any solution, the
teacher may find it beneficial to seek the perspective of a colleague or mentor. Here
the teacher shares their interpretation of the incident. In the light of this discussion
the teacher may modify their analysis, and the solution to the problem.

Brookfield's 'critical reflection'

Brookfield (1995) argues that teachers' reflection on practice should be a process of
'hunting assumptions', where assumptions are the 'taken for granted' beliefs about
the world. He argues that there are three sets of such assumptions:

- *Prescriptive assumptions*: what we think *ought* to happen in a given situation, for
  example, adult students *ought* to be self-directed learners.

- *Causal assumptions*: if we do *x*, then *y* will happen, for example, if a teacher uses
  games and quizzes, followed by rewards, the motivation of young learners will be
  improved.

- *Paradigmatic assumptions*: the most difficult assumptions to uncover. They are
  the structuring assumptions we use to order the world into different categories, for
  example those operating within a 'conservative' paradigm may categorize learners
  as 'deserving' or 'undeserving' of their support, while those operating within an
  'emancipatory' paradigm draw on categories of 'those with or without power'.

Brookfield suggests that teachers can 'hunt' these assumptions by viewing their
practice through four 'critical lenses':

- *Our autobiographies as learners and teachers*: Brookfield sees as a prerequisite for the 'working' of the other lenses. Through self reflection Brookfield states a teacher becomes aware of the paradigmatic assumptions that influence their work. When a teacher knows what these are they can begin to test their accuracy.

- *Teachers looking at practice through their students' eyes*: For Brookfield, this allows a teacher to check whether the learners are engaging with teaching in the way intended.

- *Colleagues' experiences*: Brookfield argues that by inviting colleagues to observe practice and engage in 'critical conversations' the teacher can become aware of aspects of professional practice normally hidden.

- *Theoretical literature*: This helps to 'inform' practice. Brookfield argues it provides the teacher with 'multiple perspectives' on familiar situations. For example, reading literature on 'transforming learning cultures' (James and Biesta 2007) might provide greater insight into the motivations and learning experiences of young learners.

Criticisms of reflective practice

While reflective practice is widely accepted and some would say ubiquitous (Loughran 2006) throughout education, it is not without critics. There are at least four areas of concern: first, doubts about the efficacy of the reflective process; second, concern over the extent to which organizational cultures are 'enabling' of reflective practice; allied to this, the wider context in which teachers' practice is located may not be supportive; and, last, scepticism about teachers' commitment to reflective practice.

Some writers (for example Cornford 2002) have argued that there is a lack of empirical evidence on the efficacy of reflective practice. It is claimed that many academics have an 'ideological' commitment to reflective practice; consequently research showing reflective practice to be 'non-significant' remains unpublished. It is argued that this commitment is often to a 'critical' or 'emancipatory' reflective practice which is seen as rather abstract by many teachers (Parker 1997). Such abstractness is claimed to cause other problems. Husu et al. (2008) argue that the rather vague commitment to reflective practice presumes that everyone 'knows' how to reflect, but that some teachers need 'structured' help with the *process* of reflective practice which is not always available. Most writers making these criticisms do not suggest the abandonment of reflective practice. However, it is suggested instead that we should be sceptical about the claims made for it (Cornford 2002), and that there should be more guidance on the process of reflective practice (Husu et al. 2008)

A second criticism is that the importance of the milieu in which reflective practice takes place is overlooked in the literature. Suter (2007) found that the 'culture' within which it is enacted is crucial to its success. He found managerial regimes and levels of peer support to be as important as individual teachers' dispositions. Teachers interviewed for the research commented that their relationship with managers was an important consideration when embarking on reflective practice. Some stated that managers actively encouraged suggestions made as a result of reflection, while others commented these would not be welcomed, and in some instances were actively discouraged. In the same research, it was found that some teachers were working in teams where dialogue, trust and collaboration meant that teachers were comfortable in voicing concerns about their own professional practice, but others felt that this might be seen as a sign of weakness or incompetence. Such a critique can be developed to acknowledge the wider socio-economic context. In much the same way as we can interrogate managerial processes for the affordances they offer for reflective practice, so too can we question the wider structural and policy context in which teachers work. Such an analysis points toward an expansive notion of practice, one that moves beyond a focus on individual practitioners and aligns with a rather more political understanding of education.

Finally, Suter (2007) notes the dangers of reflective practice becoming 'routinized', just one more thing that the teacher is required to do alongside all the other paperwork required to keep up to date. When one considers the workload of teachers in the LLS, it is difficult not to sympathize with the view of some teachers that they do not have the time to reflect deeply on their practice, perhaps making a cursory note of an evaluation on a session plan which may or may not be followed up later. This perfunctory approach to reflective practice is an example of 'strategic compliance' (Shain and Gleeson 1999) where teachers comply minimally with what is required by management, creating the space for what they consider to be the 'real' job of teaching. It is ironic that some teachers come to regard as a chore that which is meant to 're-professionalize' them. But we should be attentive to the way in which notions of reflective practice can themselves become technicized and accented towards managerial interests – after all they can be used to keep us all up to the mark and in this sense are inherently contradictory (Avis 1994). Suter did find, however, that strategic compliance is by no means universal, and that some teachers will, with the right support, engage in reflective practice to enhance teaching and learning.

16

Mentoring in teacher education

Wayne Bailey, Chris Blamires, Liz Dixon and Denise Robinson

In this chapter:

- What is mentoring?
- Mentoring teachers in lifelong learning
- The role of the mentee
- Being observed in the classroom
- Conclusion

Mentoring in lifelong learning and its use in the support of trainee teachers is still relatively undeveloped and under-researched. Although mentor support is commonplace in many occupations and is often used to induct new teachers in lifelong learning, mentoring of trainee teachers in the sector was undertaken only sporadically until the Ofsted survey of 2003. This survey found that trainees lacked appropriate support for subject specialist development and attributed the deficiency to poorly developed mentoring systems (Ofsted 2003). The Government's response, in *Equipping Our Teachers for the Future*, accepted this view, stating that 'Subject-specific skills must be acquired in the teachers' workplace and from vocational or academic experience. Mentoring, either by line managers, subject experts or experienced teachers in related curriculum areas is essential' (DfES 2004: 8).

This chapter focuses on mentor support for trainee and newly-qualified teachers in lifelong learning. The concept of mentoring is discussed, together with important aspects of the mentoring relationship. The specific focus on mentoring trainee teachers helps to make the discussion concrete and detailed; in addition, many readers of this book will be trainees who are currently being mentored and may themselves be mentors in the future. This chapter will be of value to such readers in understanding their current and future roles in mentoring. However, many of the concepts and approaches discussed are transferable to other mentoring situations and the chapter is also intended to be helpful outside the immediate context of teacher education.

What is mentoring?

Megginson and Clutterbuck (1999: 3) define mentoring as 'Off-line help by one person to another in making significant transitions in knowledge, work and thinking'. In this definition, 'off-line' is taken to mean a relationship outside the organizational hierarchy and without any line management authority. Similar definitions are used by Rodd (2007) for mentoring teachers and by Mumford (1995) in his work on managers. The principle used is that, having no managerial responsibility for the *mentee* (the usual term for the person being mentored), the mentor is more able to be impartial. The relationship therefore has greater potential for mutual trust, empathy, cultural sensitivity, critical friendship and openness, without being supervisory and linked to specific management priorities. Mumford captures this argument succinctly when he observes 'a boss is not a mentor to a subordinate' (1995: 4). Mentoring may therefore be seen as a 'protected' relationship with the purpose of developing the mentee from apprenticeship to independence. This relationship will involve learning and experimentation and the development of competencies rather than coverage of specific course content. Ultimately, the effectiveness of mentoring for new or trainee teachers will depend on how successfully the mentoring relationship develops.

Mentoring teachers in lifelong learning

A variety of skills and attributes are needed to enable both mentor and trainee to get the best out of their relationship. Clearly, the main objective of mentoring is to support the trainee's development, both in achieving a teaching qualification and in providing a sound basis for CPD. A mentor needs to be friendly and approachable, build rapport with trainees and offer the right blend of challenge and support. The mentor needs to encourage trainees to reflect on their development and, in discussions, to listen actively and ask probing questions. These qualities are discussed in more detail below.

Be friendly and approachable in order to help build rapport

Mentors need to be actively interested in the development of trainees (Carter and Francis 2001) and to have a *mentoring attitude*, which involves the mentor valuing their own learning and that of their trainee in order to assist the trainee's development. A mentoring attitude can be developed by being open-minded, responsible and wholehearted in the relationship with trainees. Building rapport is a crucial part of the mentoring process and a 'culture of trust' must be developed (Taylor 2002). It is important that the trainee feels that their mentor cares about their development. The mentor must maintain 'transparency', by having clear and open expectations of the mentor–trainee relationship (Wallace and Gravells 2007). Confidentiality is an important aspect of a trusting relationship, as is being patient and non-judgemental.

Sharing what Egan (2002) calls 'empathic highlights' can also inspire trust. This involves the mentor sharing their understanding of the trainees' key experiences, behaviours and feelings. Egan asserts that they are 'empathic' because they are driven by the mentor's desire to understand their trainee and to communicate this understanding, and that they are 'highlights' because they focus on the key points that the trainee is making. Similarly, mentors also need to share their own experiences and critical incidents with trainees; this can in turn help the mentor and trainee trust one another.

Listen actively and question appropriately

Mentors can engage in *active listening* by maintaining regular eye contact and giving full attention to the trainee. Active listening helps to ensure that the mentor is open to all information and is free to follow, rather than to lead, the trainee (Wallace and Gravells 2007). Questioning skills are also important. The use of open, probing questions enables issues to be considered in detail and to be fully explored. Similarly, questions that connect ideas or events can also promote new understandings, helping trainees to explore the cause of an incident as well as its effects (Wallace and Gravells 2007). Conversely, the excessive use of closed questions and leading questions that invite particular answers can be detrimental to the trainee's development.

Encourage reflection

Reflective practice models currently dominate teacher education and it is therefore important that a trainee's understanding of critical reflection is developed by the mentor. Mentoring is not only about personal support; it should also provide professional development by challenging trainees' ideas and beliefs (Le Cornu 2005). Mentors should encourage trainees to take a critical stance towards their practice, which in turn encourages them to evaluate their teaching through reflection (Halai 2006). Boud et al. (1985: 37) discuss the role of a facilitator in assisting the process of reflection, particularly in describing events as objectively as possible and in being aware of affective barriers to learning (see Chapter 8). In contrast to Egan (see above), they note that 'It is vital that facilitators offer no interpretations or analyses of their own' and that 'The single most important contribution facilitators can make is to give free and undivided attention to the learner'.

Offer the right amount of challenge and support

There is abundant evidence that challenge is an appropriate mentoring strategy. Butcher (2003: 38) explains that 'challenge is seen as a discourse in which a mentor can guide, advise and question their student teachers in a collaborative context'. Challenge needs to be specific and focused and must involve a mentor setting tasks which could introduce conflicting ideas or even involve the trainee questioning their own assumptions (McNally and Martin 1998). Yet, if trainees are to be challenged then appropriate support mechanisms are needed. According to Butcher (2002: 198) challenge should be used 'in the context of a supportive and trusting training relationship'. This in turn fosters an atmosphere of empathy and trust as outlined earlier in this chapter. If challenge is used inappropriately, this can lead to the trainee leaving teacher training altogether (Stanulis and Russell 2000). There is also evidence to suggest that effective mentoring requires challenge and support that encompasses appropriate mechanisms for feedback (Stanulis and Russell 2000; Butcher 2002).

McNally and Martin (1998) propose a model of mentoring that involves both challenge and support. They discuss three types of mentors:

- The *laissez-faire* mentor sees their role as nurture and support, but offers little or no challenge to trainees.

- The *imperial mentor* has strong views and is interventionist, but offers little support to the trainee as the needs of the novice teacher are not seen as important.

- The *collaborative mentor* combines challenge and support, empowering trainees to engage in critical reflection as they develop.

Having a collaborative mentor brings clear benefits to trainees; however, the balance between challenge and support is crucial (Stanulis and Russell 2000; Butcher 2002). Too much challenge without support may lead to the trainee withdrawing or retreating due to lack of trust between trainee and mentor. In contrast, support without challenge does nothing more than confirm the status quo without developing the trainee; support combined with challenge is more likely to enable trainees to grow. Experienced in-service trainees may both require and expect more challenge from the outset of the mentoring relationship, although this cannot be assumed in advance. On the other hand, novice trainees (whether pre-service or in-service) may require more support than challenge in the first instance, a balance to be reviewed as the trainee develops. The model shown in Figure 16.1 gives a useful indication of how the varying combination of support and challenge impacts on the novice trainee.

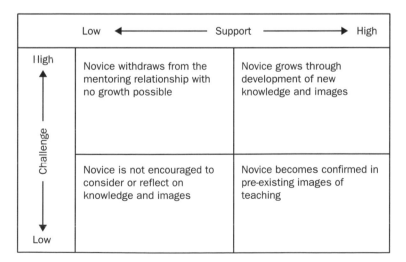

Figure 16.1 Support and challenge in mentoring novice trainees
Source: Elliott and Calderhead (1993)

The role of the mentee

As discussed in Chapter 3, the Reform Agenda has introduced requirements for FE teachers and those in the wider Learning and Skills sector to achieve an appropriate teaching qualification. This has meant a shift in the trainee population towards teachers in WBL and ACL contexts in addition to those in FE colleges. These developments imply a great increase in the number of teachers needing mentors to support their training, as well as considerable diversity in the contexts within which mentoring takes place. As teacher training reforms in the sector take effect, and the great majority of serving teachers achieve qualifications, trainees will largely be either pre-service or newly appointed staff with little teaching experience.

The skills acquisition model of Dreyfus and Dreyfus (1980) can be applied to inexperienced trainees. They identify the following stages: novice; advanced beginner; competent; proficient; and expert. According to this model, the novice trainee may have a rigid adherence to taught rules or plans and limited situational perception. Novices may hesitate in undertaking reflection in and on action. The role of the mentor is to draw out deeper understanding from the mentee enabling them to view situations holistically rather than in terms of individual aspects. The mentor needs to encourage reflective practice so as to aid trainees in their decision making.

The role of the mentee is closely related to the approach or model of mentoring that is adopted (consciously or unconsciously) by the mentor, as well as the previous teaching experience of the mentee. As noted earlier, models of mentoring tend to incorporate some aspect of reflective practice; the role of the mentor within this approach is one of supporting a professional colleague on a mutual basis of development and for experienced mentees this may well be appropriate. However, due to the changing profile of in-service teacher training, new entrants after 2010 will be much less likely to have substantial teaching experience and this model may become less appropriate, at least in the initial stages of trainee development.

Various approaches may be useful with less experienced mentees. Furlong and Maynard (1993) suggest that a flexible framework which reflects the growing knowledge and skill of the mentee is preferable. A novice mentee can initially be introduced to professional culture as well as skills-based development. With growing experience, they may be offered more responsibility and move away from peripheral participation to one closer to the centre of the professional community (Hankey 2004). Using communities of practice to analyse mentees' experiences with their mentors, Maynard (2000) suggests that mentees need to 'manage' their mentor as well as their own learning and that mentors can strongly influence the quality of their experience. This is confirmed in work by Hankey (2004) and Cullimore (2006).

Some guidelines for college-based mentees are presented in *Mentoring Towards Excellence* (LSC 2001: 154). These include, as a pre-requisite, an attitude of openness to the process. Mentees 'should possess: a commitment to their own development; honesty and openness about their own behaviour; a positive approach to the value of feedback; [and] time and willingness to develop relationships with their mentor'. Further protocols for mentees drawn from this document are given in Figure 16.2.

Protocols for mentees
Mentoring may be defined as a means of developing individuals to their potential. Mentoring can be used in different ways at different stages in an individual's career. Whatever the reason for using a mentor, as the mentee, you should possess the following:

- Commitment to your own development
- Honesty and openness about your own behaviour
- A positive approach to the value of feedback
- Time and willingness to develop a relationship with your mentor
- Willingness to listen and clarify your understanding
- Willingness to learn about the organization and about possible new ways of working
- The ability to accept the support and encouragement offered by the mentor and to consider advice in the spirit it is offered
- Willingness to challenge your own assumptions
- Willingness to consider options suggested by the mentor which you had not previously considered
- Willingness to review and reflect on your own behaviour and performance
- The wish to take responsibility for your own personal development
- Acknowledgement to share in the decision-making process to ensure the maximum outcomes from the mentor relationships.

Figure 16.2 Guidance for mentees
Source: LSC (2001: 155)

Being observed in the classroom

The observation of teaching is widespread in lifelong learning and teachers can expect to be observed on both a formal and informal basis. As well as having a place in quality assurance processes, classroom observation can help teachers to develop as professionals, and will often be a significant part of a mentoring relationship – either when the mentor observes and gives feedback to the trainee, or when the trainee observes their mentor. Observation can have a profound impact on organizational culture and may lead to a more open climate, greater trust between colleagues and the development of strong professional relationships (Marriott 2001). However, some teachers may feel threatened by observation of their practice, and may view the process with apprehension. This section considers a number of contexts in which teaching observations take place, highlighting their positive aspects while acknowledging that the experience of being observed may not always be unproblematic.

Observation in initial teacher training

Teaching observations have always been an important part of ITT and are an essential element of the professional development of trainee and novice teachers. Observations contribute to the assessment process in ITT and provide trainees with feedback on their progress and development. In order to achieve a teaching qualification, the trainee will be required to demonstrate that they have achieved a satisfactory standard based on a series of observations during the course. Where possible, trainees should themselves observe other teachers in order to learn from their practice; this will also help to broaden the trainee's experience of lifelong learning, particularly if the teacher observed works in a different context to the trainee.

Although the nature of observations for ITT is generally developmental and supportive, they contribute to summative as well as formative assessment and decisions have to be made as to whether or not the trainee has reached the standard required. For most trainees in lifelong learning, these decisions will be based on the LLUK standards discussed in Chapter 3. However, awarding institutions need to align their assessment criteria with current inspection frameworks and it is therefore likely that trainees will be assessed against the criteria used by Ofsted specifically for grading trainees in the course of ITT inspections (Ofsted 2008b: 29–31). Because trainees are developing towards qualified teacher status, these criteria differ from those used in inspecting college provision other than ITT.

Conduct of initial teacher training observations

Within the present system of initial teacher training, observations will normally be carried out by either a course tutor or the trainee's mentor. In the case of in-service trainees, practical teaching experience is gained through employment as a teacher and the timing of observations will therefore depend on the trainee's pattern of work. For this reason, in-service observations are normally arranged by negotiation between the trainee and the observer. Pre-service trainees, whose practical teaching is based on a placement in an appropriate organization, may have less control over the scheduling of observations. In particular, pre-service trainees may be teaching classes normally taken by their mentor, who could observe at any time – at least in principle. Nevertheless, even pre-service trainees will normally have some say in when they are observed. Although it may be tempting for a trainee to attempt to 'steer' observers towards lessons in which they are confident, it can be more beneficial to be observed in a more challenging situation which gives greater scope for developmental feedback (Cosh 1999).

Observers need to be able to make sense of the learning session and the trainee should provide them with copies of planning documents (lesson plan and scheme of work) as well as learning resources and assessment materials relating to the lesson. Some courses require trainees to provide a written rationale for the lesson. This would include information such as the background and context for the session, a brief profile of the learners in the group, known learning support needs, an outline of the overall approach (including strategies for assessment and differentiation) and any specific areas on which the trainee might wish to have feedback.

The observer may stay for the whole or part of a session. In either case it is important that the trainee receives both verbal and written feedback following the observation; verbal feedback provides the opportunity for dialogue and clarification, while written feedback provides a more detailed and permanent record for the person observed. In many ways, the process and content of feedback will relate to the principles of mentoring discussed above, although of course the feedback on an observation can be highly specific and deal with immediate practical issues while they are still fresh in the mind. However, observers need to go beyond procedural details, encouraging the trainee to reflect upon the issues arising and identify some specific areas for further development. It is possible that having received their feedback, the trainee or teacher who was observed will not agree with the comments and judgements of the observer. Nevertheless, the feedback can still provide a catalyst for further reflection on the issues raised.

Peer observations

Peer observations take place between colleagues, either as an informal means of developing their own practice or as a formal part of quality assurance systems. Mentoring relationships will normally involve an element of peer observation, possibly including reciprocal observations between mentor and mentee. Peer observation may be useful to individuals or groups of colleagues who are keen to explore and experiment with new ideas or problematic areas of practice. A fresh viewpoint in a supportive environment may stimulate insight, discussion and collaboration among colleagues. However, if feedback is overwhelmingly confirmatory it may become merely an exercise in mutual congratulation (Cosh 1999). As with mentoring relationships, an appropriate balance of challenge and support is necessary if peer observation is to be effective as a developmental tool.

Peer observation may be used for the purpose of appraisal, and this can sometimes be detrimental to teacher confidence and to a supportive teaching environment (Cosh 1999). As noted earlier, many authors regard an 'off-line' relationship (Megginson and Clutterbuck 1993: 3) as the most productive in building a mentoring climate based on mutual trust. Similar considerations suggest that peer observations may work best when they are outside a line-management relationship or quality assurance system.

The focus of peer observations may be chosen by the observer or the person observed. In the first model, standard pro-formas provide a framework to direct the observation towards certain predetermined issues. This may be helpful to inexperienced observers and may serve institutional agendas, but can be restrictive. By contrast, an observed led model allows the person being observed to set the agenda and to highlight, prior to the observation, certain key issues on which they would like the observer to give feedback. A strongly developmental focus is therefore possible, although considerable experience may be needed if the required balance of challenge and support is to be achieved.

Conclusion

It should be clear from this chapter that the quality of relationships is crucial to the effectiveness of both mentoring and peer observation. Achieving the right balance of support and challenge, and accepting that both parties can learn from the process, will allow mentoring and observation to be a constructive professional development experience. Teaching is becoming a much more open and collaborative activity, with a broader range of people being welcomed into classrooms and professional discussions. Mentoring and peer observation have the potential to be valuable elements in creating and maintaining the new communities of practice arising from this process.

17

Coaching
Alison Iredale and Judith Schoch

In this chapter:

- What is coaching?
- Experiential learning and coaching
- Social and situated theories of learning and coaching
- Getting the best from the relationship

I deeply believe that traditional teaching is an almost completely futile, wasteful, overrated function in today's changing world.

Carl Rogers (1983: 137)

What is coaching?

Carl Rogers (1902–87) is a major figure in humanist psychology, a leading progenitor of the counselling movement, as well as a force behind the development of the interest in person-centred therapies. He was also an apostle of student-centred learning, and advocates of coaching have been drawn to Carl Rogers for theoretical inspiration.

Today's coaches are often to be found working in the corporate world of human resources, frequently as consultants, and normally on a one-to-one basis. In that context, those being coached are usually referred to as 'clients' or as 'coachees', and despite the term 'client' carrying some negative consumerist connotations, it will be used in this discussion (coachee having an association with transport). A term such as 'trainee' would certainly be antithetical to the ethos of coaching. Central to the role of a coach is the facilitation of learning, and a fundamental tenet is that learning is controlled by the learner.

There are similarities between coaching and mentoring, and readers are advised to read Chapter 16 before this one. Part of the role of a mentor is to support development, providing advice and encouragement as well as challenging assumptions. It has been suggested that coaching is more concerned with the specific issue of the acquisition and refinement of 'skills' (Clutterbuck 2005; Jones et al. 2008). This understanding may have its basis in the fact that 'coaching' is frequently associated with sports, often with a focus on physical skills rather than on 'the total development of the individual' (Jones et al 2008: 3). Coaching, however, often goes beyond skills development. Arguably, the core of coaching is concerned with the engendering of attitudes and dispositions in order for an individual to be successful *on their own terms*. Not all mentors will adopt a coaching approach in their role, though Jenny Rogers (2007: 179) suggests they will be 'far more powerful' if they do. In recent years coaching has become fashionable, and a number of specialist sub-categories have emerged, including 'life coaching', 'business coaching' and 'conflict coaching'. Here we intend to consider coaching more generically.

Informal coaching is frequently incorporated into everyday situations where there are opportunities for learning and development, and in such circumstances the individuals involved are unlikely to attempt to distinguish between activities that may involve a mix of coaching, mentoring, facilitating, counselling, and teaching and training. There are, however, particular skills and attributes associated with effective coaching that can make a real difference to performance, whether used with groups of learners in the classroom, or with individuals at work.

Within business organizations, as is the case with mentoring, it is not unusual for coaching to be carried out by a line manager who is well placed to see how a person works on an everyday basis. With this 'operational coaching', however, there is the possibility that reflective and transformational dimensions in the process will be neglected in the face of the imperatives of 'getting the job done'. In essence, coaching techniques are being employed, but this kind of arrangement would not fit a purist vision of coaching.

Coaching in lifelong learning organizations, and in particular as part of CPD for teachers, is a relatively recent phenomenon. Since *Success for All* (DfES 2002a), coaching has enjoyed a much increased profile within training and development interventions. Starr (2003), discussing sports coaching, highlights the seeming contradiction of a world class athlete being coached by someone without world class status. Conversely, a world class athlete may lack the attributes required to coach effectively. In most situations coaching is about intuitive facilitation, and about inspiration, more than it is about the transmission of technique. Using the accumulated expertise of staff in an organization can effect change in a focused way, relating to performance criteria established from external quality enhancement measures such as the *Framework for Excellence* (LSC 2007b). This performative approach is, however, unlikely to nurture human potential in the way envisaged by Carl Rogers.

In the context of organizations in the LLS the coach is usually a qualified teacher and sometimes a close colleague of 'the client'. Here the recipient of the coaching is usually identified through an appraisal process, which may include assessments of their teaching undertaken by managers. In addition to the formally designated position of coach, there are several roles within initial teacher training for the LLS which may require coaching related sensibilities. These include teacher/ trainer, mentor, learning support worker and academic skills tutor. Another descriptor currently finding currency is that of 'critical friend', a term which is normally used to describe an informal role where a colleague seeks to provide a realistic and thought-provoking 'sounding board' and 'listening ear' to bring clarity to a person's thinking.

Experiential learning and coaching

Chapter 8 presented an overview of some key learning theories, including experiential learning, which is a foundational element underpinning the philosophy of coaching. The nature of coaching recognizes that people learn in different ways. John Dewey (1859–1952) argued for experience to be an important part of the educational process. Dewey was particularly interested in the nature of reflection, and the non-linear process of learning, paving the way for Kolb's (1984) model of experiential learning. Both the coach and the client need to be aware of this embodiment of learning as a holistic activity, taking into account the experiences of both parties.

> An experience is always what it is because of a transaction taking place between an individual and what, at the time, constitutes his environment, whether the latter consists of persons with whom he is talking . . ., the subject talked about . . .; the book he is reading . . .; or the materials of an experiment . . .
>
> (Dewey 1938: 43–4)

Dewey's thinking has a great deal to offer coaching practice, particularly in the areas of observation, reflection and deliberation. In traditional Inuit culture, when the young observe hunting activities they are not instructed what to do, as this is considered the least effective method of learning. Similarly, coaching practice uses observation as a key strategy for success, along with listening, questioning and reflection (Starr 2003: 48). The observational process is reciprocal, and the coach must in some sense expose or 'open up' elements of the client's needs, powers and potential trajectories. There is a complex and mutual process of envisioning.

A major method of assessing the work of teachers in relation to the quality of their teaching and the effectiveness of the learning processes which they manage is by observation. In the case of a trainee teacher this is carried out 'on them' primarily by a teacher educator or by their mentor, but they also routinely see their tutor, their mentor and their peers teaching. A qualified teacher might be observed by a member of their management team. In all these instances feedback provided is generally intended to be supportive and developmental, but, unless carefully managed, any power imbalances can mitigate against an encounter with the potential to enhance performance.

Social and situated theories of learning and coaching

There is a clear imperative for a coach to situate facilitation within a context which is meaningful to the client. For Lave and Wenger (1991) learning is a function of the activity, context and culture in which it occurs. They have suggested a movement from cognitive development to socially situated practice where learning is embedded in activity, and this activity needs to be close to 'real life' in order to be meaningful (see Figure 17.1 below). There is a distinction, however, between learning and performance, between the potential for competence and actual competence, and this lies at the heart of coaching practice.

Social and situated learning theories view learning as problematic, especially when there is a significant length of time between the learning and the performance. Classrooms are economically viable, traditionally recognized places of learning, but they are artificial. The knowledge required by a learner can be distilled into a classroom setting, bringing together learners with similar needs, but knowledge into action requires individuals to work together, and this requires a shared purpose. Wenger (1998: 6) described such a group as a 'community of practice' stating,

> [w]e all belong to communities of practice. At home, at work, at school, in our hobbies – we belong to several communities at any given time. And the communities of practice to which we belong change over the course of our lives. In fact, communities of practice are everywhere.

The (generally) one-to-one nature of the coach/client relationship may place it in tension with social theories of learning. The social environment is a crucial dimension in the dynamics of coaching, but some elements of the coach/client nexus rest on exclusion (of others) and on an element of closure to enable the client to engage with and develop self-understandings.

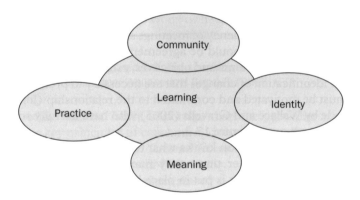

Figure 17.1 Components of a social theory of learning
Source: Wenger (1998: 5)

Getting the best from the relationship

Coaching is a process that has the capacity to identify opportunities for improvement, motivate through targets, facilitate the development and application of knowledge and skills, and to provide individualized constructive feedback. Carl Rogers (1983) stated his desire to wave an imaginary wand that would cause teachers to forget that they were teachers, to develop a 'complete amnesia' for the teaching skills they had acquired. Instead he wanted to find each teacher 'holding the attitudes and possessed of the skills of a *facilitator of learning* – genuineness, prizing, and empathy' (p.135, original emphasis). Rogers saw the approaches of a teacher and a facilitator as different – a teacher would ask, 'How can I make the mug hold still while I fill it from the jug with these facts that the curriculum planners and I regard as valuable?'. In contrast, a facilitator would ask, 'How can I create a psychological climate in which

supportive of the client. According to Sparrow (2008) more organizations are using a combination of coaching and mentoring, or choosing to ignore the subtle differences between them. Clutterbuck (2005) suggest this can be a useful approach. Mentors may need to coach their mentees to help them improve their performance in certain areas (Wallace and Gravells 2005). This might support the development of trainee teachers when applied to mentor observations of their teaching.

The theory of coaching is still under development, and there are many emergent models. It is important that coaching interventions are applied with due sensitivity and recognition of the primacy of the client in the relationship. Principles such as trust and confidentiality do not sit easily with systems designed for management, quality assurance, audit, or performance monitoring. Coaching offers great potential when applied in the right way in an appropriate environment for the benefit of the client. The coach/client relationship is a privileged one in both senses of the word – and it should not be abused.

PART 3

Working in the lifelong learning sector

18

Getting to know the organization

James Avis, Julie Dalton, Liz Dixon, Ann Jennings, Kevin Orr and Jonathan Tummons

---

In this chapter:

- Your first visit
- Structures and hierarchies
- Informal networks
- Managerialism and performativity
- The staffroom

This chapter has two interrelated tasks. First, it seeks to help pre-service trainees prepare for a college placement. To reflect this intention, some sections are written in the second person, addressed to 'you' as the trainee. Second, the chapter aims to provide a conceptual framework for understanding college relations. Newly appointed teachers may also find this chapter useful.

Your first visit

'Be prepared for anything' is useful guidance for someone attending a placement college for the first time. Some colleges may interview you before offering a placement, others will assume that you are suitable because you have already been interviewed for your ITT course. In this case they may introduce you to staff, discuss your teaching and placement plans and show you where you will be working.

Prepare for the visit as you would for a job interview. Study the college website, which should contain maps, lists of courses and news events. Some give information on policies and procedures and many offer a virtual tour of the premises. The Internet can provide a wealth of information, including Ofsted reports and job vacancies.

If possible, go to the college before the visit. How far is it from the bus or train station? If driving, do not assume that you will be able to park on-site – college car parks are often reserved for staff and formal visitors. If you visit during a normal college day you will see students and staff, and will be able to assess the character and ethos of the college. Many colleges now have some form of dress code for staff, and it is helpful to be aware of this before your first formal visit.

Your appearance is important, and first impressions count. You should appear clean, neat and tidy. Many organizations do not allow jeans to be worn and consider tattoos or body piercing inappropriate. Staff are often regarded as role models for students, with the same expectation applying to trainee teachers. It is advisable to dress modestly and smartly and to cover any tattoos and piercings if possible. As a guest in the organization, you may have to make an attempt to 'fit in'.

Prepare some documentation for the visit and organize it so that you can easily find what you need. The staff you are meeting may have seen your CV, but do not assume this – communication within large organizations can be difficult. Have your contact details and times of placement ready to give to the member of staff you will be working with. It is advisable to take more than one copy as you may be working in more than one section. Take your ITT course enrolment card with you as proof of identity, as well as any course documents needed by college staff. Some college Human Resource departments may need evidence of your Criminal Record Bureau (CRB) check. Take a notebook and pen so that you can take notes. As in a job interview, be prepared to 'sell' yourself – there may be other students needing placements at the college so you may have competition.

Be early rather than late, but not too early. College staff are busy and may not appreciate someone turning up half an hour early. Go to reception unless you have been told otherwise. Be prepared to explain clearly who you are and who you are meeting. Turn off your mobile telephone. You will probably be asked to make an entry in the visitors' book, giving your name and the name of the person you are to see, the name of your university, college or other training provider and the time of arrival. You may be given a visitor identity badge. You will probably be asked to wait for the member of staff to come and collect you. If you are waiting in the reception area, take the opportunity to look through the college leaflets and information sheets often situated there.

If you feel nervous take a few deep breaths. Look cheerful, smile, appear enthusiastic and confident. You have something to offer the college. As you are led to the staff room or office, make a mental note of your location: rooms and corridors may be numbered or colour coded. Make a note of where facilities such as toilets and drinks machines are located.

The rest of the visit very much depends on who you are meeting. It may be someone with cross-college responsibility for trainees on teaching placements. Alternatively, it may be your mentor or another member of staff from your vocational/ discipline area. Before the visit, consider questions you need to ask; you will probably think of further questions during the visit. Remain polite and courteous. Discuss what is required but do not be overfamiliar.

You might want to discuss the research you have done and show that you are familiar with some of the courses the college offers. You may have read the latest college Ofsted report. If this was favourable, you might comment; if not, it may be better not to draw attention to this. Note how people address one another. It is usual nowadays for first names to be used, but in a few colleges and vocational areas more formal terms of address are used. Remain professional and discreet at all times.

Structures and hierarchies

The organizational structures of a college or other provider are often a prominent feature of its life. The organizational charts distributed at induction events for new staff indicate specific lines of responsibility and communication between different areas, departments or directorates. Similarly, the procedures and paperwork that accompany the work of the teacher are grounded in the structures and hierarchies of the organization. Self-assessment reports, probation reports for new staff, line management meetings, appraisals: these and other procedures follow the formal structures of the organization in terms of reporting, quality assurance and administration.

Informal networks

As a new member of staff or trainee on placement, spend some time getting to know the organization. As well as knowing about formal procedures, it is also important to develop a realistic awareness of timescales and possible delays in these systems so that you can plan work in good time. For example, printing services may have a heavy workload and large-volume photocopying may not be possible on a same-day basis. Circumventing such procedures, which is often possible in large organizations, may help in the short term but will not make you popular with colleagues or the college hierarchy.

Whatever the ethics, it is certainly the case that staff will often find ways to do what is expected but not necessarily in ways that coincide with formal organizational practices and procedures. Such *inventive resourcefulness* is a characteristic of any community of practice, and a FE college is a collection of many such communities. This inventive resourcefulness is part of the *shared repertoire* of the community of practice, and it is through the forming and re-forming of informal networks of practice that it is shared and learned (Tummons 2008).

As a way of understanding the FE college workplace, inventive resourcefulness can be seen as an aspect of work-based learning. From this point of view, there is no theoretical distinction between learning how to complete a requisition form correctly and learning how to acquire the requisitioned article by other means. Both are part of the workplace, but only one is officially sanctioned by established policies and procedures.

Becoming part of these informal networks is not straightforward. They will look and behave differently across different colleges, and even within the same college will vary between different staffrooms and departments. A workplace mentor can serve as a useful conduit on such occasions. Taking time to make introductions and ask questions can also be helpful. Generally, it is through participation, trial and error and experience that inventive resourcefulness is learned and developed. Informal networks of practice, participation and activity are therefore an important way to learn about the organization.

Managerialism and performativity

Prior to the Further and Higher Education Act of 1992, FE colleges were controlled by local education authorities; as noted elsewhere (see Chapters 2, 5 and 21) management structures often reflected patriarchal relations. However, following incorporation, increasingly strident forms of managerialism developed (Randle and Brady 1997). These were frequently set within a rather aggressive form of bullying masculinity (Kerfoot and Whitehead 1998). During this period there were significant numbers of redundancies, with many established members of staff taking early retirement.

Partly as a reaction to the rigours of incorporation and with the retirement of many male senior staff, the climate of management has moderated and a less 'masculine' culture exists, partly due to an increase in the number of women principals. However, despite the changes that have taken place, colleges remain set within a performative context. That is to say, a context in which activity is focused upon measurable outcomes with an emphasis upon meeting targets set by the state or it intermediaries. Targets may relate to year-on-year improvement in student performance, scores in satisfaction surveys, efficiency gains, and so on. Targets for individual teachers and the degree to which previous targets have been met may be discussed in appraisals.

There is a real question about the way in which we conceptualize waged labour within FE. The move towards managerialism undermined previous forms of control, breaking away from the rhetoric of professionalism and collegiality. It also accented the division between managers and teachers as well as highlighting potential antagonisms surrounding professional autonomy and the intensification of labour. Not everyone would accept this analysis. Some writers argue that FE teachers occupy contradictory positions involving both teaching and elements of managerial responsibility (Simkins and Lumby 2002). Others suggest that there is a possibility of progressive alliances that cross over hierarchical divisions. Gleeson and Shain (1999) describe the different orientations held by those working in the sector, including unwilling, willing and strategic compliance. Unwilling compliers are those most likely to take redundancy or early retirement, willing compliers accept managerialism whereas strategic compliers adopt a pragmatic stance. For Gleeson and Shain, these orientations are not tied to particular institutional positions and could just as easily be inhabited by senior management as well as rank and file staff. Strategic compliers seek to wrest progressive possibilities from the conditions in which they find themselves. The difficulty with this particular orientation is that such a stance could easily be appropriated by a particular form of managerialism, thereby becoming a veneer for managerial control.

Edwards (1980) reminds us that there are various ways through which managerial control is enacted. These range from the patriarchal to those based upon what we now call managerialism. Forms of management that celebrate the creativity and contribution of the labour force may be as much about control as the more authoritarian types. The strategy developed by management will be in part shaped by the institutional context as well as the power relations that are in play. Neither should we forget the impact of the management orientation of a particular principal, who may wish to accent a specific aspect of the prevailing management regime. For while performativity and target setting are currently ubiquitous, the way in which they are accented may vary from institution to institution, with some seeking to mitigate their effects while others seemingly relish the rigours involved. Finally, we should remember that different managerial regimes may well co-exist within a particular college, whereby particular sections or departments mediate the current regime in ways that afford staff more or less autonomy.

The staffroom

Although teachers spend a great deal of time in classrooms, the staffroom is another important space in their professional lives. The staffroom is typically a place where teachers have a physical base and are likely to spend varying amounts of time during their working day, engaged in a range of activities both social and work-related. In books on teaching and learning or teacher training, discussion of the staffroom is uncommon. The staffroom is arguably a taken-for-granted space, and as such, perhaps mistakenly, afforded little significance when trainees are prepared for their teaching practice or when considering trainees' learning on placement.

Perhaps it is the highly distinctive nature of individual staffrooms which make any general observations or comment difficult to distil into a few paragraphs. Any staffroom is likely to have its own particular culture; the complexity of these cultures may be influenced by such factors as the individuals who populate the space, the curriculum areas or shared specialisms of the staff and the physical size and layout of the environment. Biott and Easen (1994: 71) note the significance of context and suggest that teachers work in interwoven social structures created partly by themselves and partly by management and organizational arrangements and processes. The staffroom may be defined by its own characteristics, explicit and implicit rules and boundaries, and could be said to represent a microcosm of social and professional life. It may offer some clues as to the history, culture and practices of the institution as a whole and may also reflect social and political concerns of the time.

A staffroom is both a private and public space and the balance and interplay of these may indicate the culture and values associated with it. On approaching a staffroom it is interesting to note the detail of access and what it signifies about the staffroom itself and the institution as a whole. Is there open access to the room? Do individuals knock on entering? What clues do signs give – 'Staff Only', 'Please knock before entering' – ? Are students and visitors welcomed into the staffroom space? It is possible that the culture and values of any particular staffroom may be highly idiosyncratic and may mirror or diametrically oppose the culture and values of the institution as a whole.

Allocation of space and working areas may be clearly defined and territorial, where each member of staff has a clearly demarcated space. That space may double as a place of work and recreation. On entering a staffroom for the first time one might encounter a space which has clearly defined boundaries associated with particular individuals; indeed, that personalized space may speak volumes about those who occupy the area. On the other hand the space may be much less clearly defined with shared areas designated for 'hot-desking'. This is arguably a telling reflection of working practices in a sector whose responses are typically short term, rapid and reactive and where the emphasis lies on product as opposed to process. It may also reflect the transient, temporary and unstable nature of employment for many staff on short-term or part-time hourly paid contracts.

We might also consider the nature of the conversations and exchanges which take place in staffrooms. What proportion of time is devoted to conversations about teaching and learning? This may be highly significant for a trainee teacher who may be expecting and looking for opportunities to speak with their mentor and colleagues about teaching, learning and wider educational issues.

It is interesting to reflect on the individual and shared characteristics and culture of the teachers who populate the staffroom. Is it a noticeably gendered space, and if so, what are its defining characteristics? Is there a higher proportion of male or female staff? Is this linked in any way to the curriculum area? Is it an orderly, tidy space or is it chaotic or highly individualized? Is the desk space occupied by individuals and personalized by artefacts such as photographs, notices or personal belongings or is it a neutral place devoid of any defining characteristic? Within any institution, a staffroom is likely to be populated by different groups and individuals who may be constituted according to shared curriculum areas or subject disciplines. They may include teachers and support staff employed under different types of contracts and with different conditions of service. Indeed, a trainee teacher may find difficulty in distinguishing the myriad individuals using the staffroom. Yeomans (1986) noted that teachers' interactions were frequent, if sometimes fleeting, and that their personal and professional concerns were rarely kept separate, claiming also that flat hierarchies meant that those with leadership and management roles were not easily distinguished.

Does this staffroom culture suggest a place where, irrespective of numbers, layout or proximity, teachers operate in isolation or is there an indication of working together with notions of collegiality or collaboration? What is the impact of that culture on the trainee teacher who may be a newcomer or is in the process of 'becoming' a teacher? The staffroom may be a place where new and developing teachers seek to access guidance and support from experienced staff and colleagues. However, 'Individuals or cohorts of individuals will experience different kinds of affordances, depending on their affiliation, associations, gender, language skills, employment status and standing in the workplace' (Billett 2004: 116). These differentiations may be apparent within the confines of the staffroom and may help to explain the extent to which individuals or groups are included or choose to involve themselves in workplace activities. While some trainee teachers may have only limited formal contact with permanent staff in a staffroom, it is likely that they will be influenced by them and learn from them in an informal, *ad hoc* manner. This is likely to be brought into sharp focus in the staffroom environment where teachers learn and respond to the implicit and explicit values, practices and hierarchies which pertain to that place. Other aspects of identity such as gender, race, age, sexual orientation may also play a part in determining the extent to which individuals are perceived by others and feel themselves to 'fit in'. On observing the staffroom it is likely we will encounter a unique culture characterized by the teachers who inhabit that space. For any trainee or new teacher, the staffroom can be a rich source of reflection and is likely to offer insights into the wider aspect of a teacher's life beyond the confines of the classroom.

19

Health, safety and well-being
Julie Dalton and David Neve

In this chapter:

- Risk
- Legal responsibilities
- Health and safety in the workplace
- Bullying and harassment
- The Independent Safeguarding Authority and the Criminal Records Bureau
- Security
- *Every Child Matters* and *Youth Matters*

Risk

According to Ulrich Beck (1992), processes of modernization have generated unprecedented levels of risk. These arise from new technologies, increased mobility, the environmental consequences of economic activity and other features of globalization. Educational establishments can be seen as places brimming with the potential for harm – both physical and psychological. Furedi (1997) critiques what he sees as a disabling tendency for Western society to become absorbed by concerns for safety and the anticipation of threat; this climate can stifle thinking, limit creativity and bind academics and learners in bureaucratic procedures. Ecclestone and Hayes (2009) have argued that there is a damaging tendency for teachers to regard students as vulnerable. Concerns with issues such as stress, bullying and harassment have led to a plethora of policies and committees that feed (and feed on) a discourse of caution, and thereby perpetuate 'victimhood'. Places of learning, however, like other workplaces, leisure spaces, and the domestic sphere, do harbour dangers – especially in vocational training areas. There *are* responsibilities, and these need to be taken seriously.

Legal responsibilities

This book will not provide an exposition on the law in relation to teaching in the LLS, not least because information and case law are subject to rapid change. JISC (2002) provides useful guidance, explaining that:

Duty of care is the obligation to exercise a level of care towards an individual, as is reasonable in all the circumstances, to avoid injury to that individual or his or her property.

Duty of care is therefore based upon the relationship of the parties, the negligent act or omission and the reasonable foreseeability of loss to that individual.

A negligent act is an unintentional but careless act which results in loss. Only a negligent act will be regarded as having breached a duty of care. Liability for breach of a duty of care very much depends on the public policy at the time the case is heard.

In the FE and HE system duties of care will govern relations with a wide variety of groups including, but not limited to, employees, students and even visitors.

Any individual facing a work-related legal issue should seek current legal advice (this is normally available via trade unions for members).

Health and safety in the workplace

All employers have legal duties relating to workplace safety, the operation of day-to-day activities, and the way that equipment or substances are handled and stored. Under the terms of the Health and Safety at Work Act (HSWA 1974) employees also have responsibilities, reflecting the fact that good safety practice stems from working collaboratively. Governors play an important role in establishing health and safety policy at the institutional level, and the governing body will have the main role in management and responsibility for health and safety, together with the allocation of sufficient funds to ensure safe working and that health practices are compliant.

The Health and Safety Executive (HSE) enforces health and safety law. The HSE has legal powers backed up by the criminal courts, and through its inspectors can issue improvement notices or prohibition orders. It is worth emphasizing that any breaches of Health and Safety law under the 1974 Act are likely to result in a criminal offence being committed and action being taken. Employers and employees are often subject to legal action in this form. For example, in April 2008 a college was fined £14,000 with £18,000 costs following an incident in which a lecturer was burned by the explosion of a nitric acid container (UCU 2008).

The HSE education website (http://www.hse.gov.uk/) is a useful source of guidance and carries the following brief list of responsibilities:

- provide all necessary information, instruction, training and supervision to enable individuals to be safe
- provide and maintain a safe place of work with safe entry and exit
- provide and maintain a working environment that is safe and without risk to health
- provide and maintain systems of work that are safe
- arrange for the safe use, handling, storage and transport of articles and substances.

The website also identifies employees' duties as follows:

- to take reasonable care of the health and safety of themselves and of others who may be affected by what they do or forget to do
- to cooperate with the employer on health and safety matters
- not to misuse any equipment that is provided for safety purposes (for example, fire extinguishers or safety goggles)
- to follow instructions from the employer on health and safety matters and attend relevant health and safety training
- to report hazards and defects observed in the workplace.

Employees should refer to the health and safety policy which employers are legally required to provide. This must be in writing and must be updated according to need. Further information on the responsibilities of employers is also available on the UCU website. For advice and guidance related to specific vocational areas it would be wise to check the various Sector Skills Councils.

Risk assessment

> Some of the 'elfandsafety' stories are just myths . . . But our research shows that behind many of the stories, there is at least a grain of truth . . . Of course the untold story is that many organizations manage risks sensibly, responsibly and proportionately.
>
> > Bill Callaghan, Chair of the Health and Safety Commission
> > (HSE 2006a)

An effective risk assessment is a key tool in the management of risks. The National Union of Teachers (NUT; 2003: 1) published guidance defining risk assessment as

> . . . an important tool in ensuring health and safety at work. It means, simply, that employers set out to identify hazards to health and safety, evaluate the risk of harm resulting from those hazards and take appropriate action to protect employees and others.

In the LLS, teachers in vocational areas such as hairdressing, beauty therapy or construction will have experience of industry-based risk assessment. As teachers or trainers, health and safety will be a central part of course content as well as classroom practice. Particularly in NVQ qualifications, this will probably entail assessing trainees in safe working practices and risk assessment. More generally, in any educational setting risks posed by the teaching environment must be considered, together with any specific risks presented by learning activities. Practical workshops are potentially hazardous places. Computer workshops, and off-campus field trips or study visits, also present varying degrees of risk and teachers must undertake appropriate risk assessment.

Some likely risk assessment categories are summarized here:

- *General risks*: (management of the Health and Safety at Work Regulations)
- *Exposure to substances which may cause damage to health*: (Control of Asbestos at Work Regulations; Control of Lead at Work Regulations)
- *Computers and workstations*: (Health and Safety [Display Screen Equipment] Regulations)
- *Hazardous lifting or carrying*: (Manual Handling Operations Regulations)
- *Noisy environments which could cause damage to hearing*: (Control of Noise at Work Regulations)
- *Fire Safety*: (Regulatory Reform [Fire Safety] Order)

It is important that teachers consider how these categories might affect their specialist subject.

Teachers need to carry out risk assessments regularly in relation to their working areas. Risk assessments do the following:

- provide an assessment and evaluation of risks which might occur as a result of training and educational activities and document corrective and or preventative action;
- demonstrate performance standards for the control of risks;
- help organizations reduce risks to the lowest level, providing a safe system of work;
- the setting up of well-managed risk assessments enables trainers and teachers to model what trainees will need to do in the workplace.

Who is responsible for risk assessments?

The employer has legal responsibility for risk assessment. In the LLS this will normally mean the governing body of the organization. The NUT recognize that in practice the risk assessment process will need to be delegated by the employer to someone who manages the process, and someone who carries out risk assessments, on the employer's behalf. The extent to which teachers should be involved in risk assessment will depend on two things: first, their conditions of service, professional duties and any management responsibility which they have for health and safety matters; and, second, whether they are competent to take part in the process on the employer's behalf.

Risk assessments can be (and often are) completed on a single page and need not be complicated. HSE (2006b) advocate a five stage plan.

1 Identify the hazards.
2 Decide who might be harmed and how.
3 Evaluate the risks and decide on precaution.
4 Record your findings and implement them.
5 Review your assessment and update if necessary.

Bullying and harassment

There are a number of broad categories of bullying and harassment that may concern teachers. These can be summarized as:

- learner to learner
- teacher to learner
- learner to teacher
- management to employee.

Websites may prove useful in exploring aspects of bullying and harassment. *Bullying Matters* (2009) refers to bullying in the workplace as follows:

> Workplace bullying makes people's working lives a misery and can have devastating effects on an individual's health, family and career . . . Bullying impacts on staff turnover, health, morale, production and performance and can result in costly lawsuits as well as damaged reputation and public confidence.

Harassment may refer to a spectrum of offensive actions and behaviours that are experienced as threatening or disturbing, and beyond those sanctioned by society. Sexual harassment refers to persistent and unwanted sexual advances. In general terms, harassment involves behaviour that is unwanted, unwarranted and likely to cause detriment and stress to sufferers. It can take the form of physical, verbal and emotional abuse, gestures and the written word. Cyber forms of harassment and bullying are now common through email, text messages and web-based social networking.

In effectively managed working environments there should be written policies on harassment and bullying – and allegations should be documented. There should be a programme of staff development related to the policies and procedures. For further information a short list of relevant websites is provided below.

- **ACAS** at http://www.acas.org.uk
- **Government advice** at http://www.teachernet.gov.uk
- **TUC** at http://www.tuc.org.uk

The teacher unions are normally able to provide guidance and representation for their members.

The Independent Safeguarding Authority and the Criminal Records Bureau

The Independent Safeguarding Authority (ISA) assesses people wishing to work or volunteer with vulnerable people. It uses data gathered by the CRB – an executive agency of the Home Office set up to help employers make safer recruitment decisions. There are two types of CRB checks, enhanced disclosures and standard disclosures. Both require a fee to be paid by those using the service. 'List 99' is a

DCSF maintained list of people unsuitable for or barred from working with children, or young and vulnerable people, following criminal prosecutions. The CRB's work has increased following a number of high profile cases in the residential care and educational sectors. All people employed to work with children and vulnerable adults should undergo a CRB assessment before taking up employment.

Security

Theft

The theft of personal items and institutional equipment is commonplace, with institutions combating this by issuing identity cards to staff and learners, and by installing security systems and CCTV. The opportunity to steal valuable items has increased with the use of mobile phones, mp3 players and laptop computers. Simple steps can be taken to avoid such thefts. Valuable items should not be left in an unlocked teaching area or office. Items should be security marked or locked down wherever possible, and should not be displayed more than necessary.

Computer security

Harmful programs can spread between unprotected computers, especially when connected through networks. In the best practice users will have up-to-date anti-virus software running at all times. Because the risks are high most educational institutions will provide specialist advice and guidance to users. Institutional policies on the use of computer facilities should be read carefully, as there will normally be restrictions on what can be accessed and these restrictions may affect teaching activities (see also Chapter 11).

Many learners and teachers do not take sensible precautions in relation to the security of computer files. It is wise to ensure that files stored on computer hard drives are 'backed up' at regular intervals by writing them to CD, DVD or similar secondary storage systems. Some social software provides users with a free account and storage space for files. These files can be made public, for sharing across a community, or locked for personal use. The servers used for these services are themselves backed up, duplicated or triplicated, and therefore a reasonably secure environment is created.

Unfortunately, the large networks that exist in universities and colleges are often targets for mass emailings and malicious requests. It is important to exercise caution when suspect mail finds its way into personal mailboxes. It is not uncommon for hoax email messages to warn of viruses that do not exist. Other hoax messages often spread, and advice should be sought from the institution's computing services staff. Personal computers are best protected with an anti-virus package, which will automatically update itself as new threats appear.

Every Child Matters and *Youth Matters*

This section will consider the broader context of staying safe, being healthy and making a positive contribution. These aims are part of The Children's Act 2004 and are outcomes inspected by Ofsted. In 2003 the Government published its *Every Child Matters* (ECM; HM Government 2003) Green Paper, outlining a new approach to the well-being of children and young people up to the age of 19. This was a response to Lord Laming's Report (DoH/The Home Office 2003) into the circumstances surrounding the abuse and murder of eight-year-old Victoria Climbié. ECM (DfES 2003: 13) identified the need 'to ensure we properly protect children at risk of neglect and harm within a framework of universal services which aims to prevent negative outcomes and support every child to develop their full potential'.

The focus of ECM is on enabling young people to meet five key outcomes:

- *being healthy*: enjoying good physical and mental health and living a healthy lifestyle
- *staying safe*: being protected from harm and neglect and growing up able to look after themselves
- *enjoying and achieving*: getting the most out of life and developing broad skills for adulthood
- *making a positive contribution*: to the community and to society and not engaging in anti-social or offending behaviour
- *economic well-being*: overcoming socio-economic disadvantages to achieve their full potential in life.

(DfES 2003d: 7)

The Education Act 2002 required local authorities and the governing bodies of schools and FE institutions to 'carry out their functions with a view to safeguarding and promoting the welfare of children' (HM Government 2003: 76). This duty came into force on 1 April 2004.

The aims of ECM, are unlikely to meet with criticism from any reasonable source but the initiative and policy are not unproblematic. Hoyle (2008: 10) has argued the following:

> Central to the *Every Child Matters* way of thinking is a re-enforcement and perpetuation of a focus on visible 'symptoms' in the lives of children, young people and families. A shallow focus obviates any critical dialogue about the structural inequalities in contemporary England from which such 'symptoms' can emerge. For example, public services are required to work with each other to provide services that ensure children and young people can 'Be Healthy' – in the outcomes framework this broad outcome is reduced to, reducing infant mortality; obesity; conception and sexually transmitted infection among under 18s; and the use of Class A drugs . . . attention at both national and local level is diverted away from deep and widening health inequalities between advantaged and disadvantaged communities . . .

Hoyle further criticizes the way in which ECM invades children's rights to privacy, and what he regards as a tendency to 'centralization of credit: diffusion of blame' that is inherent within ECM.

Every Youth Matters

The Green Paper *Youth Matters* (HM Government 2005) constituted a development of ECM (DfES 2003d) with a view to improving the services available to support young people through enhanced coordination and use of technology. It would seek to engage young people, through various initiatives, including volunteering. Government has proposed a targeted programme of reform for youth services (DCSF 2007a). Targeted youth support aims to help vulnerable young people achieve the ECM outcomes. The most important goal for post-compulsory providers is to 'raise young people's aspirations and help them to achieve and feel positive towards learning. This includes helping them to be engaged and stay engaged in the wider range of learning opportunities becoming available for 14–19-year-olds' (p. 6). The Green Paper *Raising Expectations: Staying in Education and Training Post-16* (DfES 2007) recognized that 'vulnerable' and 'low achieving' young people were those most likely to leave education at the age of 16. Consequently, it was proposed that young people should be required to remain in education or training until the age of 18 (Simmons 2008) and that new 14–19 diplomas, with a mix of practical and theoretical study, would be made available.

The Every Youth Matters (EYM) agenda suggests three areas of necessary improvement. First, the reform of the curriculum and qualifications, which will engage and challenge more young people; second, improvements to advice and guidance; and, third, improvements in youth services to ensure there are more outlets for young people and that they can undertake wider activities.

For teachers in post-compulsory education and training the emphasis will be on working with local authorities and other agencies to deliver an entitlement which will go beyond anything that one provider could offer. There will be a need to share resources and information, to work within a multi-agency team and to have awareness of the information, advice and guidance available to young people within the local authority. Impartial information, advice and guidance must be available within institutions.

Issues of 'well-being' have emerged as an important element in New Labour social policy. Indeed, there has been a convergence of initiatives that, with a focus on multi-agency working, have seen aspects of the education, social welfare and health systems intersect. Educational institutions now constitute a critical site where connections between health and education for young people are expected to mirror government imperatives for 'joined up' thinking. A greater emphasis on social inclusion has meant that young people with special educational needs (SEN) and/or behavioural, emotional or social difficulties (BESD) are likely to be educated in 'mainstream' institutions within the LLS. There is also a growing number of young people identified as suffering from mental health and psychological problems. Greater student diversity demands much of teachers, who must adopt differentiated strategies. Teachers are expected to promote learning environments conducive to well-being. At the same time, however, they face unprecedented pressures to raise educational standards. These apparently contradictory drives may be incompatible. Pressures to raise standards are not always reconcilable with the type of 'caring' relationship that promotes well-being.

The policy thrust of New Labour may be seen as a positive development which is indicative of a concern to alleviate disadvantage and to facilitate equality of opportunity. Alternatively, it can be regarded as an attempt to mask inherent inequalities through initiatives that, while ostensibly enabling, place responsibility on individuals to comply with economic imperatives that are unlikely to serve their best interests.

20

Administration and course management
Frances Marsden and Andrew Youde

In this chapter:

- Maintaining records
- Managing a course
- Curriculum management
- Managing teaching staff
- Marketing
- Working with administrative staff
- Awarding bodies
- Committee membership
- Conclusion

This chapter provides an overview of the main administrative functions relating to teaching in the LLS. Jackson and Wallis (2006: 251) state:

> Post-compulsory education is living through an extended period of unprecedented upheaval and change in a climate of increased public accountability. A culture of target setting, action planning and monitoring underpins the allocation of public funding . . .

Effective administrative procedures assist the maintenance of accurate course records and student information systems, enhance institutional quality assurance processes, and serve the need to respond to the requirements of external funding bodies (such as SFA and HEFCE) or inspection (for example, Ofsted and the QAA). Teachers and administrators have an important inter-professional relationship and academics normally carry course management responsibilities.

Maintaining records

The first priority for a teacher will be their pedagogic work. Teacher education courses normally incorporate significant reference to the wider work of curriculum development and evaluation, though it is frequently the case that the administrative role of a teacher is only appreciated in the workplace. While the maintenance of records may be experienced as a bureaucratic imposition there is a clear link between effective administration and a positive learning experience.

Registers of attendance are key records and it is important that they are completed accurately for external audit purposes and possible Educational Maintenance Allowance (EMA) requirements. Each institution will have its own attendance monitoring system, often utilizing electronic attendance monitoring systems with the data automatically downloading to the Management Information System (MIS). While summative achievement is usually monitored centrally, formative assessment records are normally maintained and reviewed by individual teachers. It is the responsibility of all teachers to prepare teaching materials, teach students, assess work and monitor student progress. Each of these activities should be evidenced.

Government funded FE is inspected primarily by Ofsted, as are teacher training courses, with the QAA reviewing most HE. Ofsted (2007: 7) aim to 'promote a culture of self-assessment among providers' with the inspection team judging its accuracy. Strengths and weaknesses are identified through the self-assessment process supported with relevant quantitative data supplemented with qualitative analysis.

Managing a course

A course leader's role will involve management of the following areas:

- the annual course evaluation
- the curriculum
- the course team.

Annual course evaluation

A course leader is heavily involved in the processes of course evaluation. O'Connell (2005: 197) outlines the importance of self-assessment by course teams. Each team should consider its strengths and weaknesses, informing the production of an action plan to monitor progress. This process can be rationalized by the use of standard forms derived from Ofsted's inspection handbooks, or similar documentation. Institutional training will normally guide this process and keep course teams abreast of changes in inspection frameworks. Advice regarding the grading of the course will be provided as part of this training, as a valid grade forms part of the annual evaluation process which will usually involve a meeting with the senior management team (SMT). For a new course leader this could be a development process where targets are agreed, however, these meetings can be quite judgemental. Many institutions follow Drucker's (1993) 'Management by Objectives' philosophy, and targets will usually be agreed around the following areas:

- Attendance
- Retention
- Progression

- Achievement
- Measures of value added.

Key information from the self-assessment process will normally be used to inform an institutional self-evaluation report that will be reviewed by inspectors during their visit.

Of increasing importance to course leaders is obtaining, evaluating and implementing student feedback. As students are increasingly regarded as 'customers' they sometimes adopt a consumer mentality in relation to what they may regard as a service they have purchased. It is important that systems should be in place to provide a 'voice' for students – student feedback is an important means of improving provision. Common methods of obtaining student feedback are through questionnaires, focus groups and staff/student liaison meetings, however, informal discussions with students often provide more immediate feedback. A transparent and collegial process for responding to formal feedback is essential. Ofsted (2007: 150) consider the ways in which courses 'meet the needs and interests of learners'; how student feedback systems inform self-evaluation documents will inform their judgements.

Curriculum management

Careful management of the curriculum and fostering a team approach to the planning, preparation and delivery of teaching is important. Where there is duplication of teaching within a subject area, the course leader should encourage a culture of openness and sharing. Each lecturer will produce schemes of work, lesson plans and resources and these can be stored electronically on shared networks for others to adapt and use. If this planning and preparation is divided equitably, a whole team ethos can be encouraged and duplication saved. O'Connell (2005) outlined the benefits of teamwork in the success of a college, with the sharing of resources and the acknowledgment of good practice being integral to this; he recommends that ground rules should be established for team behaviour.

It is important that planning of timetables and the allocation of teaching rooms and office accommodation for staff are equitable. The course leader may find they have to negotiate with senior managers and other course leaders for appropriate rooming resources.

A department may work with a specific awarding body, with resources tailored to meet their requirements, however, the responsibility to select the most appropriate body and possible optional modules generally lies with the course leader. This decision should be made in consultation with the institution's examination officer, who will probably have developed a relationship with each awarding body. An important administrative aspect of a course leader's role is the accurate collation of examination entries, and it is necessary to work closely with the course team to ensure that students are entered correctly. Errors in the process can be expensive for the institution, with late entry fees incurred and stress and uncertainty for students and staff. The examination entry process will normally be driven by the examination officer.

Managing teaching staff

Institutions are seeking to use teaching staff more flexibly. A course leader should follow basic human resource management (HRM) practice by undertaking a job analysis and matching this to the qualities of the course team to allocate teaching responsibilities (Stredwick 2005). It is unlikely that a course leader will be allocated enough time to fully manage the staff and curriculum. The professionalism of the teaching staff in undertaking their individual responsibilities is crucial, and this is fostered by open culture where help can be requested as required. Troman (2003) argues that educational relationships cannot be maintained without a strong bond of trust and engendering this is important. Regular course team meetings, appropriately recorded, will facilitate the efficient management of curriculum and staff while encouraging a team culture.

Chairing of meetings requires care to ensure that the agenda is followed, the debate is focused, and participants feel they can contribute. It is not unusual for senior managers to have a teaching commitment and therefore to attend course team meetings. This can be intimidating for a new course leader, however, it can provide an opportunity to draw on their expertise and to demonstrate competent running of a course. An administrative colleague may take the minutes at team meetings, though this is not always the case and course leaders may have to minute and disseminate the proceedings. The minutes will then feed into the institution's quality assurance procedures.

Course management is complex work as teams increasingly have to integrate full-time, part-time and temporary supply staff. This teamwork is facilitated by a system of centrally storing key documents such as teaching resources, schemes of work and lesson plans to enable sharing. The course leader needs to ensure that monitoring systems are explained to all team members.

Besides the day-to-day course management outlined above, institutions require formal systems of teacher accountability for quality monitoring and the course leader will be integral to these processes. Appraisals, observations of teaching, peer review of teaching and student feedback mechanisms are commonly used methods of ensuring accountability and enabling professional development. Most institutions will have these performance management systems embedded within their quality assurance procedures.

Performance management systems and appraisals are an important aspect of educational human resources management. For probationary teachers, appraisals form part of their induction process. Bush and Middlewood (2005: 176) state that performance management systems 'are based on a rational model of goal-setting and reviewing, and have the aim of connecting organisational and individual planning' and, depending on the culture of the organization, these may be carried out in a judgemental or developmental manner. A course leader needs to allocate sufficient time to carry out individual appraisals sensitively within a suitable and private environment. There should be negotiation regarding the time and place.

Like appraisals, teaching observations can be carried out in a developmental or judgemental manner and the course leader should be aware that colleagues can find the process stressful. While there will be an institutional process of teacher observations, a course leader should, in line with institutional policies, provide opportunities for peer observation of teaching to support and encourage innovative practice. This can help to alleviate the stress of the formal observation process, and this could be further relieved by the introduction of some team teaching. Team teaching facilitates creativity within a safe and supportive environment, allowing natural mentoring, and it also provides continuity should absences occur.

Marketing

Due to the variety of choices available to applicants, marketing activities have increased in importance within the LLS. The growing amount of information within the public domain such as inspection reports and league tables necessitates the consistent promotion of a corporate brand. The increasing competition within the sector with the aim of efficiency gains ensures that marketing will continue to be an important aspect of corporate strategy.

Traditionally, 'above the line' (media based advertising) methods have been adopted, but more recently there has been an increased prominence of 'below the line' (for example direct mail, public relations activities, customer care) relationship marketing. Lumby (2001: 59) argued that FE Colleges' primary marketing objective had been 'bums on seats' with a lack of focus on meeting the needs of customers (students). A course will commonly be promoted via the institution's website, prospectus and through leaflets, all of which will be produced by marketing personnel with detail provided by the course leader. This will result in accurate course information being promoted within the vision of the marketing strategy. Further marketing communications will usually take the form of open days, taster sessions and presentations to feeder institutions, all of which the course leader will be expected to actively engage with.

Institutional websites are increasingly being used to market courses with online application processes common. Course leaders find that a growing number of enquiries are generated by email, and they must be prepared to respond via the same channels. Email communication provides an easy system of storing potential student contact information for future promotions. A potential applicant's first action when researching an institution will often be to search the website, and a course leader should use this opportunity to promote positive aspects of their departments, such as photographs and examples of student success.

A total quality management (TQM) philosophy states that everyone within an institution has an important role to play in the quality and image it portrays. Fidler and Atton (1999) endorse this by stressing the importance of a receptionist as a first point of contact being as crucial to marketing as the role of any lecturer. Both academic and administrative staff need to ensure that all external contacts are dealt with in a professional and helpful manner. A potential applicant will search for other courses if they are dissatisfied with their first contact.

Internal marketing targets stakeholders within the institution, and in the educational context it is relations with students and with all categories of staff that provide the most obvious opportunities. O'Connell (2005: 142) stresses the importance of the quality of internal marketing. Successful internal marketing will entail the course leader developing a provision that helps students recognize that they are important and that they will benefit from a quality provision. Interesting trips and visits, a supporting intranet, and being treated with respect are all factors that create satisfied students who become ambassadors for the institution, providing a powerful marketing tool. This notion is at the heart of relationship marketing which is becoming an increasingly important phenomenon (Harwood et al. 2008).

Meeting recruitment targets is always important in the LLS, and this is a pressure on course leaders. An institution's commitment to effective marketing will go a long way to achieving the required numbers. In conclusion the course leader has an important role in marketing, but the most vital aspect of this is running a course with high-achieving and happy students.

Working with administrative staff

Teachers, trainers and lecturers work with a wide variety of administrative professionals who are able to guide and support them. A positive relationship with administrative staff can alleviate some of the pressures of teaching.

The prominence of self-governance in the LLS has led to an increased professionalization of administrative roles, which has not always been fully appreciated. O'Connell (2005) felt that where problems in relationships between academic and support staff have occurred this has followed teachers ignoring procedures and placing unrealistic demands on support staff. Bush and Middlewood (2005: 38) recommend that effective work between higher level teaching assistants and lecturers depends on:

- clarity of roles
- recognition of the different but complementary skills each brings to the partnership
- mutual respect
- agreement about what are the common goals
- opportunity for good communication.

It is important for a teacher or trainer to understand the value of different administrative roles. Fostering an open dialogue will help build mutually beneficial relationships. To develop respect between academic and support staff O'Connell (2005) recommends that teachers should communicate with support staff in a positive manner to encourage improved service; however, he argues, this is a two-way responsibility.

Many organizations now have a 'business manager' (Bush and Middlewood 2005), who heads a department of support staff including those working in finance (bursars), management information systems, marketing, HRM and student support. To illustrate the increasing professionalism of support staff roles Donovan (2005) outlines the changing roles of examinations officers, which include the development of their own professional institute and framework for training and development. Degree courses are now available specifically for educational administrators, with many senior administrative managers holding masters level qualifications and above. Institutions are increasingly seeking to harmonize the working conditions for all staff (Lumby 2001), with many having a common pay spine.

Awarding bodies

Lecturers in the LLS deliver qualifications from a variety of awarding bodies. Each of these has their own support mechanisms for lecturers, which we will consider below.

Of primary importance is for a teacher to gain familiarity with the syllabi, and copies of these should be available within academic departments. The syllabi guide the production of schemes of work and lesson plans. Resources are normally freely available to download from the website, or paper copies are available by contacting the awarding body. Specimen assessment materials, past examination papers, marking schemes and exemplar student responses are valuable documents together with coursework assessment guidance. Coursework will often come under the scrutiny of an external moderator and it is usual for the course leader to prepare for this event with the teaching team being available to discuss specific issues. All teachers will be involved in preparation for external moderation by ensuring that all coursework is assessed accurately and to deadline, and that a sufficient sample is internally moderated.

Awarding bodies are increasingly proactive in the CPD of teachers, offering training days and a range of conferences. While these events are useful there is often a financial fee and they can use a large proportion training budgets and therefore need to be selected carefully. Feedback from these events should be disseminated throughout the department. Another opportunity for continued CPD is undertaking assessment work for an awarding body. Specific training is given for examiners over and above what is offered to teachers, and it can be an opportunity to earn some extra money (depending on institutional policies) while further developing assessment skills.

Committee membership

Committees and working parties allow teachers at all levels to contribute to the decision-making process and take ownership of agreed outcomes (Bush and Middlewood 2005). A new teacher should volunteer to join a group to which they feel their skills will contribute, while those with more experience are likely to be invited to join a wide range of committees during a successful career. Common examples of committees are:

- Equality and diversity
- Student welfare and guidance
- Teaching and learning
- e-learning
- Health and safety
- Research

Internal committees provide an overview of how the organization operates, together with an understanding of the decision-making process and its impact. Working parties are often formed from a committee membership for specific short-term issues with a remit to report back their findings. For example, an e-learning software working party could be formed from the e-learning committee, and would report back their findings for consideration.

Within a committee environment a new academic may feel unable to express their opinion fully, or may have not fully formed their opinions surrounding the debate. New staff should not be afraid to ask questions to clarify the discussion, particularly if institutional terminology is being used. Familiarity with the operation of the committee builds confidence, and contributions will become more frequent. New committee members often provide a valuable external perspective.

Conclusion

This chapter has provided an overview of aspects of administration for teachers in the LLS, and its importance to the success of an institution. Reference has been made to teachers' responsibilities in meeting funding and inspection body requirements; however, on a day-to-day basis the important administrative routines are maintaining records, particularly completing registers accurately and monitoring student progress. For other administrative tasks a teacher should utilize the appropriate support staff wherever appropriate, and should value their professionalism. A collegial approach underlines that all have an important role to play in the quality of an institution's provision, the creation of its image, and, crucially, the provision of a rewarding student experience. For a course leader particular attention needs to be paid to:

- course evaluation processes
- managing the curriculum
- managing the course team.

To be successful in undertaking these activities a course leader would need to foster a team culture, with a strong ethos of mutual trust among fellow professionals.

21

Evaluation and quality assurance

Roy Fisher, Alison Iredale, Ros Ollin and Denise Robinson

In this chapter:

- The audit culture and professional autonomy
- Evaluating teaching and learning
- Methods of evaluating teaching
- Evaluating the curriculum
- Retention
- Ofsted

The audit culture and professional autonomy

> It is essential that principals have a firm grasp of modern management techniques so that they have a better knowledge of such matters as performance statistics . . .
>
> (From *The Administration of Technical Colleges*,
> Charlton et al. 1971: 153)

The idea of running educational institutions on management principles is not new, but the extent to which colleges and universities have been required to adopt systems in which staff must comply with a culture of control, measurement and audit is unprecedented. The consequences of this ideological shift have included the casualization of work, the imposition of inspection regimes, funding mechanisms based on performance indicators, and the introduction of industrially derived quality systems. Educational and academic values have often been sublimated and, even by the mid-1990s, the following sentiment from Crombie et al. (1995: 61) seemed appropriate:

> [W]e need constantly to remind ourselves of the essentially moral and social purpose – not only of education but also of training. Jerome Bruner's three questions 'What makes people human?' 'How did they become so?', 'How might they be more so?' have sadly become instead 'What makes people wealthy?', 'How do they become so?' and 'How might they be more so?'

Quality *assurance* (QA) systems in education are concerned with safeguarding academic standards through systematic monitoring. The QA process is normally conducted through devices such as validation and revalidation procedures, annual course evaluation, module surveys, the use of student and employer feedback, and the monitoring of statistics relating to recruitment, retention, progression, achievement, success and destinations. Quality *enhancement* (QE) focuses on the improvement of performance and of learning experiences, and has generally been conceptualized as subordinate to QA. In recent years, however, QE has become more prominent although a universally accepted definition has yet to emerge (HEA 2008).

During the early years following incorporation, effectiveness and quality concerns within FE institutions focused on the recently established structures and procedures associated with governance and management. They have now reached all aspects of the operation of educational institutions, including teaching and learning, and scholarship and research. HE has not been immune, developing a culture of league tables and accountability that threatens to undermine some of the values associated with the idea of a university (Morley 2003; Evans 2004).

It is important that teachers in the LLS are able to conceptualize themselves as professionals. Elliott (1998) has connected the working practices of FE lecturers and their sense of the value of what they do. This underlines the necessity of recognizing the centrality of teaching and learning in questions of college effectiveness, and the crucial task of ensuring that these are given a higher profile in the debates surrounding quality. As conditions of employment have changed the processes of teaching and learning have been altered by stealth, sometimes within a disarming rhetoric of educational progressivism (especially in relation to curriculum change associated with competence based awards).

Avis (2002: 81–2) has argued that

Lying behind managerialism is a set of taken-for-granted assumptions. Management becomes the means by which a society's economic success can be pursued. The goal is unequivocal – the end to be pursued is known [economic success]. The question then becomes one of means, with the development of human and social capital seen as central to this process. Management becomes a quasi-technical pursuit to devise the appropriate means to attain the desired end . . . Managerialism through the use of targets, performance indicators and the like sets the terrain on which individuals are to act.

Among the key factors in the identity of a professional is the capacity to make decisions in a relatively independent way. The autonomy of teachers has been eroded both by routine monitoring systems and by external inspection regimes. Rennie (2003) provides an account of the negative impact of Ofsted inspections on the morale of FE staff. It would, however, be an overstatement to present teachers in the sector as lacking confidence and wholly at the mercy of managers and inspectors, or to imply that processes of evaluation are implicitly negative. Effective and critical evaluation is an important dimension of professional practice.

Evaluating teaching and learning

The terms 'assessment' and 'evaluation' are often confused. Assessment relates to the measurement and testing of performance; evaluation considers the 'value' or worth of what has taken place. The results of assessment generally inform evaluation.

Individuals and organizations operate within value systems, and these cause them to place worth on some experiences rather than others. Evaluation is not a neutral process, but is framed within cultural values and practices. For example, government departments, driven by targets, are likely to value statistical indications of qualifications achieved. In this context, evaluation is also linked to accountability and 'value for money'. In contrast, community organizations delivering education in disadvantaged areas may place a greater value on learning experiences which promote self-esteem and enjoyment of learning. These two sets of values are not mutually exclusive, but they can create tensions. The community organization may well rely on funding from government and quantitative rather than more subtle qualitative evaluation may need to be emphasized.

Teaching to maximize the achievement of qualifications (often evaluated statistically), and teaching to create a love of the subject/skill can create a sense of being pulled in two directions. The organizations in which teachers work are driven by the need to obtain funding, linked to performance judged through inspections. Evaluating teaching and the curriculum takes place within this performative context. The LLUK Standards ask teachers to evaluate their practice in terms of 'efficiency and effectiveness'. Who defines what is 'efficient' and 'effective'? While it is important to work within government and organizational requirements, teachers need to consider their values and beliefs, and to ensure that evaluation processes give meaningful information for use in developing understanding and skills. If teachers only think 'inside the box', then possibilities for changing ineffective policies or for asserting good practice will be limited.

Evaluating teaching

The influence of Ofsted over how teaching and learning are evaluated has increased significantly since the late 1990s. The Common Inspection Framework (CIF; Ofsted 2005b) has had benefits, including an increased focus on the learner. Organizations in the LLS have often used the CIF as a basis for evaluation. The LLUK professional standards require teachers to evaluate, drawing on learner feedback and learning theories. Apart from the development of technical teaching skills, evaluation involves becoming more aware of the promotion of equality, inclusivity and differentiation.

When planning how to evaluate teaching, it might be asked:

- What is the purpose?
- What information is needed?
- Who is this information for?
- What methods will be best?
- What evidence will inform development?

Many teaching evaluations are conducted at the level of the group. For example:

- Have the learning outcomes been achieved?
- Has this session been enjoyable?
- Has everyone felt included?
- Have the students learned what was intended?
- Did students learn anything not anticipated?

Groups are made up of individuals, so a teacher may wish to differentiate evaluation by focusing on particular students, for example: What have I observed about Nasreen today? What has she learned?

Methods of evaluating teaching

Evaluation mainly works on the principle that to be effective there should be a range of perspectives. As with other aspects of teaching, the type of learner needs to be taken into account. The most useful information gives the teacher an insight into how learners experienced the session and what they learned. Evaluation of this kind uses information from the learners to give feedback to the teacher.

Evaluation of teaching through silent watching and listening

This is often ignored in texts on teaching, but teachers can gain information about learners' experience by observing and listening. It is important to bear the following in mind:

- Where learners are working independently, or in small groups, avoid unnecessary intervention and observe how each individual approaches the task or relates to others. Body language can provide useful information.
- Listen carefully to a learner's exact words; these can give valuable information about *how* they understand. 'Errors' can give insight into how learners might be helped.

These observations are from the teacher's perspective. Other means involve the learners more directly.

Written evaluations of teaching

Examples include the following:

- *Questionnaires*: 'happy sheets' with smiley/frowning faces; tick boxes with yes/no answers; rating scales asking for responses to aspects of the session; headings and space for 'open' written comments.
- *'Sticky notes'*: everyone is given a sticky note on which they comment about the

session and then post on the wall. This can be extended by asking different people to comment about particular aspects of the session, then displaying the notes under headed sections.

- *'Lucky dip'*: students are given blank sheets of paper and asked to write anonymously the 'best' and 'worst' things about the session. The students fold the sheets identically and drop them into a container. The container is then passed round and each student picks out and reads a paper without commenting themselves. Alternatively, the teacher can read out all the comments.

Spoken evaluations of teaching

An *individual* example is the verbal 'Round Robin': going round each student in turn asking them the same question, for example, one of the following:

- What is the most important thing you learned today?
- What have you enjoyed most/least today?
- Say one thing that surprised you about the session today.
- What are you most proud of in what you achieved today?

A group example uses small group/pair work. Using flip charts to coordinate and present group/pair feedback, or one group member reporting back from the group, for example, feedback on:

- things we would have liked more/less of;
- what we would keep the same/what we would have preferred to be done differently;
- tips for the teacher – 'things you can do to motivate us'.

These are some ways to obtain information about teaching. However, it is only when an analysis of results leads to action to improve that evaluation becomes worthwhile.

Evaluating the curriculum

There are many approaches to curriculum evaluation, underpinned by a variety of values. The four examples below illustrate a range of positions that can be adopted in this context:

- Tyler's (1949) objectives model leads to evaluation based on whether objectives have been achieved.
- Eisner's (1985) 'connoisseurship' model is based on the notion of education as artistry. An evaluator takes the role of connoisseur and critic, feeding back what they perceive and helping those involved to view their work from a critically constructive 'expert' perspective.

- Scriven's (2001) formative evaluation model emphasizes the developmental aspect of evaluation.
- Kirkpatrick's (1998) 'four level' model is based on review of:

  1 Reactions of learners
  2 Actual learning – resulting increase in knowledge/skills
  3 Transfer of behaviour – improvement in real life behaviours
  4 Results – impact on organization

Curriculum evaluation is likely to involve formal procedures and organizations operate a variety of systems as part of their quality improvement processes and these often derive from Tyler's (1949) objectives model. Curriculum evaluation may be ongoing, or it may occur towards the end of a course and will draw on a range of sources such as:

- assessment results linked to targets for achievement;
- student feedback, often through written questionnaires;
- course tutor and course team feedback.

Within a quality improvement cycle this information is fed into the organizational system and is considered at senior level. Areas for improvement are identified and actions are taken, monitored and fed back. At an organizational level, curriculum evaluation will take into account achievement of intended outcomes of the course, and the number of successful student completions.

Ofsted influences institutional approaches to curriculum evaluation, both through the CIF and through an increased focus on organizational self-evaluation. Ofsted's (2006) report on 'best practice' praised approaches to evaluation which clearly integrate into management systems and use performance indicators as a means of measurement of success.

For the individual teacher, there could be a different starting point for course evaluation. In the evaluation process, the values and philosophy underpinning the aims of the course should be taken into account. In evaluating a course, a teacher might ask: 'What did I *really* want to achieve by the end of the course with this student/group?' Here it is tempting to focus on the stated learning outcomes for the course, which will be couched in terms of knowledge and skills. However, there may be broader and more fundamental aims, such as developing learners' self-esteem and empowerment, the ability to be independent learners or to be caring members of society. Curriculum evaluation against these kinds of values might lead to these questions:

- How have the teaching/learning and assessment methods helped or hindered these aims?
- How has the overall learning environment (social/cultural/environmental) helped or hindered these aims?
- What might be changed to better achieve these broader aims?

Evaluation leading to improvement

Evaluation is used to monitor quality and bring about improvement. However, perceptions of quality may vary according to the nature of the value system underpinning them. The demands of target-driven evaluation can create pressures for teachers who are working to provide rewarding learning experiences. In this situation, it is important that teachers and managers keep a critical eye on how different types of evaluation are used, to ensure that these provide valid and reliable information for improvement.

Retention

The post-incorporation funding methodology ensured that student retention became a major concern in FE. The existence of a 'retention problem' was underlined by various studies undertaken in the 1990s (for example, Martinez and Munday 1998). More nuanced understandings of the retention issue began to emerge (Bloomer and Hodkinson 2000) recognizing that an outcomes-based approach might not best serve either the evaluation of quality or the development needs of young people.

The cultural capital and skills needed for a learner to progress derive, according to Halsey et al. (1997), largely from social class. Bloomer and Hodkinson (2000) have shown that the learner's journey can be haphazard, involving a set of connections with education. The decision to withdraw from a course can be a positive one for an individual, involving a complex interplay between the costs and benefits of staying or leaving. From the institutional perspective, however, the impact of a student leaving is generally seen as negative with regard to funding and performance indicators.

Retention and achievement research has tended to focus on ideas derived from the institutional perspective. Analysis is generally about how well an educational institution keeps learners, and its efficiency in maximizing achievements against a set of benchmarks compared to other institutions. If an institution concentrates attention on achieving benchmarks teachers inevitably focus on enrolment related decisions. Yorke and Longden (2004) highlight the risks of 'taking the safe option' at the point of entry to a course, rather than working to improve the overall quality of the learning experience.

Concepts such as 'retention' (keeping students on the course), 'attrition' (normally the rate of withdrawal on a course), and 'progression' and 'achievement' can have slightly differing sectoral or institutional definitions – it is important to clarify the precise meaning in any specific context. In recent years there has been significant progress in improving retention rates, but there are particular challenges in supporting and retaining learners beyond secondary education. Many learners, whether straight from school or after a break from education, need to develop learning skills and well as to manage time around work and domestic commitments. Good teachers will identify the learning skills needed by students and will develop these integrally within the curriculum. The starting point is analysis of data relating to recruitment, retention, progression and achievement to review existing courses, and to consider whether new provision may be needed. This is often termed 'curriculum mapping'.

Analysis of data can reveal courses which have poorer retention than similar or linked provision. Trends can be analysed, such as early withdrawals, issues for particular groups of learners (such as part-timers or those with specific disabilities) and gender- or ethnicity-related factors may be identified. Teachers can use 'live' data, for example, where a course has relatively poor retention early in the academic year the recruitment strategy should be reviewed. Did applicants received appropriate guidance prior to entry? Did they have the stated entry qualifications and attributes, and were they prepared for the demands of the course? Once learners are enrolled careful monitoring of attendance and performance can pinpoint the effectiveness of initial assessment tools which identify not only levels of literacy and numeracy, but also more affective skills. An understanding of the profile of each learner, and a dialogic analysis of strengths and areas for development, provides a starting point for progress towards the stated goal. Without this it is not possible to be clear about how far an individual learner is able to commit to the demands of the course.

Ofsted

Today's inspection procedures are enforced through the Education and Inspections Act 2007; this saw a merger of various agencies. The newly extended Office for Standards in Education, Children's Services and Skills (Ofsted) came into being on 1 April 2007, bringing together the Adult Learning Inspectorate (ALI), the Commission for Social Care Inspection (CSCI), Her Majesty's Inspectorate of Court Administration (HMICA) and the Office of Her Majesty's Chief Inspector of Schools (the former Ofsted). Ofsted is now responsible for inspection of provision that includes 3.6 million learners in colleges and 1.3 million in the workplace or the community.

A brief history

Prior to 1993 Her Majesty's Inspectors (HMIs), alongside the FE advisers from LEAs, were responsible for the inspection of FE. HMIs date back to 1839 and, even at that point, their work included the observation of teachers (Norton Grubb 1999). The stated purpose was for the monitoring of public funds and for school improvement. HMIs provided advice and were regarded as 'wise practitioners'. Up to 1993 inspections in FE colleges occurred every ten years or so. With the introduction of the National Curriculum in schools, the HMI 'wise-guidance' model was considered no longer appropriate and in 1993 Ofsted was born. Thus began the standardization of procedures and approaches to making judgements, including grading and the publication of reports on individual schools and, later, colleges. The focus for the basis of the judgements was on observing teachers and discussion with staff and students.

The year 1993 brought the FEFC into existence. The main thrust of the inspection arm of the FEFC was to ensure that the newly independent FE colleges maintained standards. The focus of this regime was on teaching together with an emphasis on procedures and systems associated with the new status of FE colleges with responsibility for estates, human resources, finance and administration. The Learning and Skills Act 2000 moved funding from the FEFC to the newly formed LSC and also removed inspection powers from the FEFC. The Act stated that the LSC was responsible for

> (a) the quality of the education and training within its remit (b) the standards achieved by those receiving that education and training; and (c) whether the financial resources made available to those providing that education and training are managed efficiently and used in a way which provides value for money.
>
> (DfEE 2000: part 1, ch. 1, p. 5)

FE colleges now found themselves responsible to at least three government-directed bodies with some remit for standards: the LSC, Ofsted and ALI.

ALI had been set up under the Learning and Skills Act 2000 to be concerned with the inspection of adult and work-based learning. It was responsible for work-based learning for all aged over 16; provision in FE for people aged 19 and over; Learndirect provision; adult and community learning; training funded by Jobcentre Plus; and education and training in prisons (this 'at the invitation of Her Majesty's Chief Inspector of Prisons'). Ofsted now had responsibility for the joint inspection of FE colleges with ALI.

The stated purpose of inspections

Inspections prior to 1993 had a remit to provide guidance; after this date this system was one of regulation rather than advice. However, Ofsted annual reports and occasional papers do offer examples of good practice. This does not include the kind of direct support that ALI formerly provided. Neither would the Ofsted approach necessarily be regarded as one that incorporated a dispassionate analysis of the data; rather Ofsted were seen to support government policy (Smith 2000). In the incorporation of ALI within Ofsted it would be the remit and culture of Ofsted that dominated.

Impact and issues arising from inspections

A number of issues are raised by practitioners in relation to inspection regimes.

- *Stress*: as inspection brings judgements on teaching teachers often experience stress; furthermore, considerable time and effort is put into preparation for inspections (Wallace and Gravells 2007).
- *Balance of power*: the relationship of the inspector to both the teacher and the institution is unequal; the inspection process can lead to the closure of an institution.
- *Improvement in qualifications of learners*: research points to little improvement in achievement or, indeed, a negative effect (Cullingford 1999; Fielding 2001). A study of school results indicated that

> there exists no evidence that the occurrence of an Ofsted visit has beneficial effects on the exam performance outcome of the school following the

inspection. Indeed, the results show a small but well-determined *negative* direct effect on exam results: Ofsted inspections seem to affect adversely student performance in the year of the visit

(Rosenthal 2004: 144).

- *Use of statistics and other data*: does the focus on data (for example, retention and achievement) and comparison to national benchmarks tend to shift attention to that which can be measured?

- *A 'snapshot' approach to inspections*: do teachers and others give a false impression by simply adapting to the presence of the inspector?

The culture and practices of Ofsted may be regarded as congruent with a government philosophy of control through measurement. The notion of the 'coasting college' has emerged. A 'coasting college' is one that, although achieving satisfactory grades, is regarded as not striving to achieve the relevant government targets. Special measures or a 'notice to improve' can be applied such that if the college does not improve it may be required to merge.

Alternatives?

While most practitioners accept that inspections are a permanent feature of public service, critics have presented alternatives. The inspection system has offered some leeway to institutions that perform well (a 'lighter touch'). Fielding (2001: 695) has highlighted 'the conceptual and practical inadequacy of "accountability" as an agent of reciprocal public engagement in a participatory democracy. In its stead a more robust, more open notion of "reciprocal responsibility" is offered as a more fitting means of professional and communal renewal.'

Fielding's work exposes the way which the accountability regime can impact negatively on trust and openness. Important skills in teaching are qualitative and there are intuitively based dimensions to practice that are not easily observable. The work of Ofsted may be taken to represent a quest for greater rigour and a concerted response to Government imperatives to drive up standards; more pessimistically, it can be seen as an example of a culture in thrall to performativity and audit.

22

Career planning and continuing professional development

Robin Simmons and Martyn Walker

In this chapter:

- The FE context
- Employment and roles in FE colleges
- Job applications
- The interview
- The first post and career progression
- Part-time teaching and agencies
- Creating and maintaining a curriculum vitae
- Staff appraisal and planning CPD
- Trade unions
- Getting promotion
- In transition

This chapter surveys a range of issues related to obtaining a teaching post in the LLS, and considers some factors relating to CPD. Employment practices often differ markedly from those in schools; indeed, there are diverse approaches within the LLS broadly (including training organizations), and even between different FE colleges. Universities and other HEIs have their own approaches and these may differ according to specific subject areas. This chapter deals primarily with teaching posts in FE colleges and is informed by interviews conducted with human resource managers during 2008. However, we believe that some general principles can be sensibly but cautiously applied to job seeking and recruitment across different parts of the education system. Readers applying to particular institutions should study carefully their specific institutional context and procedures.

The FE context

A post in FE is unlikely to be a lecturer's first experience of formal employment (given our focus on FE in this chapter we shall use the term 'lecturer'). Unlike the situation in schools, teaching may be a second, or even third, career for the majority of

FE lecturers. Entering FE teaching after extensive previous employment is not a new trend: as Ainley and Bailey (1997: 2) stated 'the basic work of the colleges has always been the teaching of theory and practice of the skills used in everyday occupations' and this is still true today.

Readers seeking a first post should recognize that teaching will bring new challenges. The education system in England has undergone rapid and extensive change since the 1990s and FE has perhaps experienced the most profound effects (Hyland and Merrill 2003). For several decades after World War Two, LAs ran the majority of both school and post-school education in England. While most state funded schools remain under the auspices of LAs, almost all post-compulsory education and training is outside their control. Following the 1992 Further and Higher Education (F and HE) Act, FE, sixth-form and specialist colleges in England were removed from LEA control. This process, known as incorporation, ended a period of almost fifty years of municipal responsibility for FE. From 1 April 1993 local authorities ceased to plan and manage FE; individual colleges became self-governing and, for the first time, direct employers of their staff.

Nowadays college principals are regarded, perhaps primarily, as business managers or 'chief executives'. In contrast, their traditional role under LEAs tended to be more a combination of 'chief academic' and 'senior administrator'. The LEA took the role of employer, budget maker, estates manager and much else besides (Reeves 1995). The system of national collective bargaining that existed meant that managers were detached from the determination of pay and conditions and their role was mainly confined to administering arrangements negotiated elsewhere.

Despite the traditionally localized nature of FE, national pay bargaining had been established as early as the 1920s. Following the 1944 Education Act there was the requirement for standard national pay scales and the creation of the 'Burnham FE Committee' to preside over such issues. Over time the remit of national bargaining grew and eventually, in the early 1970s, became enshrined in what was known as the 'Silver Book' agreement for teaching staff. There were tight limits on the maximum number of teaching hours, the number of teaching sessions and the continuity of work that could be required of a teacher. There were also detailed arrangements for additional payment and the remission of teaching hours in recognition of non-teaching duties performed (Waitt 1980). Incorporation brought an end to this. Lecturers were forced off the 'Silver Book' onto more 'flexible' localized contracts of employment.

There is an extensive literature on the changed circumstances of FE teachers since incorporation which, in addition to increased class contact hours, include additional administrative duties and reduced holidays, high levels of managerial control and a culture that often emphasizes 'business' values. In a study of over 3000 staff working across FE, Villeneuve-Smith et al. (2008) found that over 85 per cent believed that they were making a valuable social contribution. However, in almost every dimension of their labour, working conditions were challenging, and over 90 per cent regularly worked beyond their contracted hours. A new or aspiring teacher should be aware that workloads are often heavy. Teaching in all parts of the LLS can be interesting and stimulating, but for a successful career it is necessary to be hard working, committed and resilient.

Employment and roles in FE colleges

In FE colleges provision ranges from vocational courses to professional programmes and traditional academic subjects. In private training organizations and work-based learning contexts there are, of course, a vast range of job-specific courses. While most FE lecturers primarily teach their subject specialism, many are likely to teach in other areas that challenge the boundaries of their knowledge. Flexibility and the ability to apply knowledge and skills across traditional subject boundaries are, in the reality of day-to-day teaching in FE, useful attributes.

Aspiring applicants looking for their 'ideal' post may well have a long wait. While a sociology graduate may obtain a post teaching their subject on GCSE, AS/A2 and Access to Higher Education courses they may also teach modules in health and social care, media studies and other vocational courses. Similarly, an accountant may secure an FE post in a business studies department which entails teaching a broad range of business subjects. This can be stretching, but it will broaden knowledge and experience, putting the lecturer in a position to take directions that they may not have previously considered. Experiencing the range of learning programmes in colleges, and seizing some of the unexpected opportunities that arise can be rewarding and interesting.

Government policy and the pressure of changing funding regimes contribute to the diversification of FE. For example, in the four colleges consulted to inform this chapter (referred to henceforth as Colleges A, B, C and D respectively), College B had recently decided to concentrate on vocational subjects rather than the GCE 'A' Levels. College C tended to focus mainly on provision at level 2 and below, and had a relatively large proportion of students with special educational needs.

With the fall in numbers of 16–18-year-olds as a result of demographic change and the decline in funding for adult education, College B had taken the decision to concentrate on the skills agenda and new apprenticeship programmes. All teachers in College B were now referred to as 'lecturer/assessors'. This reflected a change in approach to teaching and learning in order to provide the flexibility of staff to support learners in their workplaces. In some institutions 'assessors' are paid less than 'lecturers', but at College B all were paid lecturers' salaries. College D employed 'tutors', 'academic support tutors' (to work with students on all courses) and 'study skills and learning support tutors' for work with students with learning difficulties.

Before making a job application it is important to consider the curriculum offered, the approaches to learning and the culture prevailing in the college. It is advisable to read the college's literature with care; to explore their website; and, if practicable, to visit beforehand. Researching the institution's history, ambitions and status will enable an applicant to assess whether or not they would be comfortable working there. To be positive and optimistic is recommended – but it is also vital be realistic and constructively critical in conducting a job search.

Job applications

The Internet has made job searching much easier, and a number of specialist websites exist. This enables those contemplating a career in the sector to explore the number and geographical distribution of opportunities, to identify exactly what employers are asking for, and to carefully consider the usual terms and conditions of employment. In addition, the *Guardian* newspaper (Tuesday is education jobs day) and the *Times Educational Supplement* (TES), available each Friday, are sources of information.

The first time a potential employer has contact with an applicant is normally when they receive a request for an application form and further details, either by letter or telephone or, more commonly nowadays, through an email or web download. A job description and person specification will usually be included in the application pack. Both should be given careful consideration. The job description provides details about the post, enabling the potential applicant to check whether or not this is the job they want. The person specification will include a list of essential and desirable criteria. To be successful an applicant must meet all the 'essentials' and as many as possible of the desirable criteria. The application will require several hours of preparation. Applicants should not underestimate their abilities and experience; they should think carefully through their skills and strengths and match them to the job description and person specification. A positive and optimistic approach to self-appraisal is good, but under no circumstances should an applicant be untruthful. In the unlikely event a teaching post was secured in this way, any gaps in experience and ability would soon be exposed.

The essential criteria for a post will include academic qualifications, and candidates are expected to produce their original certificates either at interview or on appointment. All college managers who gave their views for this chapter stressed the importance of presenting a good, well written application. College B liked applicants to complete the form online, which was seen as part of the assessment process. It also preferred candidates to identify useful selling points, including examples of the applicant's experience to date. In the case of recently qualified teachers these might include staff development undertaken while on teaching practice and any extra-curricular activities. College B also liked to know what else an applicant may have been involved with outside teaching. For example, being a member of a parent-teachers' association, being a school or college governor or having been a student representative at university. For applicants to vocational posts in College D it was expected that they would have at least NVQ level 3 qualifications. College D sent out guidance notes to aid completion of the application form, as well as equal opportunities and CRB-related information. CRB checks are standard practice throughout the sector, and those with concerns about their own records in this respect should seek advice before applying either for teacher training or for teaching posts. The information for applicants pack from College D made it clear that no CV should be included.

The second time that an applicant contacts a college is the point when they are formally entering the application process. This requires time and care. It is common for the prospective employer to require a letter in support of an application. Grammar and spelling should be correct. The 'further particulars' supplied by the college should be carefully studied. Such information helps to build a picture of what the job is all about. It can be included in discussions during the interview day or perhaps during the interview itself. Applicants should strive to be well informed and knowledgeable – not just about their subject, but also about the job and the place where they want to work.

The interview

A letter inviting attendance at a job interview is encouraging for an applicant. It should be read carefully. Candidates for interview are usually met by a member of the senior management team who will provide an overview of the college and clarify the logistics of the day. There will probably be a brief tour of the college, or at least of the department. This provides an opportunity to see the facilities and equipment and generally assess the environment. Candidates should remember that the selection process begins from the moment they report to reception. Punctuality is essential. Whatever form of transport is chosen, a candidate should make sure that they have enough time to find the college. Where the interview is some distance from home colleges will normally pay for overnight accommodation, as well as reasonable travel expenses. It is surprising how many candidates get basic issues like times and locations wrong. It is important to plan, be punctual, be prepared and to be positive.

Nowadays it is usual for the interview process to include a presentation, or even for candidates to be required to teach a class. Formal interviews are still an important part of the selection process, but a 'micro-teaching' scenario allows the applicant to be assessed in a more realistic environment. Where applicants are asked to teach or present for, say, 15 or 20 minutes they need to think carefully about what they are going to do. The presentation should be engaging and lively, and any resources to be used should be remembered. Several (say six) copies of any materials should be available for distribution to the panel. Applicants should be prepared to answer questions or contribute to any discussion about the presentation. Colleges C and D used presentations as part of the selection process.

As five or six candidates may be called for interview and arrangements may involve a tour, presentations and formal interviews, interviewees for a post in an FE college need to be prepared to be in attendance all day. Inevitably, this will involve some waiting around. It is wise to resolve to use all parts of the day constructively. An interviewee may get the opportunity to talk to members of staff or chat to students. It is likely that there will be times when a group of interviewees is left alone in a waiting area. Again, this time should be used effectively. Teaching can be a 'small world', and it is quite possible that fellow interviewees will meet again. The whole day should be treated as a learning experience – even if an interviewee does not get the job, they can find out what sort of backgrounds the other candidates have, gain insight into the workings of the organization they are visiting, and build useful professional networks.

Candidates should keep a copy of their application form and letter as a reminder. An interviewee needs to show that they are familiar with the main details of the post. Such details may, for example, include a policy about teaching and learning, so when answering a question on support for learners, an interviewee has an opportunity to show that they have read and support the policy.

Personal appearance at an interview is crucial – interviewees should be smart and presentable. College managers expect interviewees to be dressed and groomed appropriately, as this indicates respect for the organization. Colleges expect staff to be appropriately dressed during the daily routine of their work, and to be role models for students who will later be applying for jobs in the respective vocational fields.

As previously mentioned, many colleges expect, as part of the selection process, to see candidates plan and deliver a presentation. College A arranged for a group of students to be 'taught' by each candidate for 20 minutes on the same theme. Students gave feedback on the session and academic staff made formal notes to feedback to the interviewing panel. The assessment criteria for this part of the process included subject knowledge and lesson planning (including the production of a lesson plan for a full 90 minutes), presentation skills, interaction with the group and responsiveness to individual students.

College B set tasks as part of the selection process relating to the subject areas the new post holder would teach. College B's human resource manager explained that 'Perhaps a rather mundane module will be selected by the curriculum manager and the candidates will be expected to give a short presentation on how they might approach teaching it in a creative and innovative way'. College C stressed that the interview panel wanted to see the candidates 'in action' rather than merely theorizing about teaching and learning.

Candidates should not be discouraged by a letter of rejection. It is common, particularly in applying for a first post, to submit many applications. If an applicant has not been successful it is strongly recommended that they should contact the college for feedback that may be helpful in future applications. Much of the general research undertaken and personal details prepared for an application can be re-used to support future applications.

The first post and career progression

Institutions in the LLS invest in professional development. Newly appointed full-time staff are generally inducted into the organization over several weeks, and are often allocated a mentor. At College A, mentors were allocated from a different but culturally similar curriculum area to that of the new appointee. The intention was for the mentor to be someone who could be confided in. The process usually lasted for one year and might include some observation of teaching. All staff at College A were observed teaching once a year, with new appointees visited in the classroom within six months of starting work. These observations were usually carried out in the context of the annual staff review system (see below). Similarly, all new teachers at College C were observed teaching in the first term after appointment. Peer review of teaching, where individuals are annually observed and provided with feedback by a colleague, is now standard practice – and these normally relatively informal systems provide opportunities to receive (and provide) constructive feedback.

It is wise to take advantage of training opportunities offered by an employer and to apply for staff development funding for appropriate events that are offered externally. At College A, staff were funded to attend meetings arranged by examinations boards. It is crucial that lecturers keep up to date both with their specialist area and with wider developments in education generally. FE is fast moving; policy can change quickly and knowledge can quickly become outdated.

Many colleges will provide financial support to staff undertaking award bearing qualifications, including higher degrees. This may also include some release from teaching or other duties. It is, however, now common practice that should an employee leave within two years of completing an award, they may be asked to repay some or all of the financial assistance given. Career-minded lecturers normally make the most of events and courses – even if, in the case of the latter, a lot of the work will be done in their own time.

Part-time teaching and agencies

LLS institutions have tended to employ relatively more staff on a part-time and/or temporary or fractional basis than is the case in schools. On vocational courses the use of staff who are recent or current practitioners gives learning currency, and helps to foster valuable links with industry and commerce. Notwithstanding this, the commercialization of FE that accompanied incorporation led colleges to utilize their staff more intensively and to focus on productivity. One consequence of this has been an increased workload for staff. Another has been intensified use of part-time and temporary lecturers and the use of casually employed agency staff. Such practices, perhaps, peaked during the 1990s but it is probably fair to state that the workforce is employed on more fluid and 'flexible' terms than was the case when colleges were under the control of LAs.

College A rarely contacted teaching agencies and it kept general inquiries for part-time or hourly paid teaching in a 'pool' for possible contact. This college encouraged those who wanted to be considered for part-time employment to send in a completed application form (not curriculum vitae) around May or June. Rather than assume the college will contact them, those seeking work would probably benefit from making another inquiry in late August when student recruitment is underway. Unlike the schools sector, it is difficult for college managers to estimate recruitment numbers with accuracy until close to the beginning of term. The number and range of courses that can run is influenced by student recruitment. Applicants should not be surprised if they are contacted shortly before a course begins and asked to teach at short notice. Those not employed at the start of the academic year may be approached later on. Opportunities can arise as staff change jobs or due to other unforeseen circumstances, and some courses commence at different times of the year.

College B used teaching agencies for all its hourly paid 'lecturer/assessors'. Such an arrangement gave the College flexibility to respond to student enrolments. The use of teaching agencies also offers colleges the advantage of the agency taking responsibility for CRB checks and allows the college to have reduced responsibilities under employment law. College B, however, otherwise treated its agency staff in the same way as those with permanent contracts. The College stated that it had often appointed full-time staff from those that had initially worked for the College via the agency. Should a post become vacant and they applied in the normal way, agency staff were well-placed for selection. All agency staff had access to College activities, including mentoring to support high standards in teaching and learning, and had the same opportunities for CPD as staff employed directly.

College C did not use agency staff, employing all its part-time teachers directly. Although it had, in the past, considered using an agency, the College believed that direct employment offered a range of advantages – not least in ensuring continuity for students and encouraging harmonious staff relations. College D appointed 'associate staff' employed on variable contracts. These provided flexibility in relation to staffing requirements on a yearly basis and they had the same employment rights as all full-time staff at the College. They also had the same opportunities as full-time staff regarding in-house training and professional development.

Creating and maintaining a curriculum vitae

Some colleges stipulate that a curriculum vitae (CV) should not be included with application forms and letters of application. Once appointed to post, whether part-time or full-time, it is wise to maintain a CV as a record of ongoing development, including additional qualifications, CPD activities, and teaching and management responsibilities. While the colleges in this sample did not request a CV at the application stage, all highlighted the importance of maintaining one. Trainee teachers should construct a CV during their training and use it when completing application forms. In addition, many awarding bodies expect to see CVs from staff who teach and manage their courses. Universities and sector-wide bodies, such as the City and Guilds of London Institute (CGLI), normally specify the format to be used.

Staff appraisal and planning CPD

Most colleges have an appraisal system in which the appraiser (usually a line manager) and the appraisee discuss annual performance in relation to individual progress, challenges, professional development, agreed targets and career advancement. Such systems can be seen as part of the culture of performance management that has grown over recent years. However, there is a requirement to engage in CPD once in post. Since September 2007 all newly qualified teachers have been required by the sector skills council LLUK to complete at least 30 hours a year of CPD which supports the needs of students. Orr (2008) argues that this requirement should be seen as an opportunity to engage in meaningful activities that enhance skills and knowledge.

College A conducted appraisals for all teaching staff at the start of the academic year with a mid-year review around January or February. The meetings usually lasted between one to two hours and included feedback from teaching observations, training analysis for the future, and agreed targets. The mid-year review provided the opportunity to see 'how things are going'. College B had an appraisal scheme for all staff with performance indicators. The form used by College B allowed appraisees to identify areas of success, areas had not gone as well, and key targets for the following twelve months. Where targets had been met, supporting evidence was to be produced. For example, the claim 'I am a really good teacher', would need to be supported with internal and external observations, including grades awarded. The appraisee was expected to compare their successes with national benchmarks which were provided by LSCs. The college provided annual training for both appraisees and appraisers.

Recently qualifying LLS staff should join the IfL. For those teaching on higher education courses it would be appropriate to join the HEA. The IfL and HEA websites advise on how to join and the benefits offered.

College A required all new staff to attend in-service Certificate in Education or PGCE courses where appropriate. As well as providing a teaching qualification, this enabled staff to keep abreast of current developments and engage with broader debates. New appointments were advised regarding 'value added' issues, benchmarking and assessment and all new teaching staff were inducted into the College's quality assurance systems, assessment criteria for their subject areas and support for dealing with challenging behaviour in the classroom.

College B provided five days per year for CPD, two of which focused on cross-college development activities, while the remaining three days were designated for team development and could be used, for example, for team or directorate updating, training, developing new courses or working with employers. The college worked with three other institutions as part of its peer quality group. The colleges worked together in relation to issues of self-assessment and teaching observations.

In addition to ongoing activities, College C had an annual 'staff development week' in which current issues of priority were addressed and, although some sessions were optional, all staff were required to take part in certain activities. College D included the annual salary review in an appraisal process based on objectives (not competences) and on evidence as to how these were met.

Trade unions

Whether an individual joins a trade union is, of course, a matter of choice. As well as providing collective bargaining over terms and conditions, both at an institutional and a national level, workplace union representatives can also provide valuable services to their members and may be able to assist in any disputes or difficulties. Unions such as the UCU and the Association of Teachers and Lecturers (ATL) provide programmes of professional development and training. Furthermore, unions offer a range of free or discounted services, such as legal advice and insurance.

Since the incorporation of FE in the early 1990s the relationship between college employers and trade unions has often been difficult. Although localized disputes sometimes took place under local authority control, generally industrial relations were benign and local authorities tended to cushion teachers from excessive exploitation. Work relations tended to be collegial; with college managers usually adopting a relatively low profile. Incorporation changed this situation: college principals and other managers were given greatly increased responsibilities based on the belief that 'more forceful management organised on a decentralised basis and held accountable for performance would ensure greater control of costs and lead to better public services' (Winchester and Bach 1995: 304).

The early years of incorporation saw some well publicized instances of 'macho management' (Randle and Brady 1997). FE was marked by turbulent industrial relations and New Labour inherited a sector in crisis when it came to power in 1997. Although, as Williams (2003: 314) argues, many of the inherent conflicts of interest remain, there has also been some shift in stance and a more conciliatory and pragmatic approach to running FE emerged under New Labour. There has been increased funding and a higher profile for the sector, including some impressive building projects that are transforming the image of FE. This perhaps derives from the present Government's identification of colleges as central to delivering the human and social capital deemed necessary for economic prosperity.

College A recognized two trade unions, the UCU and ATL. The college claimed a good working relationship with union representatives and regular meetings were held between the unions and management. College B encouraged individual staff to join a union. College C recognized one trade union for teaching staff, the UCU. College D had an employer forum of elected staff (one representative to 50 staff covering all areas, including academic, technical and administrative and estates). Any employee in the college who 'had an issue' could, if they wished, invite a union representative to these meetings.

Getting promotion

There are a number of options to consider in relation to promotion – one of which is moving into a management role. Colleges tend to have different structures and job titles can vary, but typically a main grade teacher may apply for a 'curriculum manager' or 'programme manager' post as a move into first-line management. In addition to retaining an element of teaching, normally such roles require the management of staff, budgets and resources as well as the curriculum. Before applying for such a job it is important to be aware that they are usually demanding. Those keen to gain further promotion may, after a few years as a curriculum manager, consider pursuing a head of school or faculty role, from which they can subsequently go on to more senior positions. Pay can be relatively attractive in such roles, but they also carry considerable levels of responsibility and pressure. The higher up the organizational hierarchy staff move the less likely they are to have contact with students.

Managing in the complex and changing LLS is challenging. College A expected staff wishing to move to more senior posts to have gained complex knowledge regarding funding and budgetary systems. Aspiring managers were expected to know about income and expenditure to demonstrate readiness for posts with first- and second-line budgetary responsibilities. In addition, marketing, human resources, sector-wide and government policies were all areas in which managers were expected to have expertise.

College B wanted ambitious lecturers to become involved with cross-college activities. The College has designed its own 'Aspiring Managers Course' which covered themes such as managing meetings, managing staff and writing reports. Those who wished to pursue this were allocated a manager mentor they worked closely with. There was also the opportunity to work in other parts of the college. A 'lecturer/assessor' may, for example, work closely with a MIS colleague. Working on projects with managers across the College provided the opportunity for colleagues to present their work to the senior management team and to 'get noticed'. Few, if any, colleges look negatively on staff applying for promotion externally. Those seeking internal promotion indicate that they are interested in advancing. Either way, those keen to progress should display a willingness to take on additional responsibilities as and when opportunities arise.

For those that wish to retain more contact with learners the role of 'advanced practitioner' offers an alternative to entering a line manager's post. Being appointed as an advanced practitioner gives insight into quality assurance systems and assessing colleagues in preparation for Ofsted and other inspections. At College B, for example, many staff were encouraged to become advanced practitioners, or mentors to new staff, and to become involved in developing new courses.

In transition

All learning is a process of transition, with the implication, but not the guarantee, of a positive trajectory. There is a sense in which this characteristic is amplified in the LLS, which itself is often a 'place between'. FE, in particular, bridges the worlds of school and work for some, and the worlds of school and HE for others. The LLS is diverse, complex and demanding. These factors make it a stimulating area of education in which to teach and to learn. Given the presence of both vocational and academic curricula, ranging from foundation level to HE awards, and the extraordinary diversity of its learners, lifelong learning is a field where the ability to constantly develop and adapt is important.

The disparate backgrounds of teachers and trainers working in FE have made it historically difficult for them to formulate a common professional identity (Clow 2001) and, many, given the importance of vocational knowledge and practice 'retain strong allegiances to their first occupational identity' (Robson et al. 2004: 187). Gleeson et al.'s (2005: 449–50) study of FE professionalism found that

> [e]ntering FE is, for many, less a career choice or pathway than an opportunity at a particular moment in time. As Ruth notes: '. . . nobody leaves school saying, Oooh I want to be a basic skills teacher! It's something you come to via a variety of routes.' The transition into FE is not a smooth one. It often coincides with lifestyle changes, career breaks, redundancy, divorce and relocation, circumstances after divorce.

This is another sense in which colleges and training organizations can be experienced as liminal spaces, not only transitory zones for the students within them, but also for the staff who teach there. As Vähäsantanen and Eteläpelto (2009) have pointed out, teachers are positioned in roles which mediate between policy and practice – another aspect of being between sometimes conflicting forces. Sector reform and curriculum reform have an impact in the classroom and the staffroom, and in recent years these pressures have been intense. Negotiating these transitions and the associated tensions demands up-to-date knowledge and high level skills, optimism and tenacity. While it would be Utopian to claim that all teachers in this sector have a vocation in the other sense of that word – a 'calling' based on a commitment to particular values imbued with an ethos of human progress – there is no doubt that many have, and that this helps. The LLS is now highly regulated, but at the same time it offers teachers and trainers the opportunity to make an important contribution, not only to improved educational standards in the abstract sense, but more concretely to individual learners. For those who find this an exciting prospect, a career in teaching or training, however carefully planned or however much a consequence of chance, is likely to offer a highly rewarding experience.

Bibliography

Abrams, D. and Houston, D. (2006) *Equality, Diversity and Prejudice in Britain: Results from the 2005 National Survey*, Report for the Cabinet Office Equalities Review. Canterbury: University of Kent.

Ainley, P. (1993) *Class and Skill: Changing Divisions of Knowledge and Labour*. London: Cassell.

Ainley, P. (1994) *Degrees of Difference: Higher Education in the 1990s*. London: Lawrence and Wishart.

Ainley, P. (2001) From a national system locally administered to a national system nationally administered: the new leviathan in education and training in England, *Journal of Social Policy*, 30(3): 457–76.

Ainley, P. (2008) The cruellest con of all, *Times Higher Education Supplement*, 7 February.

Ainley, P. and Bailey, B. (1997) *The Business of Learning: Staff and Student Exeriences of Further Education in the 1990s*. London: Cassell.

Alexander, C. (2004) Imagining the Asian gang: ethnicity, masculinity and youth after 'the riots', *Critical Social Policy*, 24(4): 526–49.

Alexander, S. and McKenzie, J. (1998) *An Evaluation of Information Technology Projects in Australian Higher Education*. Canberra: Australian Government Publishing Services.

Allen, M. and Ainley, P. (2007) *Education Make you Fick, Innit?* London: Tuffnell.

Althusser, L. (1971) Ideology and ideological state apparatuses (notes towards an investigation), in L. Althusser *Lenin and Philosophy and Other Essays*. London: New Left Books.

Anderson, R. (2006) *British Universities Past and Present*. London: Hambledon Continuum.

Apple, M. (1990) *Ideology and Curriculum*, 2nd edn. London: Routledge.

Apple, M. (2000) *Official Knowledge: Democratic Education in a Conservative Age*. London: Routledge.

Apple, M. (2006) *Educating the 'Right' Way: Markets, Standards, God and Inequality*. London: Routledge.

Apple, M. and Beane, J. (2007) *Democratic School: Lessons in Powerful Education*, 2nd edn. Portsmouth, NH: Heinemann.

Archer, M.S. (1979) *Social Origins of Educational Systems*. London: Sage.

Attwood, G., Croll, P. and Hamilton, J. (2003) Re-engaging with education, *Research Papers in Education*, 18(1): 75–95.

Ausubel, D.P. (1963) *The Psychology of Meaningful Verbal Learning*. New York: Grune and Stratton.

Avis, J. (1991) The strange fate of progressive education, in CCS Education Group (eds), *Education Limited*. London: Unwin Hyman.

Avis, J. (1994) Teacher professionalism: one more time, *Education Review*, 46(1): 63–72.

Avis, J. (1995) Post-compulsory education: curricular forms, modernisation and social difference, *International Studies in the Sociology of Education*, 5(1): 57–75.

Avis, J. (1999) Shifting identity – new conditions and the transformation of practice: teaching within post-compulsory education, *Journal of Vocational Education and Training*, 51(2): 245–64.

Avis, J. (2002) Imaginary friends: managerialism, globalisation and post-compulsory education and training in England, *Discourse: Studies in the Cultural Politics of Education*, 23(1): 75–90.

Avis, J. (2003a) Re-thinking trust in a performative culture, *Journal of Education Policy*, 18(3): 315–32.

Avis, J. (2003b) Work-based knowledge, evidence informed practice and education, *British Journal of Education Studies*, 51(4): 369–89.

Avis, J. (2005) Beyond performativity: reflections on activist professionalism and the labour process, *Journal of Education Policy*, 20(2): 209–22.

Avis, J. (2007a) Post-compulsory education and training: transformism and the struggle for change, *International Studies in Sociology of Education*, 17(3): 195–209.

Avis, J. (2009) *Education, Policy and Social Justice: Learning and Skills*, revised edn. London: Continuum.

Avis, J. and Bathmaker, A-M. (2004) The politics of care – emotional labour and trainee FE lecturers, *Journal of Vocational Education and Training*, 56(1): 5–19.

Avis, J. and Bathmaker, A-M. (2006) From trainee to FE lecturer: trials and tribulations, *Journal of Vocational Education and Training*, 58(2): 171–89.

Avis, J., Bathmaker, A-M. and Parsons, J. (2002a) Communities of practice and the construction of learners in post-compulsory education and training, *Journal of Vocational Education and Training*, 54(1): 27–50.

Avis, J., Bathmaker, A-M. and Parsons, J. (2002b) 'I think a lot of staff are dinosaurs': further education trainee teachers' understandings of pedagogic relations, *Journal of Education and Work*, 15(2): 181–200.

Avis, J., Bloomer, M., Esland, G., Gleeson, D. and Hodkinson, P. (1996) *Knowledge and Nationhood: Education, Politics and Work*. London: Cassell.

Ball, S. (1995) Education, majorism and the 'curriculum of the dead', in P. Murphy, M. Selinder, J. Bourne and M. Briggs (eds), *Subject Learning in the Primary Curriculum*. London: Routledge.

Ball, S.J. (2008) *The Education Debate*. Bristol: The Policy Press.

Barber, B. (1963) Some problems in the sociology of professions, *Daedalus*, 92(4): 669–88.

Barer, R. (2007) *Disabled Students in London: A Review of Higher and Further Education, Including Students with Learning Difficulties*. London: GLA.

Barker, P. (2002) On being an online tutor, *Innovations in Education and Teaching International*, 39(1): 3–13.

Barnett, R. (2003) *Beyond All Reason: Living with Ideology in the University*. Buckingham: Open University Press.

Barton, D. and Tusting, K. (eds) (2005) *Beyond Communities of Practice: Language, Power and Social Context*. Cambridge: Cambridge University Press.

Barton, D., Hamilton, M. and Ivanič, R. (2000) *Situated Literacies: Reading and Writing in Context*. London: Routledge.

Bathmaker, A-M. and Avis, J. (2005) Becoming a lecturer in further education in England: the construction of professional identity and the role of communities of practice, *Journal of Education for Teaching*, 31(1): 47–66.

BBC (2003) *Clarke Criticised over Classics*, 23 January. Available at http://news.bbc.co.uk/1/hi/education/2712833.stm (accessed 5 January 2004).

Beale, D. (2004) The impact of restructuring in further education colleges, *Employee Relations*, 26(5): 465–79.

Beck, U. (1992) *Risk Society: Towards a New Modernity*. London: Sage.

Beckett, D. and Hager, P (2000) Making judgements as the basis for workplace learning: towards an epistemology of practice, *International Journal of Lifelong Education*, 19(4): 300–11.

BECTA (2008a) *Technology Strategy for Further Education, Skills and Regeneration: Implementation Plan for 2008–2011*. Coventry: BECTA.

BECTA (2008b) *Safeguarding Children Online: A Guide for School Leaders*. Coventry: BECTA.

Beetham, H. (2007) An approach to learning activity design, in H. Beetham and R. Sharpe (eds), *Rethinking Pedagogy for a Digital Age*. London: Routledge.

Bhavnani, R., Mirza, H.S. and Meetoo, V. (2005) *Tackling the Roots of Racism: Lessons for Success*. Bristol: Policy Press.

Biesta, G. (2004) Against learning: reclaiming a language for education in an age of learning, *Nordisk Pedagogik*, 23: 70–82.

Billett, S. (2001) Learning through work: workplace affordances and individual engagement, *Journal of Workplace Learning*, 13(5): 209–14.

Billett, S. (2002a) Workplace pedagogic practices: co-participation and learning, *British Journal of Educational Studies*, 50(4): 457–81.

Billett, S. (2002b) Toward a workplace pedagogy: guidance, participation and engagement, *Adult Education Quarterly*, 53(1): 27–43.

Billett, S. (2004) Learning through work: workplace participatory practices, in H. Rainbird, A. Fuller and A. Munro (eds), *Workplace Learning in Context*. London: Routledge.

Biott, C. and Eason, C. (1994) *Collaborative Learning in Staffrooms and Classrooms*. London: David Fulton.

Black, P. and Wiliam, D. (1998) *Inside the Black Box: Raising Standards Through Classroom Assessment*. London: King's College.

Black, P., Harrison, C., Lee, C., Marshall, B. and Wiliam, D. (2003) *Assessment for Learning: Putting it into Practice*. Maidenhead: Open University Press.

Blair, T. (2002) PM's speech on tackling poverty and social exclusion. Available at http://www.number10.gov.uk (accessed 4 November 2002).

Blewitt, J. and Cullingford, C. (2004) *The Sustainability Curriculum: The Challenge for Higher Education*. London: Earthscan.

Bloom, B. (ed.) (1956) *Taxonomy of Educational Objectives, Handbook 1: Cognitive Domain*. New York: Longman.

Bloomer, M. and Hodkinson, P. (2000) Learning careers: continuity and change in young people's dispositions to learning, *British Educational Research Journal*, 26(5): 583–98.

Blum, P. (2001) *A Teacher's Guide to Anger Management*. London: RoutledgeFalmer.

Board of Education (1944) *Teachers and Youth Leaders*, McNair Report. London: HMSO.

Boud, D., Cohen, R. and Walker, D. (1993) *Using Experience for Learning*. Buckingham: Society for Research into Higher Education and Open University Press.

Boud, D., Keogh, R. and Walker, D. (1985) *Reflection: Turning Experience into Learning*. London: Kogan Page.

Bourdieu, P. (1974) The school as a conservative force: scholastic and cultural inequalities, in J. Eggleston (ed.), *Contemporary Research in the Sociology of Education*. London: Methuen.

Bourdieu, P. with Wacquant, L. (1989a) Towards a reflexive sociology: a workshop with Pierre Bourdieu, *Sociological Theory*, 7(1): 26–63.

Bourdieu, P. (1989b) Social space and symbolic power, *Sociological Theory*, 7(1): 14–25.

Bourdieu, P. (1996) *The State Nobility: Elite Schools in the Field of Power*. Cambridge: Polity Press.

Bourdieu, P. (1990) *The Logic of Practice*. Cambridge: Polity Press

Bourdieu, P. and Passeron, J. (1990) *Reproduction in Education, Society and Culture*, 2nd edn. London: Sage.

Bowles, S. and Gintis, H. (1976) *Schooling in Capitalist America*. London: Routledge and Kegan Paul.

Brine, J. (2006) Lifelong learning and the knowledge economy: those that know and those that do not – the discourse of the European Union, *British Educational Research Journal*, 32(5): 649–65.

Brockbank, A. (2006) *Facilitating Reflective Learning Through Mentoring and Coaching*. London: Kogan Page.

Brookfield, S. (1995) *Becoming a Reflective Teacher*. San Francisco, CA: Jossey Bass.

Brookfield, S.D. (2005) *The Power of Critical Theory for Adult Learning and Teaching*. Maidenhead: Open University Press.

Brown, G. (2007) Speech to the nation, London's Imagination Gallery, London, 11 May.

Browne, R.B. (ed.) (2005) *Popular Culture Studies Across the Curriculum*. Jefferson: McFarlane and Company Inc., Publishers.

Bruner, J.S. (2006) *In Search of Pedagogy Vol. 1: The Selected Works of Jerome S. Bruner*. Abingdon: Routledge.

Bullying Matters (2009) *Is Your Business at Risk?* Available at http://www.bullyingmatters. co.uk/index. php?pageid=12 (accessed 20 February 2009).

Bunt, G.R. (series editor) *Faith Guides for Higher Education*. Higher Education Academy. Available at http://www.ecu.ac.uk/guidance/religionandbelief/guidance.htm (accessed 1 July 2009).

Bush, T. and Middlewood, D. (2005) *Leading and Managing People in Education*. London: Sage Publications.

Butcher, J. (2002) A case for mentor challenge? The problem of learning to teach post-16, *Mentoring and Tutoring*, 10(3): 197–220.

Butcher, J. (2003) 'Sink or swim': learning to teach post-16 on an 11–18 Postgraduate Certificate of Education, *Teachers' Development*, 7(1): 31–57.

Byron, T. (2008) *Safer Children in a Digital World: the Report of the Byron Review*. Nottingham: DCSF Publications.

Callaghan, J. (1976) Towards a national debate, *Education*, 148(17): 332–3.

Cantle, T. (2001) *Community Cohesion – A Report of the Independent Review Team*. London: Home Office.

Cantle, T. (2005) *Community Cohesion: A New Framework for Race Relations*. Basingstoke: Palgrave.

Cantor, L. and Roberts, I. (1972) *Further Education in England and Wales*, 2nd edn. London: Routledge and Kegan Paul.

Carr, D. (2003) *Making Sense of Education*. London: RoutledgeFalmer.

Carr, W. (1995) *For Education: Towards a Critical Education Enquiry*. Buckingham: Open University Press.

Carter, M. and Francis, R. (2001) Mentoring and beginning teachers' workplace learning, *Asia-Pacific Journal of Teacher Education*, 29(3): 249–62.

Casanova, J. (1994) *Public Religions in the Modern World*. Chicago: University of Chicago Press.

Cassidy, S. (2004) Learning styles: an overview of theories, models, and measures, *Educational Psychology*, 24(4): 419–44.

Challis, M. (1993) *Introducing APEL*. London: Routledge.

Charlton, D., Gent, W. and Scammells, B. (1971) *The Administration of Technical Colleges.* Manchester: Manchester University Press.

Child, D. (2004) *Psychology and the Teacher,* 7th edn. London: Continuum.

Chitty, C. (2004) *Education Policy in Britain.* Basingstoke: Palgrave Macmillan

Clow, R. (2001) Further Education teachers' constructions of professionalism, *Journal of Vocational Education and Training,* 53(3): 407–19.

Clutterbuck, D. (2004) *Everyone Needs a Mentor.* London: CIPD.

Clutterbuck, D. (2005) *Coaching and Mentoring in Education.* Burnham: Clutterbuck Associates.

Coffield, F. (2005) *Learning Styles: Help or Hindrance?* London: Institute of Education.

Coffield, F. (2006) Running ever faster down the wrong road, Inaugural Lecture, London University Institute of Education, London, 5 December.

Coffield, F. and Edward, S. (2008) Rolling out 'good', 'best' and 'excellent' practice. What next? Perfect practice? *British Educational Research Journal,* iFirst Article: 1–20.

Coffield, F., Moseley, D., Hall, E. and Ecclestone, K. (2004) *Should We Be Using Learning Styles? What Research Has to Say to Practice.* Trowbridge: Learning and Skills Research Centre.

Colley, H. (2006) Learning to labour with feeling: class, gender and emotion in childcare education and training, *Contemporary Issues in Early Childhood,* 7(1): 15–29.

Colley, H. and James, D. (2005) Unbecoming tutors: towards a more dynamic notion of professional participation. Paper presented at the Changing teacher roles, identities and professionalism conference, King's College, London, 16 May.

Colley, H., James, D., Tedder, M. and Diment, K. (2003) Learning as becoming in vocational education and training: class, gender and the role of vocational habitus, *Journal of Vocational Education and Training,* 55(4): 471–97.

Colley, H., James, D. and Diment, K. (2007) Unbecoming teachers: towards a more dynamic notion of professional participation, *Journal of Education Policy,* 22(2): 173–93.

Collis, B. and Moonen, J. (2001) *Flexible Learning in a Digital World: Experiences and Expectations.* London: Kogan Page.

Commission for Black Staff in FE (2002) *Challenging Racism: Further Education Leading the Way.* London: Commission for Black Staff in FE.

Commission for Racial Equality (1999) *Open Talk, Open Minds.* London: CRE.

Condie, R. and Munro, B. (2007) *The Impact of ICT in Schools: A Landscape Review.* Coventry: BECTA.

Connor, H., Tyers, C., Modood, T. and Hillage, J. (2004) *Why the Difference? A Closer Look at Higher Education Minority Ethnic Students and Graduates,* Research Report RR552. London: DfES.

Cornford, I. (2002) Reflective teaching: empirical research and some implications for teacher education, *Journal of Vocational Education and Training,* 54(2): 219–35.

Cosh, J. (1999) Peer observation: a reflective model, *ELT Journal,* 53(1): 22–7.

Cowan, K. (2006) *How to Monitor Sexual Orientation in the Workplace.* Stonewall Workplace Guides. Available at www.stonewall.org.uk/education_for_all/research/1790.asp (accessed 14 January 2007).

Cowley, S. (2003) *Getting the Buggers to Behave 2.* London: Continuum.

Crawley, J. (2005) *In at the Deep End.* London: David Fulton Publishers.

Creanor, L. (2002) A tale of two courses: a comparative study of tutoring online, *Open Learning,* 17(1): 57–68.

Creanor, L., Tinder, K., Gowan, D. and Howells, C. (2006) *LEX: Learner Experiences of E-learning.* Available at http://www.jisc.ac.uk/elp_lex.html (accessed 29 October 2008).

Crombie White, R., Pring, R., and Brockington, D. (1995) *14–19 Education and Training: Implementing a Unified System of Learning.* London: RSA.

Cullimore, S. (2006) Joined-up training: improving the partnership links between a university

PGCE (FE) course and its placement colleges, *Research in Post-Compulsory Education*, 11(3): 303–17.

Cullingford, C. (ed.) (1999) *An Inspector Calls. Ofsted and its Effect on School Standards*. London: Kogan Page.

Cullingford, C. and Daniels, S. (1999) Effects of Ofsted inspections on school performance, in C. Cullingford (ed.) *An Inspector Calls: Ofsted and its Effect on School Standards*. London: Kogan Page.

Cummins, J., McNicholl, A., Love, D. and King, E. (2006) *Improving the Diversity Profile of the Learning and Skills Sector Workforce: Report for the DfES*. London: Office for Public Management Ltd.

Cunningham, B. (2007) All the right features: towards an 'architecture' for mentoring trainee teachers in UK further education colleges, *Journal of Education for Teaching*, 33(1): 88–97.

Davies, J. and G. Biesta (2007) Coming to college or getting out of school? The experience of vocational learning of 14–16-year-olds in a further education college, *Research Papers in Education*, 22(1): 23–41.

Davies, P. (2000) The relevance of systematic reviews to educational policy and practice, *Oxford Review of Education*, 26(3/4): 365–78.

Davies, P., Slack, K., Hughes, A., Mangan, J. and Vigurs, K. (2008) *Knowing Where to Study? Fees, Bursaries and Fair Access*. Stoke-on-Trent: Institute for Educational Policy Research and Institute for Access Studies, Staffordshire University.

Deem, R., Hillyard, S. and Reed, M. (2007) *Knowledge, Higher Education and the New Managerialism: The Changing Management of UK Universities*. Oxford: Oxford University Press.

DCSF (Department for Children, Schools and Families) (2007a) *Targeted Youth Support: Integrated Support for Vulnerable Young People – A Guide*. London: TDA.

DCSF (Department for Children, Schools and Families) (2009) *14–19 Education and Skills*. Available at http://www.dcsf.gov.uk/14–19/index.cfm?go=site.home&sid=51&pid=421 &ctype=FAQ &ptype=Single (accessed 2 February 2009).

DCSF/DIUS (Department for Children, Schools and Families / Department for Innovation, Universities and Skills) (2008) *Raising Expectations: Enabling the System to Deliver*. Norwich: TSO.

DES (Department of Education and Science) (1966) *The Supply and Training of Teachers for Further Education*, Russell Report. London: HMSO.

DES (Department of Education and Society) (1991) *Education and Training for the 21st Century*. London: HMSO.

DfEE (Department for Education and Employment) (1999) *A Fresh Start: Improving Literacy and Numeracy*, Moser Report. London: DfEE.

DfEE (Department for Education and Employment) (2000) *Learning and Skills Act 2000*. London: HMSO.

DfEE (Department for Education and Employment) (2001) *Skills for Life: The National Strategy for Improving Adult Literacy and Numeracy Skills*. London: DfEE.

DfES (Department for Education and Skills) (2002a) *Success for All: Reforming Further Education and Training: A Discussion Document*. London: HMSO.

DfES (Department for Education and Skills) (2002b) *Success for All: Reforming Further Education and Training: Our Vision for the Future*. London: DfES.

DfES (Department for Education and Skills) (2003a) *Introducing Access for All: Supporting Learners with Learning Difficulties and Disabilities Across the Curriculum*. Nottingham: DfES Publications.

DfES (Department for Education and Skills) (2003a) *Subject Specialism: Consultation Document*. London: DfES.

DfES (Department for Education and Skills) (2003b) *The Future of Initial Teacher Education for the Learning and Skills Sector: An Agenda for Reform – A Consultative Paper*. London: DfES.

DfES (Department for Education and Skills) (2003c) *Towards a Unified e-Learning Strategy: Consultation Document*. London: DfES.

DfES (Department for Education and Skills) (2003d) *Every Child Matters: Summary*. London: DfES.

DfES (Department for Education and Skills) (2004a) *Equipping our Teachers for the Future: Reforming Initial Teacher Training for the Learning and Skills Sector*. Nottingham: DfES Standards Unit.

DfES (Department for Education and Skills) (2004b) *14–19 Curriculum and Qualifications Reform: Final Report of the Working Group on 14–19 Reform*. Nottingham: DfES Publications.

DfES (Department for Education and Skills) (2005a) *14–19 Education and Skills*. London: HMSO.

DfES (Department for Education and Skills) (2005b) *Higher Standards, Better Schools for All: More Choice for Parents and Pupils*. London: DfES.

DfES (Department for Education and Skills) (2005c) *Skills: Getting on in Business, Getting on at Work*. Norwich: TSO.

DfES (Department for Education and Skills) (2005d) *Harnessing Technology Strategy*. Nottingham: DfES Publications.

DfES (Department for Education and Skills) (2005e) *Every Child Matters: Change for Children*. Nottingham: DfES Publications.

DfES (Department for Education and Skills) (2006) *Further Education: Raising Skills, Improving Life Chances*. London: HMSO.

DfES (Department for Education and Skills) (2007) *Raising Expectations: Staying in Education and Training Post-16*. Norwich: HMSO.

DoH (Department of Health) and the Home Office (2003) *The Victoria Climbié Inquiry: Report of an Inquiry by Lord Laming*. Norwich: TSO.

Dewey, J. (1933) *How We Think*, 2nd ed. New York: D.C. Heath.

Dewey, J. (1938) *Experience and Education*. New York: Macmillan.

DRC (Disability Rights Commission) (2007) *Disability Discrimination Act 1995: Code of Practice Post-16*. Norwich: TSO.

DIUS (Department of Innovation, Universities and Skills) (2008a) *Further Education Colleges: Models for Success*. London: DIUS.

DIUS (Department of Innovation, Universities and Skills) (2008b) *Mission Statement and Departmental Objectives*. London: DIUS.

DIUS/DWP (Department of Innovation, Universities and Skills / Department for Work and Pensions) (2007) *Opportunity, Employment and Progression: Making Skills Work*. Norwich: TSO.

Donald, J. (1992b) *Sentimental Education: Schooling, Popular Culture and the Regulation of Liberty*. London: Verso.

Donovan, G. (2005) *Teaching 14–19: Everything You Need to Know About Teaching and Learning Across the Phases*. London: David Fulton.

Dreyfus, S. and Dreyfus, H. (1980) *A Five-stage Model of the Mental Activities Involved in Directed Skill Acquisition*. Berkeley, CA: Operations Research Center, University of California.

Drucker, P. (1993) *Post-Capitalist Society*. New York: HarperCollins.

Duckett, I. and Tatarkowsky, M. (2005) *Practical Strategies for Learning and Teaching on Vocational Programmes*. London: LSDA.

Eastwood, L., Coates, J., Dixon, L. et al. (2009) *A Toolkit for Creative Teaching in Post-Compulsory Education*. Maidenhead: Open University Press.

Ecclestone, K. (2004) From Freire to fear: the rise of the therapeutic culture in post-16 education, in J. Satterthwaite, E. Atkinson and W. Martin (eds), *The Disciplining of Education*. London: Trentham.

Ecclestone, K. and Hayes, D. (2009) *The Dangerous Rise of Therapeutic Education*. London: Routledge.

ECRE (European Council on Refugees and Exiles) (1999) *Good Practice Guide on Education for Refugees in the European Union*. London: World University Service.

ECU (Equality Challenge Unit) (2004) *Employing People in Higher Education: Sexual Orientation*. London: Equality Challenge Unit.

Education Group, Centre for Contemporary Cultural Studies (1981) *Unpopular Education: Schooling and Social Democracy in England since 1944*. London: Hutchinson.

Education Group II, Cultural Studies, Birmingham (1991) *Education Limited: Schooling and Training and the New Right Since 1979*. London: Unwin Hyman.

Edwards, R. (1980) *Contested Terrain: The Transformation of the Workplace in the Twentieth Century*. London: Heinemann.

Egan, G. (2002) *The Skilled Helper*. Pacific Grove, CA: Brooks-Cole, Thompson Learning.

Eisner, Elliot W. (1985) *The Art of Educational Evaluation: A Personal View*. London: Falmer Press.

Elliott, B. and Calderhead, J. (1993) Mentoring for teacher development: possibilities and caveats, in D. McIntyre, H. Hagger and N. Wilkin (eds), *Mentoring: Perspectives on School-based Teacher Education*. London: Kogan Page.

Elliott, G. (1998) Lecturing in post-compulsory education: profession, occupation or reflective practice? *Teachers and Training: Theory and Practice*, 4(1): 161–75.

ENTO (Employment National Training Organisation) (2006) *National Occupational Standards for Coaching and Mentoring in a Work Environment*. Leicester: ENTO.

Entwistle, N.J. and Ramsden, R. (1983) *Understanding Student Learning*. London: Routledge.

EOC (Equal Opportunities Commission) (2007) *Meeting the Gender Duty for Transsexual Staff. Guidance for Public Bodies Working in England, Wales and Scotland*. Manchester: Equal Opportunities Commission (now part of Equality and Human Rights Commission).

EPPI (Evidence for Policy and Practice Information) (2001) *Review Group Manual*. London: EPPI-centre.

Eraut, M. (2000) Non-formal learning and tacit knowledge in professional work, *British Journal of Educational Psychology*, 70(1): 113–36.

Evans, J. and Benefield, P. (2001) Systematic reviews of educational research: does the medical model fit, *British Educational Research Journal*, 27(5): 527–41.

Evans, L. (2008) Professionalism, professionality and the development of education professionals, *British Journal of Educational Studies*, 56(1): 20–38.

Evans, M. (2004) *Killing Thinking: The Death of the Universities*. London: Continuum.

Feenberg, A. (1989) The written world: on the theory and practice of computer conferencing, in R. Mason and A. Kaye (eds), *Mindweave: Communication, Computers and Distance Education*. Oxford: Pergamon Press.

FENTO (Further Education National Training Organisation) (1999) *Standards for Teaching and Supporting Learning in Further Education in England and Wales*. London: FENTO.

Fidler, B. and Atton, T. (1999) *Poorly Performing Staff in Schools and How to Manage Them*. London: Routledge.

Fielding, M. (2001) Ofsted, inspection and the betrayal of democracy, *Journal of Philosophy of Education*, 35(4): 695–709.

Fisher, R. (2004) From *Business Education Council* to *Edexcel Foundation* 1969–1996: the short but winding road from technician education to instrumentalist technicism, *Journal of Education and Work*, 17(3): 237–55.

Fisher, R. and Webb, K. (2006) Subject specialist pedagogy and initial teacher training for the learning and skills sector in England: the context, a response and some critical issues, *Journal of Further and Higher Education*, 30(4): 337–49.

Fisher, R., Harris, A. and Jarvis, C. (2008) *Education in Popular Culture: Telling Tales on Teachers and Learners*. London: Routledge.

Flinders, D. and Thornton, S. (2004) *The Curriculum Studies Reader*. London: Routledge.

Foster, A. (2005) *Realising the Potential: A Review of the Role of Further Education Colleges*. London: DfES Publications.

Foucault, M. (1980) Truth and power, in C. Gordon (ed.), *Power/Knowledge: Selected Interviews and Other Writings 1972–1977*. New York: Pantheon.

Foucault, M. (1991) *Discipline and Punish: The Birth of the Prison*. Harmondsworth: Penguin.

Fowler, B. (ed.) (2000) *Reading Bourdieu in Society and Culture*. Oxford: Blackwell.

Fryer, R.H. (1997) *Learning for the Twenty-first century: First Report of the National Advisory Group for Continuing Education and Lifelong Learning*. Available at www.lifelonglearning. co.uk/nagcell2/ index.htm (accessed 11 August 2009).

Fukuyama, F. (1992) *The End of History and the Last Man*. London: Penguin Books.

Furedi, F. (1997) *Culture of Fear: Risk-taking and the Morality of Low Expectation*. London: Cassell.

Furedi, F. (2003) *Therapy Culture*. London: Routledge.

Furlong, J. and Maynard, T. (1993) Learning to teach and models of mentoring, in D. McIntyre, H. Hagger and N. Wilkin (eds), *Mentoring: Perspectives on School-based Teacher Education*. London: Kogan Page.

Gagné, R.M. (1977) *The Conditions of Learning*, 3rd edn. New York: Holt, Rinehart and Winston.

Garber, M. (2003) *Academic Instincts*. Princeton: Princeton University Press.

Gee, J.P. (1996) *Social Linguistics and Literacies: Ideology in Discourses*, 2nd edn. London: RoutledgeFalmer.

Gee, J. (2003) *What Video Games Have to Teach us About Learning and Literacy*. Basingstoke: Palgrave Macmillan.

Gee, J. (2004) *Situated Language and Learning: A Critique of Traditional Schooling*. London: Routledge.

Gibbs, G. (1995) *Discussion with More Students*. Oxford: Oxford Centre for Staff and Learning Development, Oxford Brookes University.

Giddens, A. (1998) *The Third Way: The Renewal of Social Democracy*. Oxford: Polity.

Giddens, A. and Pierson, C. (1998) Interview 3: structuration theory, *Conversations With Anthony Giddens: Making Sense of Modernity*. Cambridge: Polity Press.

Gilliat-Ray, S. (2000) *Religion in Higher Education: The Politics of the Multi-faith Campus*. Aldershot: Ashgate.

GLA (Greater London Authority) (2006) *Towards Joined Up Lives: Disabled and Deaf Londoners' Experience of Housing, Employment and Post-16 Education from a Social Model Perspective*. London: GLA.

Gleeson, D. (1983) Further education, tripartism and the labour market, in D. Gleeson (ed.), *Youth Training and the Search for Work*. London: RKP.

Gleeson, D. (2001) Style and substance in education leadership: further education (FE) as a case in point, *Journal of Education Policy*, 16(3): 181–96.

Gleeson, D. and Shain, F. (1999) Managing ambiguity: between markets and managerialism – a case study of 'middle' managers in further education, *Sociological Review*, 57(3): 461–90.

Gleeson, D., Davies, J. and Wheeler, E. (2005) On the making and taking of professionalism in the further education (FE) workplace, *British Journal of Sociology of Education*, 26(4): 445–60.

Golby, M. (1989) Curriculum traditions, in B. Moon, P. Murphy and J. Raynor (eds), *Policies for the Curriculum*. London: Hodder and Stoughton.

Goldsmith, M. (2008) Better coaching, *Leadership Excellence*, 25(5): 9.

Goodson, I.F. (1994) *Studying Curriculum: Cases and Methods*. Buckingham: Open University Press.

Goodson, I.F. (2003) *Professional Knowledge, Professional Lives: Studies in Education and Change*. Maidenhead: Open University Press.

Gorard, S. (2002) *The Future for Educational Research Post RAE 2001*, BERA conference debate. Available at http//:www.BERA.ac.uk (now www.beraconference.co.uk).

Gough, S. and Scott, W. (2004) *Key Issues in Sustainable Development and Learning: A Critical Review*. London: Routledge.

Grace, G. (1987) Teachers and the state in Britain, in M. Lawn and G. Grace (eds) *Teachers: the Cultures and Politics of Work*. London: Falmer.

Grace, G. (1995) *School Leadership: Beyond Education Management*. London: Falmer.

Gramsci, A. (1971) *Selections from the Prison Notebooks*. London: Lawrence and Wishart.

Grayling, A.C. (2007) *The Ties that Bind*. Available at www.equalityhumanrights.com/en/ newsandcomment/ (accessed 26 March 2008).

Green, A. (1990) *Education and State Formation: The Rise of Education Systems in England, France and the USA*. London: Macmillan.

Green, A. (1991) The peculiarities of English education, in Education Group 2, Cultural Studies, Birmingham, *Education Limited: Schooling and Training and the New Right Since 1979*. London: Unwin Hyman.

Green, B. (2006) English, literacy, rhetoric: changing the project? *English in Education* 40(1): 7–19.

Gregory, J. (2002) Principles of experiential education, in P. Jarvis (ed.), *The Theory and Practice of Teaching*. London: Kogan Page.

Gronlund, N.E. (1970) *Stating Behavioural Objectives for Classroom Instruction*. London: Collier-Macmillan.

GTC (General Teaching Council) (2003) *Department for Education and Skills Subject Specialism: Consultation Document: The Response of the General Teaching Council for England*. London: GTC.

GTC (General Teaching Council) (2006) *The Statement of Professional Values and Practice for Teachers*. London: GTC.

Haidar, E. (2007) Coaching and mentoring nursing students, *Nursing Management – UK*, 14(8): 32–5.

Halai, A. (2006) Mentoring in-service teachers: issues of role diversity, *Teaching and Teacher Education*, 22: 700–10.

Halsey, A.H., Lauder, H., Brown, P. and Stuart, A. (eds) (1997) *Education, Culture, Economy Society*. Oxford: Oxford University Press.

Hamilton, M. and Hillier, Y. (2006) Changing faces of adult literacy, language and numeracy: a critical history. Stoke-on-Trent: Trentham Books Ltd.

Hankey, J. (2004) The good, the bad and other considerations: reflections on mentoring trainee teachers in post-compulsory education, *Research in Post Compulsory Education*, 9(3): 389–400.

Hargreaves, D. (2005) *About Learning*. London: Demos.

Harkin, J. (2006) Treated like adults: 14–16-year-olds in further education, *Research in Post-Compulsory Education*, 11(3): 319–39.

Harwood T., Garry, T. and Broderick, A. (2008) *Relationship Marketing: Perspectives, Dimensions and Contexts*. London: McGraw Hill.

Hattie, J. (2009) *Visible Learning: A Synthesis of Over 800 Meta-analyses Relating to Achievement*. Abingdon: Routledge.

Hayes, D. and Wynyard, R. (eds) (2002) *The McDonaldization of Higher Education*. Westport, CT: Greenwood Press.

HEA (Higher Education Academy) (2006) *The UK Professional Standards Framework for Teaching and Supporting Learning in Higher Education*. York: HEA.

HEA (Higher Education Academy) (2008) *Quality Enhancement and Assurance: A Changing Picture*. York: HEA.

Health and Safety Executive (2006a) *HSC Tells Health and Safety Pedants to 'Get a Life': Statement by Bill Callaghan, Chair of the Health and Safety Commission*. Available at http://www.hse.gov.uk/risk/statement.htm (accessed on 20 February 2009).

Health and Safety Executive (2006b) *Five Steps to Risk Assessment*. London: HSE. Available at http://www.hse.gov.uk/risk/fivesteps.htm (accessed 20 February 2009).

Healy, M. and Jenkins, A. (draft 2001) Discipline-based educational development. A later version appeared in R. MacDonald and H. Eggins (eds) (2003), *The Scholarship of Academic Development*. Buckingham: Open University Press, pp. 47–57.

HEFCE (Higher Education Funding Council for England) (2005) *HEFCE Strategy for E-learning*. http://www.hefce.ac.uk/pubs/hefce/2005/05_12/05_12.pdf (accessed 1 February 2009).

Heron, J. (1989) *The Facilitator's Handbook*. London: Kogan Page.

Hewstone, M., Tausch, N., Hughes, J. and Cairns, E. (2007) Prejudice, intergroup contact and identity, in M. Wetherell, M. Lafleche and R. Berkley (eds), *Identity, Ethnic Diversity and Community Cohesion*. London: Sage.

HM Government (2003) *Every Child Matters*. Norwich: The Stationery Office.

HM Government (2005) *Youth Matters*. Norwich: The Stationery Office.

HM Government (2007) *The Further Education Teachers' Qualifications (England) Regulations 2007*. SI 2264. London: HMSO.

Hodgson, A. and Spours, K. (2006) The organisation of 14–19 education and training in England: beyond weakly collaborative arrangements, *Journal of Education and Work*, 19 (4): 325–42.

Hodkinson, P. (2004) Research as a form of work: expertise, community and methodological objectivity, *British Educational Research Journal*, 30(1): 9–26.

Hodkinson, P. (2005) Reconceptualising the relations between college-based and workplace learning, *Journal of Workplace Learning*, 17(8): 521–32.

Hodkinson, P. (2008) 'What works' does not work! Researching lifelong learning in the culture of audit. Valedictory Lecture, Lifelong Learning Institute, the University of Leeds, June.

Hodkinson, P. and James, D. (2003) Introduction transforming learning cultures in further education, *Journal of Vocational Education and Training*, 55(4): 389–406.

Holmberg, B. (1989) *Theory and Practice of Distance Education*. Routledge: London.

Holub, R. (1992) *Antonio Gramsci: Beyond Marxism and Postmodernism*. London: Routledge.

Hoyle, D (2008) Problematizing *Every Child Matters*, *The Encyclopaedia of Informal Education*. Available at http://www.infed.org (accessed 11 August 2008).

Huddleston, P. and Oh, S-A. (2004) The magic roundabout: work-related learning within the 14–19 curriculum, *Oxford Review of Education*, 30(1): 83–103.

Hunt, R. and Jensen, J. (2006) *The School Report: The Experiences of Young Gay People in Britain's Schools*. Stonewall. Available at http://stonewall.org.uk/education_for_all/research/1790.asp (accessed 14 January 2007).

Husu, J., Toom, A. and Patrikainen, S. (2008) Guided reflection as a means to demonstrate and develop student teachers' competencies, *Reflective Practice*, 9(1): 37–51.

Hyland, T. and Merrill, B. (2003) *The Changing Face of Further Education: Lifelong Learning, Inclusion and Community Values in Further Education*. London: RoutledgeFalmer.

IfL (Institute for Learning) (2008a) *Licence to Practise: Professional Formation*. London: IfL.

IfL (Institute for Learning) (2008b) *Promote: The Code of Professional Practice*. London: IfL.

Jackson, A. and Wallis, B. (2006) No pain, no gain? Learning from inspection, *Research in Post-Compulsory Education*, 11(3): 251–66.

Jacques, D. and Salmon, G. (2007) *Learning in Groups*, 4th edn. Abingdon: Routledge.

James, D. and Biesta, G. (eds) (2007) *Improving Learning Cultures in Further Education*. London: Routledge.

James, D. and Diment, K. (2003) Going underground? Learning and assessment in an ambiguous space, *Journal of Vocational Education and Training*, 55(4): 407–22.

Jarvis, P. (2004) *Adult Education and Lifelong Learning: Theory and Practice*, 3rd edn. London: RoutledgeFalmer.

Jeffries, P. and Hussain, F. (1998) Using the Internet as a teaching resource, *Education and Training*, 40(8): 359–65.

Jenkins, R. (1992) *Pierre Bourdieu*. London: Routledge.

JISC (Joint Information Systems Committee) (2002) *Duty of Care in the Further and Higher Education Sectors*. Available at http://www.jisclegal.ac.uk/publications/Dutyofcare.htm (accessed on 20 February 2009).

JISC (Joint Information Systems Committee) (2004) *Effective Practice with E-learning: A Good Practice Guide in Designing for Learning*. Bristol: University of Bristol JISC Development Group.

JISC (Joint Information Systems Committee) (2007) *Student Expectations Study*. Available at www.jisc.ac.uk/publications/publications/studentexpectations (accessed 24 January 2009).

JISC (Joint Information Systems Committee) InfoNet (2008) *Exploring Tangible Benefits of E-learning: Does Investment Yield Interest?* Newcastle: Northumbria University.

Johnson, D. and Johnson, F. (2006) *Joining Together: Group Theory and Group Skills*, 9th edn. London: Pearson Education Inc.

Johnson, T. (1972) *Professions and Power*. London: Macmillan.

Jones, C. (2006) *From Theory to Practice: Using Differentiation to Raise Levels of Attainment*. London: Learning and Skills Network.

Jones, C.A. (2007) *Personalised Learning: Learner Empowerment*, 14–19 Quick Guides. London: Learning and Skills Network.

Jones, C. (2007) Designing for practice: practising design in the social sciences, in H. Beetham and R. Sharpe (eds), *Rethinking Pedagogy for a Digital Age: Designing and Delivering E-Learning*. London: Routledge.

Jones, R., Hughes, M. and Kingston, K. (2008) *An Introduction to Sports Coaching: From Science and Theory to Practice*. London: Routledge.

Joseph Rowntree Foundation (2007) *Experiences of Poverty and Disadvantage*. Available at http://www.jrf.org.uk/knowledge/findings/socialpolicy/2123.asp (accessed 3 January 2008).

Kandola, R. and Fullerton, J. (1998) *Diversity in Action: Managing the Mosaic*, 2nd edn. London: Institute of Personnel and Development.

Keep, E. (2006) State control of the English education and training system – playing with the biggest train set in the world, *Journal of Vocational Education and Training*, 58(1): 47–64.

Kelly, A.V. (2009) *The Curriculum: Theory and Practice*, 6th edn. London: Sage.

Kennedy, H. (1997) *Learning Works: Widening Participation in Further Education*. Coventry: Further Education Funding Council.

Kerfoot, D. and Whitehead, S. (1998) 'Boys own' stuff: masculinity and the management of further education, *Sociological Review*, 46(3): 436–57.

Kessler, S. and Bayliss, F. (1998) *Contemporary British Industrial Relations*, 3rd edn. London: Macmillan.

Kirkpatrick, D. (1998) *Evaluating Training Programmes: The Four Levels*. San Francisco, CA: Berrett-Koehler Publishers.

Klein, P. (2003) Rethinking the multiplicity of cognitive resources and curricular representations: alternatives to 'learning styles' and 'multiple intelligences', *Journal of Curriculum Studies*, 35(1): 45–81.

Knight, P. (1995) *Assessment for Learning in Higher Education*. London: Kogan Page.

Knight, P. and Yorke, M. (2003) *Assessment, Learning and Employability*. Maidenhead: Society for Research into Higher Education and Open University Press.

Knowles, M., Holton, E. and Swanson, R. (2005) *The Adult Learner*, 6th edn. London: Elsevier.

Kolb, D.A. (1984) *Experiential Learning: Experience as the Source of Learning and Development*. Englewood Cliffs, NJ: Prentice Hall.

Kundnani, A. (2002) *The Death of Multiculturalism*. London: Institute of Race Relations. Available at http://www.irr.org.uk/2002/april/ak000001.html (accessed 3 May 2003).

Larivee, B. (2000) Transforming teaching practice: becoming the critically reflective teacher, *Reflective Practice*, 1(3): 293–307.

Lauder, H., Brown, P., Dillabough, J-A. and Halsey, A. (2006) *Education, Globalization and Social Change*. Oxford: Oxford University Press.

Laurillard, D. (2002) *Rethinking University Teaching: A Framework for the Effective Use of Learning Technologies*, 2nd edn. Abingdon: RoutledgeFalmer.

Lave, J. and Wenger, E. (1991) *Situated Learning: Legitimate Peripheral Participation*. Cambridge: Cambridge University Press.

Law, J. (2003) *Making a Mess with Method*. Lancaster: Centre for Science Studies, Lancaster University. Available at http://www.lancs.ac.uk/fass/sociology/papers/law-making-a-mess-with-method.pdf (accessed 28 June 2009).

Leadbeater, C. (2005) *Learning about Personalisation: How Can We Put the Learner at the Heart of the Education System?* Nottingham: DfES.

Le Cornu, R. (2005) Peer mentoring: engaging pre-service teachers in mentoring one another, *Mentoring and Tutoring*, 13(3): 355–66.

Leitch Review of Skills (2006) *Prosperity for all in the Global Economy – World Class Skills*. Norwich: HMSO.

Liber, O. and Holyfield, S. (2003) *Creating a Managed Learning Environment*. Available at http://www.jiscinfonet.ac.uk/InfoKits/creating-an-mle/index_html (accessed 1 November 2005).

Lipsett, A. (2009) Students opt for easy diplomas, *Guardian*, 7 January.

LLUK (Lifelong Learning UK) (2005) *Further Education Workforce Data for England: An Analysis of the Staff Individualised Record (SIR) for 2003–04*. London: LLUK.

LLUK (Lifelong Learning UK) (2007a) *New Overarching Professional Standards for Teachers, Tutors and Trainers in the Lifelong Learning Sector*. London: LLUK.

LLUK (Lifelong Learning UK) (2007b) *Addressing Literacy, Language, Numeracy and ICT Needs in Education and Training: Defining the Minimum Core of Teachers' Knowledge, Understanding and Personal Skills*. London: LLUK.

LLUK (Lifelong Learning UK) (2007c) *Inclusive Learning Approaches for Literacy, Language, Numeracy and ICT*. London: LLUK.

LLUK (Lifelong Learning UK) (2009) *Overview of About LLUK*. Available at http://www.lluk.org/3169.htm (accessed 3 February 2009).

LLUK (Lifelong Learning UK) (undated) *The Importance of Diversity in the Lifelong Learning Sector Workforce*. Available at http://www.lifelonglearninguk.org/2820.htm (accessed 26 March 2008).

Loughran, J. (2006) A response to 'Reflecting on the self', *Reflective Practice*, 7(1): 43–53.

Lovell, T. (2000) Thinking feminism within and against Bourdieu, in B. Fowler (ed.), *Reading Bourdieu on Society and Change*. Oxford: Blackwell.

LSC (Learning and Skills Council) (2001) *Mentoring Towards Excellence*. London: LSC.

LSC (Learning and Skills Council) (2007a) *Further Education, Work-Based Learning, Train to Gain and Adult and Community Learning – Learner Numbers in England: 2006/07* (DIUS Statistical First Release, Ref. ILR/SFR14). Coventry: LSC.

LSC (Learning and Skills Council) (2007b) *Framework for Excellence: Raising Standards and Informing Choice*. Coventry: Learning and Skills Council.

LSC (Learning and Skills Council) (2009) *About the LSC*. Available at http://www.lsc.gov.uk/aboutus/ (accessed 1 February 2009).

LSIS (Learning and Skills Improvement Service) (2008) *About LSIS*. Available at http://www.lsis.org.uk/AboutUs/AboutLSIS.aspx (accessed 1 February 2009).

LSIS (Learning and Skills Improvement Service) (2009) *About Subject Learning Coaches*. Available at http://www.subjectlearningcoaches. net/SLC_role.html (accessed 19 February 2009).

LTSN (Learning and Teaching Support Network) (2002) e-Learning, *Circular 3 LTSN*, December. Available at www.bbk.ac.uk/qa/docs/e-learning.doc (accessed March 2009).

Lucas, N. (1995) Challenges facing teacher education: a view from a post-16 perspective, *Forum*, 37(1): 11–13.

Lucas, N. (2004) *Teaching in Further Education: New Perspectives for a Changing Context*. London: Bedford Way Papers.

Lucas, N. (2007) Rethinking initial teacher education for further education teachers: from a standards-led to a knowledge-based approach, *Teaching Education*, 18(2): 93–106.

Lumby, J. (2001) *Managing Further Education: Learning Enterprise*. London: Paul Chapman Publishing.

Lumby, J. and Foskett, N. (2007) Turbulence masquerading as change: exploring 14–19 policy, in D. Raffe and K. Spours (eds), *Policy-making and Policy Learning in 14–19 Education*. London: Institute of Education, University of London.

Lumby, J., Harris, A., Morrison, M. et al. (2005) *Leadership, Development and Diversity in the Learning and Skills Sector*. London: LSRC.

Lyotard, J-F. (1984) *The Postmodern Condition: A Report on Knowledge*. Manchester: University of Manchester Press.

MacDonald, J. and McAteer, E. (2003) New approaches to supporting students: strategies for blended learning in distance and campus based environments, *Journal of Educational Media*, 28(2–3): 129–46.

Macpherson, W. (1999) *The Stephen Lawrence Inquiry: Report of an Inquiry by Sir William Macpherson of Cluny*, Cm 4262. London: The Stationery Office.

Maker, C. (1982) *Curriculum Development for the Gifted*. Rockville, MD: Aspen.

March, T. (1997) *Working the Web for Education*. Available at http://www.ozline.com/writings/theory.php (accessed 16 June 2008).

Marriott, G. (2001) *Observing Teachers at Work*. Oxford: Heinemann Educational Publishers.

Martinez, P. and Munday, F. (1998) *9000 Voices: Student Persistence and Dropout in Further Education*. London: Further Education Development Agency.

Marton, F. and Säljö, R. (1976) On qualitative differences in learning: I – Outcome and process, *British Journal of Educational Psychology*, 46: 4–11.

Marx, K. (1968) The eighteenth brumaire of Louis Bonaparte, in K. Marx and F. Engels (eds), *Marx and Engels Selected Works*. London: Lawrence and Wishart.

Marx, K. and Engels, F. (1968) *Selected Works in One Volume*. London: Lawrence and Wishart.

Maslow, A. (1970) *Motivation and Personality*, 2nd edn. New York: Harper and Row.

Mason, R. (1998) Models of online courses, *ALN Magazine*, 2(2). Available at http://www.aln.org/publications/magazine/index.asp (accessed 4 March 2009).

Mason, R. (2006) Learning technologies for adult continuing education, *Studies in Continuing Education*, 28(2): 121–33.

Mason, R. and Bacsich, P. (1998) Embedding computer conferencing into university teaching, *Computers in Education*, 30(3): 249–58.

Masterman, L. and Vogel, M. (2008) Practices and processes of design for learning, in H. Beetham and R. Sharpe (eds), *Rethinking Pedagogy for a Digital Age: Designing and Delivering E-learning*. Abingdon: Routledge.

May, S. (ed.) (1999) *Critical Multiculturalism: Rethinking Multicultural and Anti-racist Education*. London: Falmer.

Maynard, T. (2000) Learning to teach or learning to manage mentors? Experiences of school-based teacher training, *Mentoring and Tutoring*, 8(1): 17–30.

McCulloch, G. (2005) *The RoutledgeFalmer Reader in the History of Education*. London: Routledge.

McGhee, D. (2005) *Intolerant Britain: Hate, Citizenship and Difference*. Maidenhead: Open University Press.

McGhee, D. (2006) The new Commission for Equality and Human Rights: building community cohesion and revitalising citizenship in contemporary Britain, *Ethnopolitics*, 5(2): 145–66.

McIntyre, D., Hagger, H. and Wilkin, N. (eds) (1993) *Mentoring: Perspectives on School-based Teacher Education*. London: Kogan Page.

McLaren, P. (2005) *Capitalists and Conquerors: Critical Pedagogy Against Empire*. Lanham, MD: Rowman & Littlefield.

McNally, P. and Martin, S. (1998) Support and challenge in learning to teach: the role of the mentor, *Asia-Pacific Journal of Teacher Education*, 26(1): 39–50.

Medway, P. (2005) Literacy and the idea of English, *Changing English*, 12(1): 19–29.

Meek, M. (1991) *On Being Literate*. London: Bodley Head.

Megginson, D. and Clutterbuck, D. (1999) *Mentoring Executives and Directors*. Oxford: Butterworth Heinemann.

Meighan, R. and Siraj-Blatchford, I. (1997) *A Sociology of Educating*. London: Cassell.

MHF (Mental Health Foundation) (2009) *Mental Health Problems*. Available at http://www.mental health.org.uk/information/ (accessed 8 March 2009).

Millerson, G. (1964) *The Qualifying Associations*. London: Routledge Kegan and Paul.

Minton, D. (1991) *Teaching Skills in Further and Adult Education*. London: Palgrave MacMillan.

Modood, T. (2005) *Multicultural Politics: Racism, Ethnicity and Muslims in Britain*. Edinburgh: Edinburgh University Press.

Modood, T., Berthoud, R., Lakey, J. et al (1997) *Ethnic Minorities in Britain: Diversity and Disadvantage*. London: PSI.

MoE (Ministry of Education) (1959) *15–18: A Report of the Central Advisory Council for Education*, Crowther Report. London: HMSO.

Moore, A. (1999) Beyond reflection: contingency, idiosyncrasy and reflexivity in initial teacher education, in M. Hammersley (ed.), *Researching School Experience*. London: Falmer.

Moore, M.G. (1980) Independent study, in R. Boyd and J. Apps (eds), *Redefining the Discipline of Adult Education*. Washington, DC: Jossey Bass.

Morgan-Klein, B. and Osborne, M. (2007) *The Concepts and Practices of Lifelong Learning*. London: Routledge

Morley, L. (2003) *Quality and Power in Higher Education*. Maidenhead: SRHE and Open University Press.

Morrison, K. and Ridley, K. (1989) Ideological contexts for curriculum planning, in M. Preedy (ed.), *Approaches to Curriculum Management*. Milton Keynes: Open University Press.

Moule, P. (2007) Challenging the five-stage model for e-learning: a new approach, *ALT-J*, 15(1): 37–50.

Mumford, A. (1995) Learning styles and mentoring, *Industrial and Commercial Training*, 27(8): 4–7.

Nasta, T. (2007) Translating national standards into practice for the initial training of further education (FE) teachers, *Research in Post-Compulsory Education*, 12(1): 1–17.

National Commission on Education (1993) *Learning to Succeed*. London: Heinemann.

Nayak, A. (1999) White English ethnicities: racism, anti-racism and student perspectives, *Race, Ethnicity and Education*, 2(2): 177–202.

NCET (National Council for Educational Technology) (1993) *Differentiation: A Practical Handbook of Classroom Strategies*. Coventry: NCET.

NCIHE (National Committee of Inquiry into Higher Education) (1997) *Higher Education in the Learning Society: Report of the National Committee*, The Dearing Report. London: NCIHE.

NIACE (National Institute of Adult Continuing Education) (2006) *More Than a Language: NIACE Committee of Enquiry on English for Speakers of Other Languages Executive Summary*. Leicester: NIACE.

Nicholson, S. (2002) Socialization in the 'virtual hallway': instant messaging in the asynchronous web-based distance education classroom, *The Internet and Higher Education*, 5(4): 363–72.

Nicol, D. and Macfarlane-Dick, D. (2006) Formative assessment and self-regulated learning: a model and seven principles of good feedback practice, *Studies in Higher Education*, 31(2): 199–218.

Nixon, L., Gregson, M. and Spedding, T. (2007) Pedagogy and the intuitive appeal of learning styles in post-compulsory education in England, *Journal of Vocational Education and Training*, 59(1): 39–51.

Norton Grubb, W. (1999) Improvement or control? A US view of English inspection, in C. Cullingford (ed.), *An Inspector Calls. Ofsted and its Effect on School Standards*. London: Kogan Page.

NUT (National Union of Teachers) (2003) *Risk Assessment: NUT Health and Safety Briefings*. London: NUT. Available at http://www.teachers.org.uk/resources/pdf/risk.pdf (accessed on 20 February 2009).

Oblinger, D. and Oblinger, J. (2005) Is it age or IT: first steps toward understanding the net generation, in D. Oblinger and J. Oblinger (eds) *Educating the Net Generation*. Available at www.educause.edu/educatingthenetgen/ (accessed 24 January 2009).

O'Connell, B. (2005) *Creating an Outstanding College*. Cheltenham: Nelson Thornes.

Ofqual (2008) *Launch Brochure*. Available at http://www.ofqual.gov.uk/files/Ofqual_Launch Brochure.pdf (accessed 2 February 2009).

Ofsted (Office for Standards in Education) (1995) *Framework for the Inspections of Schools*. London: Ofsted.

Ofsted (Office for Standards in Education) (2003) *The Initial Training of Further Education Teachers: A Survey.* London: Ofsted.

Ofsted (Office for Standards in Education) (2005a) *Race Equality in Further Education: A Report by HMI.* London: Ofsted.

Ofsted (Office for Standards in Education) (2005b) *Common Inspection Framework for Inspecting Education and Training.* London: Ofsted.

Ofsted (Office for Standards in Education) (2006) *Best Practice in Self-evaluation: A Survey of Schools, Colleges and Local Authorities.* London: Ofsted.

Ofsted (Office for Standards in Education) (2007) *Handbook for Inspecting Work-related and Adult and Community Learning.* London: Ofsted.

Ofsted (Office for Standards in Education) (2008a) *Handbook for Inspecting Colleges.* London: Ofsted.

Ofsted (Office for Standards in Education) (2008b) *Grade Criteria for the Inspection of Initial Teacher education 2008–11.* London: Ofsted.

Ofsted (Office for Standards in Education) (2009) *About Us.* Available at http://www.ofsted.gov.uk/Ofsted-home/About-us (accessed 2 February 2009).

Ollin, R. and Tucker, J. (2008) *The NVQ Assessor, Verifier and Candidate Handbook: A Practical Guide to Units A1, A2 and V1, and STTTLSS Domain E*, 4th edn. London: Kogan Page.

Orr, K. (2008) Room for improvement? The impact of compulsory professional development for teachers in England's further education sector, *Journal of In-Service Education*, 34(1): 97–108.

Osborne, M., Houston, M. and Toman, N. (eds) (2007) *The Pedagogy of Lifelong Learning.* London: Routledge.

O'Toole, G. and Meyer, B. (2006) *Personalised Learning in the Post-16 Sector: A Preliminary Investigation.* London: Learning and Skills Network.

Ozga, J. and Lawn, M. (1981) *Teachers Professionalism and Class.* London: Falmer.

Pahl, K. and Rowsell, J. (2005) *Literacy and Education: Understanding the New Literacy Studies in the Classroom.* London: Paul Chapman.

Papen, U. (2005) *Adult Literacy as Social practice: More Than Skills.* London: Routledge.

Parker, S. (1997) *Reflective Teaching in the Postmodern World.* Buckingham: Open University Press.

Pearson, E. and Podeschi, R. (1999) Humanism and individualism: Maslow and his critics, *Adult Education Quarterly*, 50(1): 41–55.

Petty, G. (2004) *Teaching Today: A Practical Guide.* Cheltenham: Nelson Thornes.

Pintrich, P. and Zusho, A. (2002) Student motivation and self-regulated learning in the college classroom, in J.C. Smart and W.G. Tierney (eds), *Higher Education: Handbook of Theory and Research*, Volume XVII. New York: Agathon Press.

Polanyi, M. (1983) *The Tacit Dimension.* Gloucester, MA: Peter Smith.

Pollard, A., Collins, J., Simco, N. et al. (2005) *Reflective Teaching*, 2nd edn. London: Continuum.

Pratt, J. (2000) The emergence of the colleges, in A. Smithers and P. Robinson (eds), *Further Education Re-formed.* London: Falmer.

Prensky, M. (2001) Digital natives, digital immigrants, *On the Horizon* (NCB University Press), 9(5): 1–15.

Preston, J. (2003) White trash vocationalism? Formations of class and race in an Essex further education college, *Widening Participation and Lifelong Learning*, 5(2): 6–17.

Pring, R. (2000) *Philosophy of Educational Research.* London: Continuum.

Purdy, L. (2007) Educating gifted children, in R. Curren (ed.), *Philosophy of Education: An Anthology.* Oxford: Blackwell.

Putnam, R. (2000) *Bowling Alone.* London: Touchstone Books.

QCA (Qualifications and Curriculum Authority) (2000) *National Standards for Adult Literacy and Numeracy.* London: QCA.

QCA (Qualifications and Curriculum Authority) (2007) *Functional Skills.* Available at http://www.qca.org.uk/qca_6062.aspx (accessed 12 June 2008).

QCA (Qualifications and Curriculum Authority) (2008) *The Diploma: An Overview of the Qualification – Version 3.* London: QCA.

QCA (Qualifications and Curriculum Authority) (2009a) *QCF Implementation: New Flexible Qualifications and Credit Framework will Widen Access to Learning.* Available at http://www.qca.org.uk/qca_8152.aspx (accessed 30 June 2009).

QCA (Qualifications and Curriculum Authority) (2009b) *What is the QCF?* Available at http://www.qca.org.uk/qca_19674.aspx (accessed 30 June 2009).

Rainbird, H., Fuller, A. and Munro, A. (eds) (2004) *Workplace Learning in Context.* London: Routledge.

Ramsden, P. (1992) *Learning to Teach in Higher Education.* London: Routledge.

Randle, K. and Brady, N. (1997) Managerialism and professionalism in the 'Cinderella Service', *Journal of Vocational Education and Training,* 49(1): 121–40.

Reay, D., David, M. and Ball, S. (2005) *Degrees of Choice: Social Class, Race and Gender in Higher Education.* Stoke-on-Trent: Trentham.

Reeves, F. (1995) *The Modernity of FE: The Direction of Change in FE Colleges.* Bilston: Bilston College Publications.

Rennie, S. (2003) *Stories from the Front Line: The Impact of Inspection on Practitioners.* London: LSDA.

Rennie, S. (2006) *Promoting Equality and Diversity in Consortium for PCET Teacher Training Courses.* Huddersfield: Consortium for Post-Compulsory Education and Training.

Richardson, W. (2007) In search of the further education of young people in post-war England, *Journal of Vocational Education and Training,* 59(3): 385–418.

Ritchie, D. (2001) *Oldham Independent Review – On Oldham, One Future.* Manchester: Government Office for the Northwest.

Ritzer, G. (2008) *The McDonaldization of Society.* Los Angeles, CA: Pine Forge Press.

Robson, J. (2006) *Teacher Professionalism in Further and Higher Education: Challenges to Culture and Practice.* London: Routledge.

Robson, J. and Bailey, B. (2009) 'Bowing from the heart': an investigation into discourses of professionalism and the work of caring for students in further education, *British Educational Research Journal,* 35(1): 99–117.

Robson, J., Bailey, B. and Larkin, S. (2004) Adding value: investigating the discourse of professionalism adopted by vocational teachers in further education colleges, *Journal of Education and Work,* 17(2): 183–95.

Rodd, J. (2006) *Leadership in Early Childhood.* Maidenhead: Open University Press.

Rogers, A. (2002) *Teaching Adults.* Buckingham: Open University Press.

Rogers, B. (2004) *Cracking the Challenging Class.* Hendon: Books Education.

Rogers, C. (1983) *Freedom to Learn for the 1980s.* Columbus, OH: Charles E. Merrill Publishing Company.

Rogers, C. and Freiberg, J. (1994) *Freedom to Learn,* 3rd edn. New Jersey: Prentice Hall.

Rogers, J. (2007) *Adults Learning,* 5th edn. Maidenhead: Open University Press.

Rosenthal, L. (2004) Do school inspections improve school quality? Ofsted inspections and school examination results in the UK, *Economics of Education Review,* 23(2): 143–51.

RSA (Royal Society for the Encouragement of Arts, Manufacture and Commerce) (2002) *Professional Values for the 21st Century.* London: RSA.

Ryle, G. (1949) *The Concept of Mind.* London: Hutchinson.

Sachdev, D. and Harries, B. (2006) *Learning and Skills Planning and Provision for Migrants from the Accession States: An Exploratory Study*. London: Learning and Skills Network.

Sadler, D. (1989) Formative assessment and the design of instructional systems, *Instructional Science*, 18(2): 119–44.

Salmon, G. (2003) *E-moderating: The Key to Teaching and Learning Online*, 2nd edn. London: RoutledgeFalmer.

Scarman, Lord (1981) *A Report into the Brixton Disturbances of 11/12 April 1981*. London: Home Office.

Schön, D.A. (1983) *The Reflective Practitioner: How Professionals Think in Action*. London: Temple Smith

Schön, D.A. (1987) *Educating the Reflective Practitioner: Towards a New Design for Teaching and Learning in the Professions*. San Francisco, CA: Jossey Bass.

Scriven, M. (2001) *Evaluation Thesaurus*, 4th edn. Newbury Park, CA: Sage Publications.

SEC (Secondary Examinations Council) (1985) *Working Paper 2: Coursework Assessment in GCSE*. London: SEC.

Seifert, T. (2004) Understanding student motivation, *Educational Research*, 46(2): 137–49.

Sfard, A. (1998) On two metaphors for learning and the dangers of choosing just one, *Educational Researcher*, 27(2): 4–13.

Shain, F. and Gleeson, D. (1999) Under new management: changing conceptions of teacher professionalism and policy in the further education sector, *Journal of Educational Policy*, 14(4): 445–62.

Shaw, R. and Colimore, K. (1988) Humanistic psychology as ideology: an analysis of Maslow's contradictions, *Journal of Humanistic Psychology*, 28(3): 51–74.

Simkins, T. and Lumby, J. (2002) Cultural transformation in further education? Mapping the debate, *Research in Post-compulsory Education*, 7(1): 9–25.

Simmons, R. (2008) Raising the age of compulsory education in England: a NEET solution? *British Journal of Educational Studies*, 56(4): 420–39.

Simmons, R. and Thompson, R. (2007) Aiming higher? How will universities respond to changes in initial teacher training for the post-compulsory sector in England? *Journal of Further and Higher Education*, 31(2): 171–82.

Simon, B. (1991) *Education and the Social Order 1940–1990*. London: Lawrence and Wishart.

Sivanandan, A. (2005) *Its Anti-racism that was Failed, Not Multiculturalism that Failed*. Available at http://www.irr.org.uk/2005/october/ak000021.html (accessed 20 November 2005).

Smith, A. (2004) 'Off-campus support' in distance learning – how do our students define quality? *Quality Assurance in Education*, 12(1): 28–38.

Smith, G. (2000) Research and inspection: HMI and Ofsted, 1981–1996 a commentary, *Oxford Review of Education*, 26(3/4): 333–52.

Smithers, A. (1993) *All Our Futures: Britain's Education Revolution*. London: Channel 4 (Dispatches Report).

Social Exclusion Unit (1999) *Bridging the Gap: New Opportunities for 16–18-year-olds Not in Education, Employment or Training*. London: HMSO.

Solomos, J. (2003) *Race and Racism in Britain*, 3rd edn. Basingstoke: Palgrave Macmillan.

Sparrow, S. (2008) Spot the difference, *Training and Coaching Today*, March: 18.

Stanton, G. and Fletcher, M. (2006) 14–19 institutional arrangements in England: a research perspective on collaboration, competition and patterns of post-16 provision, *Nuffield Review of 14–19 Education and Training*, Working Paper 38.

Stanulis, R. and Russell, D. (2000) Jumping in: trust and communication in mentoring student teachers, *Teaching and Teacher Education*, 16(1): 65–80.

Starr, J. (2003) *The Coaching Manual: The Definitive Guide to the Process and Skills of Personal Coaching*. Harlow: Pearson Education.

Stasz, C. and Wright, S. (2007) *A Framework for Understanding and Comparing 14–19 Education Policies in the United Kingdom*, in D. Raffe and K. Spours (eds), *Policy-making and Policy Learning in 14–19 Education*. London: Institute of Education, University of London.

Stenhouse, R. (1981) *An Introduction to Curriculum Research and Development*. London: Heinemann.

Stredwick, J. (2005) *Introduction to Human Resource Management*, 2nd edn. Oxford: Butterworth Heinemann.

Street, B. (1984) *Literacy in Theory and Practice*. Cambridge: Cambridge University Press.

Suter, M. (2007) Constructing the reflective practitioner. Unpublished doctoral thesis, Manchester Metropolitan University.

Sweeney, J., O'Donoghue, T. and Whitehead, C. (2004) Traditional face-to-face and web-based tutorials: a study of university students' perspectives on the roles of tutorial participants, *Teaching in Higher Education*, 9(3): 311–23.

Taylor, R. (2002) Shaping the culture of learning communities, *Principal Leadership*, 3(4): 42–5.

Taylor, P.H. and Richards, C. (1979) *An Introduction to Curriculum Studies*. Windsor: NFER.

Thomas, P. (2006) The impact of community cohesion on youth work: a case study from Oldham, *Youth and Policy*, 93: 41–60.

Thompson, M. (2007) A critique of the impact of policy and funding, in G. Conole and M. Oliver (eds), *Contemporary Perspectives in E-learning Research*. London: Routledge.

Thompson, R. (2009) Social class and participation in further education: evidence from the youth cohort study of England and Wales, *British Journal of Sociology of Education*, 30(1): 29–42.

Thompson, R. and Robinson, D. (2008) Changing step or marking time? Teacher education reforms for the learning and skills sector in England, *Journal of Further and Higher Education*, 32(2): 161–73.

Thornton, M. (1998) *Subject Specialists: Primary Schools*, UCET Occasional Papers No.10. London: UCET.

Tomlinson, J. (1996) *Inclusive Learning: Principles and Recommendations*. London: Further Education Funding Council.

Tomlinson, M. (2004) *14–19 Curriculum and Qualifications Reform: Final Report of the Working Group on 14–19 Reform*. Annesley: DfES publications.

Tomlinson, S. (2005) *Education in a Post-Welfare Society*. Maidenhead: Open University Press.

Tomlinson, S. (2008) Gifted, talented and high ability: selection for education in a one-dimensional world, *Oxford Review of Education*, 34(1): 59–74.

Tooley, J. and Darby, D. (1998) *Educational Research: A Critique*. London: Ofsted.

Torrance, H. and Pryor, J. (1998) *Investigating Formative Assessment: Teaching and Learning in the Classroom*. Buckingham: Open University Press.

Tripp, D. (1993) *Critical Incidents in Teaching*. London: Routledge.

Troman, G. (2003) Teacher stress in the low-trust society, in L. Kydd, L. Anderson and W. Newton (eds), *Leading People and Teams in Education*. London: Paul Chapman Publishing.

Troyna, B. (1984) Fact or artefact? The 'educational underachievement' of black pupils, *British Journal of Sociology of Education*, 5(2): 153–66.

Tuckman, B. and Jensen, M. (1977) Stages of small-group development revisited, *Group and Organization Management*, 2(4): 419–27.

Tummons, J. (2007) *Assessing Learning in the Lifelong Learning Sector*. Exeter: Learning Matters.

Tummons, J. (2008) Assessment, and the literacy practices of trainee PCET teachers, *International Journal of Educational Research*, 47(3): 184–91.

Twining, P., Broadie, R., Cook, D. et al. (2006) *Educational Change and ICT: The Current Landscape and Implementation Issues.* Coventry: BECTA.

Tyler R. (1949) *Basic Principles of Curriculum and Instruction.* Chicago: Chicago University Press.

UCU (University and College Union) (2008) *Employers Warned After College Fined for Acid Explosion Injury.* Available at http://www.ucu.org.uk/index.cfm?articleid=3196 (accessed 8 June 2008).

Usher, R. and Edwards, R. (1994) *Postmodernism and Education.* London: Routledge.

Vähäsantanen, K. and Eteläpelto, A. (2009) Vocational teachers in the face of a major educational reform: individual ways of negotiating professional identities, *Journal of Education and Work,* 22(1): 15–33.

Vaizey, J. (1962) *Education for Tomorrow.* Harmondsworth: Penguin.

Van Maanen, J. (1995) *Representation in Ethnography.* Thousand Oaks, CA: Sage.

Vicars, M. (2007) *Sexual Orientation: A Practical Guide to Equality.* The East Coast Centre for Diversity. Available at http://www.grimsby.ac.uk/Eccd/documents/LSCDiversity-LGBT-final.pdf (accessed 12 June 2008).

Villeneuve-Smith, F., Munoz, S. and McKenzie, E. (2008) *FE Colleges: The Frontline Under Pressure? A Staff Satisfaction Survey of FE Colleges in England.* London: Learning and Skills Network.

Vizard, D. (2007) *How to Manage Behaviour in Further Education.* London: Paul Chapman Publishing.

Waitt, I. (ed.) (1980) *College Administration.* London: NATFHE.

Walhberg, M. and Gleeson, D. (2003) 'Doing the business': paradox and irony in vocational education – GNVQ business studies as a case in point, *Journal of Vocational Education and Training,* 55(4): 423–46.

Wallace, S. (2002a) No good surprises: intending lecturers preconceptions and initial experiences of further education, *British Educational Research Journal,* 28(1): 79–93.

Wallace, S. (2002b) *Managing Behaviour and Motivating Students in Further Education.* Exeter: Learning Matters.

Wallace, S. and Gravells, J. (2005) *Mentoring in Further Education: Meeting the National Occupational Standards.* Exeter: Learning Matters.

Wallis, J. (ed.) (1996) *Liberal Adult Education: The End of an Era?* Nottingham: University of Nottingham.

Warnock, H. (1978) *Special Educational Needs: Report of the Committee of Enquiry into the Education of Handicapped Children and Young People,* Cmnd 7212. London: HMSO.

Warren Little, J. (1992) *Stretching the Subject: The Subject Organisation of High Schools and the Transformation of Work Education.* Berkeley, CA: National Center for Research in Vocational Education, University of California at Berkeley. Available at http://vocserve.berkeley.edu/AllInOne/MDS-471.html (accessed 7 March 2009).

Watson, J. and Rayner, R. (1920) Conditioned emotional reactions, *Journal of Experimental Psychology,* 3(1): 1–14.

Webb, E., Jones, A., Barker, P. and van Shaik, P. (2004) Using e-learning dialogues in higher education, *Innovations in Education and Teaching International,* 41(1): 93–103.

Weeden, P., with Winter, J. and Broadfoot, P. (2000) *The LEARN Project Phase 2: Guidance for Schools on Assessment for Learning.* Bristol: CLIO Centre for Assessment Studies, University of Bristol.

Weiner, M.J. (1981) *English Culture and the Decline of the Industrial Spirit, 1850–1980.* Cambridge: Cambridge University Press.

Weller, M. (2007) *Virtual Learning Environments: Using, Choosing and Developing Your VLE.* London: Routledge.

Weller, M., Pegler, C. and Mason, R. (2005) Use of innovative technologies on an e-learning course, *Internet and Higher Education*, 8(1): 61–71.

Wenger, E. (1998) *Communities of Practice: Learning, Meaning and Identity*. Cambridge: Cambridge University Press.

Williams, S. (2003) Conflict in the colleges: industrial relations in FE since incorporation, *Journal of Further and Higher Education*, 27(3): 307–15.

Winchester, D. and Bach, S. (1995) The State: the public sector, in P. Edwards (ed.), *Industrial Relations: Theory and Practice in Britain*. Oxford: Blackwell.

Witz, A. (1992) *Professions and Patriarchy*. London: Routledge.

Yeomans, R. (1986) Hearing secret harmonies; becoming a primary staff member. Paper presented at the British educational research association annual conference, Bristol University.

Yorke, M. and Longden, B. (2004) *Retention and Student Success in Higher Education*. Maidenhead: Open University Press.

Young, M. (ed.) (1971) *Knowledge and Control: New Directions for the Sociology of Education*. London: Collier-Macmillan.

Young, M. (1998) *The Curriculum of the Future*. London: Falmer Press.

Young, M. (2003) Curriculum studies and the problem of knowledge: updating the Enlightenment? *Policy Futures in Education*, 1(3): 553–64.

Young, M., Lucas, N., Sharp, G. and Cunningham, B. (1995) *Teacher Education for the Further Education Sector: Training the Lecturer of the Future*. London: Association for Colleges / Institute of Education Post-16 Education Centre.

Young, P. (2000) 'I might as well give up': self-esteem and mature students' feelings about feedback on assignments, *Journal of Further and Higher Education*, 24(3): 409–18.

Yuval-Davis, N. (1997) Ethnicity, gender relations and multiculturalism, in T. Modood and P. Werbner (eds), *Debating Cultural Hybridity*. London: Zed Books.

Index